Shojo Beat

MY Love STORY!!

6

Story KAZUNE KAWAHARA
Art ARUKO

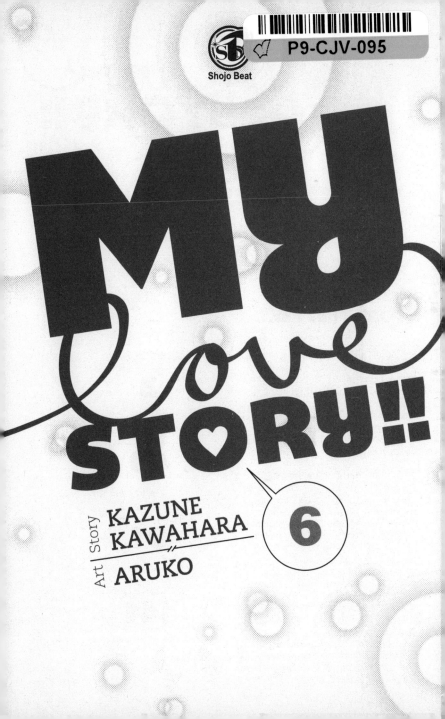

MY love STORY!!

6

CONTENTS

STORY Thus Far...

Takeo Goda, a first-year high school student, is a hot-blooded guy who is 6'6" tall and weighs 265 pounds. Boys look up to him, but the girls he falls in love with all end up liking his handsome best friend, Makoto Sunakawa! All that changes when Takeo saves Rinko Yamato from a groper on the train, and she becomes his girlfriend.

Girls other than Yamato have noticed Takeo's charms, like Sunakawa's older sister Ai and Takeo's classmate Saijo. When Saijo, who's taken to calling Takeo "Coach," tells Takeo how she really feels about him, Takeo realizes just how much he loves Yamato. He thanks Saijo for continuing to be his friend despite the fact that he can't return her feelings.

When Yamato kisses Takeo for the first time, his eyes are closed and he... doesn't notice. But once Sunakawa clues him in, Takeo immediately runs to Yamato's place for a do-over! His birthday—the day of their first kiss— is one they'll never forget.

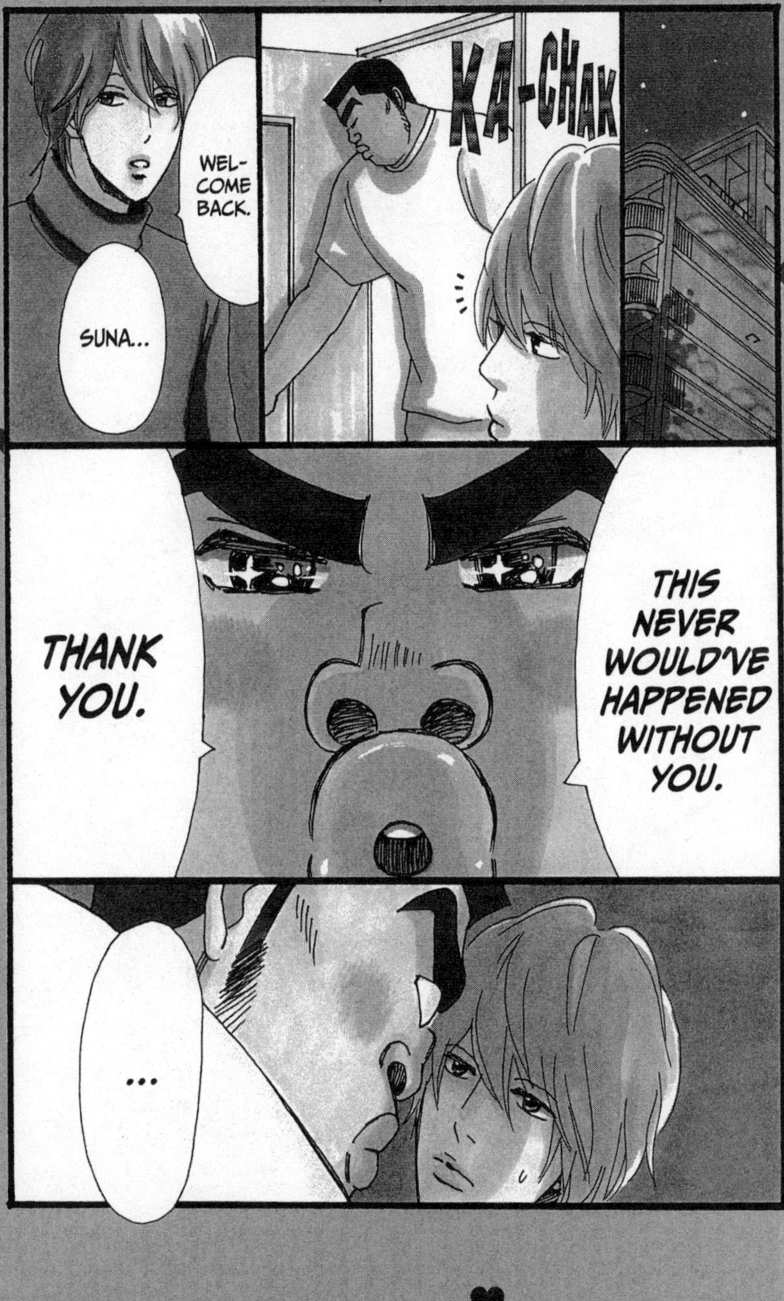
KA-CHAK
WEL-COME BACK.
SUNA...
THIS NEVER WOULD'VE HAPPENED WITHOUT YOU.
THANK YOU.
...

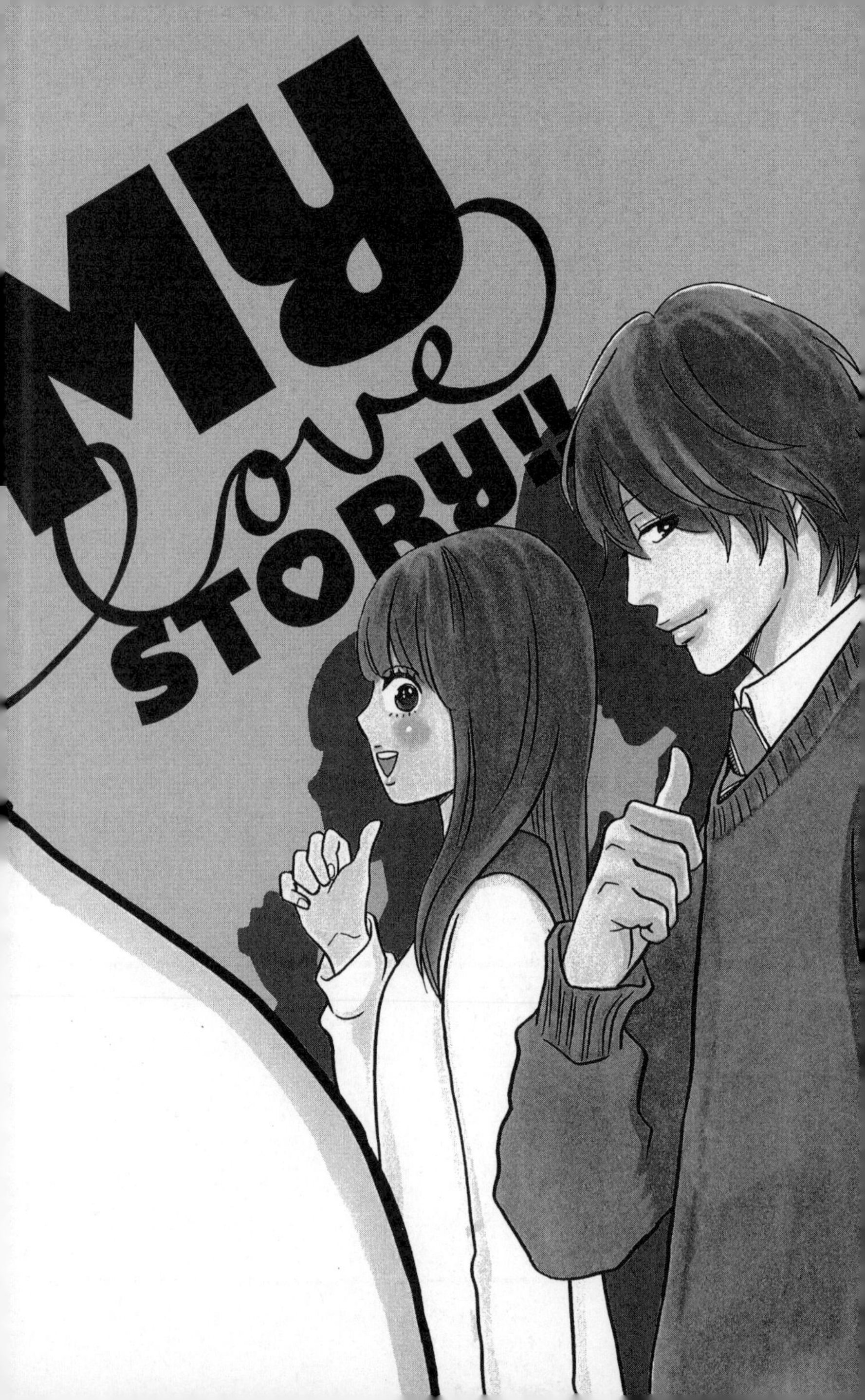
My Love STORY!!

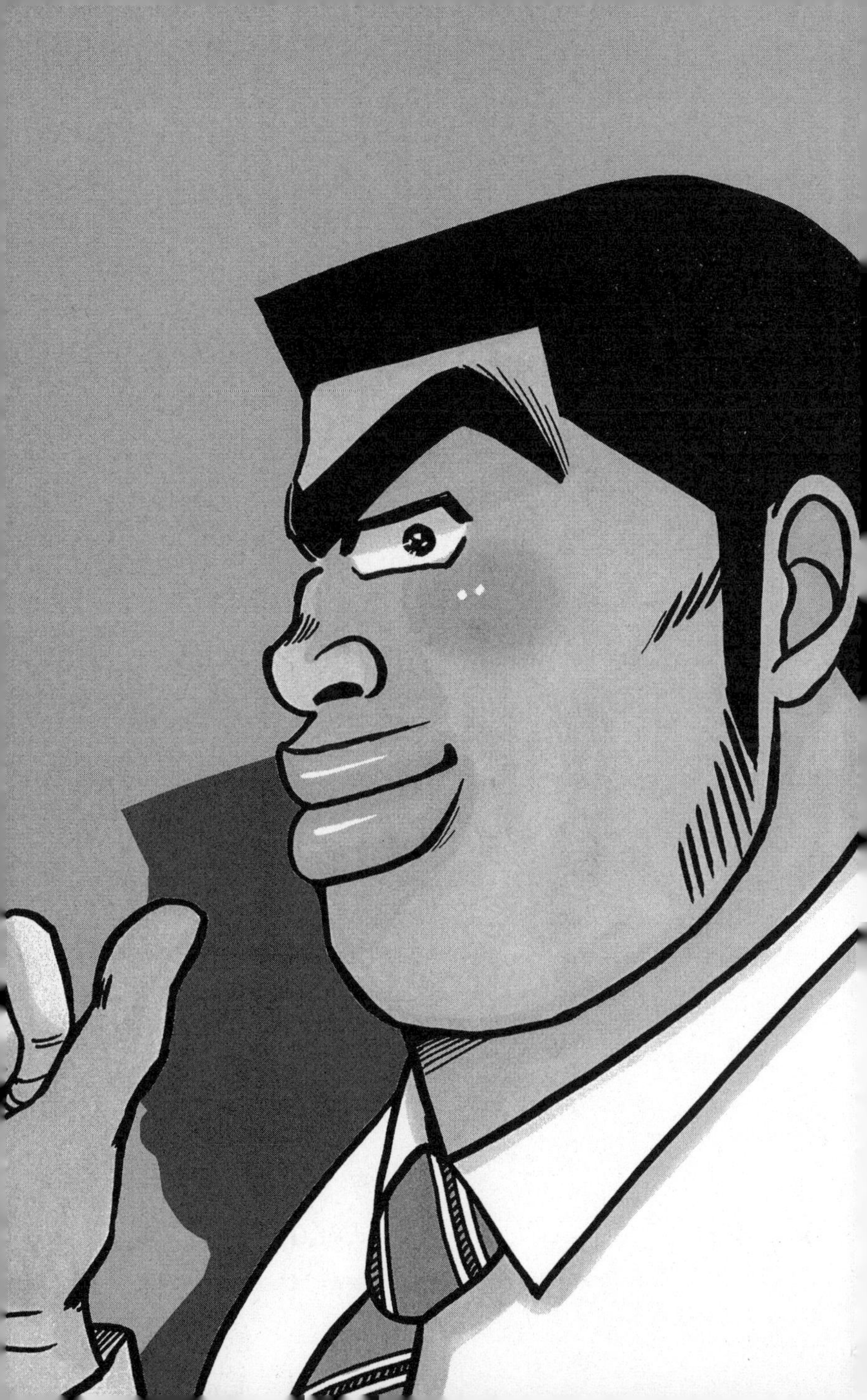

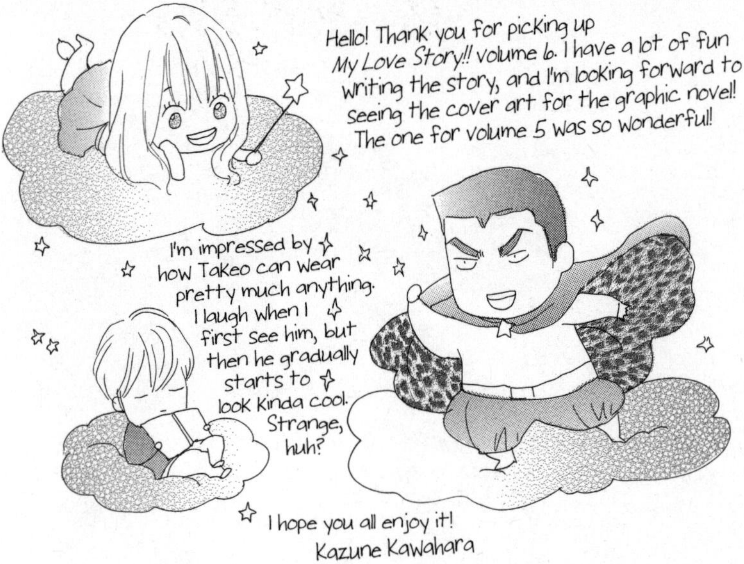
Hello! Thank you for picking up *My Love Story!!* volume 6. I have a lot of fun writing the story, and I'm looking forward to seeing the cover art for the graphic novel! The one for volume 5 was so wonderful!
I'm impressed by how Takeo can wear pretty much anything. I laugh when I first see him, but then he gradually starts to look kinda cool. Strange, huh?
I hope you all enjoy it!
Kazune Kawahara

It's volume 6! Thank you so much!

I'm always excited when I'm drawing this series. I'm very glad to be working on it. Kawahara Sensei sometimes draws really cute pictures of Takeo, Yamato and Sunakawa. I love them! I hope to see you again in the next volume.

SO PLEASED

May 2014

Aruko

A shojo manga artist who can't draw flowers...

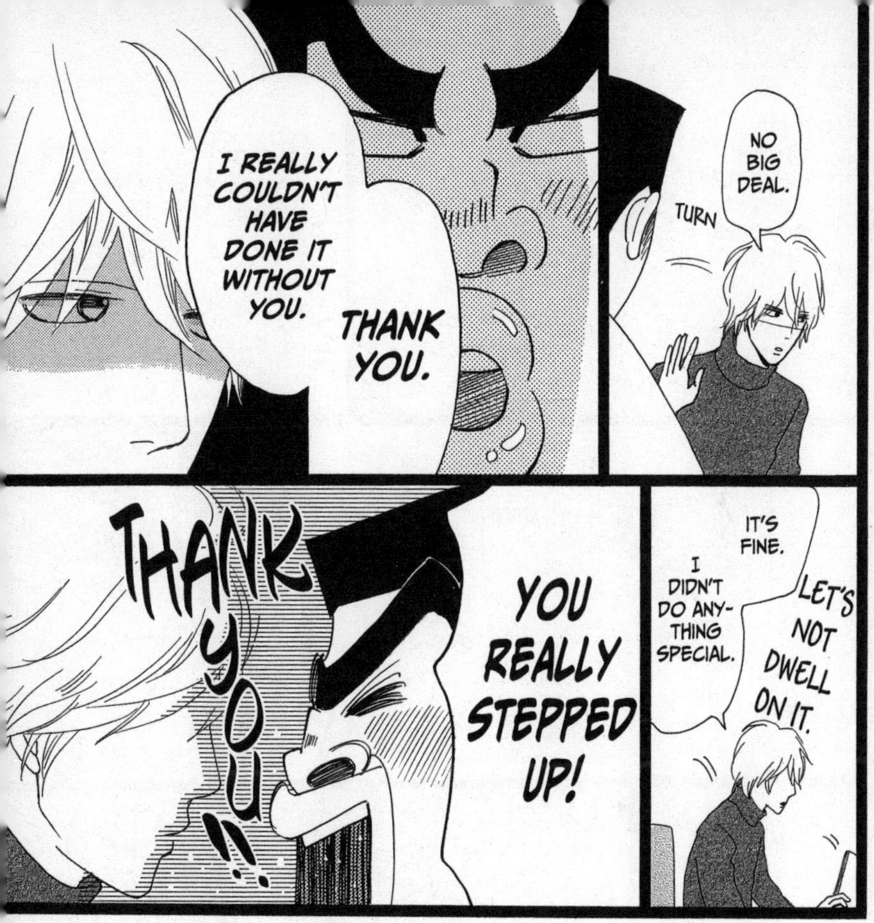
NO BIG DEAL.
TURN
THANK YOU.
I REALLY COULDN'T HAVE DONE IT WITHOUT YOU.
IT'S FINE.
I DIDN'T DO ANYTHING SPECIAL.
LET'S NOT DWELL ON IT.
YOU REALLY STEPPED UP!
THANK YOU!!

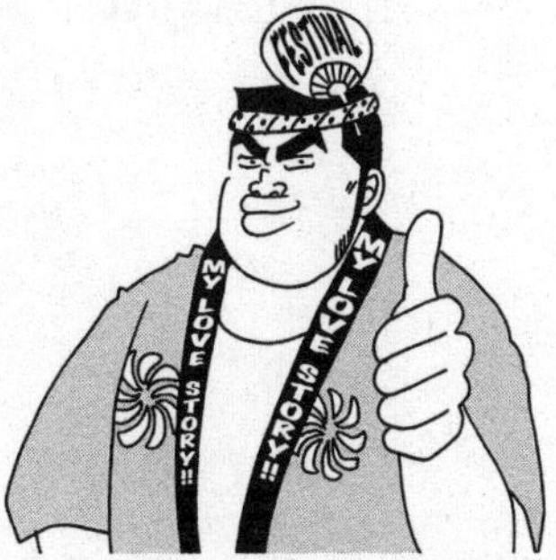
FESTIVAL
MY LOVE STORY!!
MY LOVE STORY!!

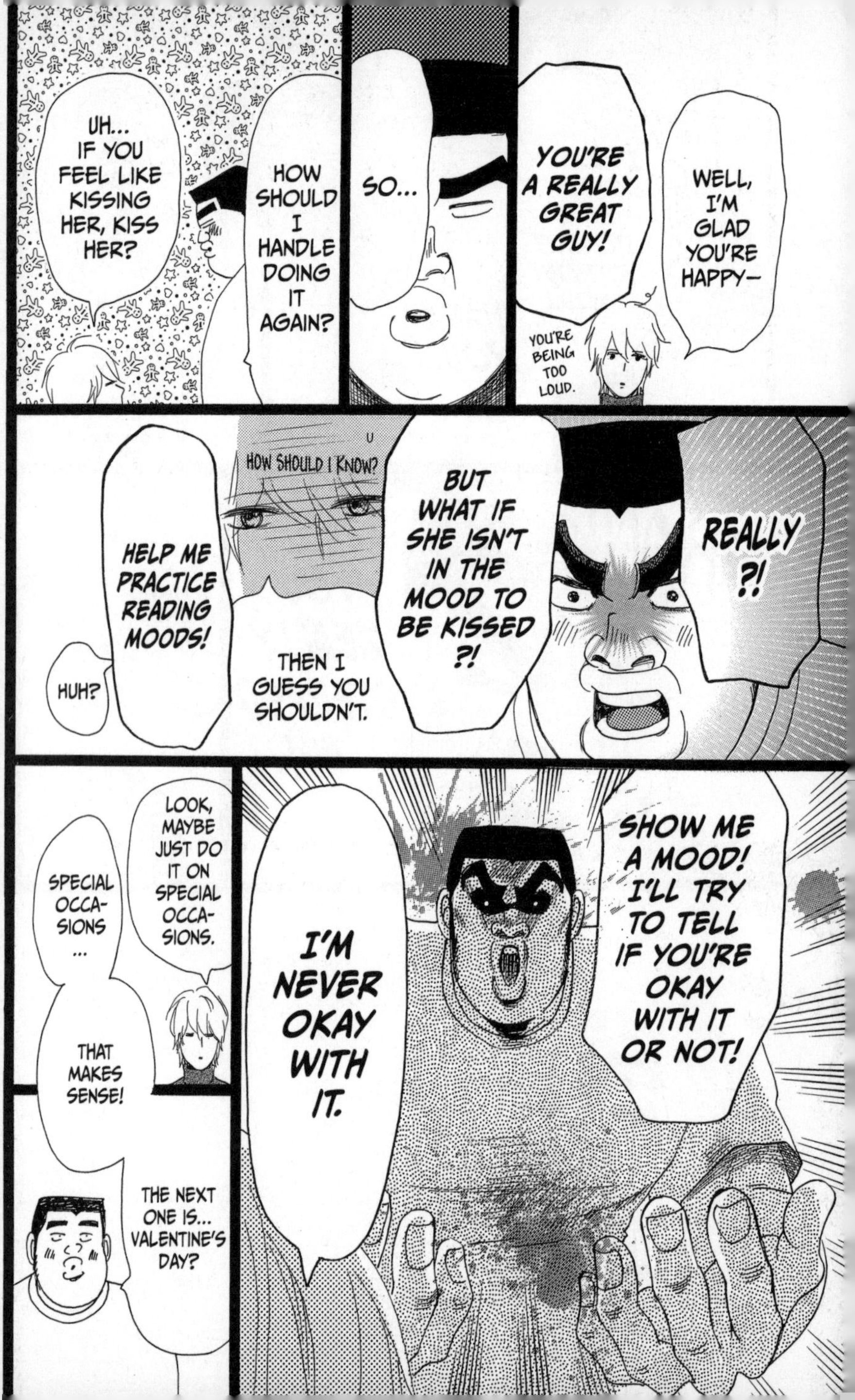
WELL, I'M GLAD YOU'RE HAPPY—
YOU'RE A REALLY GREAT GUY!
YOU'RE BEING TOO LOUD.
SO...
HOW SHOULD I HANDLE DOING IT AGAIN?
UH... IF YOU FEEL LIKE KISSING HER, KISS HER?
REALLY ?!
BUT WHAT IF SHE ISN'T IN THE MOOD TO BE KISSED ?!
HOW SHOULD I KNOW?
THEN I GUESS YOU SHOULDN'T.
HELP ME PRACTICE READING MOODS!
HUH?
SHOW ME A MOOD! I'LL TRY TO TELL IF YOU'RE OKAY WITH IT OR NOT!
I'M NEVER OKAY WITH IT.
LOOK, MAYBE JUST DO IT ON SPECIAL OCCASIONS.
SPECIAL OCCASIONS ...
THAT MAKES SENSE!
THE NEXT ONE IS... VALENTINE'S DAY?

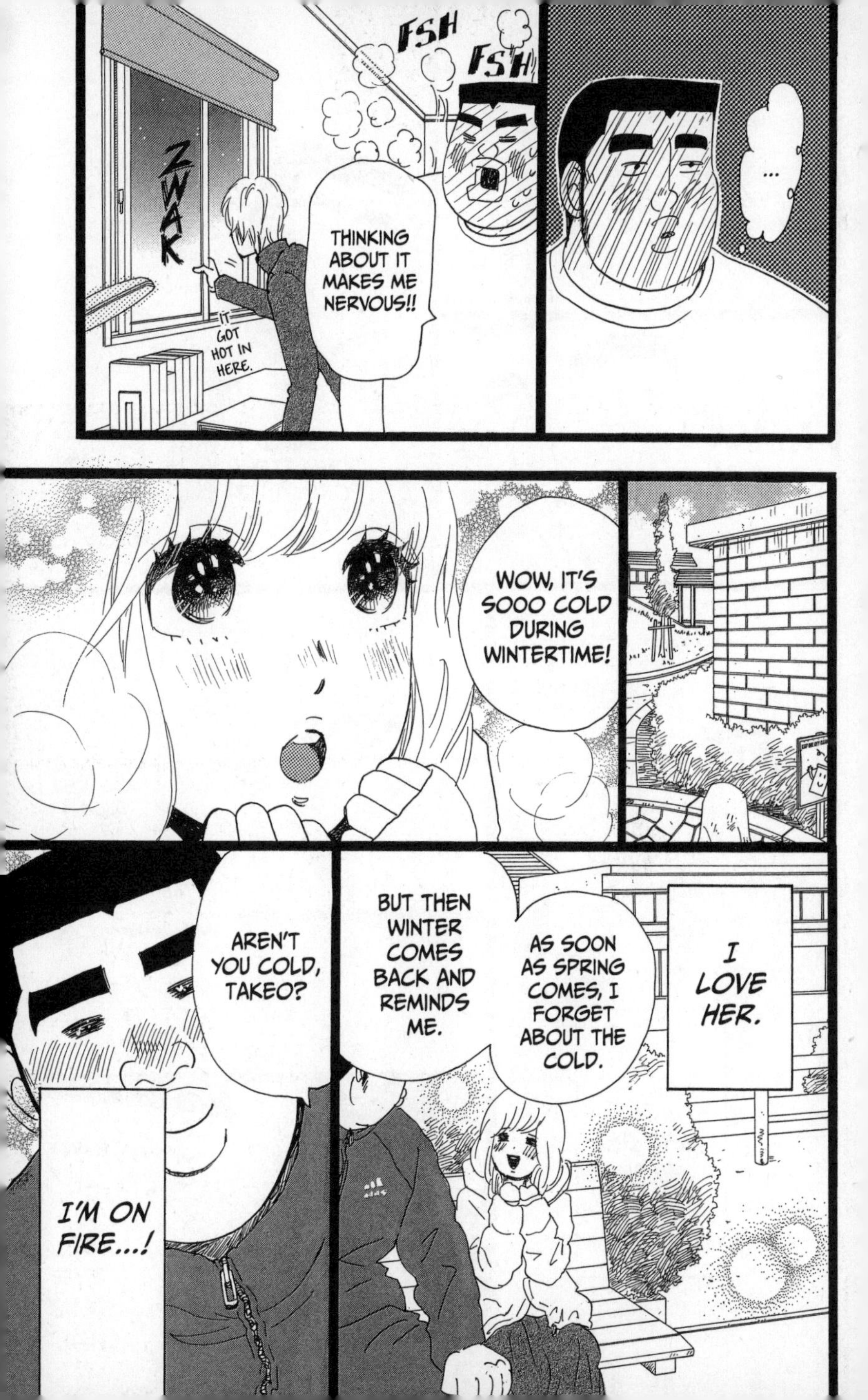
...
FSH
FSH
THINKING ABOUT IT MAKES ME NERVOUS!!
ZWAK
IT GOT HOT IN HERE.
WOW, IT'S SOOO COLD DURING WINTERTIME!
I LOVE HER.
AS SOON AS SPRING COMES, I FORGET ABOUT THE COLD.
BUT THEN WINTER COMES BACK AND REMINDS ME.
AREN'T YOU COLD, TAKEO?
I'M ON FIRE...!

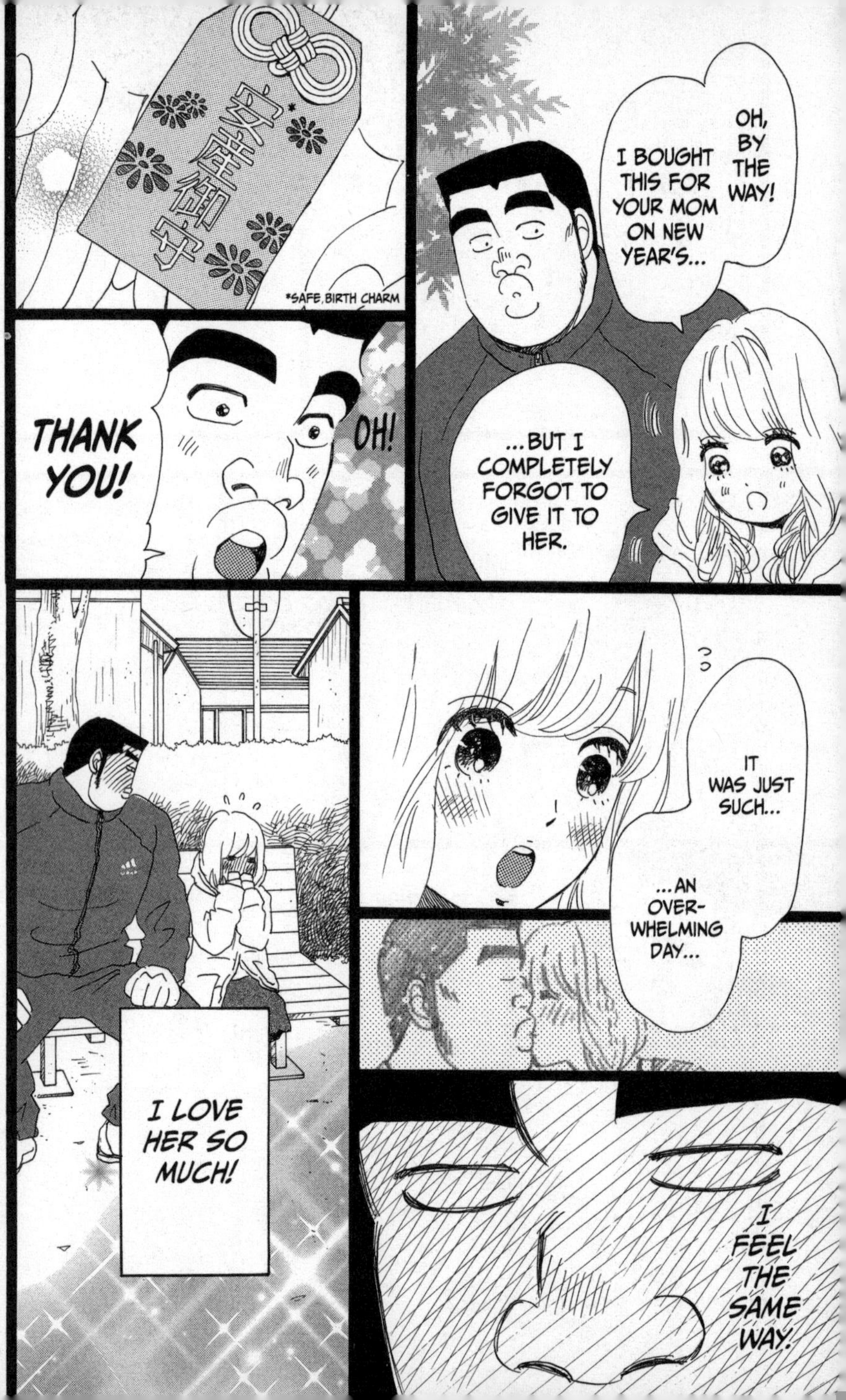
OH, BY THE WAY!
I BOUGHT THIS FOR YOUR MOM ON NEW YEAR'S...
...BUT I COMPLETELY FORGOT TO GIVE IT TO HER.
*安産御守
*SAFE BIRTH CHARM
OH!
THANK YOU!
IT WAS JUST SUCH...
...AN OVER-WHELMING DAY...
I FEEL THE SAME WAY.
I LOVE HER SO MUCH!

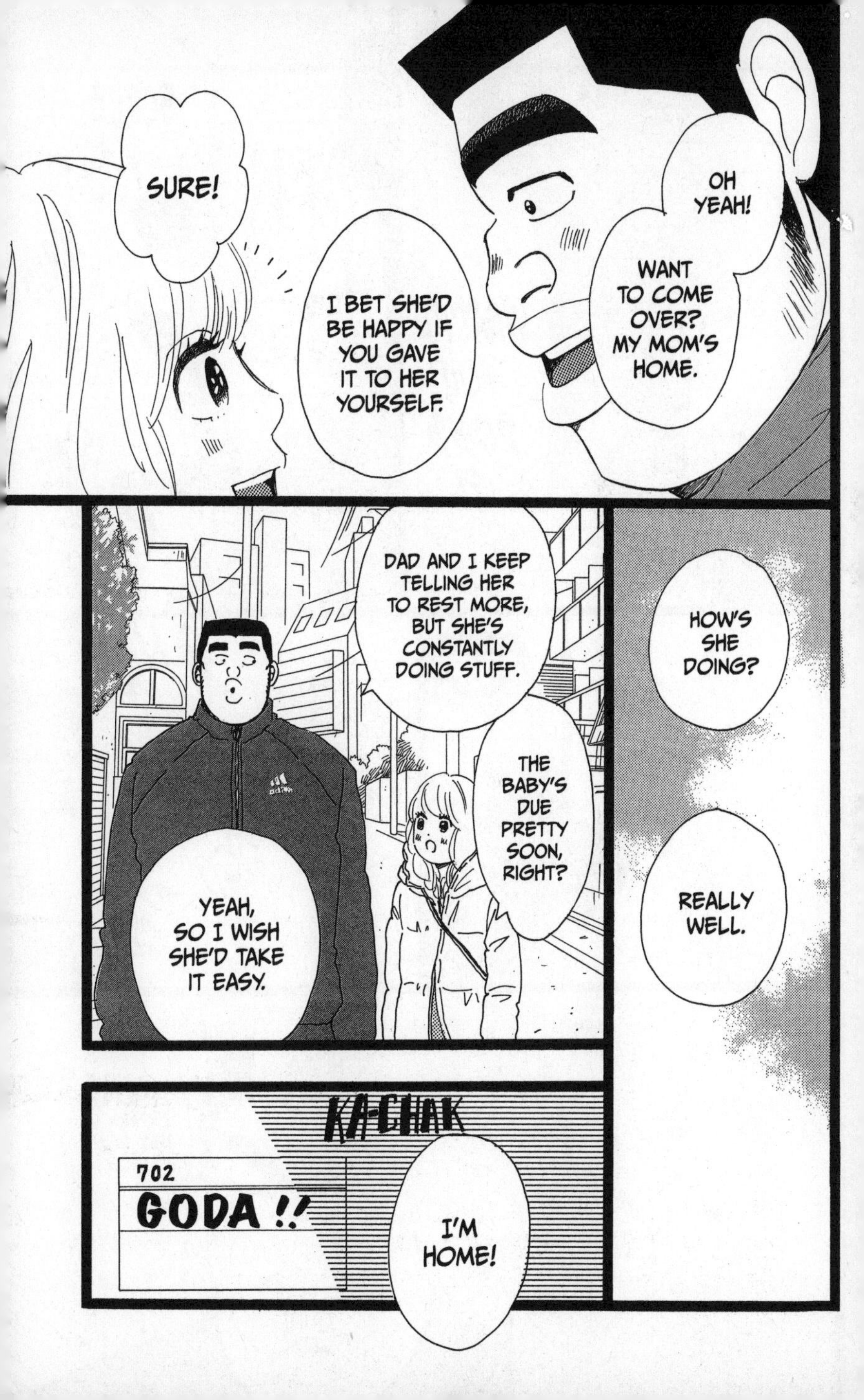
OH YEAH!
WANT TO COME OVER? MY MOM'S HOME.
I BET SHE'D BE HAPPY IF YOU GAVE IT TO HER YOURSELF.
SURE!
HOW'S SHE DOING?
REALLY WELL.
DAD AND I KEEP TELLING HER TO REST MORE, BUT SHE'S CONSTANTLY DOING STUFF.
THE BABY'S DUE PRETTY SOON, RIGHT?
YEAH, SO I WISH SHE'D TAKE IT EASY.
KA-CHAK
702
GODA !!
I'M HOME!

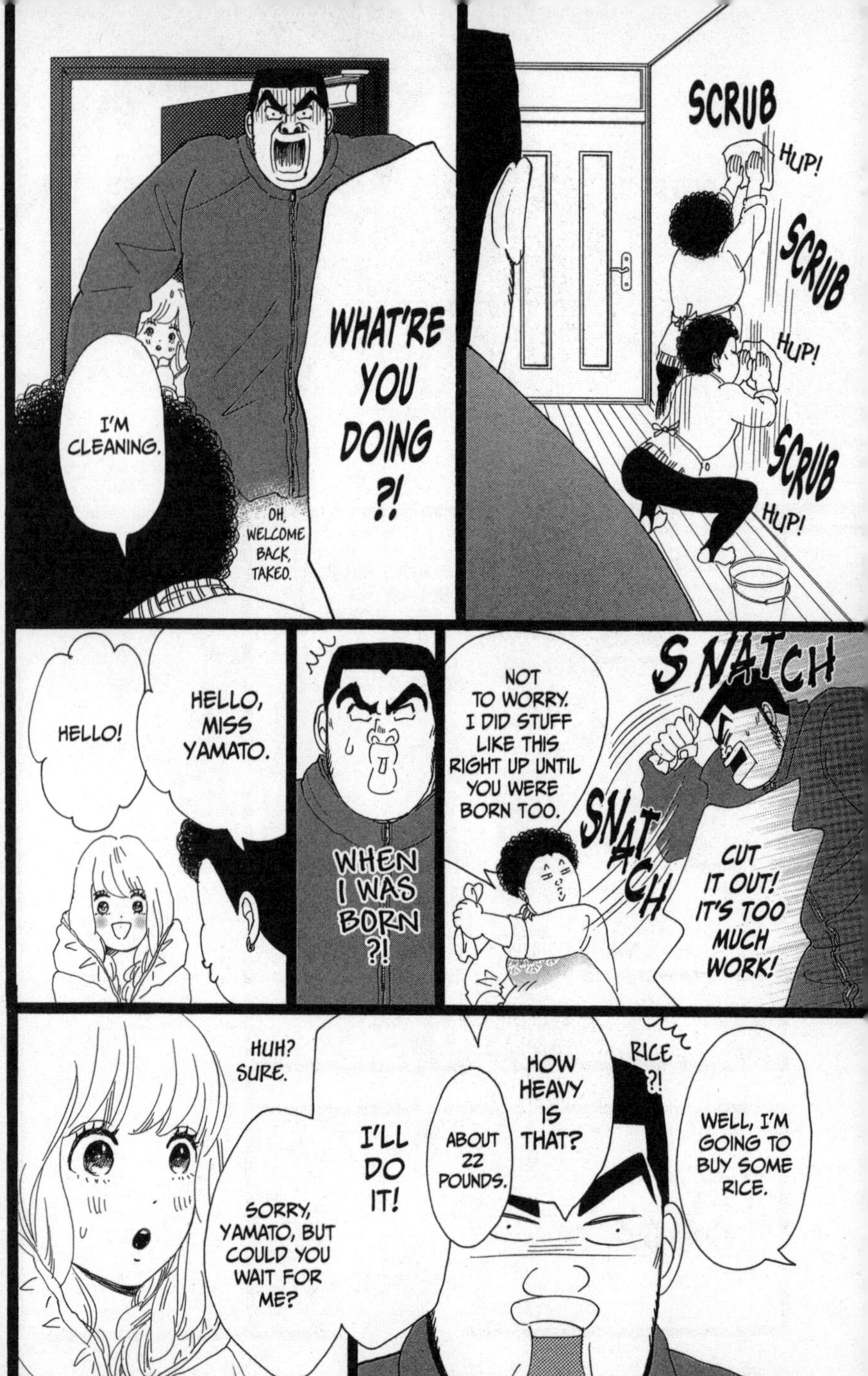
SCRUB
HUP!
SCRUB
HUP!
SCRUB
HUP!
WHAT'RE YOU DOING ?!
OH, WELCOME BACK, TAKEO.
I'M CLEANING.
SNATCH
NOT TO WORRY. I DID STUFF LIKE THIS RIGHT UP UNTIL YOU WERE BORN TOO.
SNATCH
CUT IT OUT! IT'S TOO MUCH WORK!
WHEN I WAS BORN ?!
HELLO, MISS YAMATO.
HELLO!
WELL, I'M GOING TO BUY SOME RICE.
RICE ?!
HOW HEAVY IS THAT?
ABOUT 22 POUNDS.
I'LL DO IT!
SORRY, YAMATO, BUT COULD YOU WAIT FOR ME?
HUH? SURE.

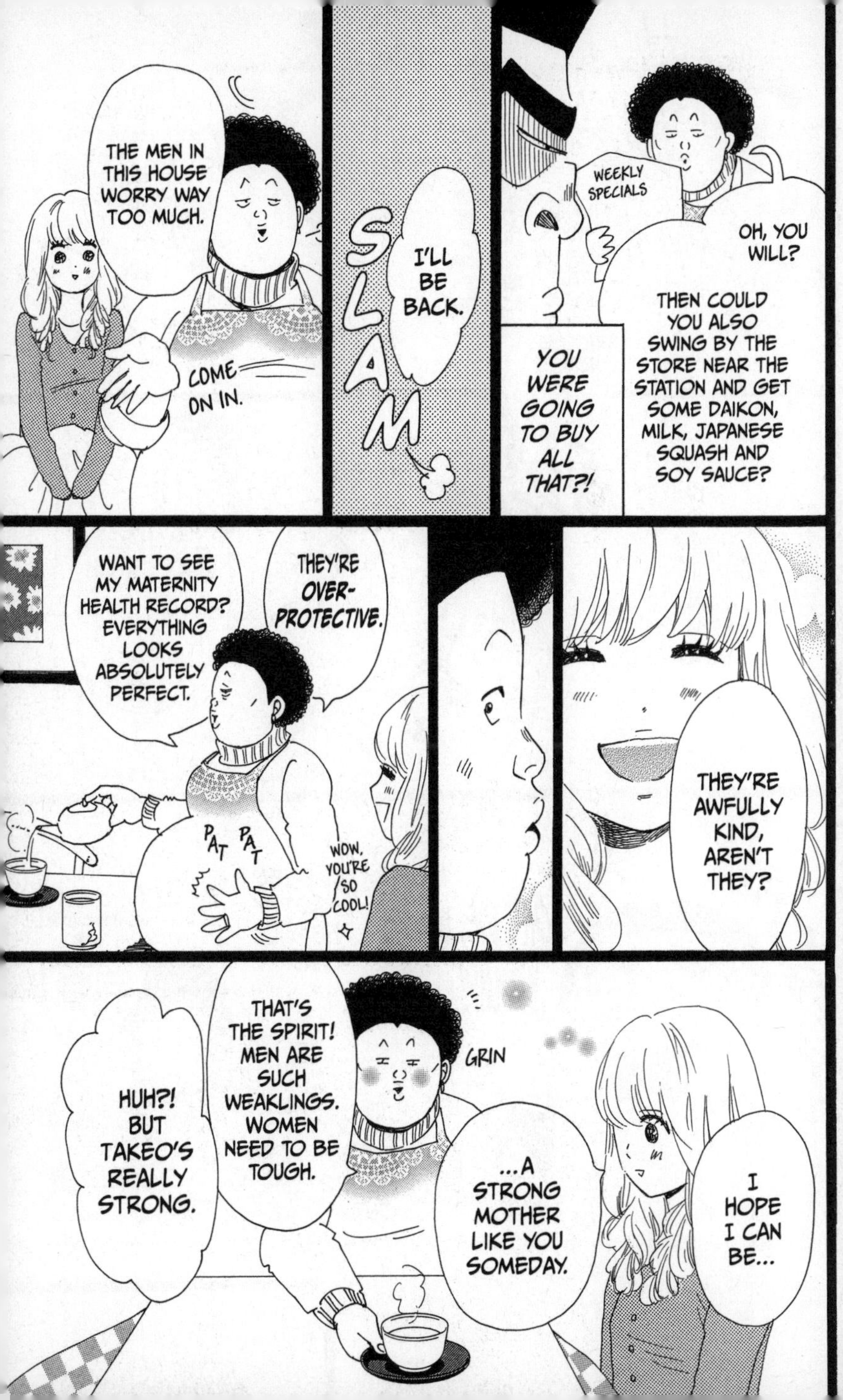
WEEKLY SPECIALS
OH, YOU WILL?
THEN COULD YOU ALSO SWING BY THE STORE NEAR THE STATION AND GET SOME DAIKON, MILK, JAPANESE SQUASH AND SOY SAUCE?
YOU WERE GOING TO BUY ALL THAT?!
I'LL BE BACK.
SLAM
THE MEN IN THIS HOUSE WORRY WAY TOO MUCH.
COME ON IN.
THEY'RE AWFULLY KIND, AREN'T THEY?
THEY'RE OVER-PROTECTIVE.
WANT TO SEE MY MATERNITY HEALTH RECORD? EVERYTHING LOOKS ABSOLUTELY PERFECT.
PAT PAT
WOW, YOU'RE SO COOL!
I HOPE I CAN BE...
...A STRONG MOTHER LIKE YOU SOMEDAY.
GRIN
THAT'S THE SPIRIT! MEN ARE SUCH WEAKLINGS. WOMEN NEED TO BE TOUGH.
HUH?! BUT TAKEO'S REALLY STRONG.

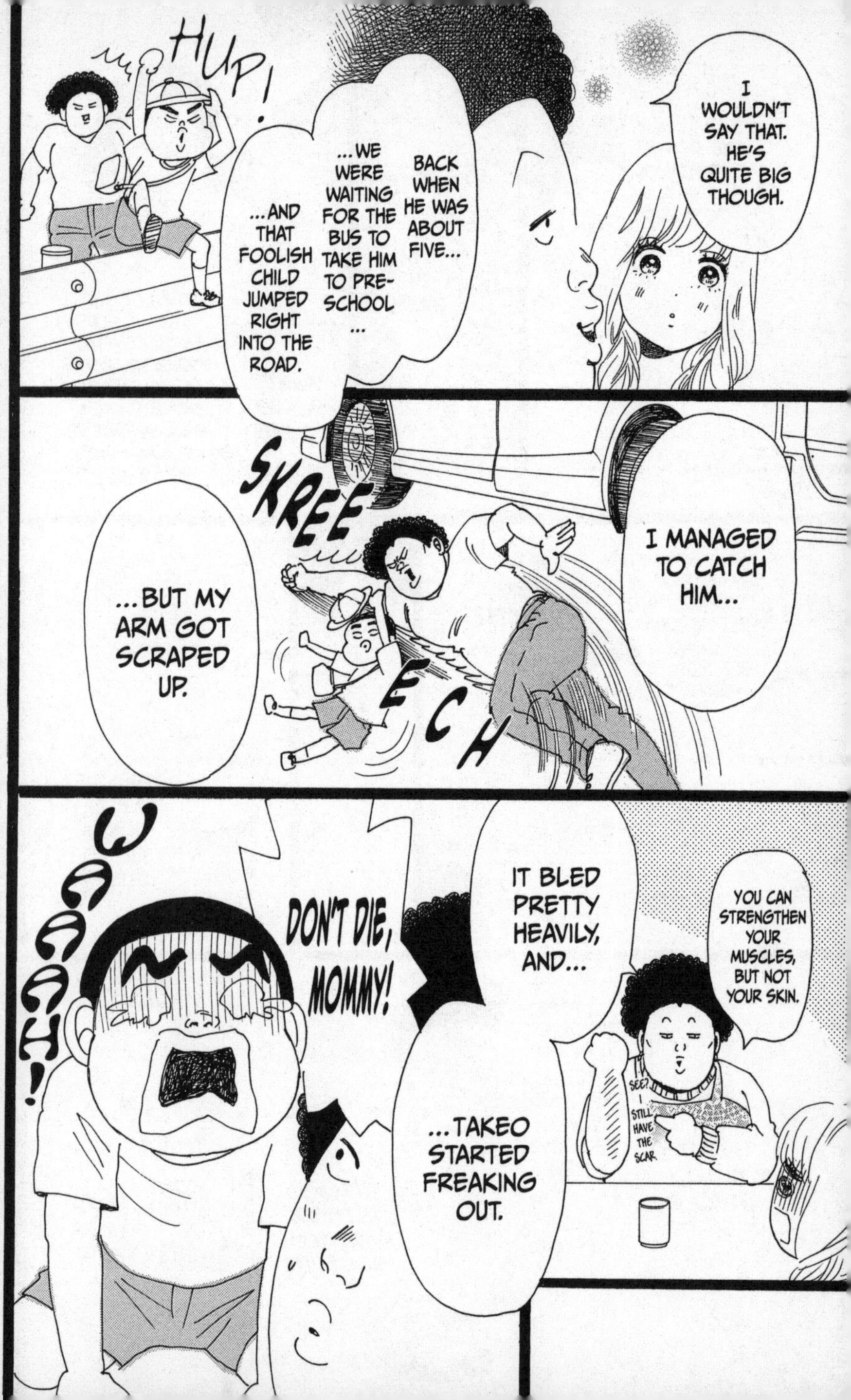
I WOULDN'T SAY THAT. HE'S QUITE BIG THOUGH.
BACK WHEN HE WAS ABOUT FIVE...
...WE WERE WAITING FOR THE BUS TO TAKE HIM TO PRE-SCHOOL...
...AND THAT FOOLISH CHILD JUMPED RIGHT INTO THE ROAD.
HUP!
I MANAGED TO CATCH HIM...
SKREEECH
...BUT MY ARM GOT SCRAPED UP.
YOU CAN STRENGTHEN YOUR MUSCLES, BUT NOT YOUR SKIN.
SEE? I STILL HAVE THE SCAR.
IT BLED PRETTY HEAVILY, AND...
...TAKEO STARTED FREAKING OUT.
DON'T DIE, MOMMY!
WAAAAH!

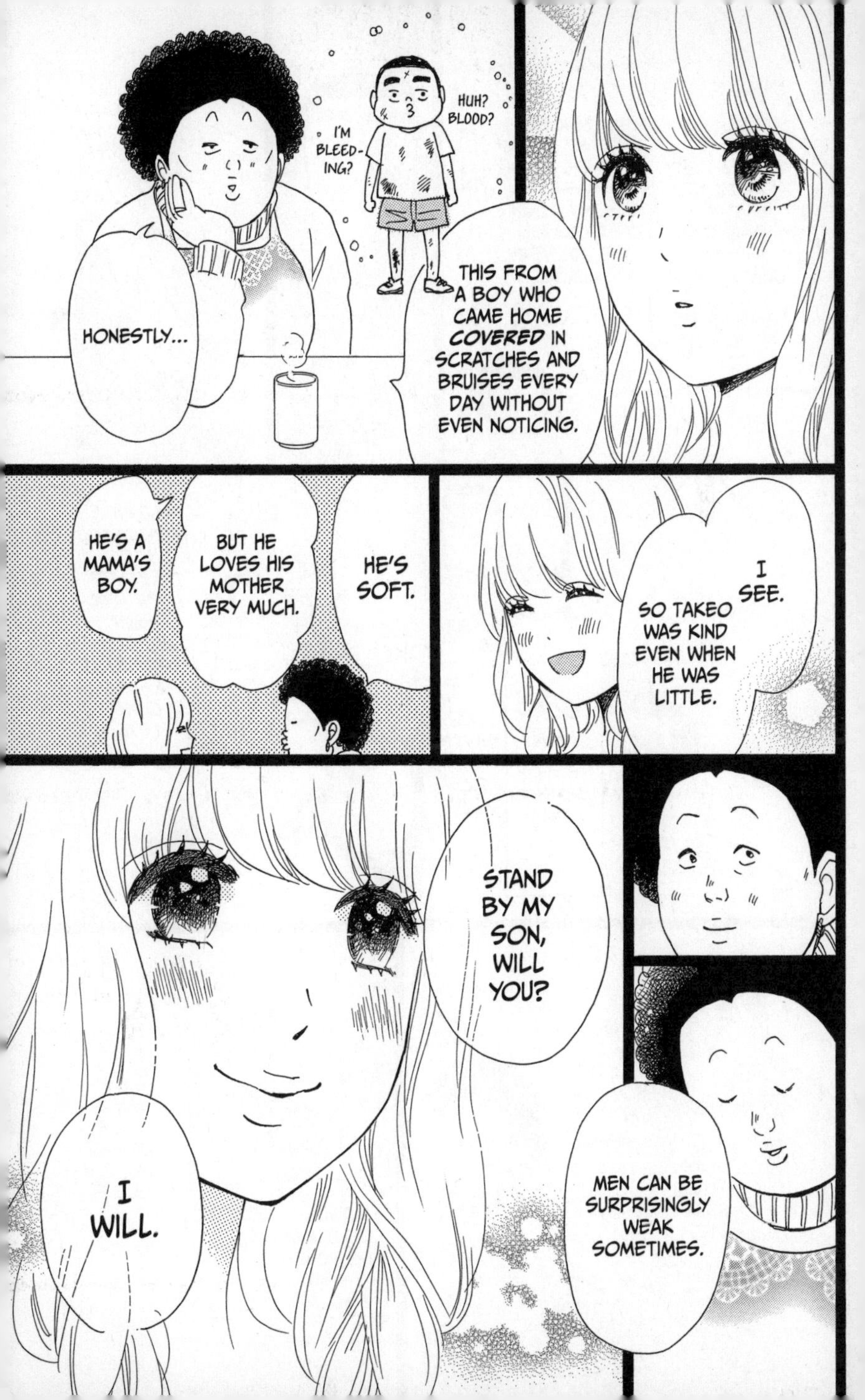
HUH? BLOOD?
I'M BLEEDING?
THIS FROM A BOY WHO CAME HOME *COVERED* IN SCRATCHES AND BRUISES EVERY DAY WITHOUT EVEN NOTICING.
HONESTLY...
I SEE.
SO TAKEO WAS KIND EVEN WHEN HE WAS LITTLE.
HE'S SOFT.
BUT HE LOVES HIS MOTHER VERY MUCH.
HE'S A MAMA'S BOY.
MEN CAN BE SURPRISINGLY WEAK SOMETIMES.
STAND BY MY SON, WILL YOU?
I WILL.

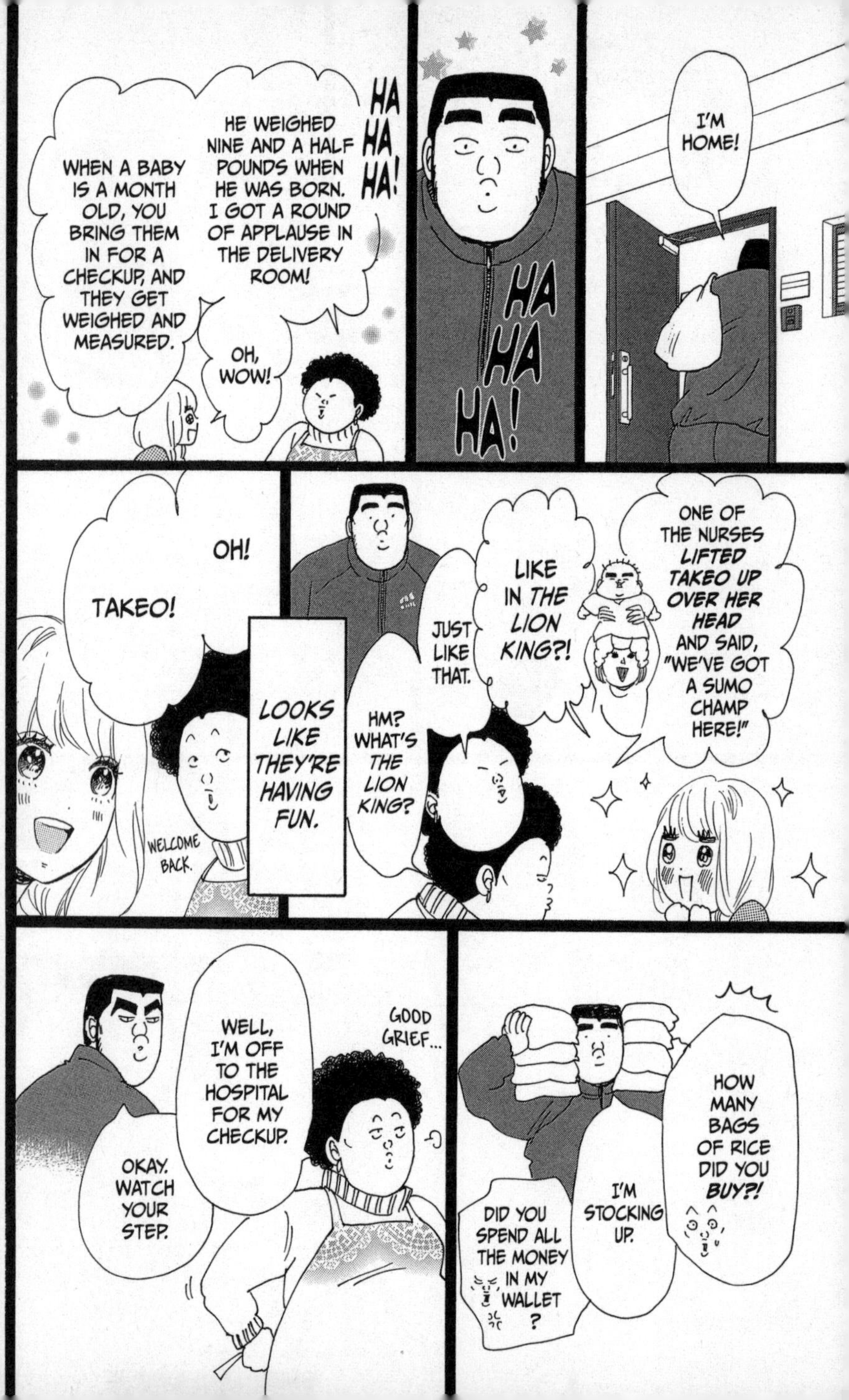
I'M HOME!
HA HA HA!
HA HA HA!
HE WEIGHED NINE AND A HALF POUNDS WHEN HE WAS BORN. I GOT A ROUND OF APPLAUSE IN THE DELIVERY ROOM!
WHEN A BABY IS A MONTH OLD, YOU BRING THEM IN FOR A CHECKUP, AND THEY GET WEIGHED AND MEASURED.
OH, WOW!
ONE OF THE NURSES *LIFTED TAKEO UP OVER HER HEAD* AND SAID, "WE'VE GOT A SUMO CHAMP HERE!"
LIKE IN *THE LION KING?!*
JUST LIKE THAT.
HM? WHAT'S *THE LION KING?*
LOOKS LIKE THEY'RE HAVING FUN.
OH!
TAKEO!
WELCOME BACK.
HOW MANY BAGS OF RICE DID YOU *BUY?!*
I'M STOCKING UP.
DID YOU SPEND ALL THE MONEY IN MY WALLET?
GOOD GRIEF...
WELL, I'M OFF TO THE HOSPITAL FOR MY CHECKUP.
OKAY. WATCH YOUR STEP.

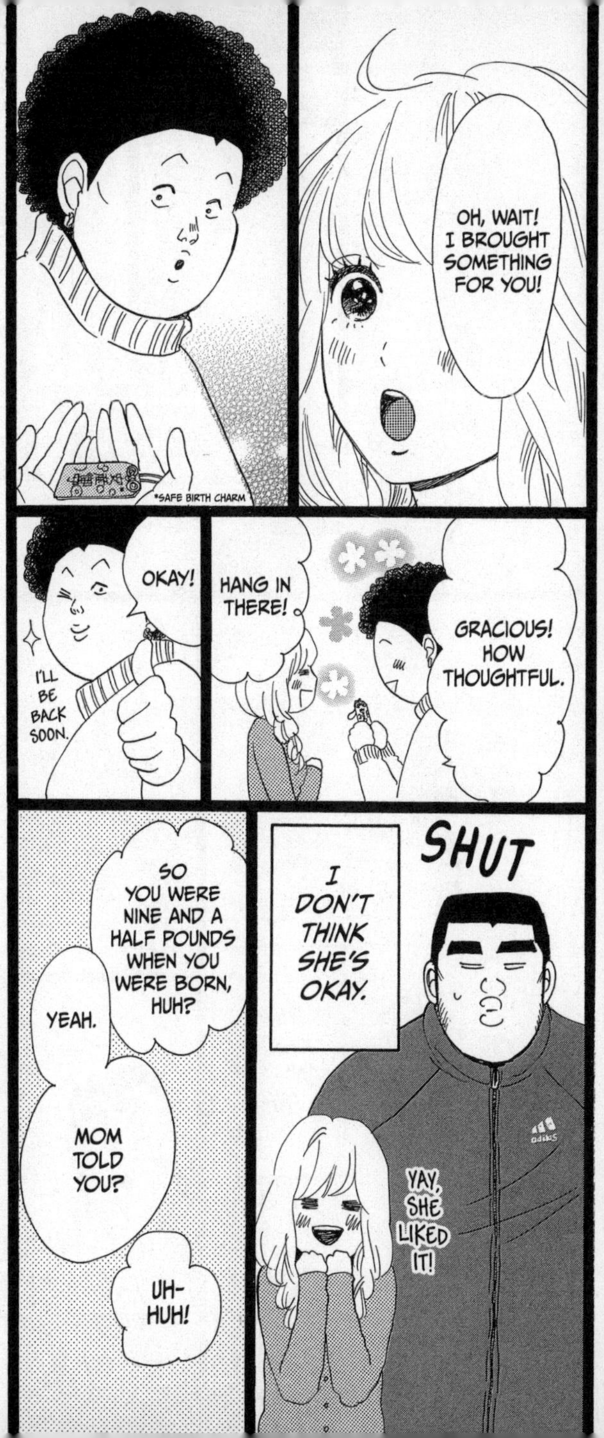
OH, WAIT! I BROUGHT SOMETHING FOR YOU!
*SAFE BIRTH CHARM
GRACIOUS! HOW THOUGHTFUL.
HANG IN THERE!
OKAY!
I'LL BE BACK SOON.
SHUT
I DON'T THINK SHE'S OKAY.
YAY, SHE LIKED IT!
SO YOU WERE NINE AND A HALF POUNDS WHEN YOU WERE BORN, HUH?
YEAH.
MOM TOLD YOU?
UH-HUH!

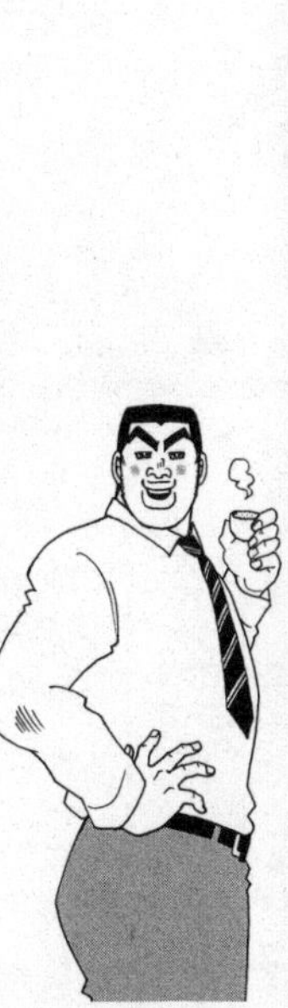

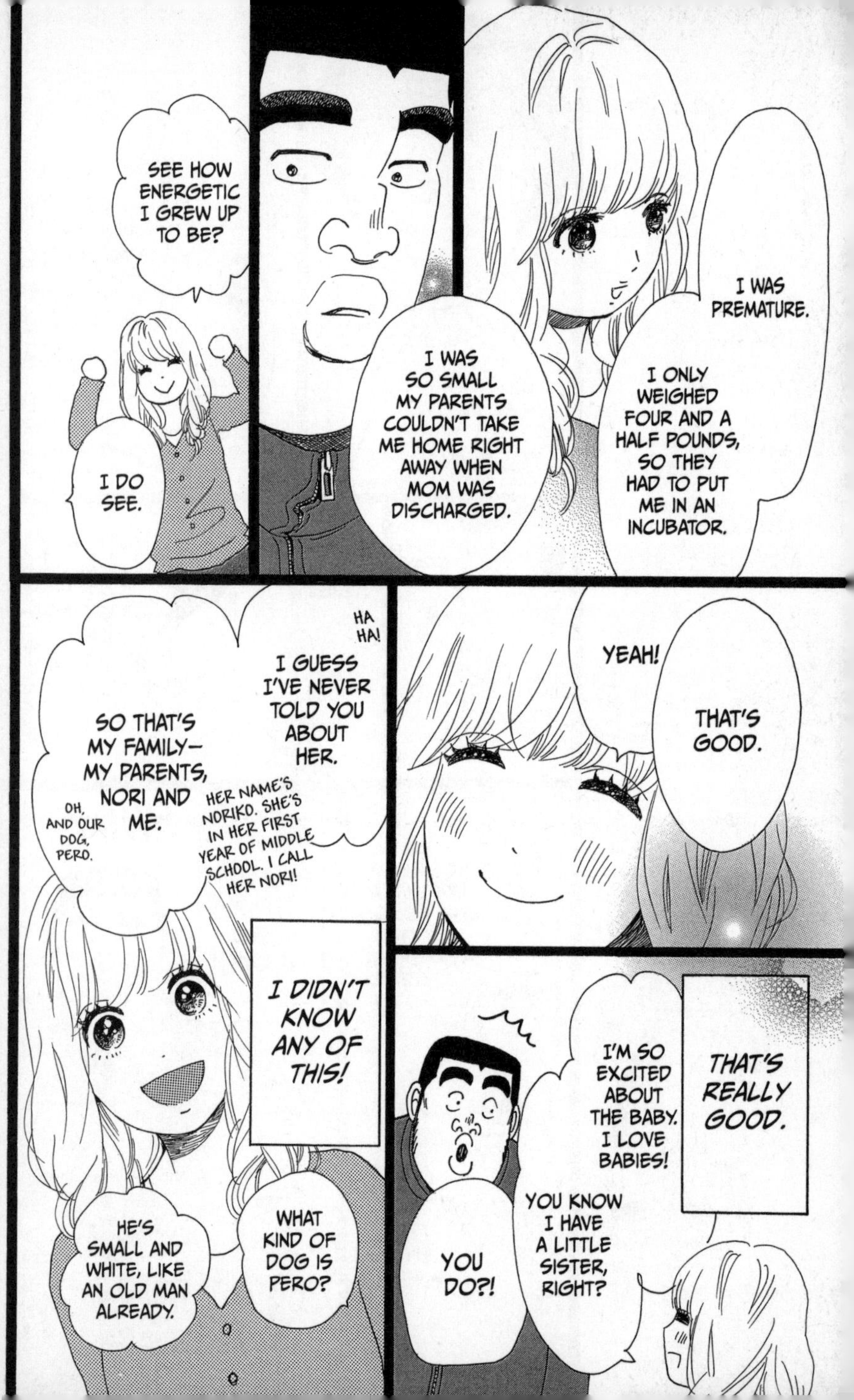
I WAS PREMATURE.
I ONLY WEIGHED FOUR AND A HALF POUNDS, SO THEY HAD TO PUT ME IN AN INCUBATOR.
I WAS SO SMALL MY PARENTS COULDN'T TAKE ME HOME RIGHT AWAY WHEN MOM WAS DISCHARGED.
SEE HOW ENERGETIC I GREW UP TO BE?
I DO SEE.
THAT'S GOOD.
YEAH!
THAT'S REALLY GOOD.
I'M SO EXCITED ABOUT THE BABY. I LOVE BABIES!
YOU KNOW I HAVE A LITTLE SISTER, RIGHT?
YOU DO?!
HA HA!
I GUESS I'VE NEVER TOLD YOU ABOUT HER.
HER NAME'S NORIKO. SHE'S IN HER FIRST YEAR OF MIDDLE SCHOOL. I CALL HER NORI!
SO THAT'S MY FAMILY—MY PARENTS, NORI AND ME.
OH, AND OUR DOG, PERO.
I DIDN'T KNOW ANY OF THIS!
WHAT KIND OF DOG IS PERO?
HE'S SMALL AND WHITE, LIKE AN OLD MAN ALREADY.

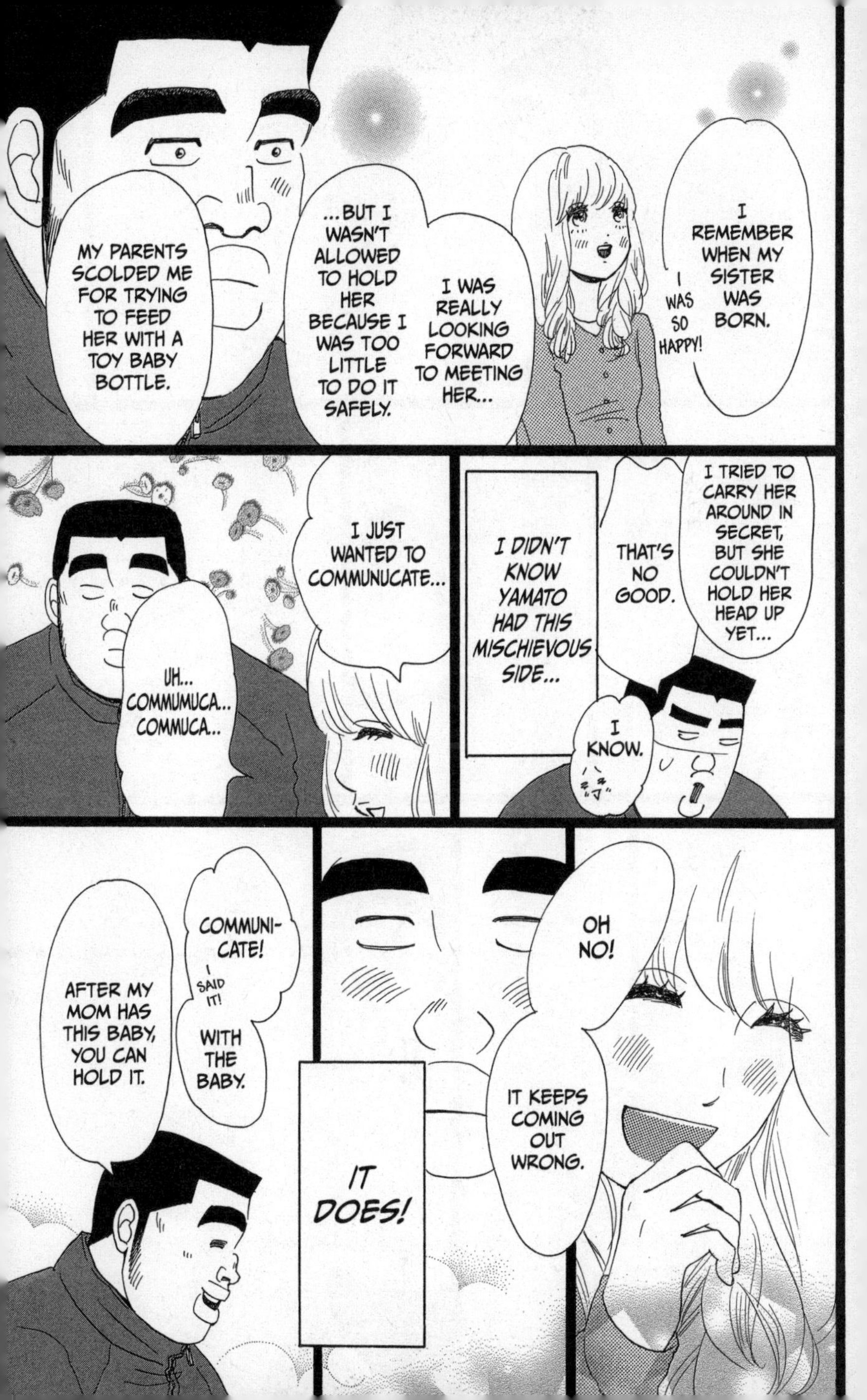
I REMEMBER WHEN MY SISTER WAS BORN.
I WAS SO HAPPY!
I WAS REALLY LOOKING FORWARD TO MEETING HER...
...BUT I WASN'T ALLOWED TO HOLD HER BECAUSE I WAS TOO LITTLE TO DO IT SAFELY.
MY PARENTS SCOLDED ME FOR TRYING TO FEED HER WITH A TOY BABY BOTTLE.
I TRIED TO CARRY HER AROUND IN SECRET, BUT SHE COULDN'T HOLD HER HEAD UP YET...
THAT'S NO GOOD.
I DIDN'T KNOW YAMATO HAD THIS MISCHIEVOUS SIDE...
I KNOW.
I JUST WANTED TO COMMUNUCATE...
UH... COMMUMUCA... COMMUCA...
OH NO!
IT KEEPS COMING OUT WRONG.
IT DOES!
COMMUNI-CATE!
I SAID IT!
WITH THE BABY.
AFTER MY MOM HAS THIS BABY, YOU CAN HOLD IT.

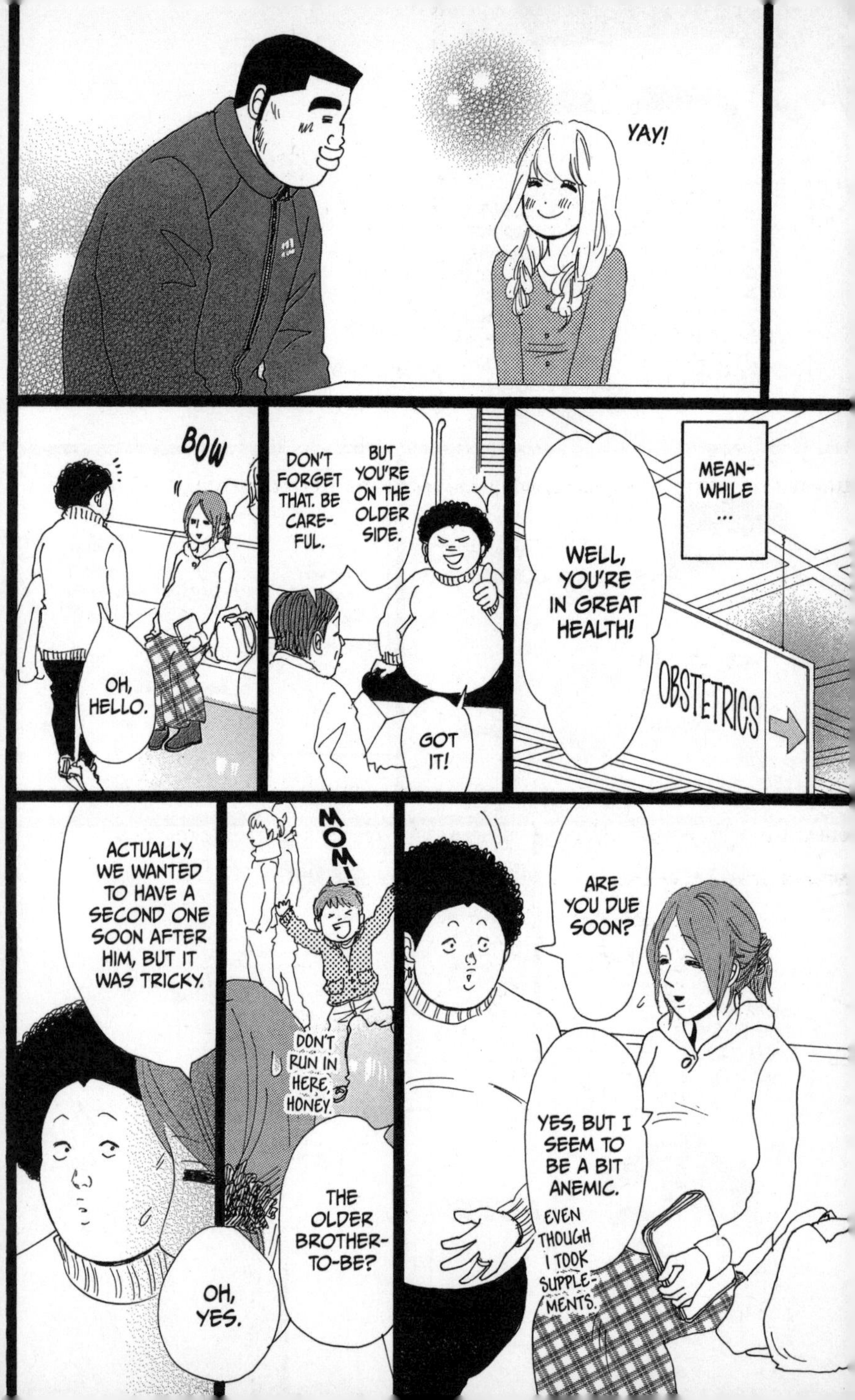
YAY!
MEAN-WHILE...
WELL, YOU'RE IN GREAT HEALTH!
OBSTETRICS
BUT YOU'RE ON THE OLDER SIDE.
DON'T FORGET THAT. BE CARE-FUL.
GOT IT!
BOW
OH, HELLO.
ARE YOU DUE SOON?
YES, BUT I SEEM TO BE A BIT ANEMIC.
EVEN THOUGH I TOOK SUPPLE-MENTS.
MOM!
DON'T RUN IN HERE, HONEY.
THE OLDER BROTHER-TO-BE?
OH, YES.
ACTUALLY, WE WANTED TO HAVE A SECOND ONE SOON AFTER HIM, BUT IT WAS TRICKY.

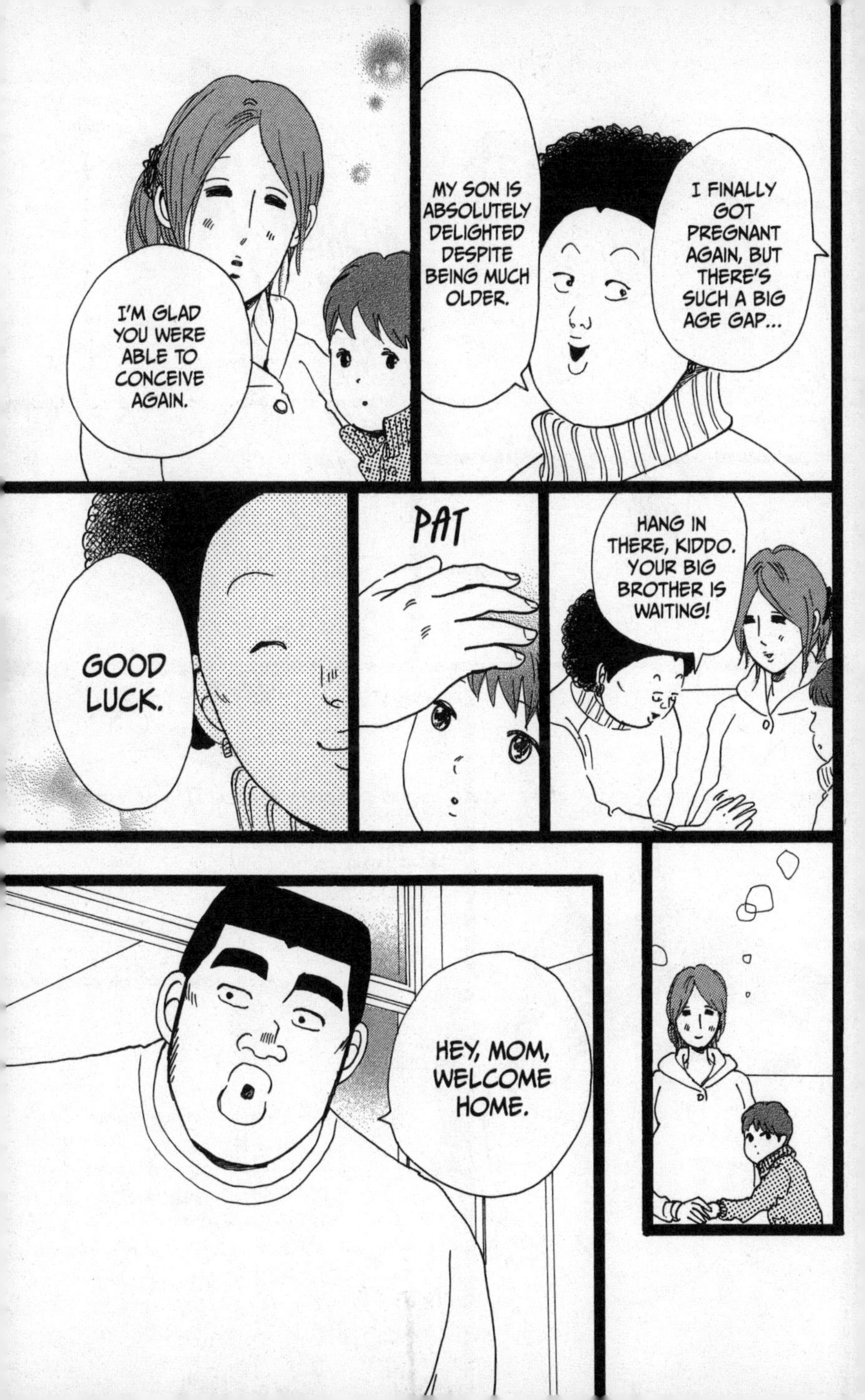
I FINALLY GOT PREGNANT AGAIN, BUT THERE'S SUCH A BIG AGE GAP...
MY SON IS ABSOLUTELY DELIGHTED DESPITE BEING MUCH OLDER.
I'M GLAD YOU WERE ABLE TO CONCEIVE AGAIN.
HANG IN THERE, KIDDO. YOUR BIG BROTHER IS WAITING!
PAT
GOOD LUCK.
HEY, MOM, WELCOME HOME.

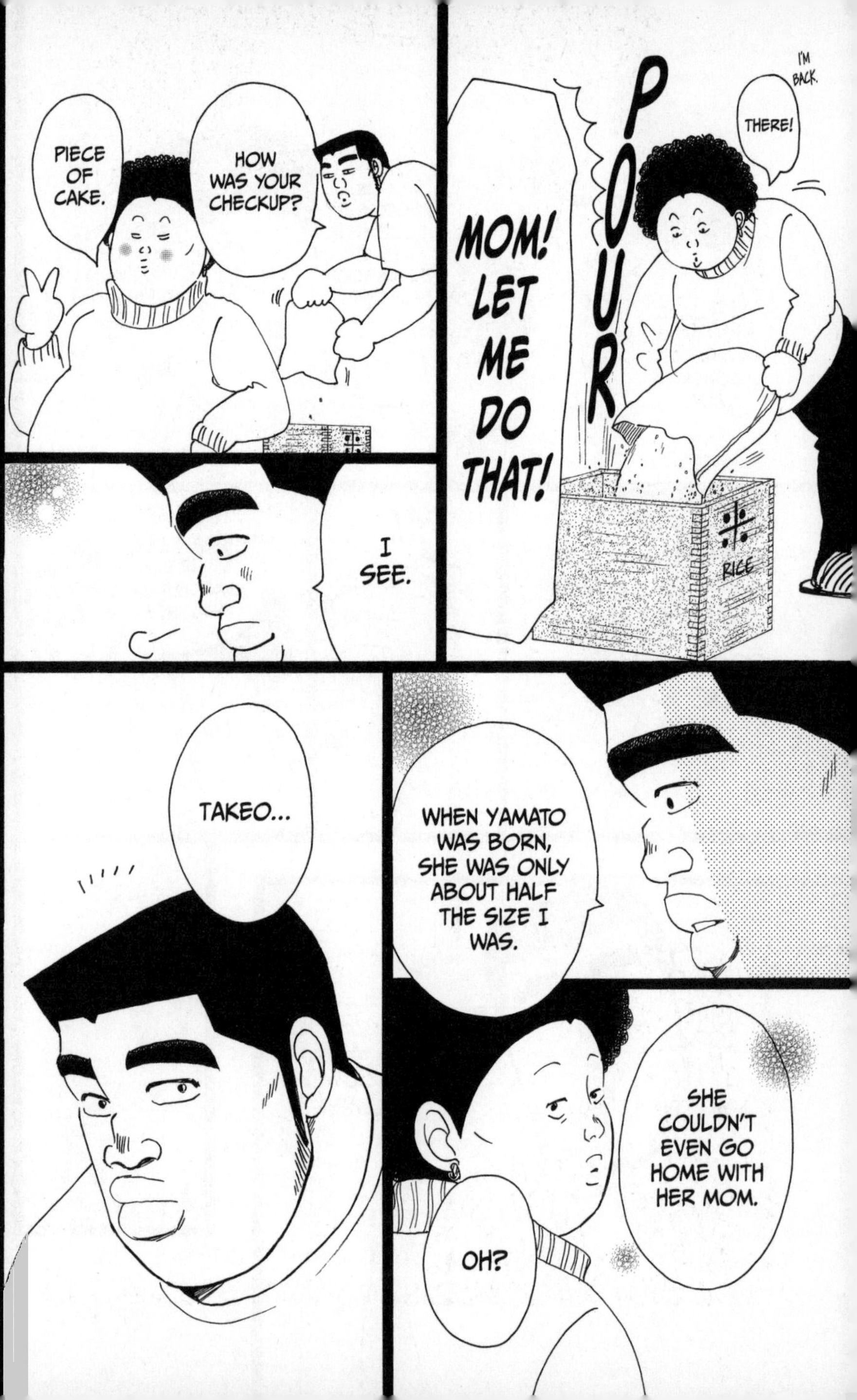
I'M BACK.
THERE!
POUR
MOM! LET ME DO THAT!
RICE
HOW WAS YOUR CHECKUP?
PIECE OF CAKE.
I SEE.
WHEN YAMATO WAS BORN, SHE WAS ONLY ABOUT HALF THE SIZE I WAS.
SHE COULDN'T EVEN GO HOME WITH HER MOM.
OH?
TAKEO...

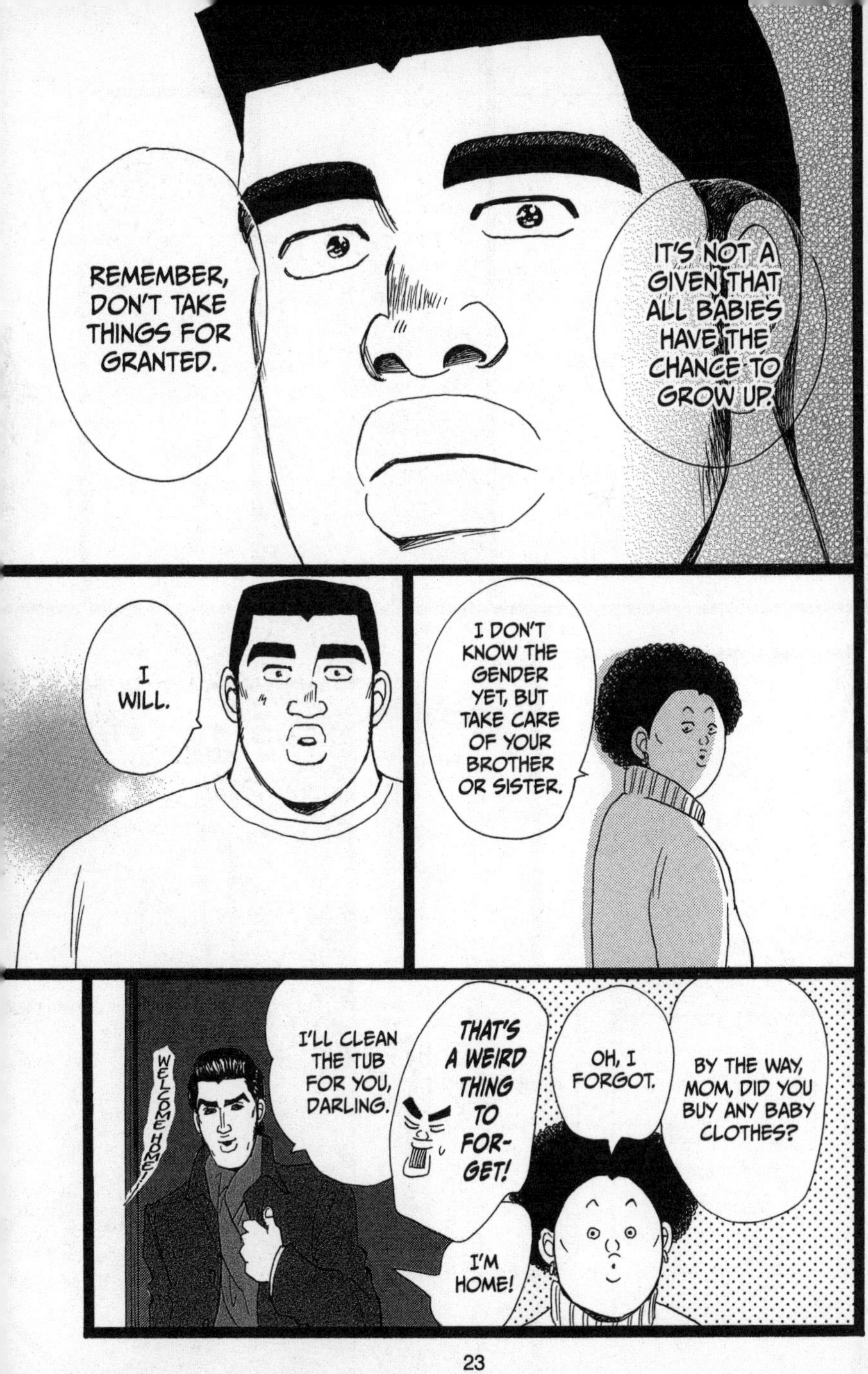
IT'S NOT A GIVEN THAT ALL BABIES HAVE THE CHANCE TO GROW UP.
REMEMBER, DON'T TAKE THINGS FOR GRANTED.
I DON'T KNOW THE GENDER YET, BUT TAKE CARE OF YOUR BROTHER OR SISTER.
I WILL.
BY THE WAY, MOM, DID YOU BUY ANY BABY CLOTHES?
OH, I FORGOT.
THAT'S A WEIRD THING TO FOR-GET!
I'M HOME!
WELCOME HOME!!
I'LL CLEAN THE TUB FOR YOU, DARLING.

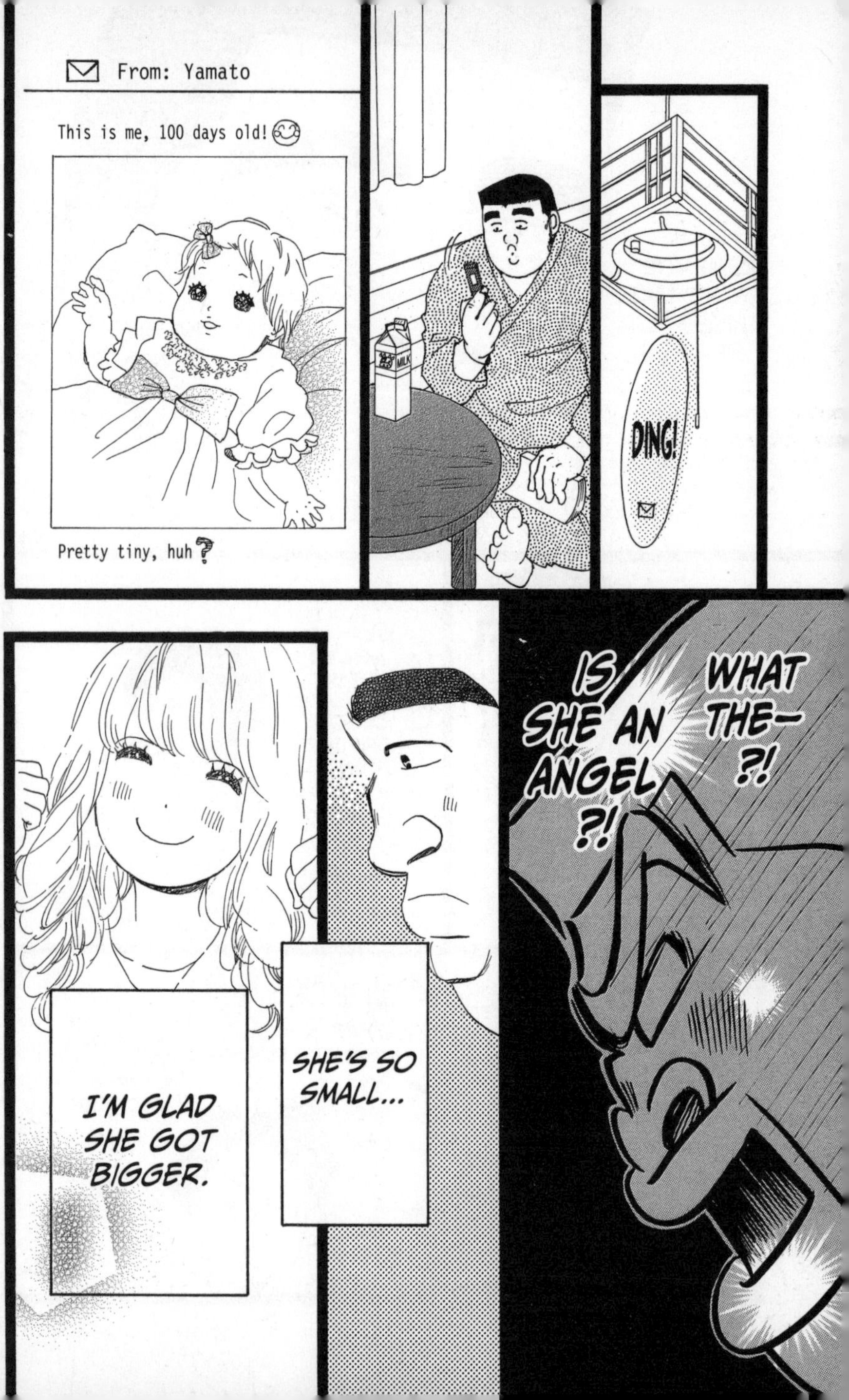
DING!
From: Yamato
This is me, 100 days old!
Pretty tiny, huh?
WHAT THE—?!
IS SHE AN ANGEL?!
SHE'S SO SMALL...
I'M GLAD SHE GOT BIGGER.

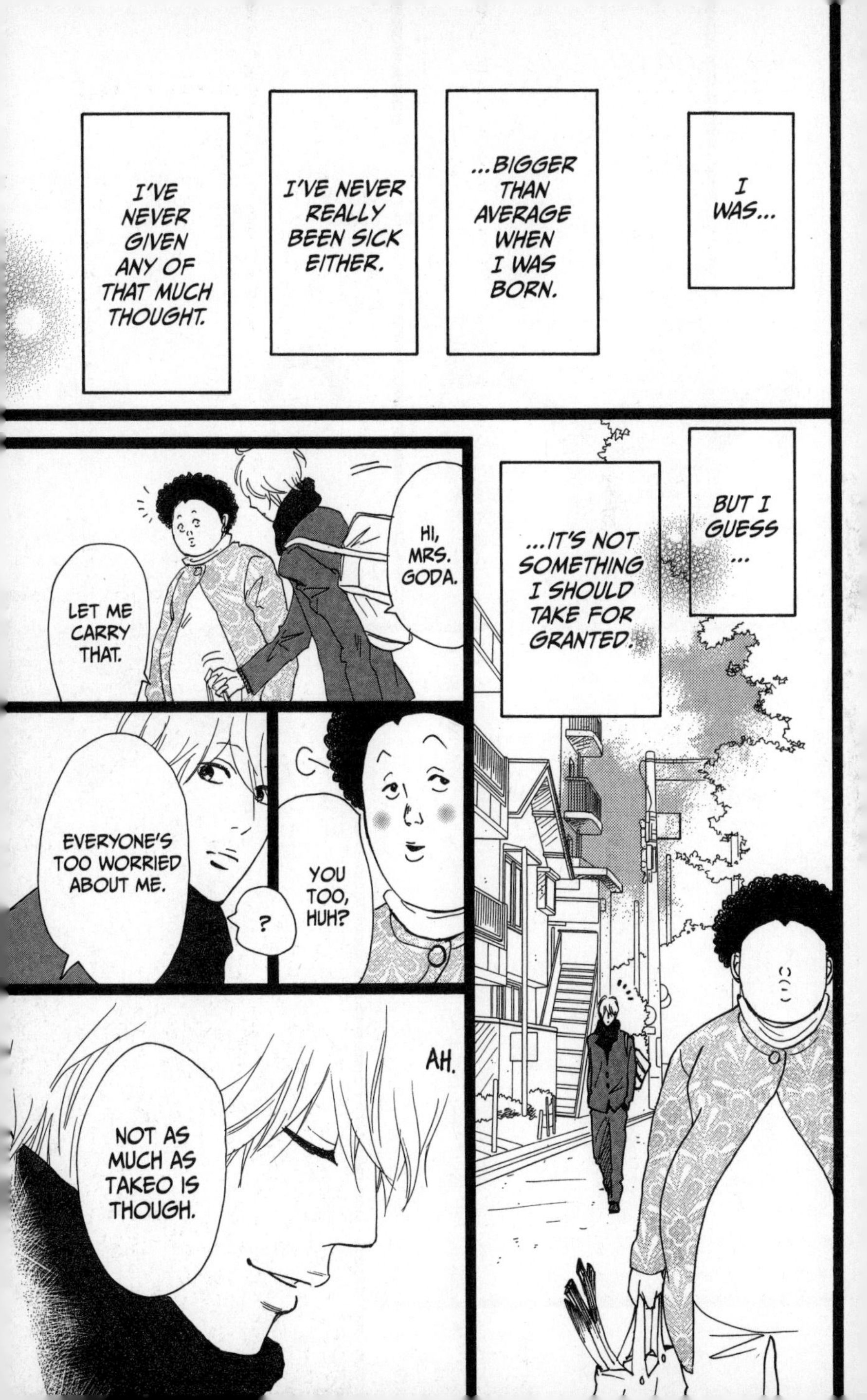
I WAS...
...BIGGER THAN AVERAGE WHEN I WAS BORN.
I'VE NEVER REALLY BEEN SICK EITHER.
I'VE NEVER GIVEN ANY OF THAT MUCH THOUGHT.
BUT I GUESS...
...IT'S NOT SOMETHING I SHOULD TAKE FOR GRANTED.
HI, MRS. GODA.
LET ME CARRY THAT.
YOU TOO, HUH?
?
EVERYONE'S TOO WORRIED ABOUT ME.
AH.
NOT AS MUCH AS TAKEO IS THOUGH.

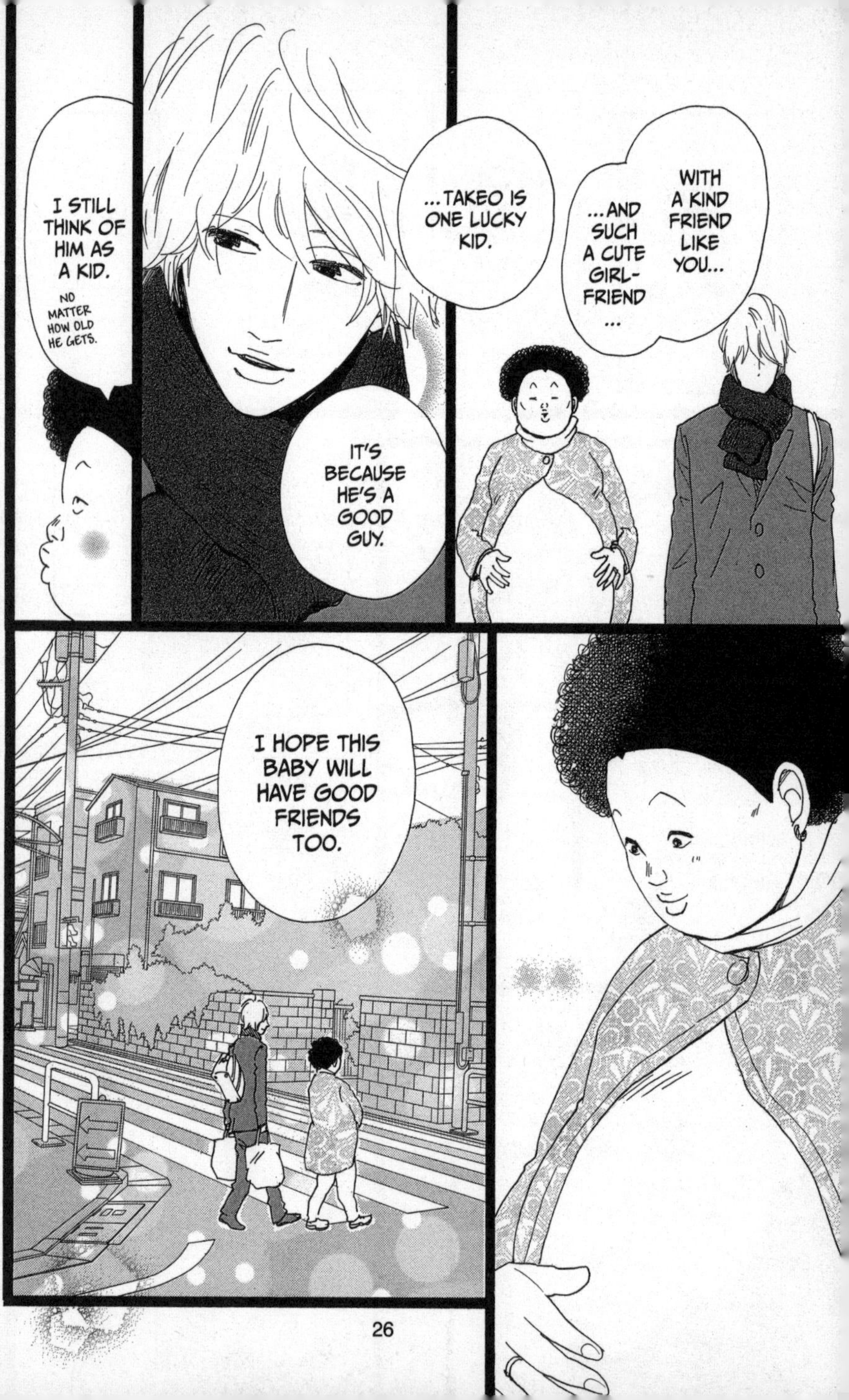
WITH A KIND FRIEND LIKE YOU...
...AND SUCH A CUTE GIRL-FRIEND ...
...TAKEO IS ONE LUCKY KID.
IT'S BECAUSE HE'S A GOOD GUY.
I STILL THINK OF HIM AS A KID.
NO MATTER HOW OLD HE GETS.
I HOPE THIS BABY WILL HAVE GOOD FRIENDS TOO.

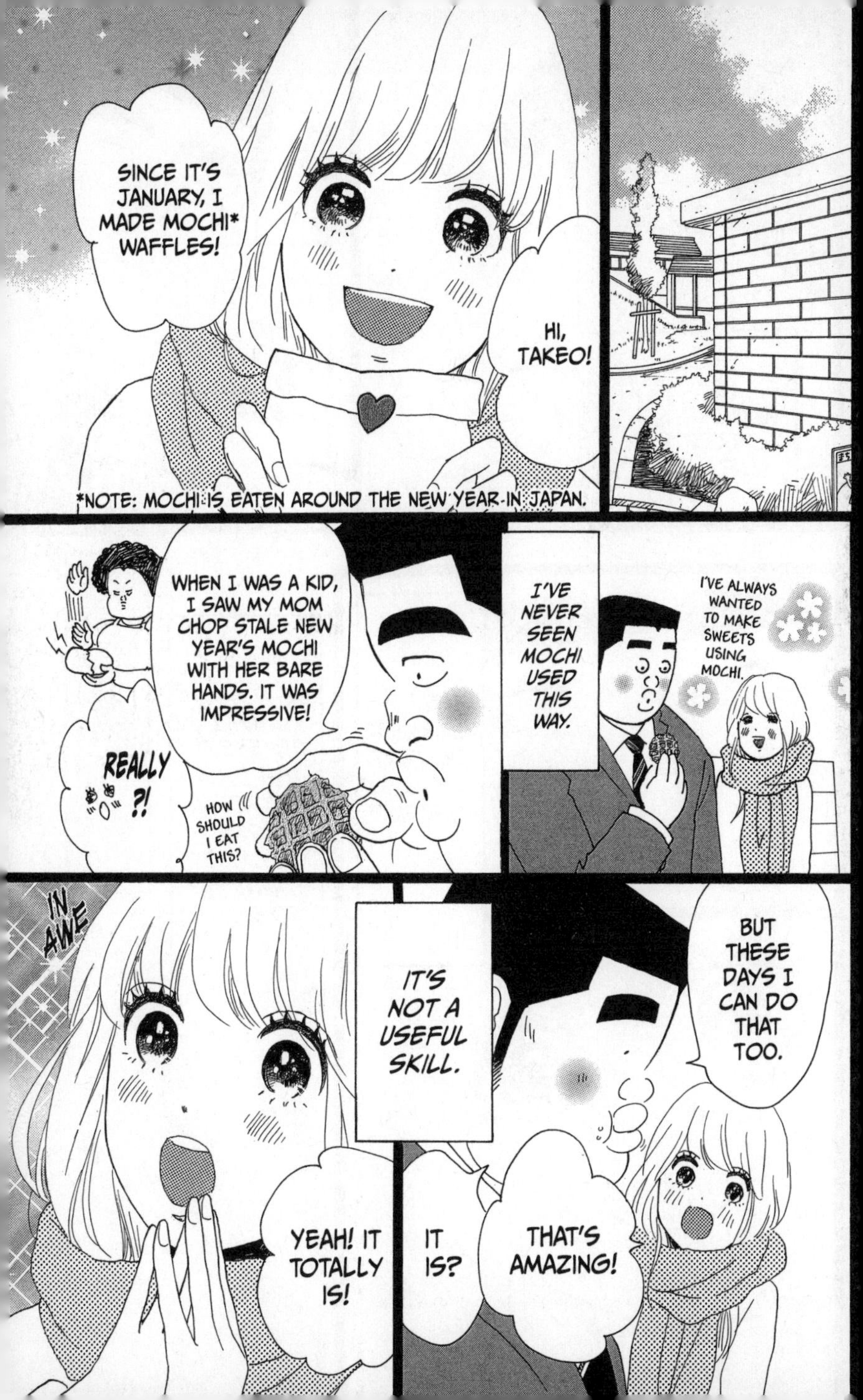
HI, TAKEO!
SINCE IT'S JANUARY, I MADE MOCHI* WAFFLES!
*NOTE: MOCHI IS EATEN AROUND THE NEW YEAR IN JAPAN.
I'VE ALWAYS WANTED TO MAKE SWEETS USING MOCHI.
I'VE NEVER SEEN MOCHI USED THIS WAY.
WHEN I WAS A KID, I SAW MY MOM CHOP STALE NEW YEAR'S MOCHI WITH HER BARE HANDS. IT WAS IMPRESSIVE!
REALLY?!
HOW SHOULD I EAT THIS?
BUT THESE DAYS I CAN DO THAT TOO.
THAT'S AMAZING!
IT IS?
IT'S NOT A USEFUL SKILL.
IN AWE
YEAH! IT TOTALLY IS!

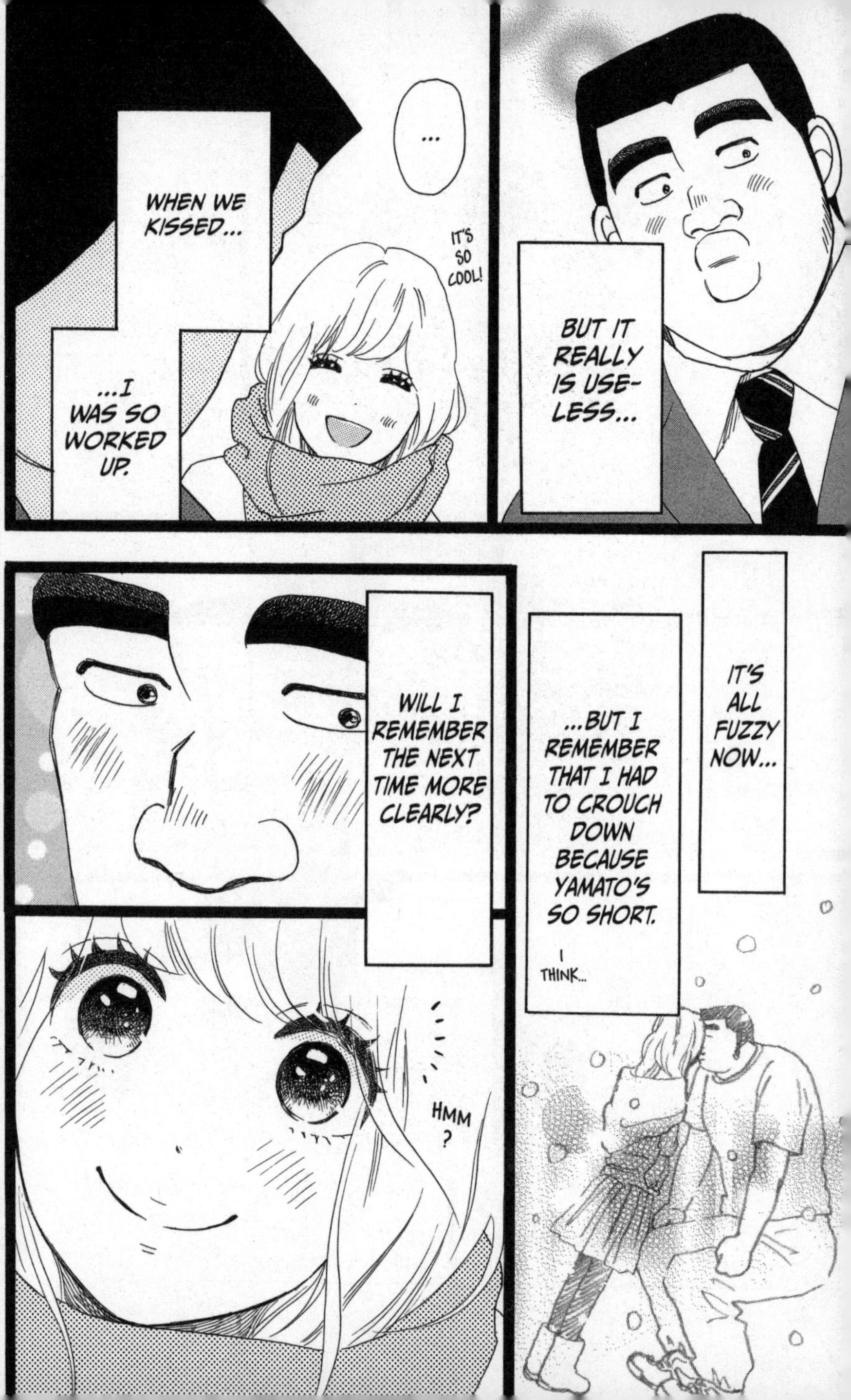
BUT IT REALLY IS USE-LESS...
...
IT'S SO COOL!
WHEN WE KISSED...
...I WAS SO WORKED UP.
IT'S ALL FUZZY NOW...
...BUT I REMEMBER THAT I HAD TO CROUCH DOWN BECAUSE YAMATO'S SO SHORT.
I THINK...
WILL I REMEMBER THE NEXT TIME MORE CLEARLY?
HMM?

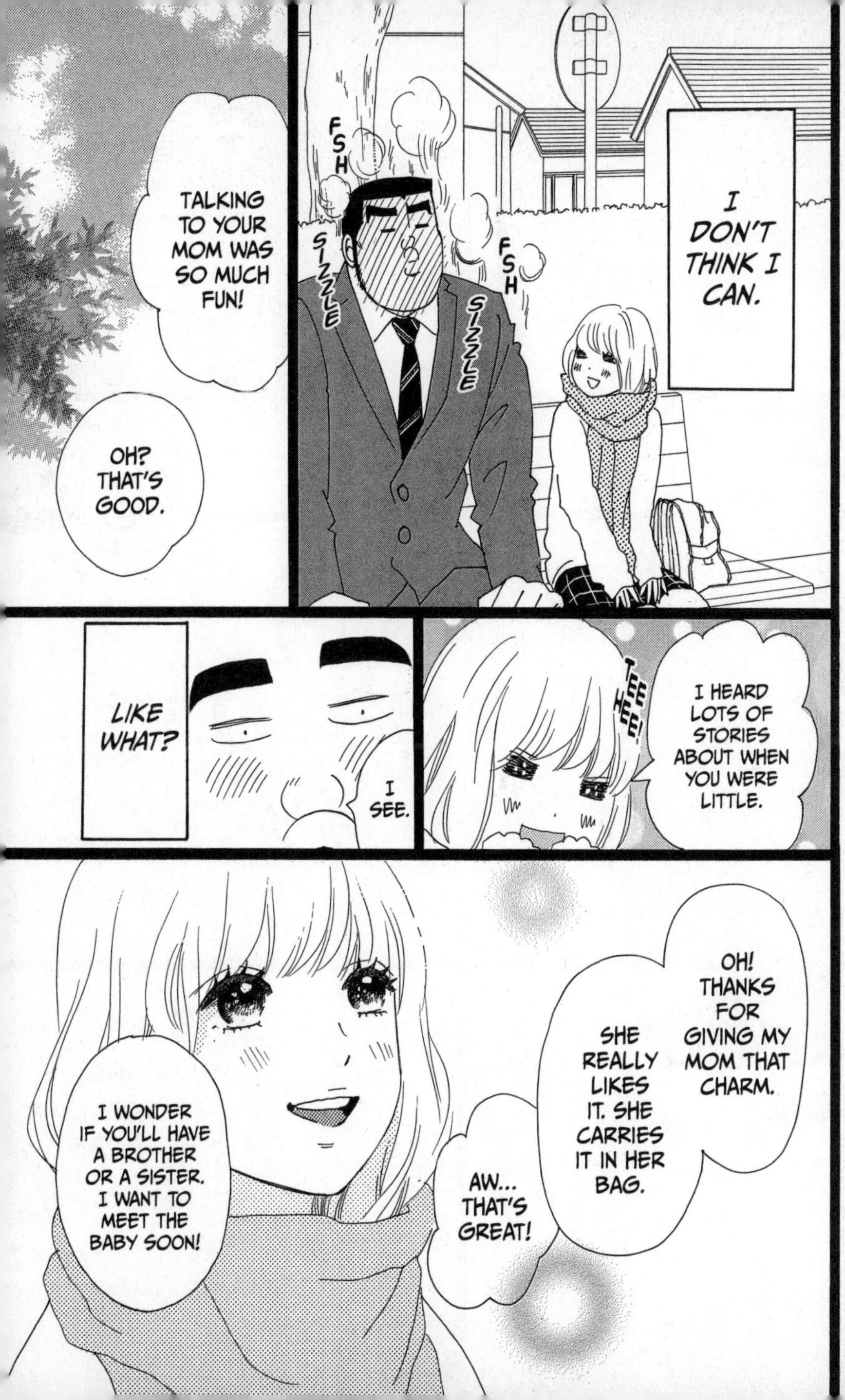
I DON'T THINK I CAN.
FSH
FSH
SIZZLE
SIZZLE
TALKING TO YOUR MOM WAS SO MUCH FUN!
OH? THAT'S GOOD.
TEE HEE!
I HEARD LOTS OF STORIES ABOUT WHEN YOU WERE LITTLE.
I SEE.
LIKE WHAT?
OH! THANKS FOR GIVING MY MOM THAT CHARM.
SHE REALLY LIKES IT. SHE CARRIES IT IN HER BAG.
AW... THAT'S GREAT!
I WONDER IF YOU'LL HAVE A BROTHER OR A SISTER. I WANT TO MEET THE BABY SOON!

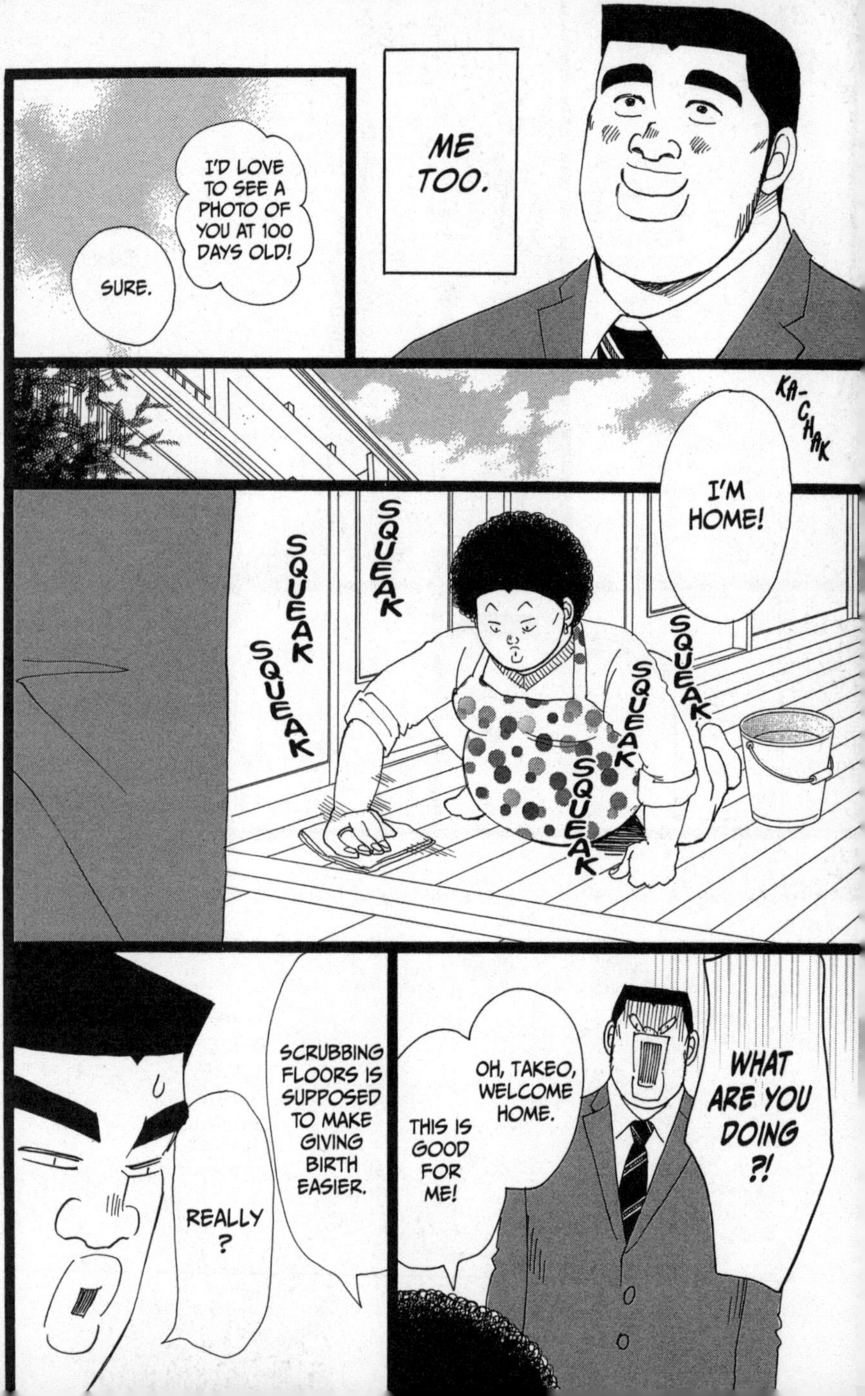
ME TOO.
I'D LOVE TO SEE A PHOTO OF YOU AT 100 DAYS OLD!
SURE.
KA-CHAK
I'M HOME!
SQUEAK
SQUEAK
SQUEAK
SQUEAK
SQUEAK
SQUEAK
WHAT ARE YOU DOING ?!
OH, TAKEO, WELCOME HOME.
THIS IS GOOD FOR ME!
SCRUBBING FLOORS IS SUPPOSED TO MAKE GIVING BIRTH EASIER.
REALLY ?

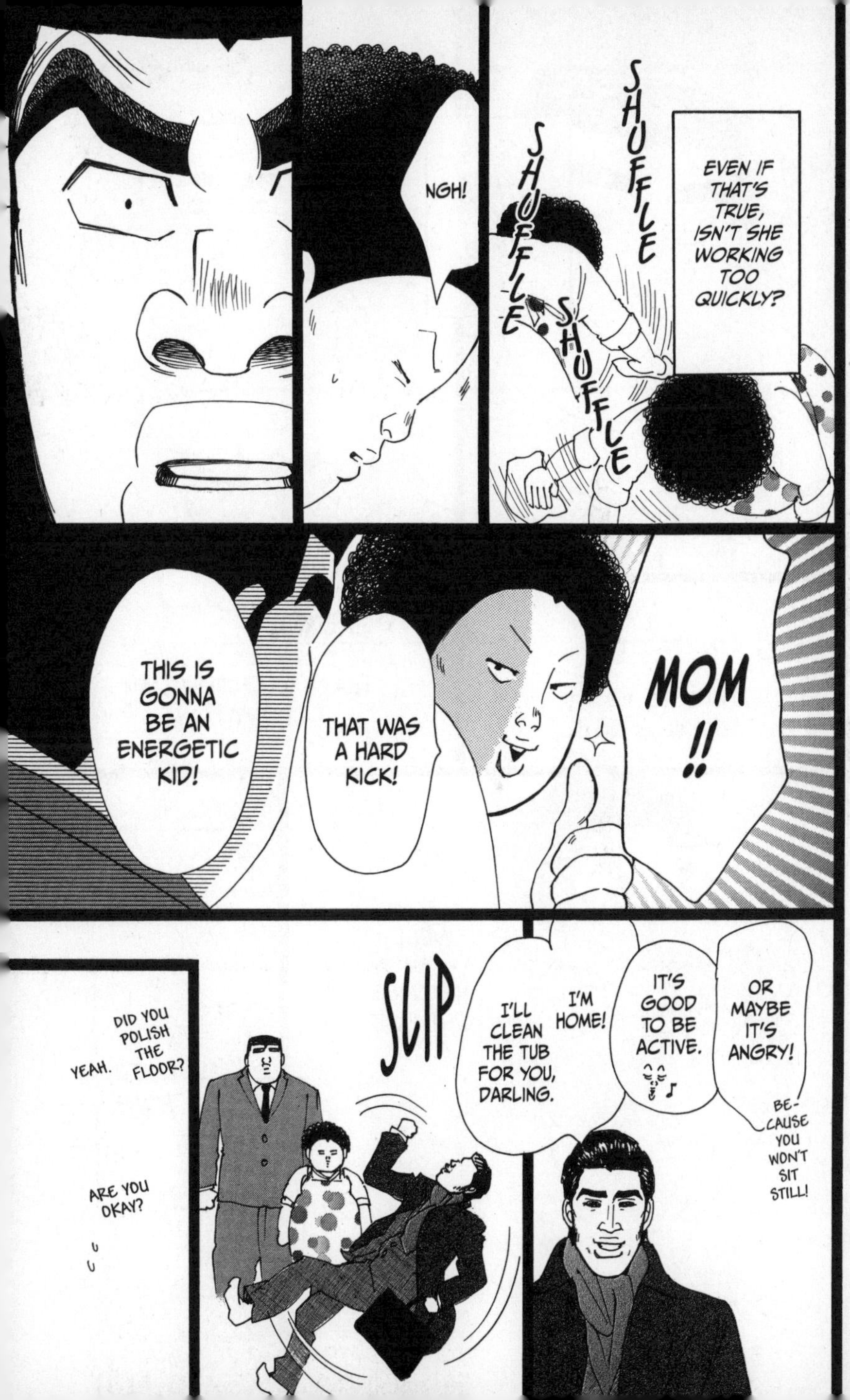
EVEN IF THAT'S TRUE, ISN'T SHE WORKING TOO QUICKLY?
SHUFFLE
SHUFFLE
SHUFFLE
NGH!
MOM!!
THAT WAS A HARD KICK!
THIS IS GONNA BE AN ENERGETIC KID!
OR MAYBE IT'S ANGRY!
BE-CAUSE YOU WON'T SIT STILL!
IT'S GOOD TO BE ACTIVE.
I'M HOME!
I'LL CLEAN THE TUB FOR YOU, DARLING.
SLIP
DID YOU POLISH THE FLOOR?
YEAH.
ARE YOU OKAY?

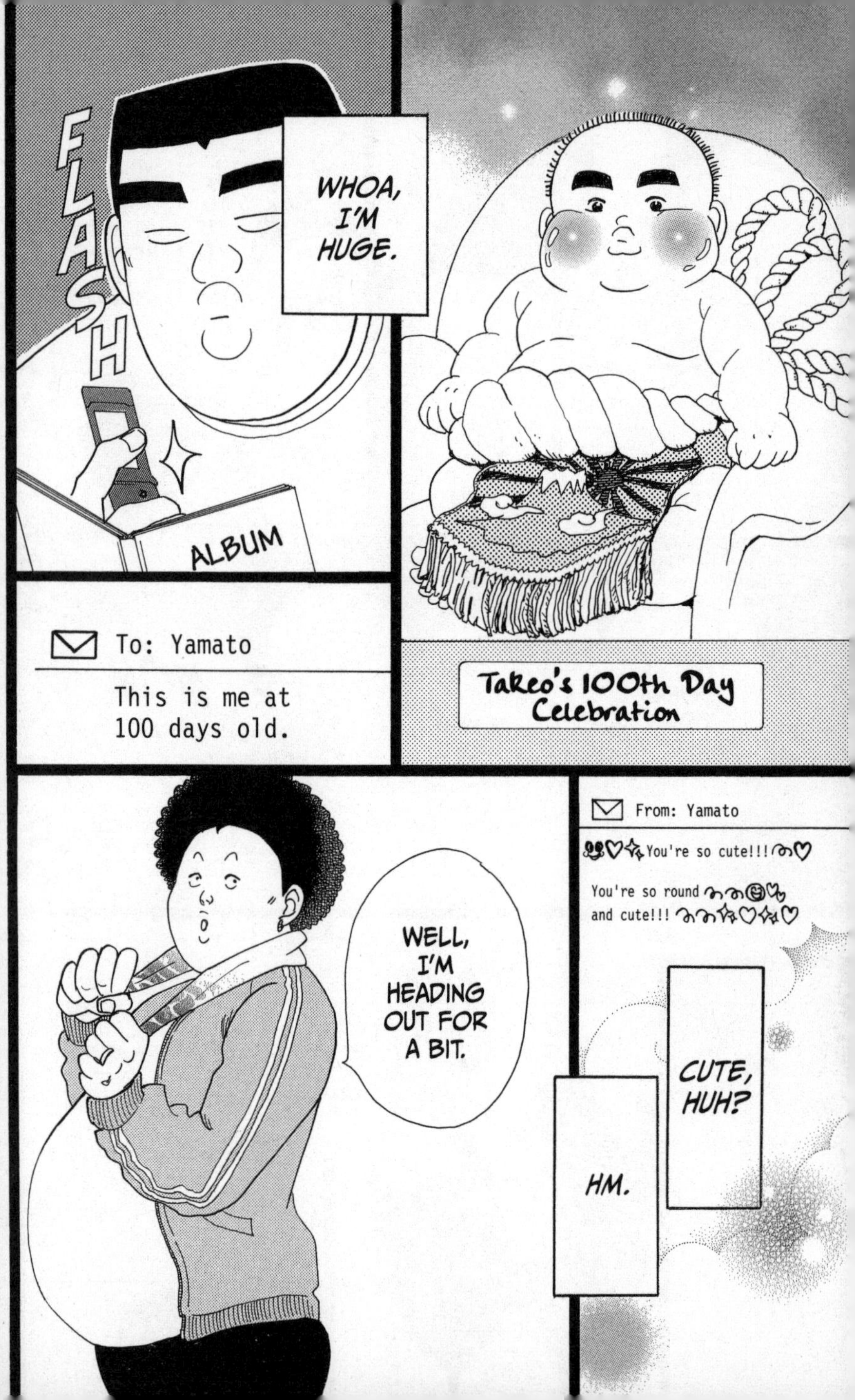

Takeo's 100th Day Celebration
FLASH
WHOA, I'M HUGE.
ALBUM
To: Yamato
This is me at 100 days old.
From: Yamato
You're so cute!!!
You're so round and cute!!!
CUTE, HUH?
HM.
WELL, I'M HEADING OUT FOR A BIT.

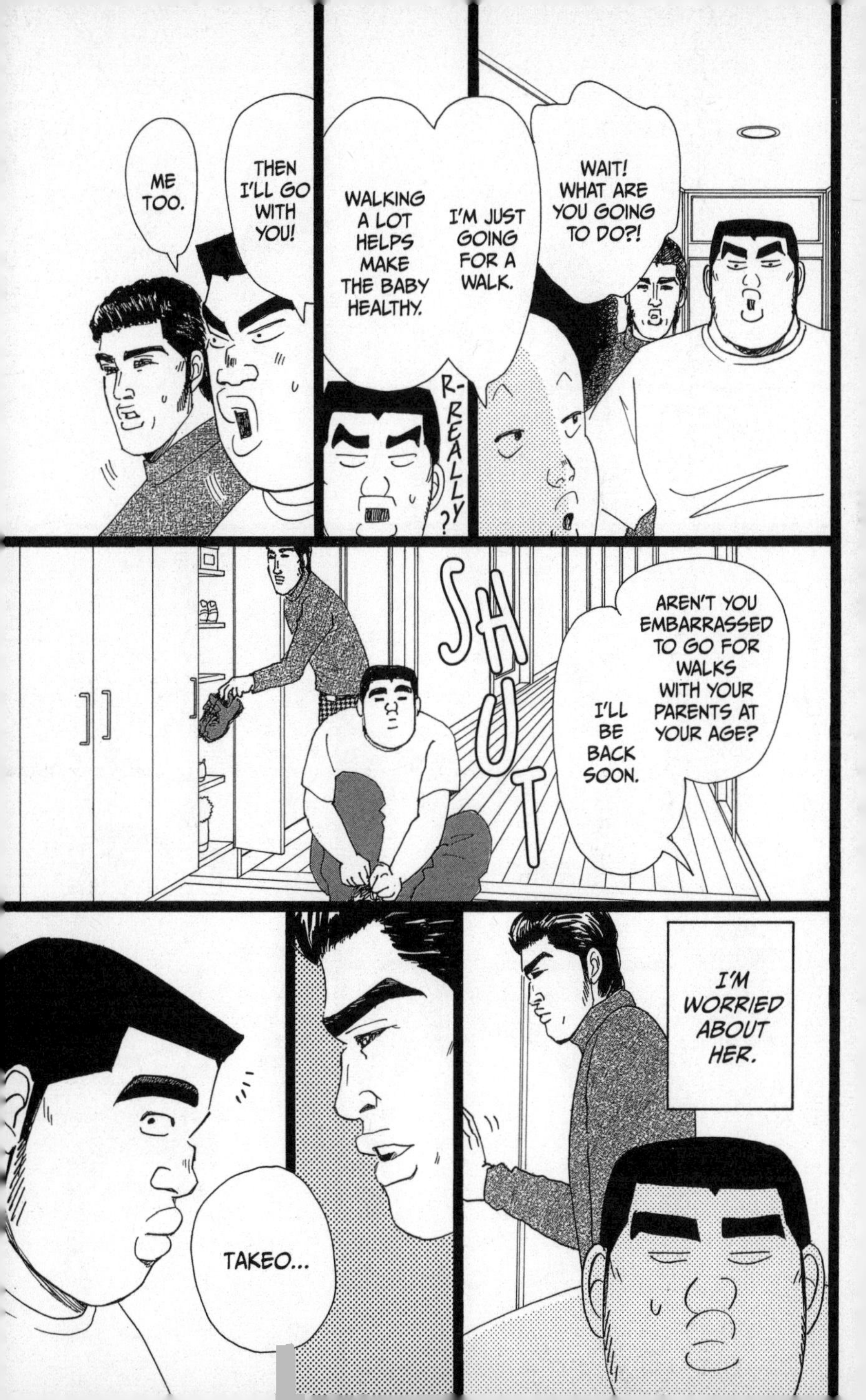
WAIT! WHAT ARE YOU GOING TO DO?!
I'M JUST GOING FOR A WALK.
WALKING A LOT HELPS MAKE THE BABY HEALTHY.
R-REALLY?
THEN I'LL GO WITH YOU!
ME TOO.
AREN'T YOU EMBARRASSED TO GO FOR WALKS WITH YOUR PARENTS AT YOUR AGE?
I'LL BE BACK SOON.
SHUT
I'M WORRIED ABOUT HER.
TAKEO...

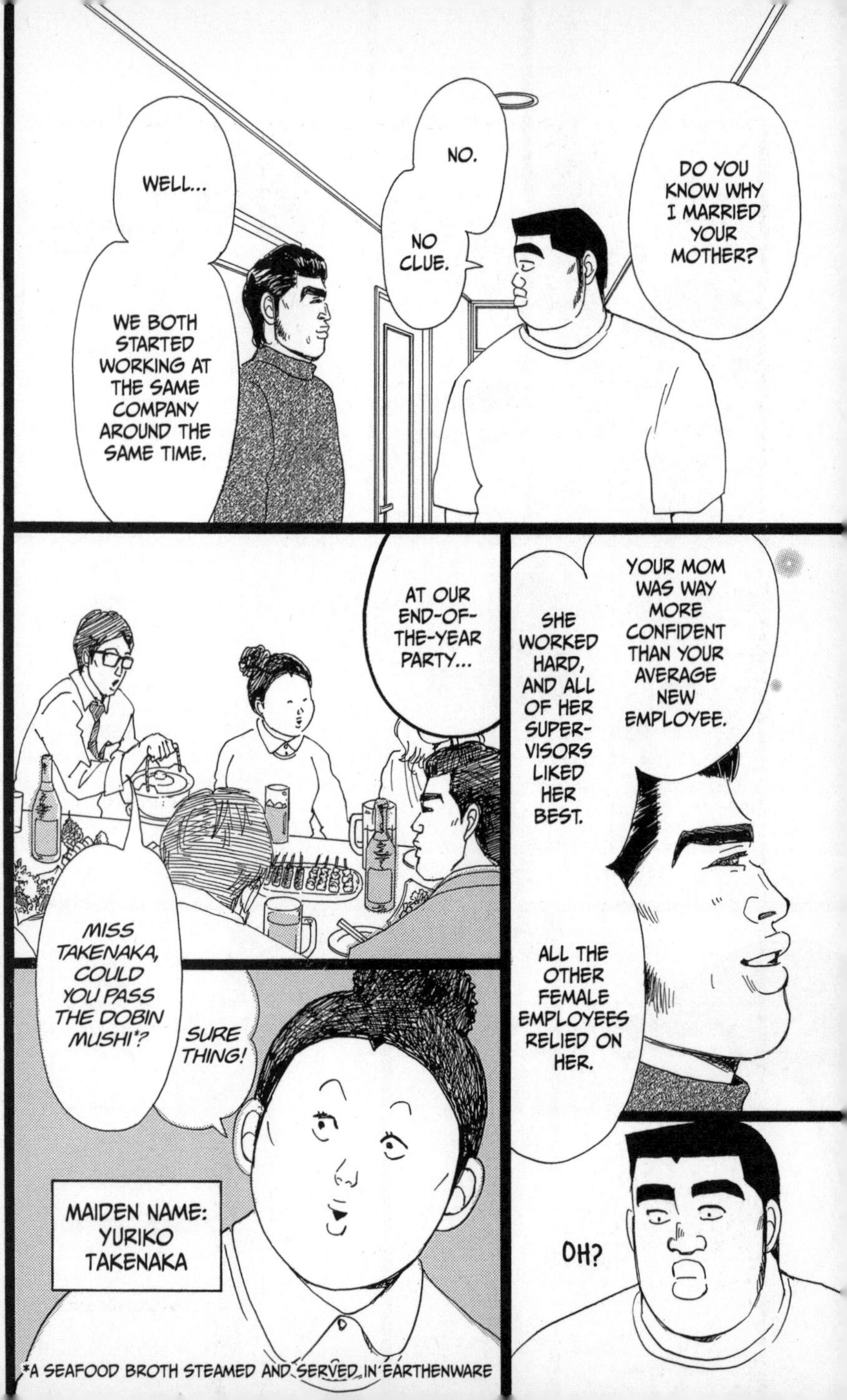
DO YOU KNOW WHY I MARRIED YOUR MOTHER?
NO.
NO CLUE.
WELL...
WE BOTH STARTED WORKING AT THE SAME COMPANY AROUND THE SAME TIME.
YOUR MOM WAS WAY MORE CONFIDENT THAN YOUR AVERAGE NEW EMPLOYEE.
SHE WORKED HARD, AND ALL OF HER SUPER-VISORS LIKED HER BEST.
ALL THE OTHER FEMALE EMPLOYEES RELIED ON HER.
OH?
AT OUR END-OF-THE-YEAR PARTY...
MISS TAKENAKA, COULD YOU PASS THE DOBIN MUSHI*?
SURE THING!
MAIDEN NAME: YURIKO TAKENAKA
*A SEAFOOD BROTH STEAMED AND SERVED IN EARTHENWARE

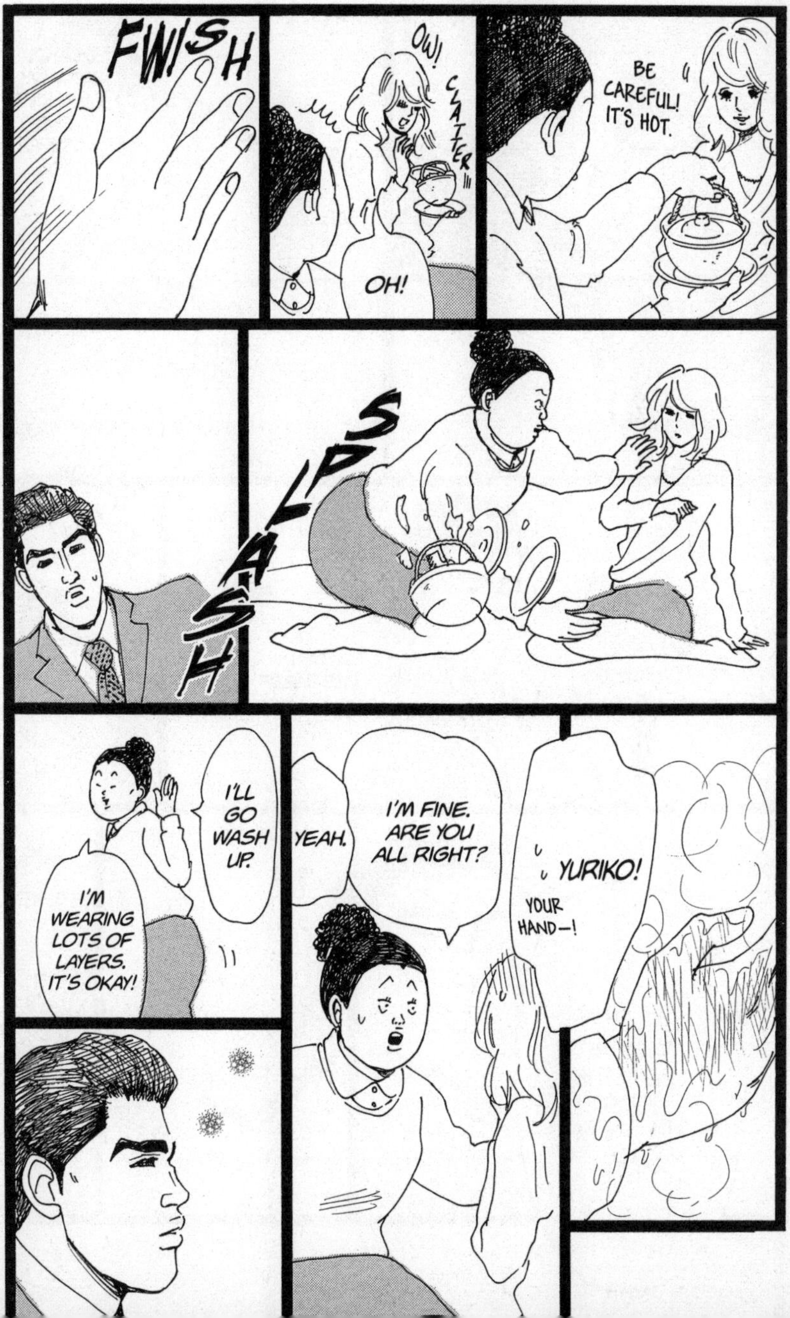
BE CAREFUL! IT'S HOT.
OW!
CLATTER
OH!
FWISH
SPLASH
YURIKO!
YOUR HAND—!
I'M FINE. ARE YOU ALL RIGHT?
YEAH.
I'LL GO WASH UP.
I'M WEARING LOTS OF LAYERS. IT'S OKAY!

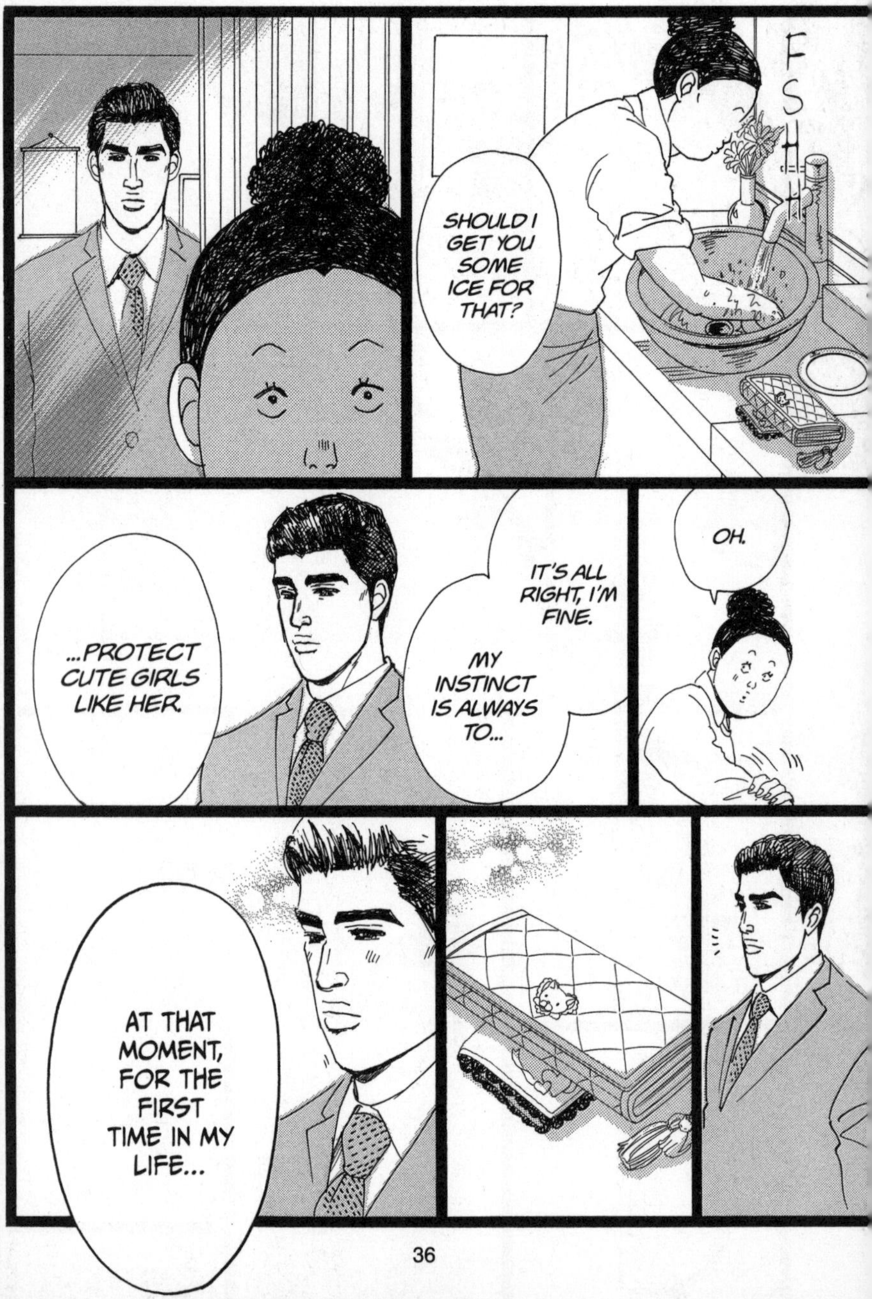
FSHH
SHOULD I GET YOU SOME ICE FOR THAT?
OH.
IT'S ALL RIGHT, I'M FINE.
MY INSTINCT IS ALWAYS TO...
...PROTECT CUTE GIRLS LIKE HER.
AT THAT MOMENT, FOR THE FIRST TIME IN MY LIFE...

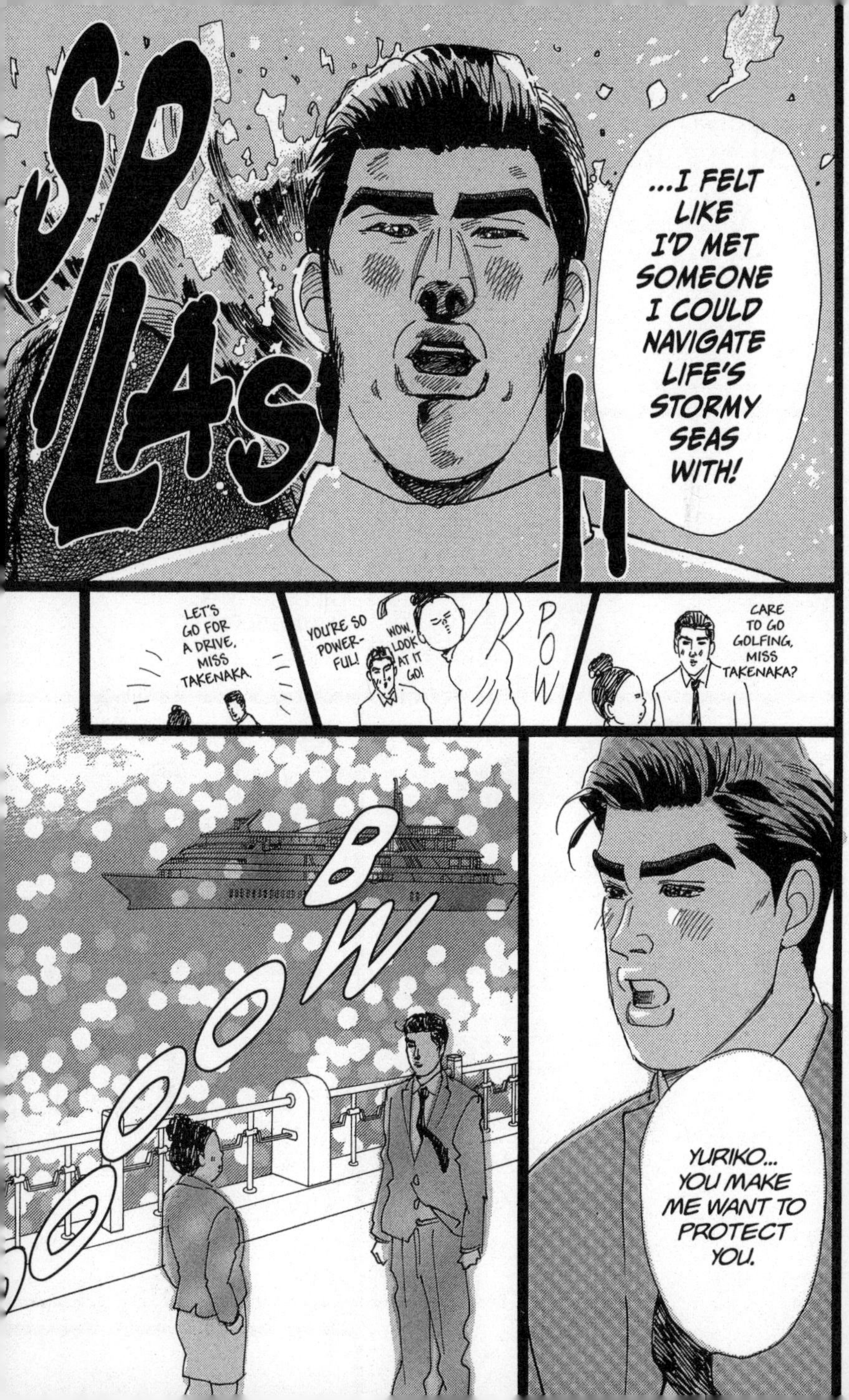
SPLASH
...I FELT LIKE I'D MET SOMEONE I COULD NAVIGATE LIFE'S STORMY SEAS WITH!
CARE TO GO GOLFING, MISS TAKENAKA?
POW
WOW, LOOK AT IT GO!
YOU'RE SO POWER-FUL!
LET'S GO FOR A DRIVE, MISS TAKENAKA.
YURIKO... YOU MAKE ME WANT TO PROTECT YOU.
BWOOOOOO

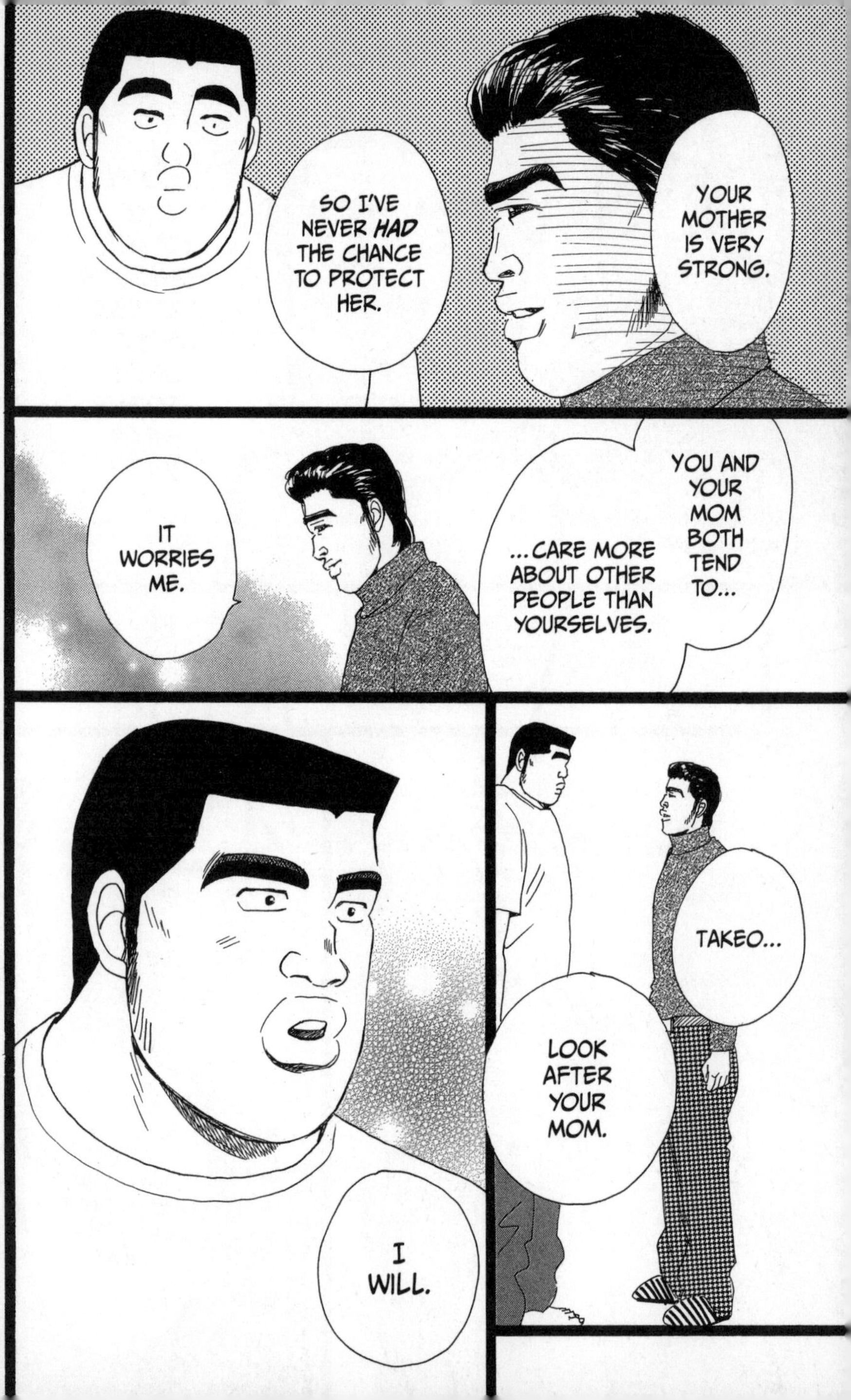
YOUR MOTHER IS VERY STRONG.
SO I'VE NEVER *HAD* THE CHANCE TO PROTECT HER.
YOU AND YOUR MOM BOTH TEND TO...
...CARE MORE ABOUT OTHER PEOPLE THAN YOURSELVES.
IT WORRIES ME.
TAKEO...
LOOK AFTER YOUR MOM.
I WILL.

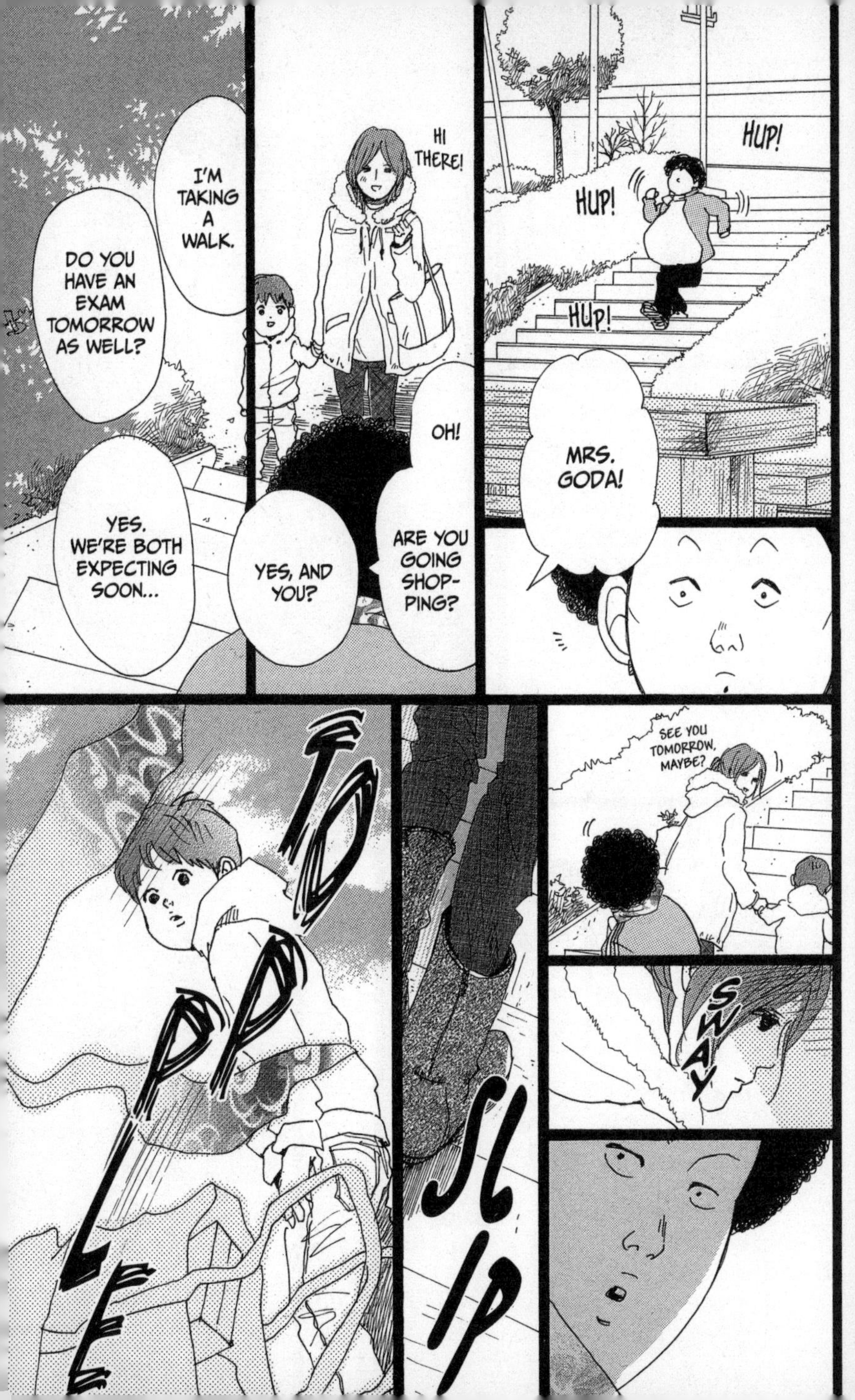
HUP!
HUP!
HUP!
MRS. GODA!
HI THERE!
OH!
ARE YOU GOING SHOP-PING?
YES, AND YOU?
I'M TAKING A WALK.
DO YOU HAVE AN EXAM TOMORROW AS WELL?
YES. WE'RE BOTH EXPECTING SOON...
SEE YOU TOMORROW, MAYBE?
SWAY
SLIP
TOPPLE

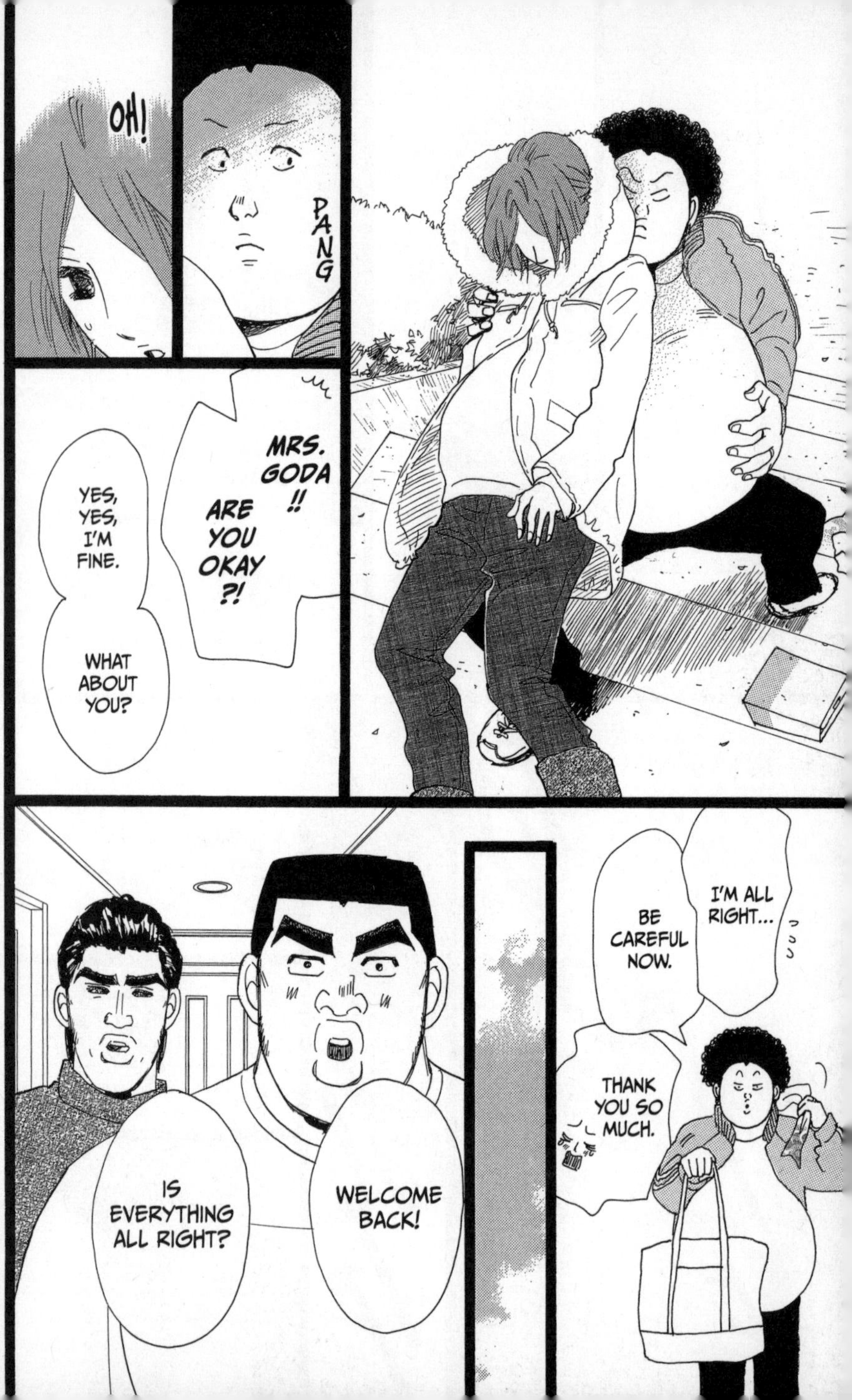
PANG
OH!
MRS. GODA!!
ARE YOU OKAY?!
YES, YES, I'M FINE.
WHAT ABOUT YOU?
I'M ALL RIGHT...
BE CAREFUL NOW.
THANK YOU SO MUCH.
WELCOME BACK!
IS EVERYTHING ALL RIGHT?

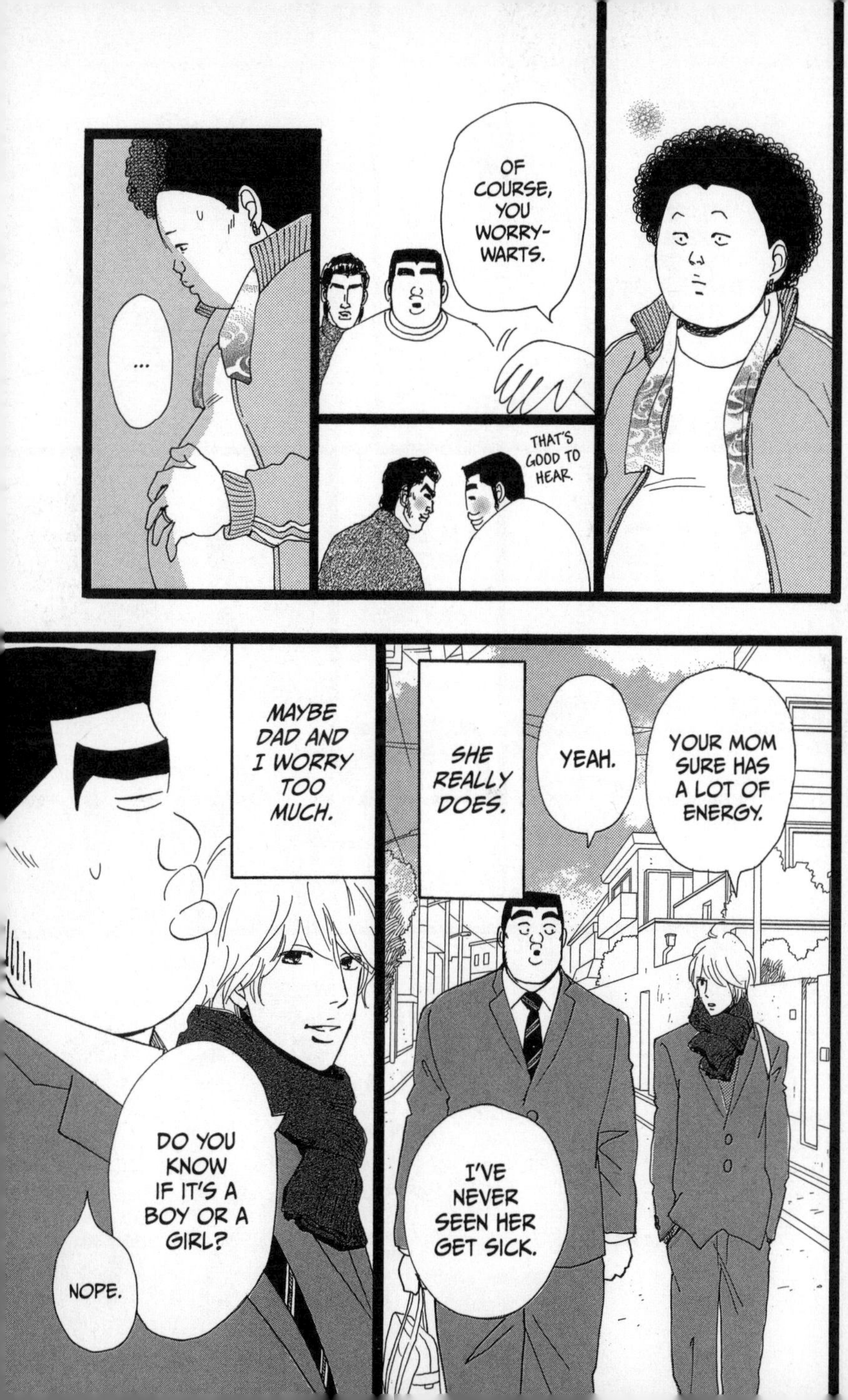

OF COURSE, YOU WORRY-WARTS.
THAT'S GOOD TO HEAR.
...
YOUR MOM SURE HAS A LOT OF ENERGY.
YEAH.
SHE REALLY DOES.
I'VE NEVER SEEN HER GET SICK.
MAYBE DAD AND I WORRY TOO MUCH.
DO YOU KNOW IF IT'S A BOY OR A GIRL?
NOPE.

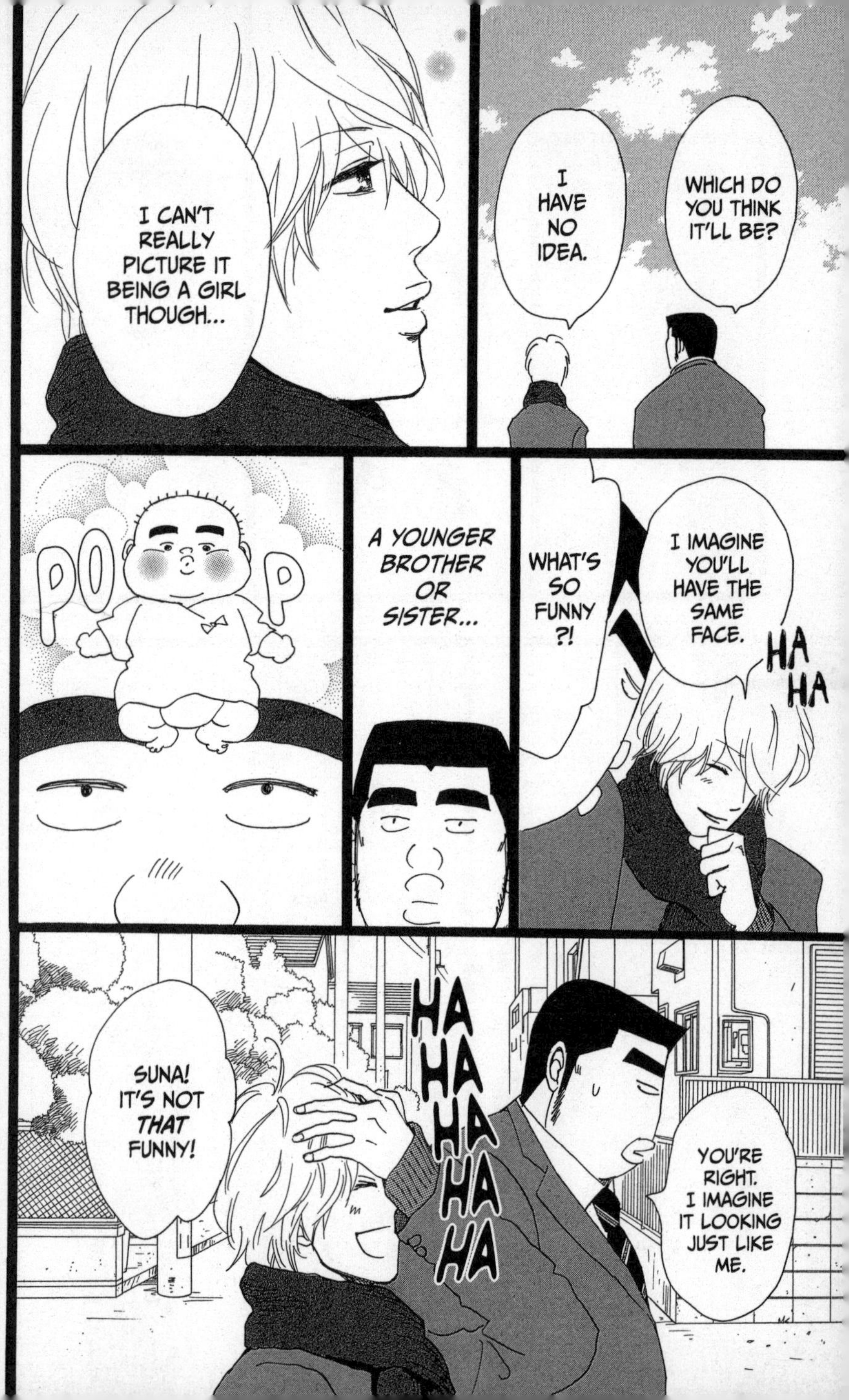
WHICH DO YOU THINK IT'LL BE?
I HAVE NO IDEA.
I CAN'T REALLY PICTURE IT BEING A GIRL THOUGH...
I IMAGINE YOU'LL HAVE THE SAME FACE.
HA HA
WHAT'S SO FUNNY ?!
A YOUNGER BROTHER OR SISTER...
POP
YOU'RE RIGHT. I IMAGINE IT LOOKING JUST LIKE ME.
HA HA HA HA HA HA
SUNA! IT'S NOT *THAT* FUNNY!

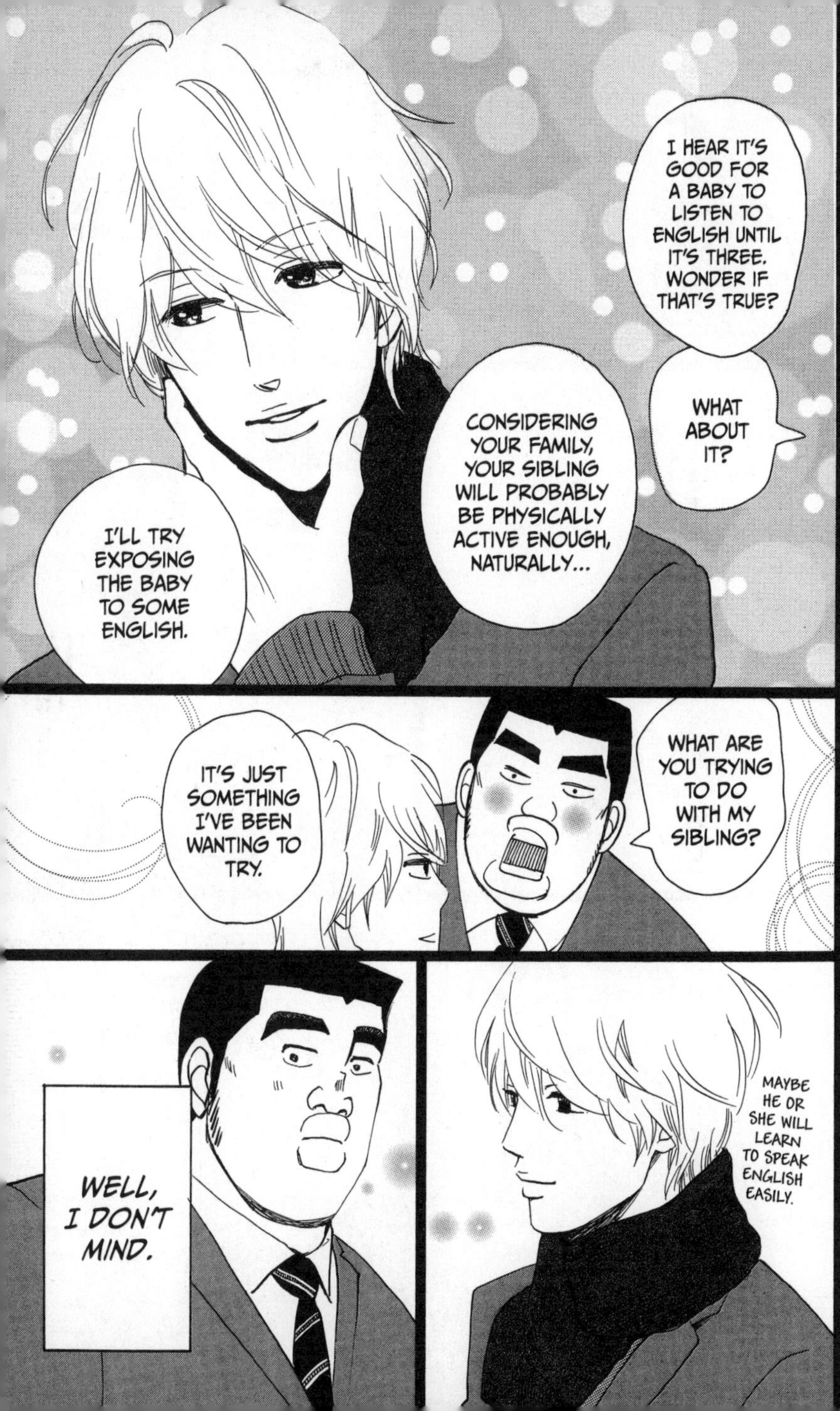
I HEAR IT'S GOOD FOR A BABY TO LISTEN TO ENGLISH UNTIL IT'S THREE. WONDER IF THAT'S TRUE?
WHAT ABOUT IT?
CONSIDERING YOUR FAMILY, YOUR SIBLING WILL PROBABLY BE PHYSICALLY ACTIVE ENOUGH, NATURALLY...
I'LL TRY EXPOSING THE BABY TO SOME ENGLISH.
WHAT ARE YOU TRYING TO DO WITH MY SIBLING?
IT'S JUST SOMETHING I'VE BEEN WANTING TO TRY.
MAYBE HE OR SHE WILL LEARN TO SPEAK ENGLISH EASILY.
WELL, I DON'T MIND.

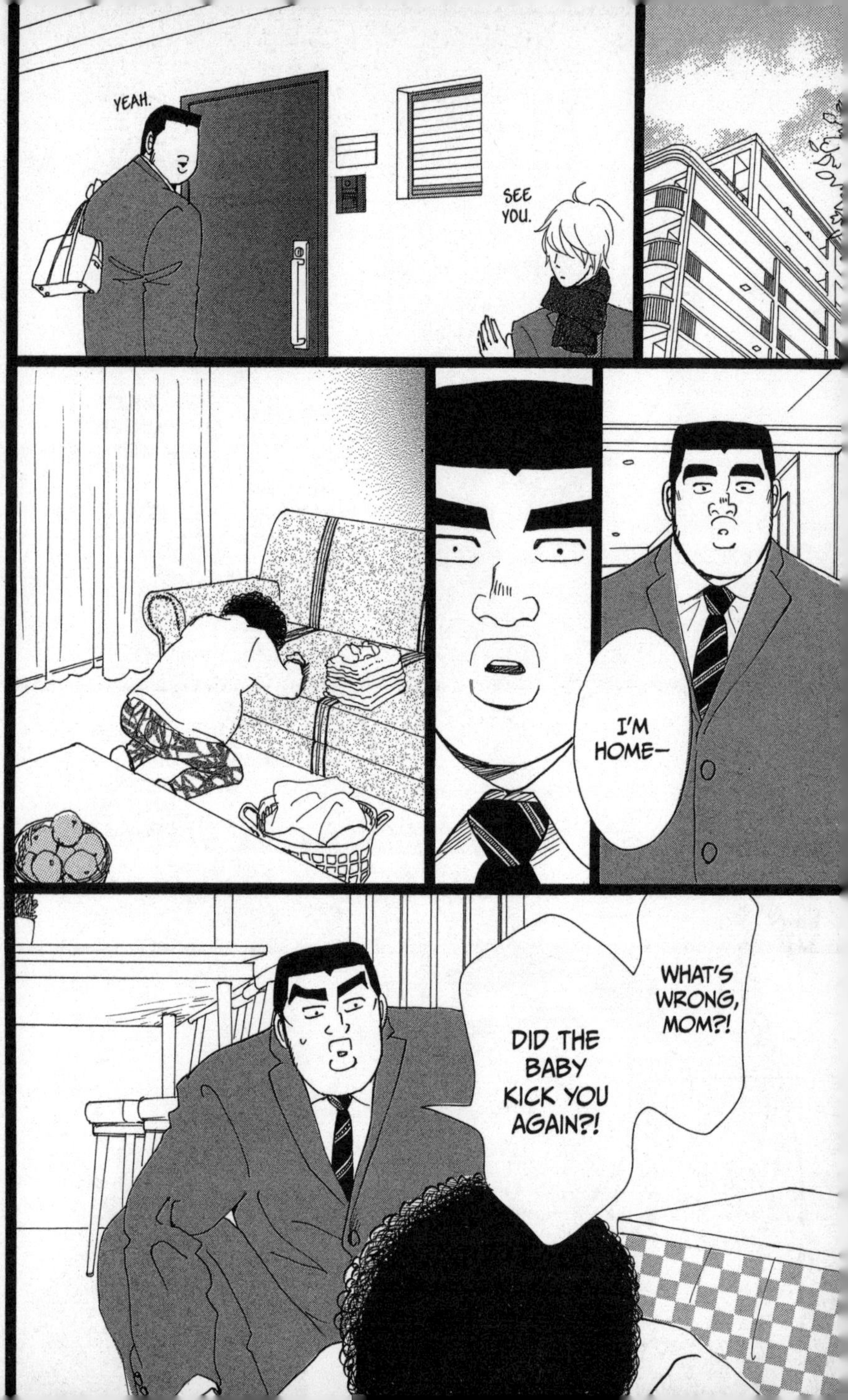
SEE YOU.
YEAH.
I'M HOME—
WHAT'S WRONG, MOM?!
DID THE BABY KICK YOU AGAIN?!

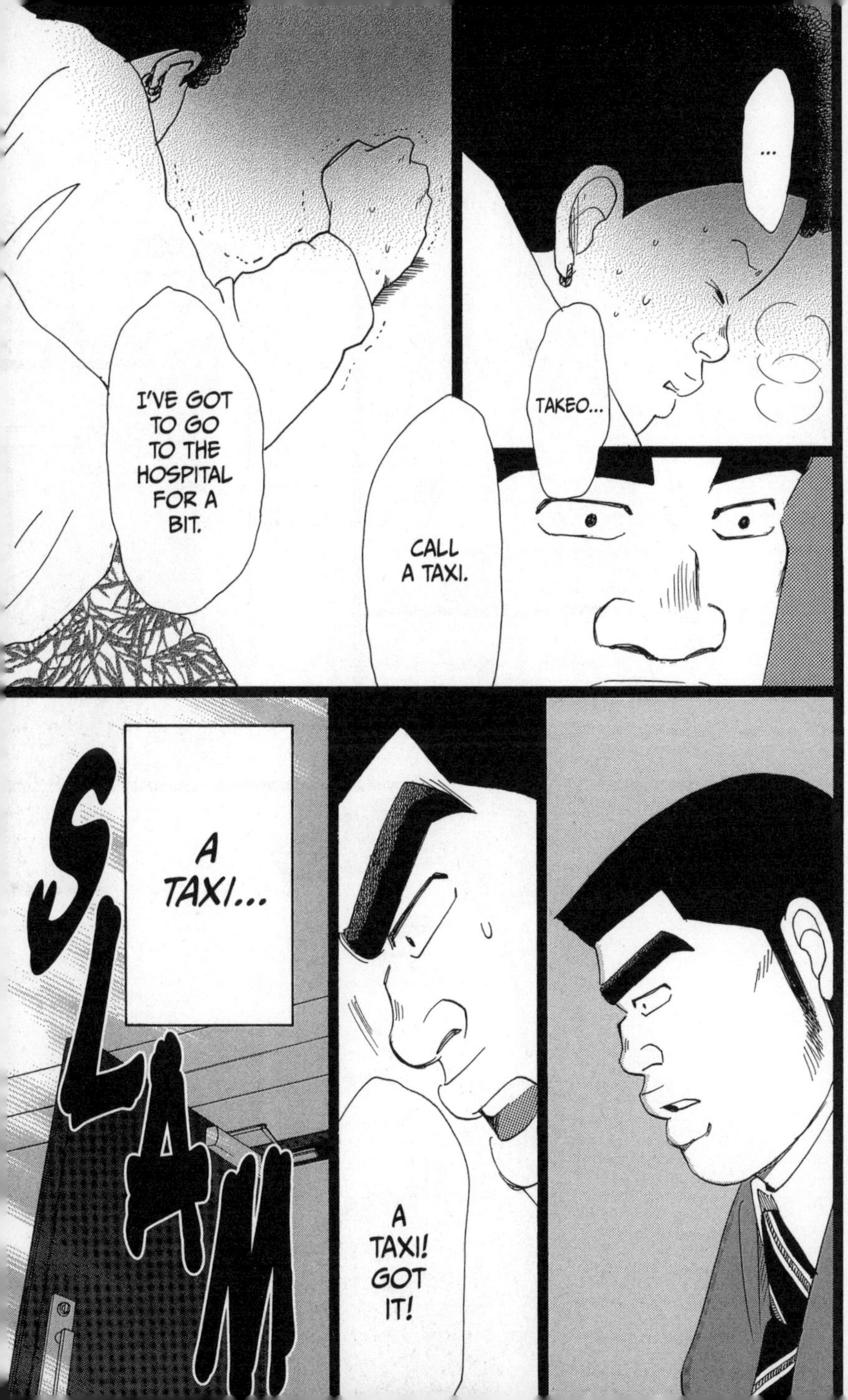
...
TAKEO...
CALL A TAXI.
I'VE GOT TO GO TO THE HOSPITAL FOR A BIT.
A TAXI! GOT IT!
A TAXI...
SLAM

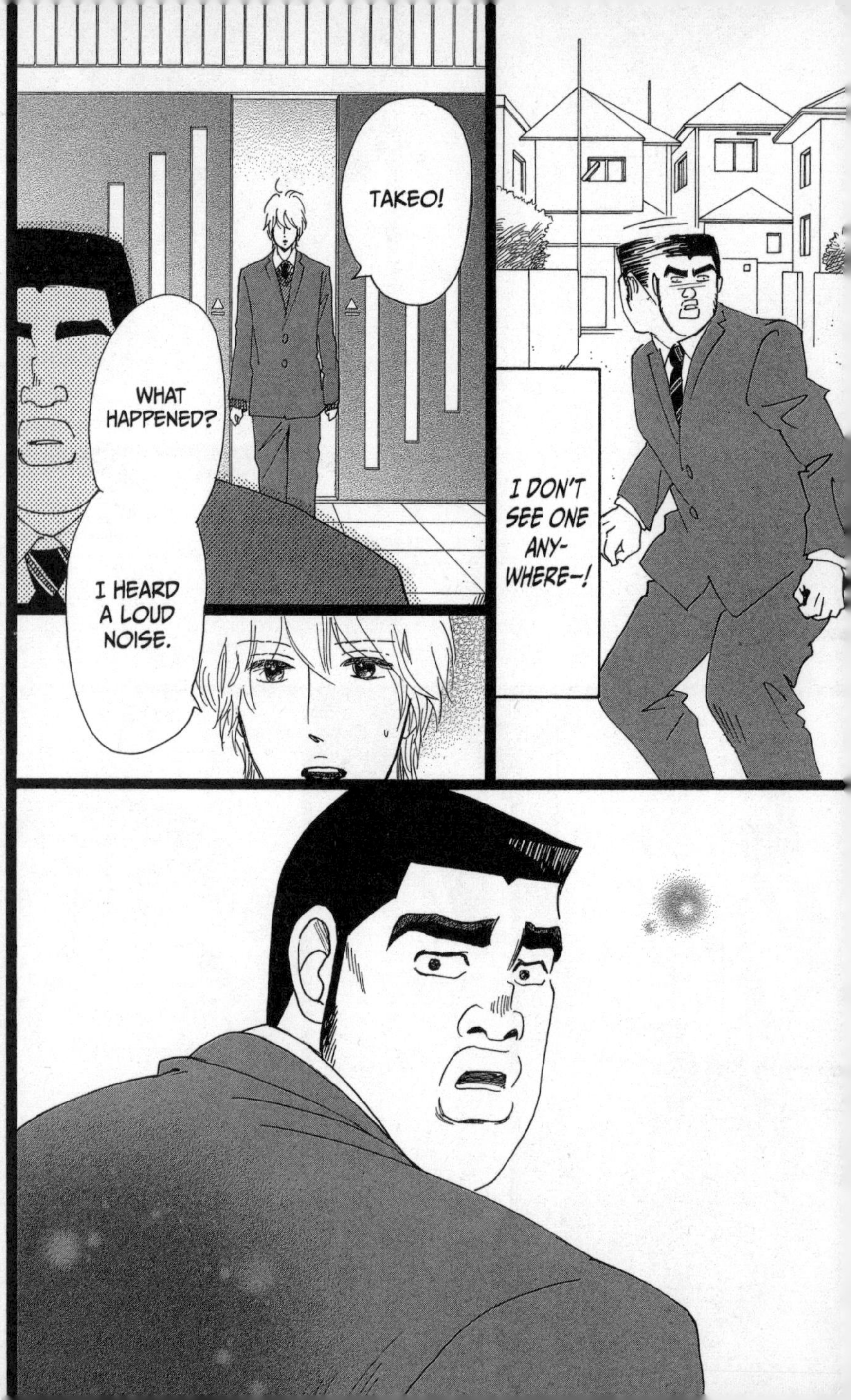
I DON'T SEE ONE ANY-WHERE—!
TAKEO!
WHAT HAPPENED?
I HEARD A LOUD NOISE.

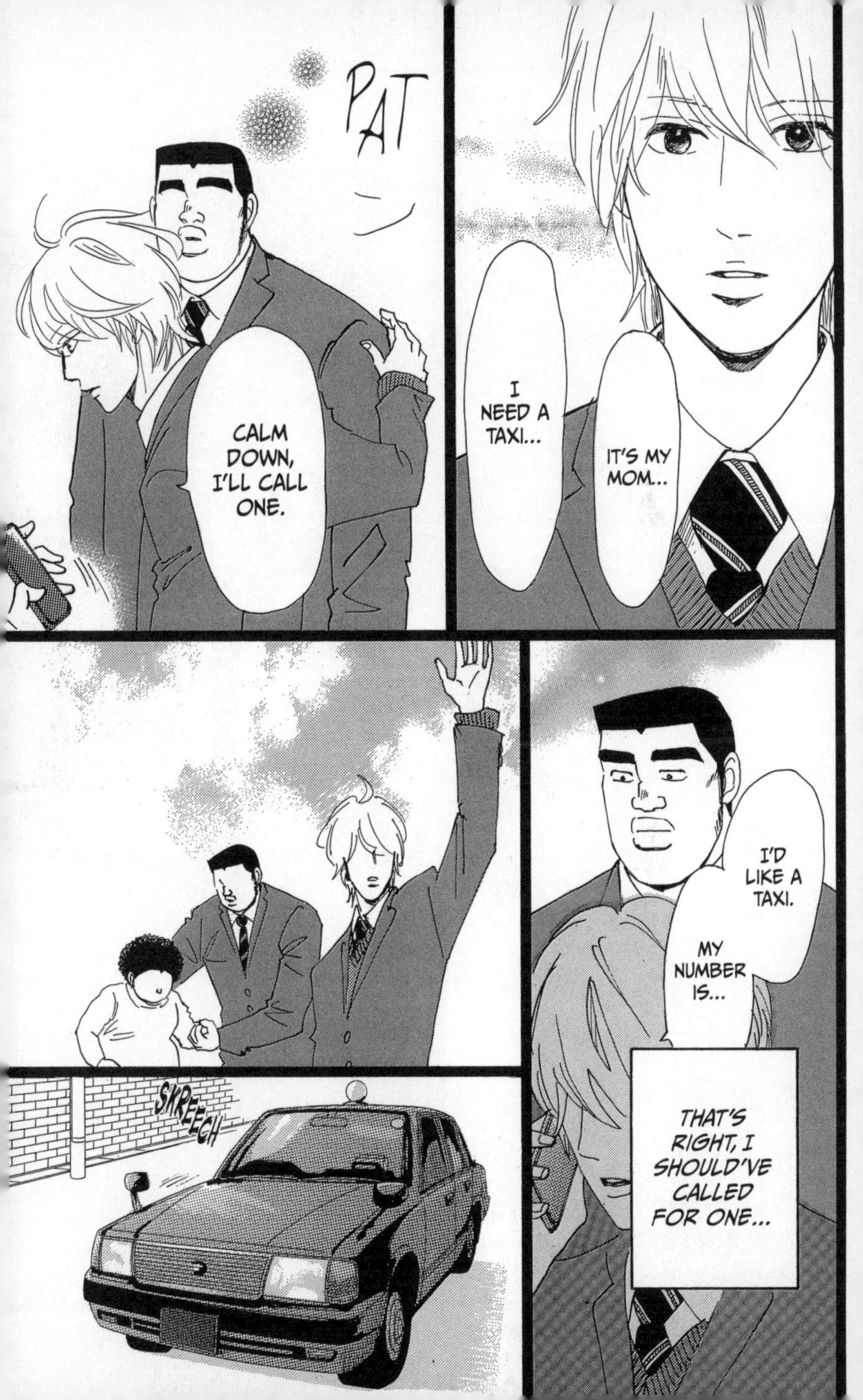
IT'S MY MOM...
I NEED A TAXI...
PAT
CALM DOWN, I'LL CALL ONE.
I'D LIKE A TAXI.
MY NUMBER IS...
THAT'S RIGHT, I SHOULD'VE CALLED FOR ONE...
SKREECH

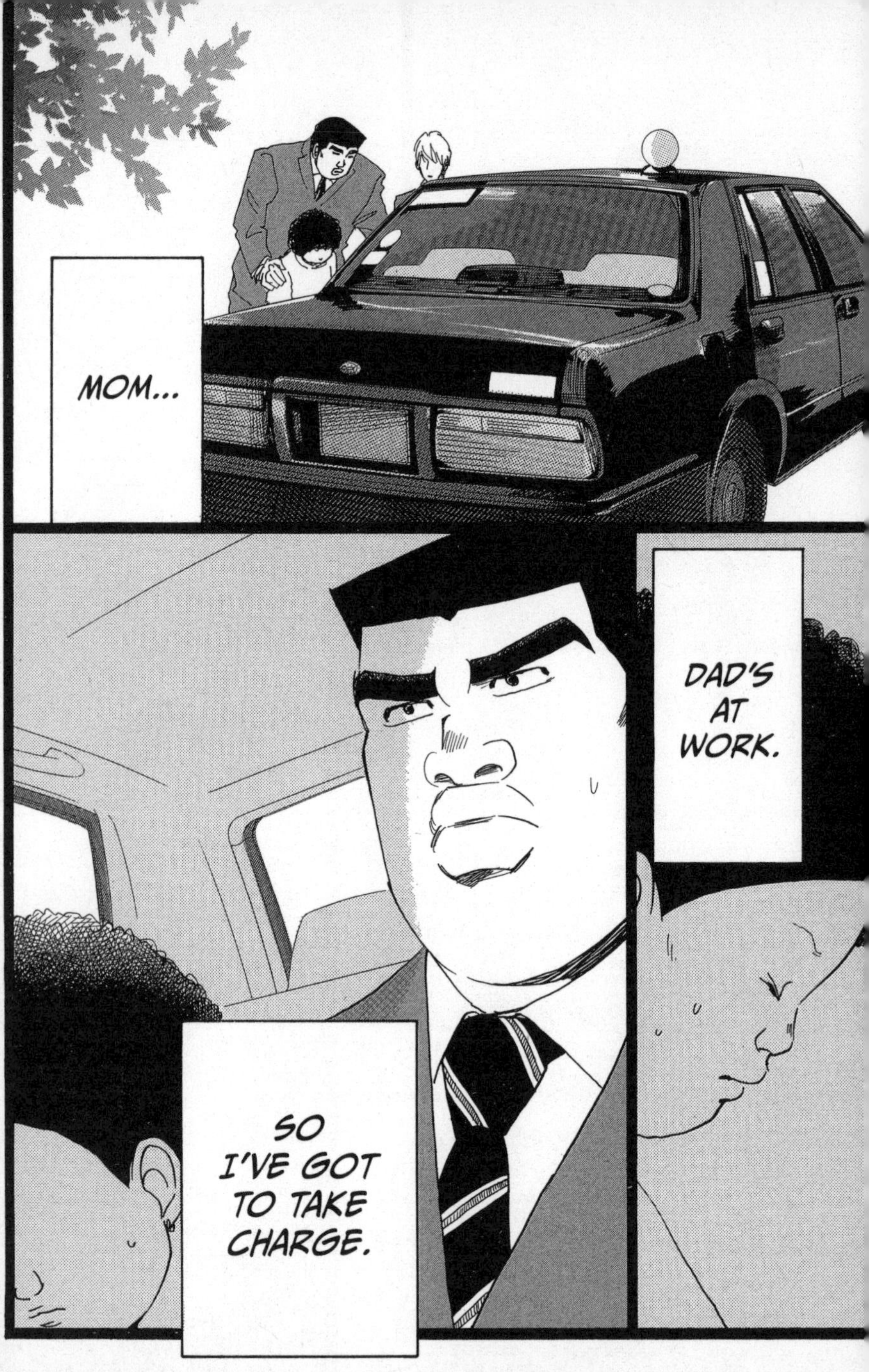
MOM...
DAD'S AT WORK.
SO I'VE GOT TO TAKE CHARGE.

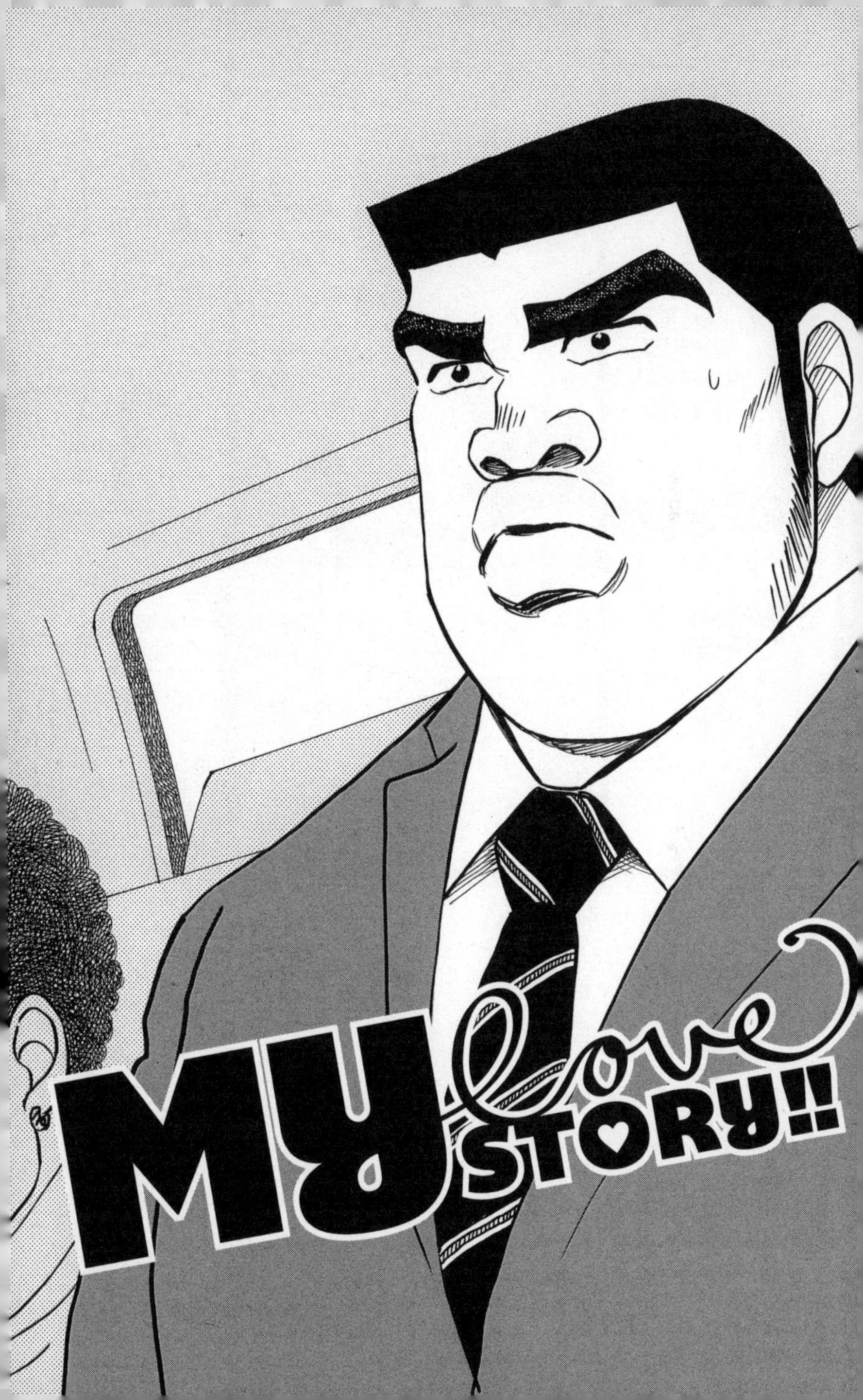
MY love STORY!!

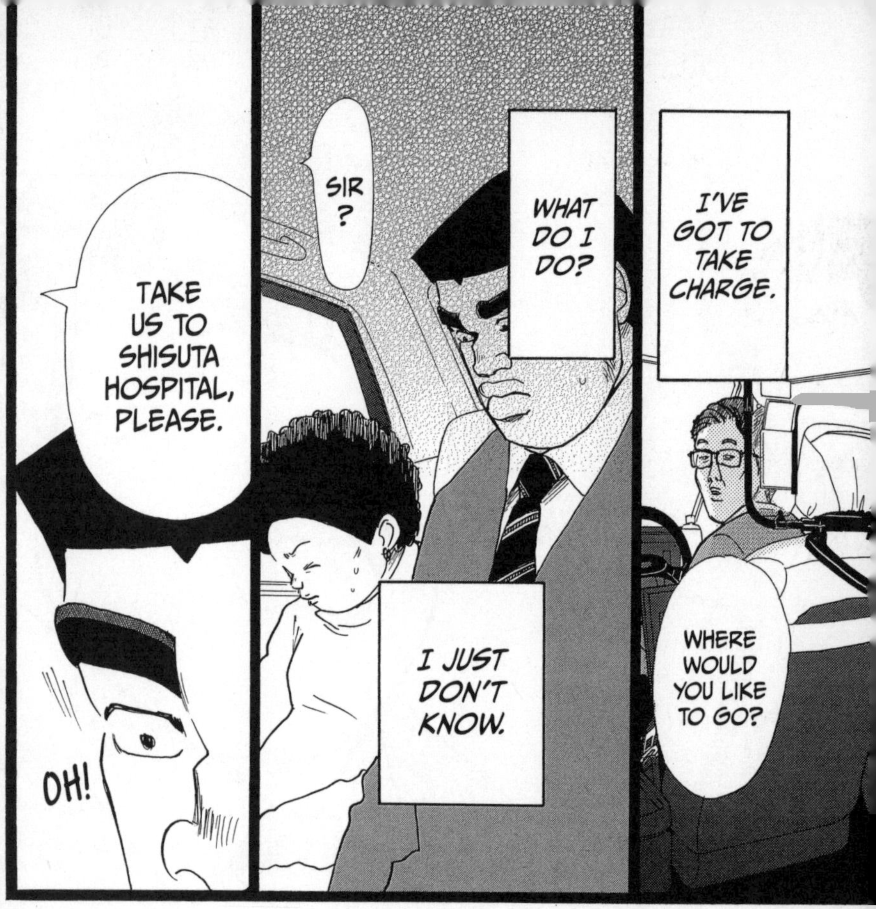
I'VE GOT TO TAKE CHARGE.
WHERE WOULD YOU LIKE TO GO?
WHAT DO I DO?
SIR?
I JUST DON'T KNOW.
TAKE US TO SHISUTA HOSPITAL, PLEASE.
OH!

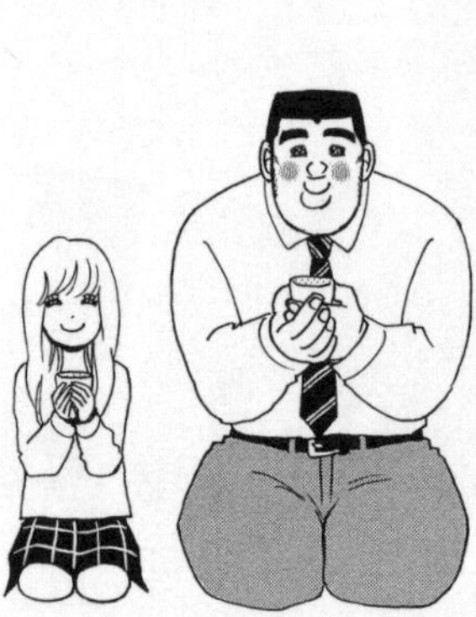

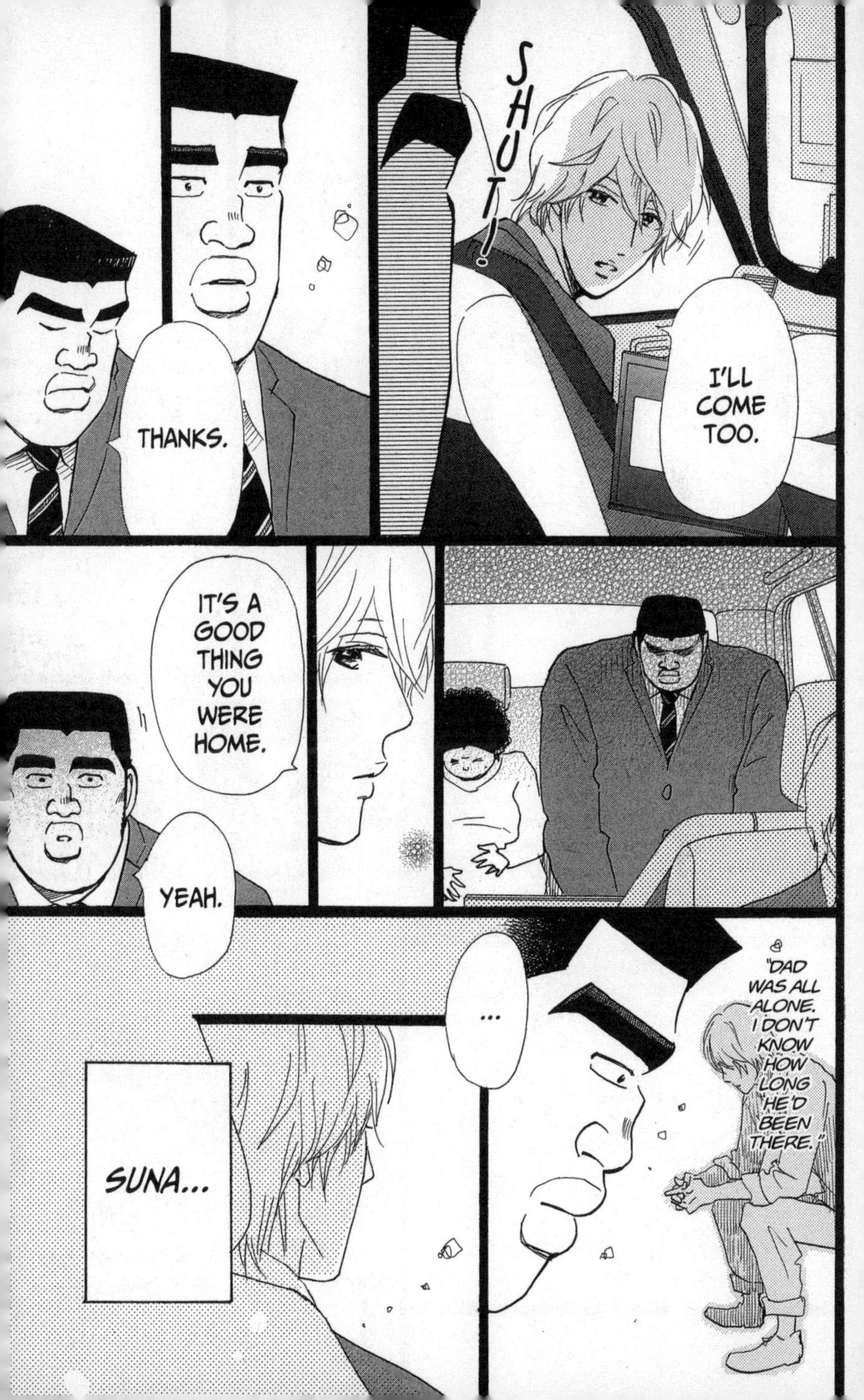
SHUT!
I'LL COME TOO.
THANKS.
IT'S A GOOD THING YOU WERE HOME.
YEAH.
"DAD WAS ALL ALONE. I DON'T KNOW HOW LONG HE'D BEEN THERE."
...
SUNA...

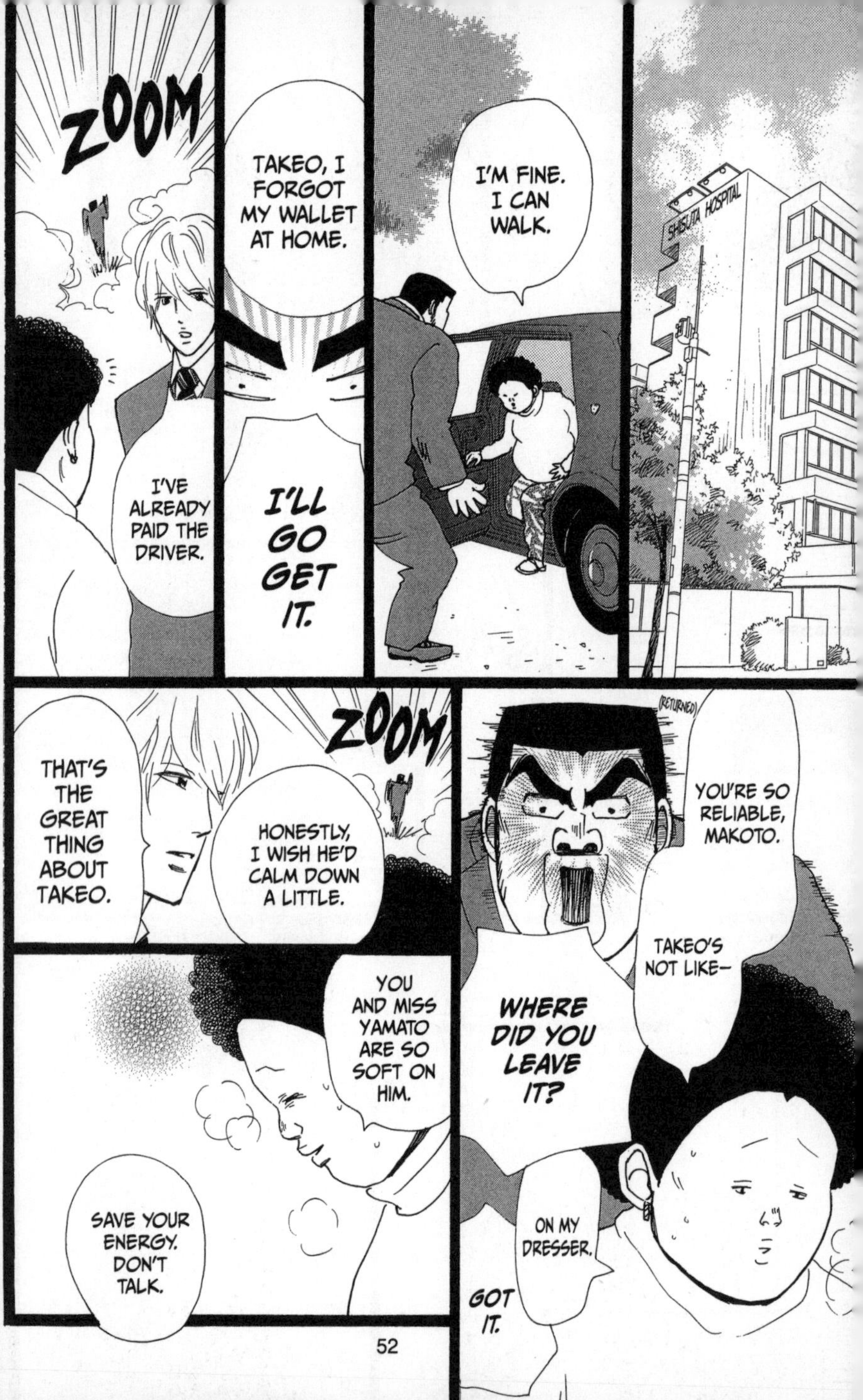
SHISUTA HOSPITAL
I'M FINE. I CAN WALK.
TAKEO, I FORGOT MY WALLET AT HOME.
I'LL GO GET IT.
ZOOM
I'VE ALREADY PAID THE DRIVER.
(RETURNED)
YOU'RE SO RELIABLE, MAKOTO.
TAKEO'S NOT LIKE—
WHERE DID YOU LEAVE IT?
ON MY DRESSER.
GOT IT.
ZOOM
HONESTLY, I WISH HE'D CALM DOWN A LITTLE.
THAT'S THE GREAT THING ABOUT TAKEO.
YOU AND MISS YAMATO ARE SO SOFT ON HIM.
SAVE YOUR ENERGY. DON'T TALK.

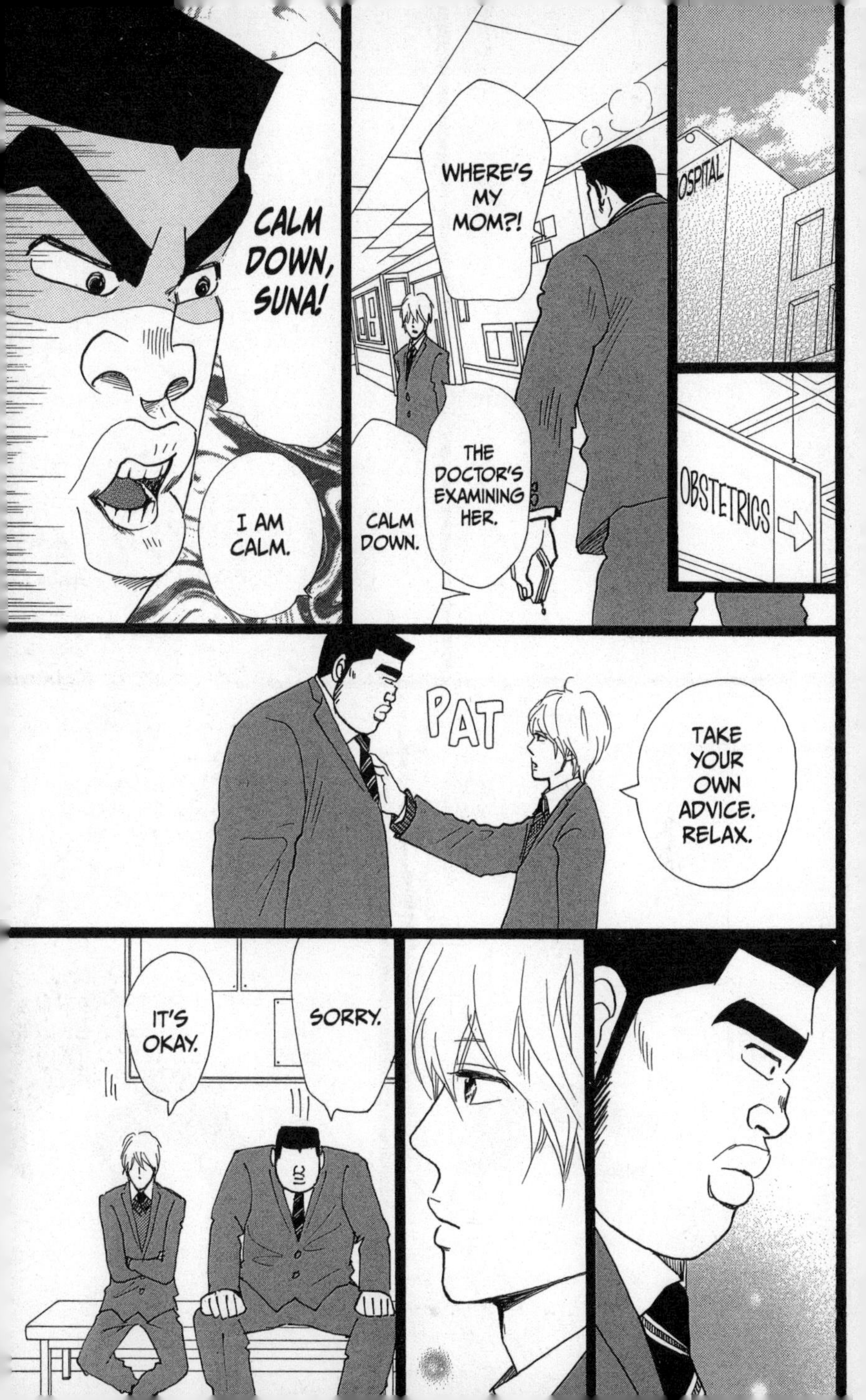
OSPITAL
OBSTETRICS
WHERE'S MY MOM?!
THE DOCTOR'S EXAMINING HER.
CALM DOWN.
CALM DOWN, SUNA!
I AM CALM.
TAKE YOUR OWN ADVICE. RELAX.
PAT
SORRY.
IT'S OKAY.

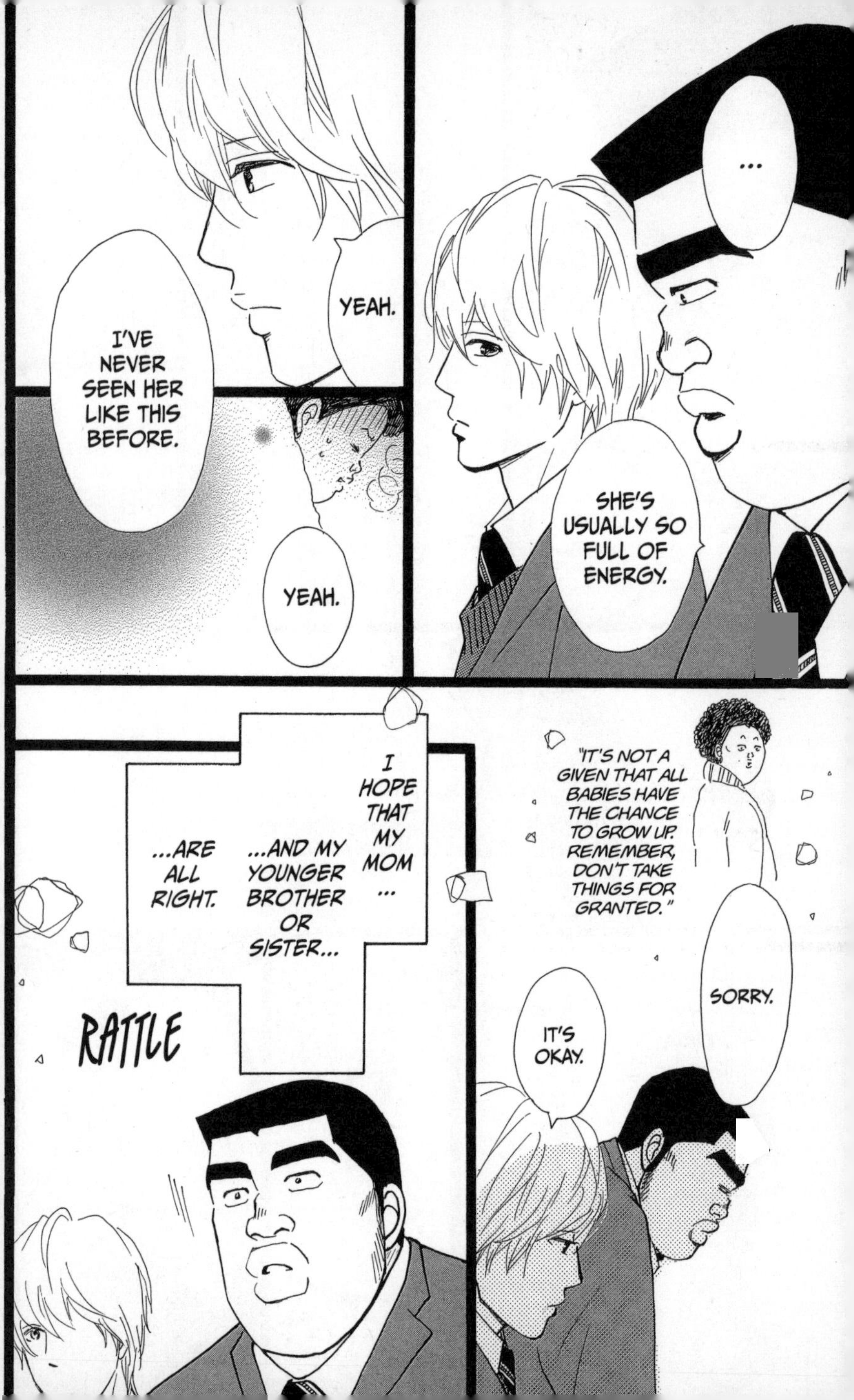
...
SHE'S USUALLY SO FULL OF ENERGY.
YEAH.
I'VE NEVER SEEN HER LIKE THIS BEFORE.
YEAH.
"IT'S NOT A GIVEN THAT ALL BABIES HAVE THE CHANCE TO GROW UP. REMEMBER, DON'T TAKE THINGS FOR GRANTED."
SORRY.
IT'S OKAY.
I HOPE THAT MY MOM...
...AND MY YOUNGER BROTHER OR SISTER...
...ARE ALL RIGHT.
RATTLE

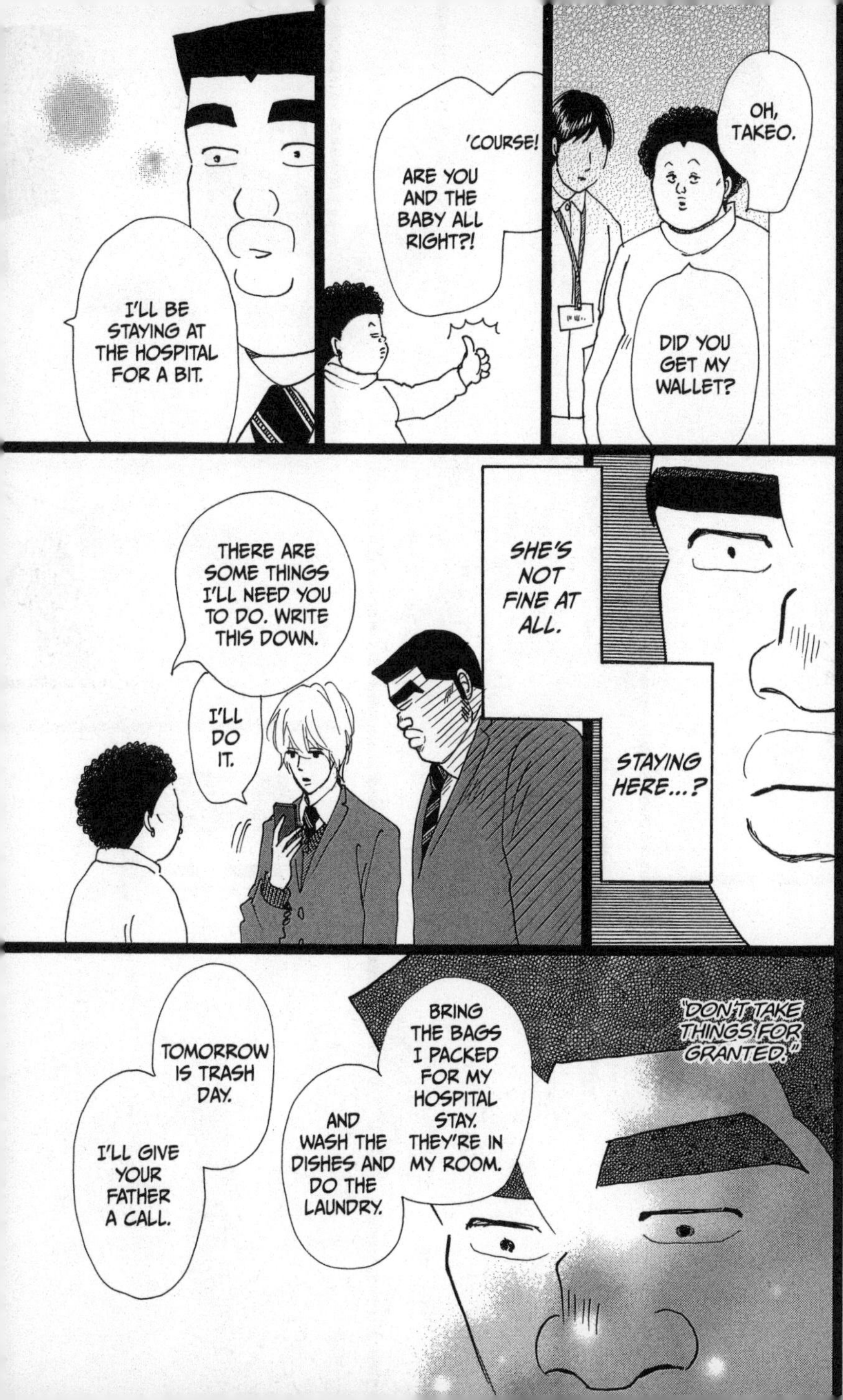
OH, TAKEO.
DID YOU GET MY WALLET?
'COURSE!
ARE YOU AND THE BABY ALL RIGHT?!
I'LL BE STAYING AT THE HOSPITAL FOR A BIT.
SHE'S NOT FINE AT ALL.
STAYING HERE...?
THERE ARE SOME THINGS I'LL NEED YOU TO DO. WRITE THIS DOWN.
I'LL DO IT.
"DON'T TAKE THINGS FOR GRANTED."
BRING THE BAGS I PACKED FOR MY HOSPITAL STAY. THEY'RE IN MY ROOM.
AND WASH THE DISHES AND DO THE LAUNDRY.
TOMORROW IS TRASH DAY.
I'LL GIVE YOUR FATHER A CALL.

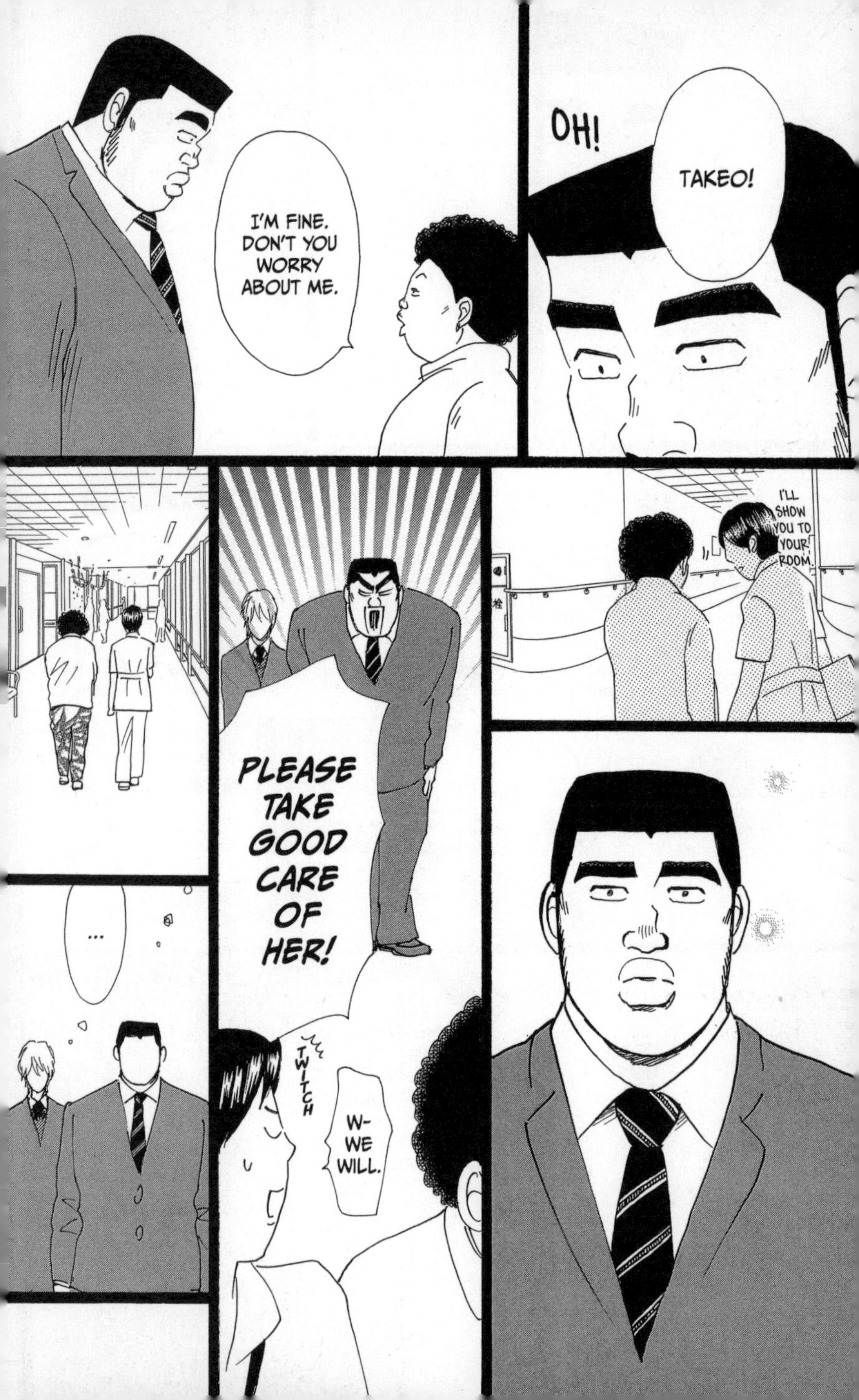
OH!
TAKEO!
I'M FINE. DON'T YOU WORRY ABOUT ME.
I'LL SHOW YOU TO YOUR ROOM.
PLEASE TAKE GOOD CARE OF HER!
TWITCH
W- WE WILL.
...

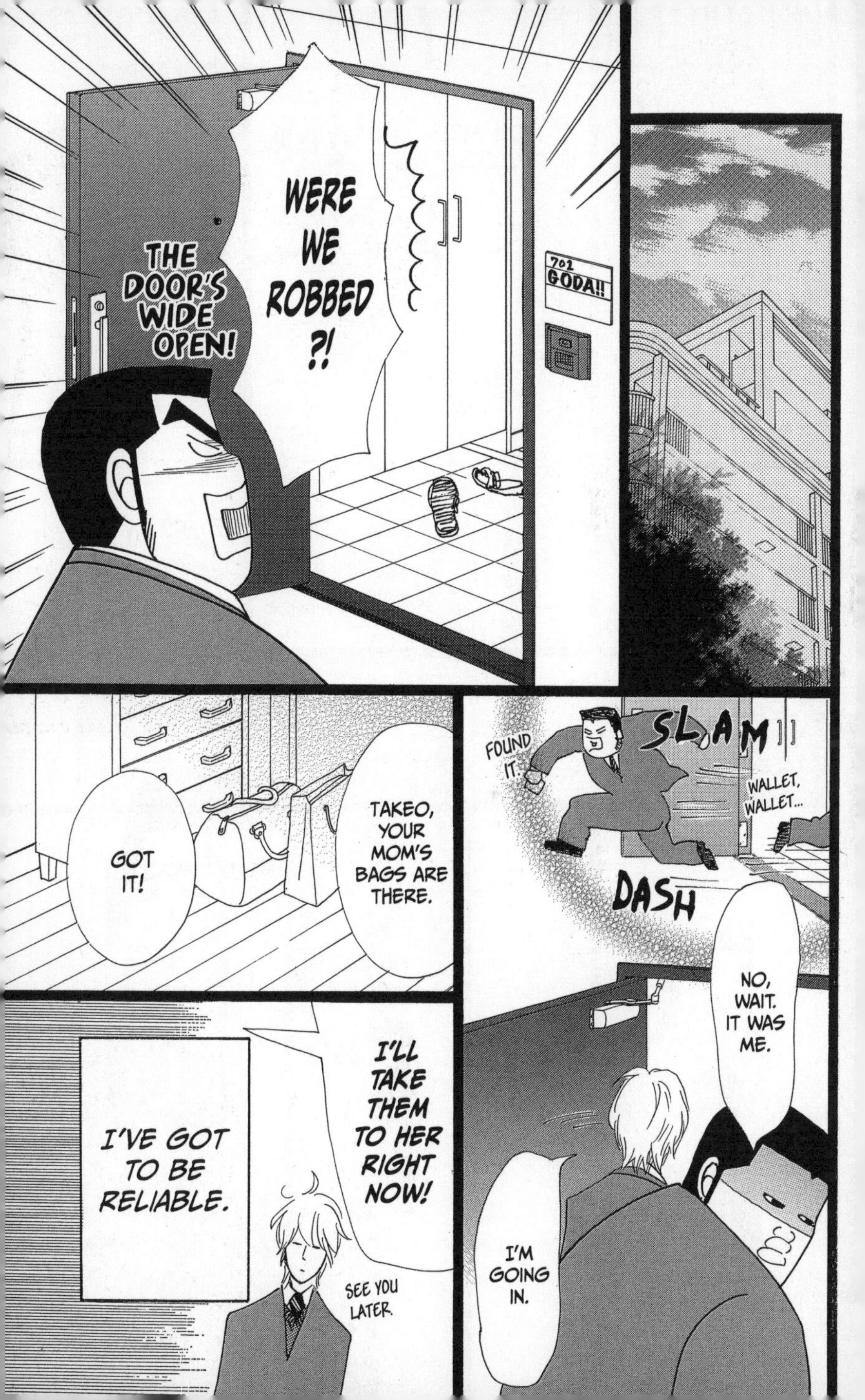
WERE WE ROBBED ?!
702 GODA!!
THE DOOR'S WIDE OPEN!
SLAM
WALLET, WALLET...
FOUND IT.
DASH
TAKEO, YOUR MOM'S BAGS ARE THERE.
GOT IT!
NO, WAIT. IT WAS ME.
I'M GOING IN.
I'LL TAKE THEM TO HER RIGHT NOW!
I'VE GOT TO BE RELIABLE.
SEE YOU LATER.

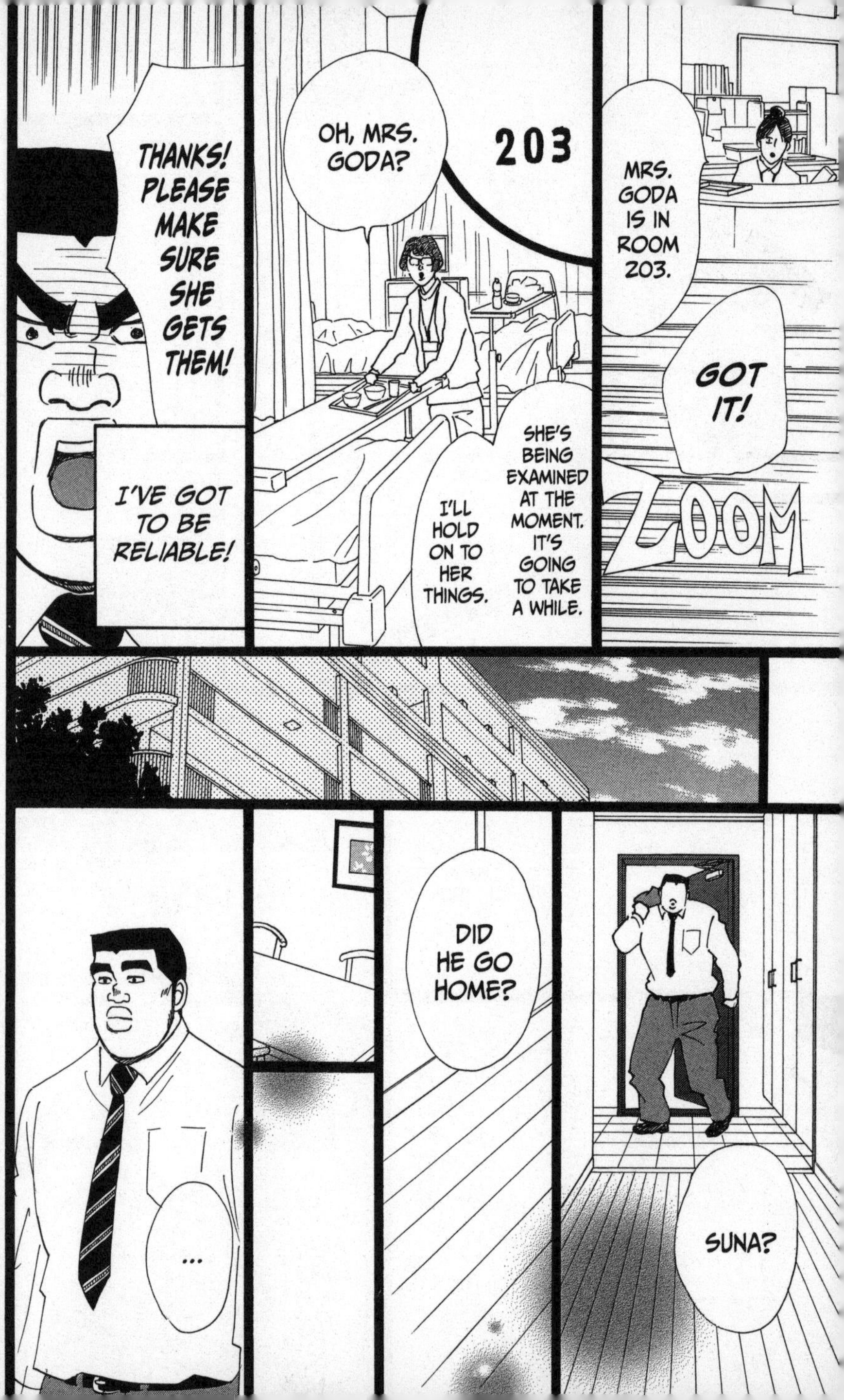
MRS. GODA IS IN ROOM 203.
GOT IT!
ZOOM
203
OH, MRS. GODA?
SHE'S BEING EXAMINED AT THE MOMENT. IT'S GOING TO TAKE A WHILE.
I'LL HOLD ON TO HER THINGS.
THANKS! PLEASE MAKE SURE SHE GETS THEM!
I'VE GOT TO BE RELIABLE!
SUNA?
DID HE GO HOME?
...

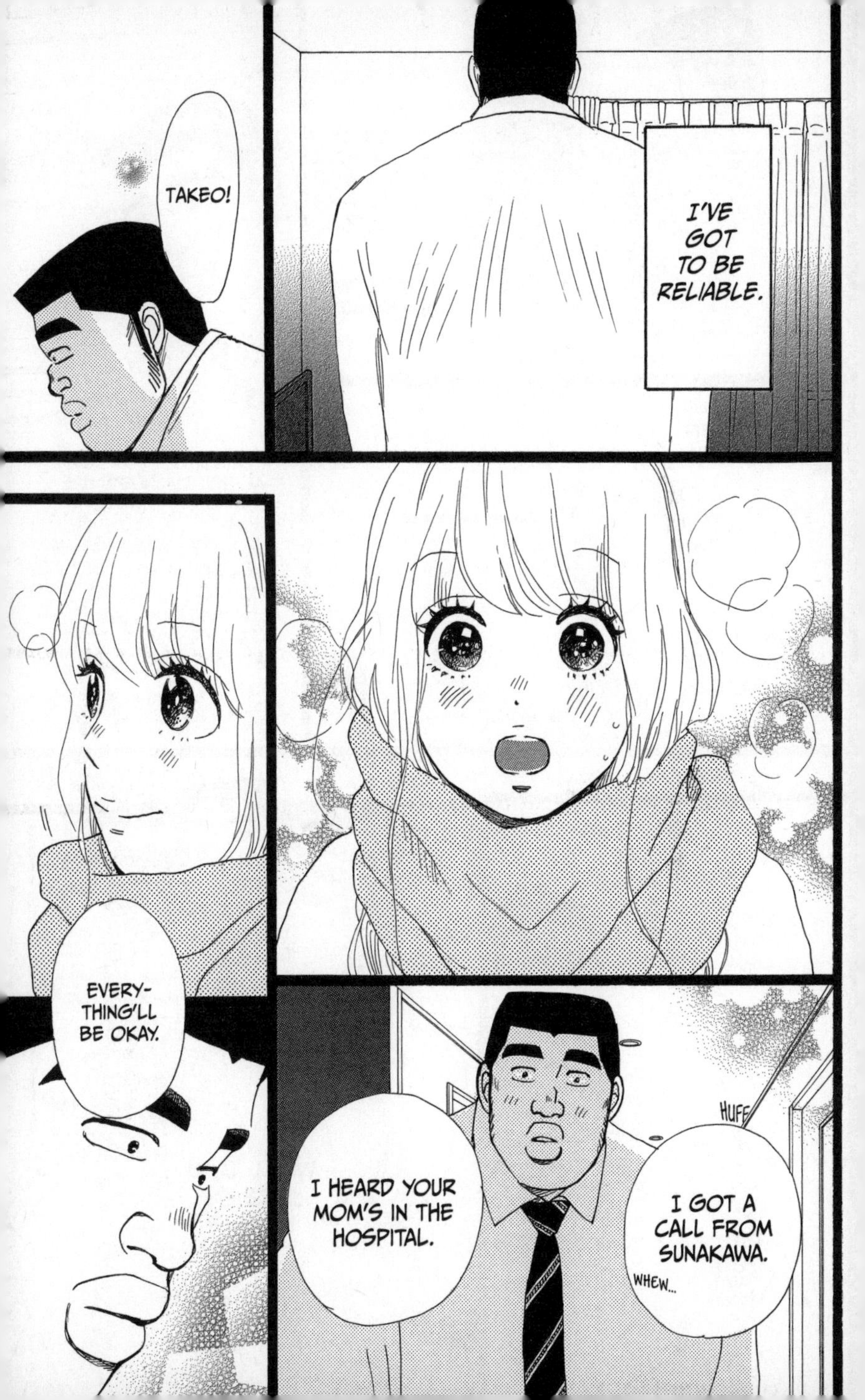
I'VE GOT TO BE RELIABLE.
TAKEO!
HUFF
I GOT A CALL FROM SUNAKAWA.
WHEW...
I HEARD YOUR MOM'S IN THE HOSPITAL.
EVERY-THING'LL BE OKAY.

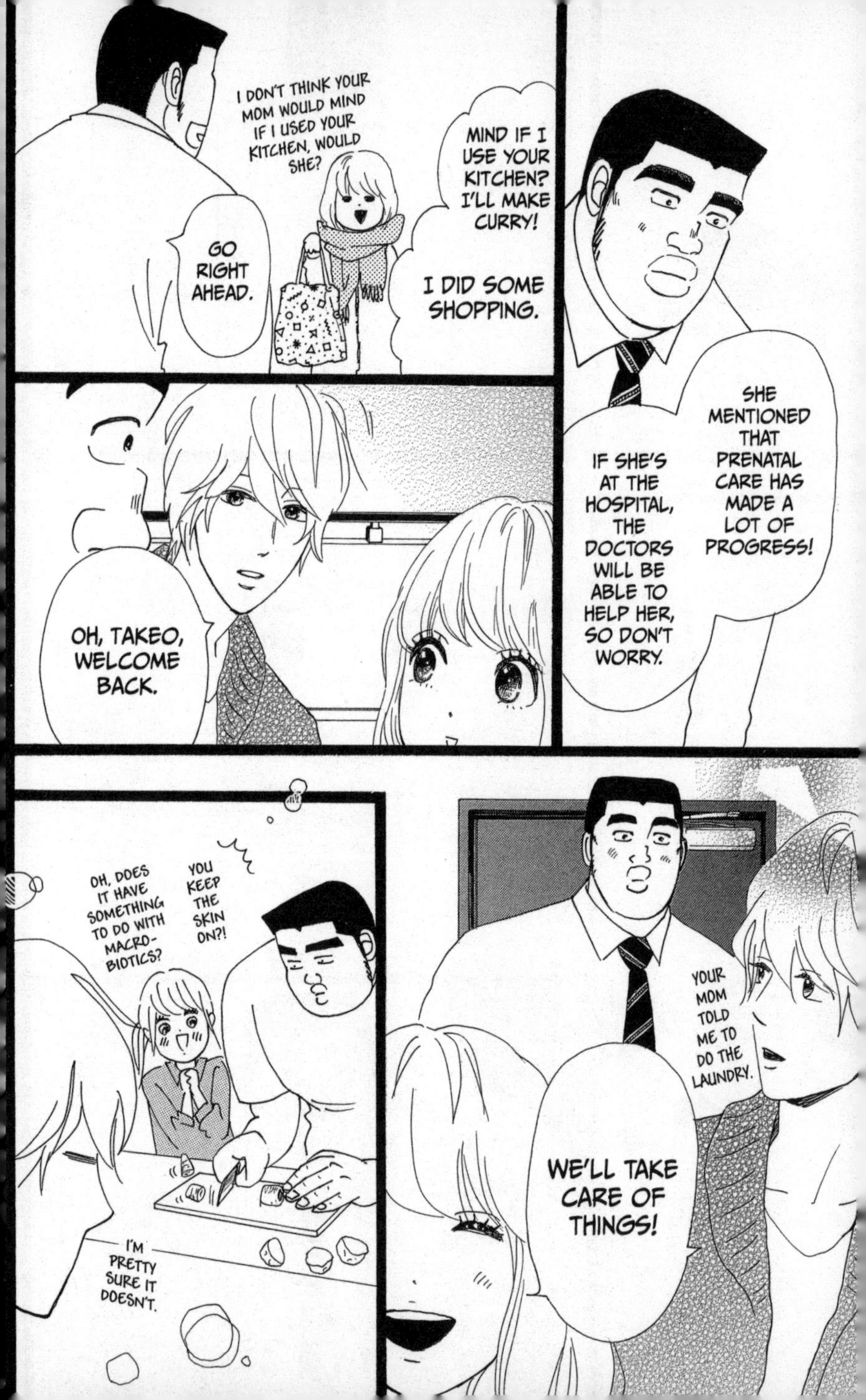
SHE MENTIONED THAT PRENATAL CARE HAS MADE A LOT OF PROGRESS!
IF SHE'S AT THE HOSPITAL, THE DOCTORS WILL BE ABLE TO HELP HER, SO DON'T WORRY.
MIND IF I USE YOUR KITCHEN? I'LL MAKE CURRY!
I DID SOME SHOPPING.
I DON'T THINK YOUR MOM WOULD MIND IF I USED YOUR KITCHEN, WOULD SHE?
GO RIGHT AHEAD.
OH, TAKEO, WELCOME BACK.
YOUR MOM TOLD ME TO DO THE LAUNDRY.
WE'LL TAKE CARE OF THINGS!
YOU KEEP THE SKIN ON?!
OH, DOES IT HAVE SOMETHING TO DO WITH MACRO-BIOTICS?
I'M PRETTY SURE IT DOESN'T.

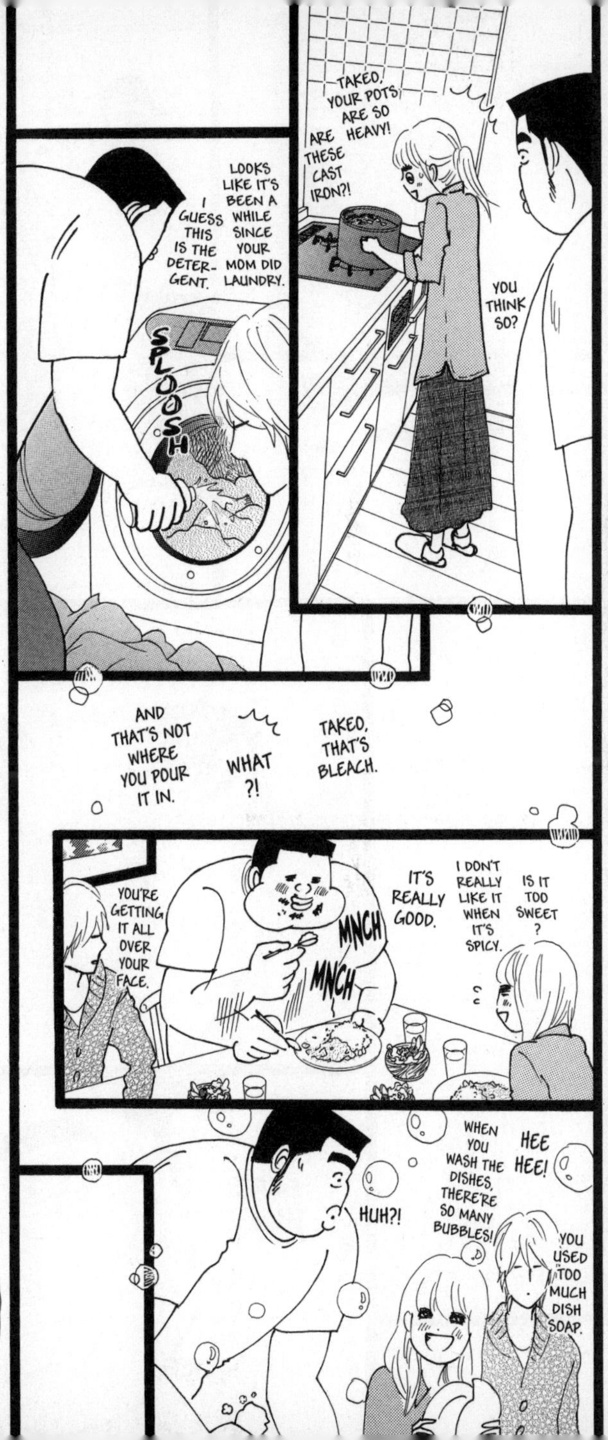
TAKEO, YOUR POTS ARE SO HEAVY! ARE THESE CAST IRON?!
YOU THINK SO?
LOOKS LIKE IT'S BEEN A WHILE SINCE YOUR MOM DID LAUNDRY.
I GUESS THIS IS THE DETERGENT.
SPLOOSH
TAKEO, THAT'S BLEACH.
WHAT?!
AND THAT'S NOT WHERE YOU POUR IT IN.
IS IT TOO SWEET?
I DON'T REALLY LIKE IT WHEN IT'S SPICY.
IT'S REALLY GOOD.
MNCH
MNCH
YOU'RE GETTING IT ALL OVER YOUR FACE.
HEE HEE!
WHEN YOU WASH THE DISHES, THERE'RE SO MANY BUBBLES!
YOU USED TOO MUCH DISH SOAP.
HUH?!

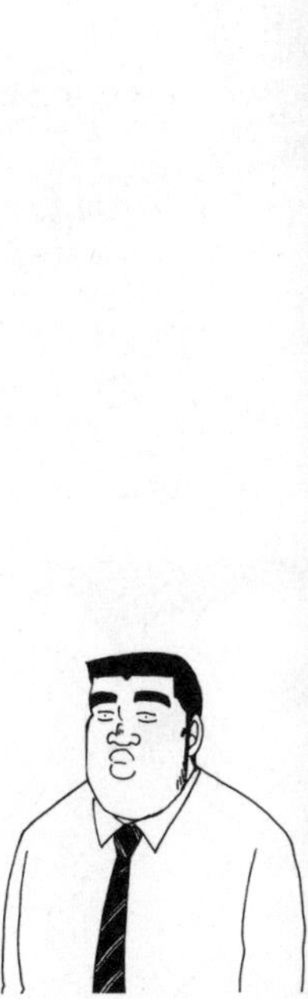

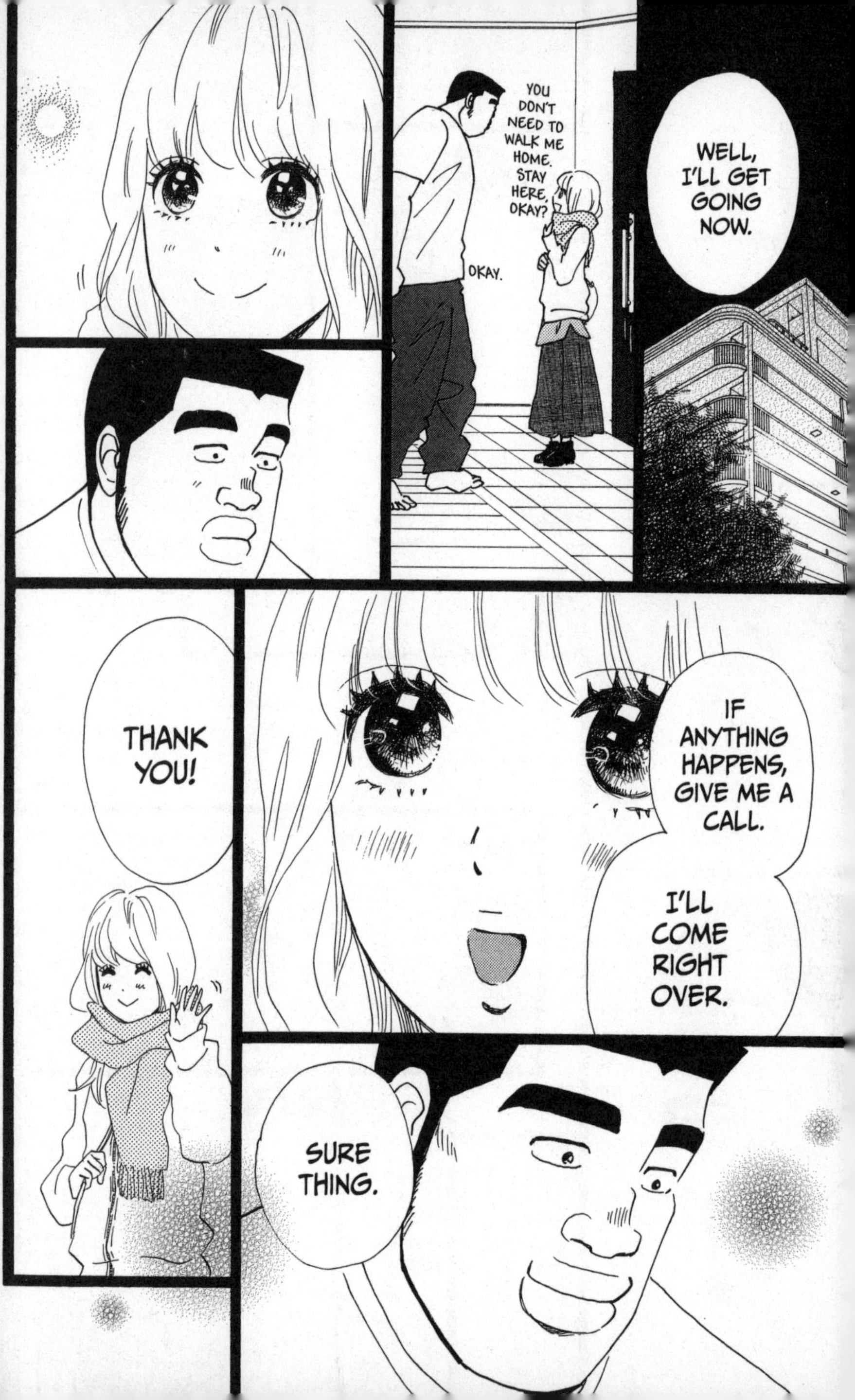
WELL, I'LL GET GOING NOW.
YOU DON'T NEED TO WALK ME HOME. STAY HERE, OKAY?
OKAY.
IF ANYTHING HAPPENS, GIVE ME A CALL.
I'LL COME RIGHT OVER.
SURE THING.
THANK YOU!

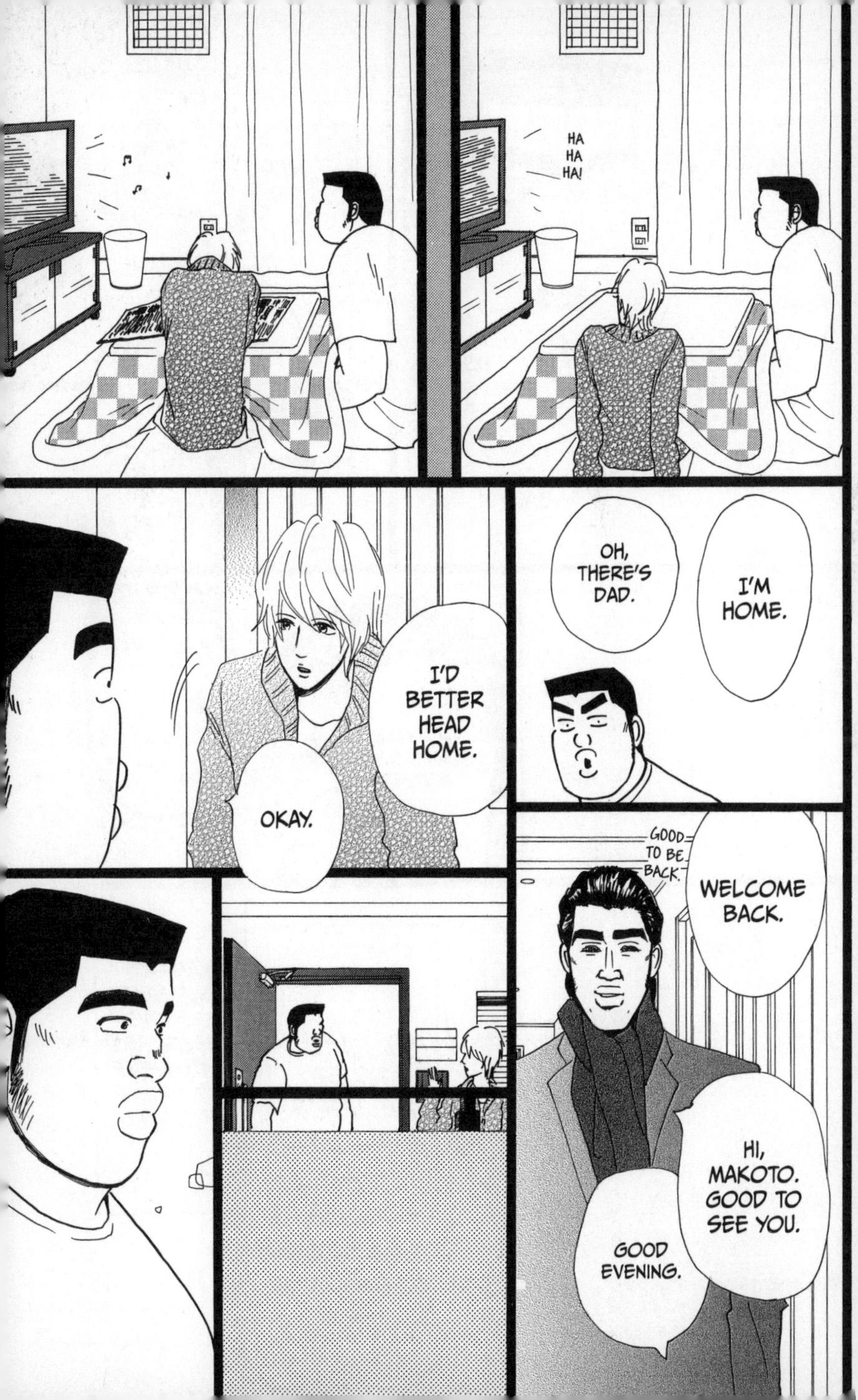
HA HA HA!
I'M HOME.
OH, THERE'S DAD.
I'D BETTER HEAD HOME.
OKAY.
WELCOME BACK.
GOOD TO BE BACK.
HI, MAKOTO. GOOD TO SEE YOU.
GOOD EVENING.

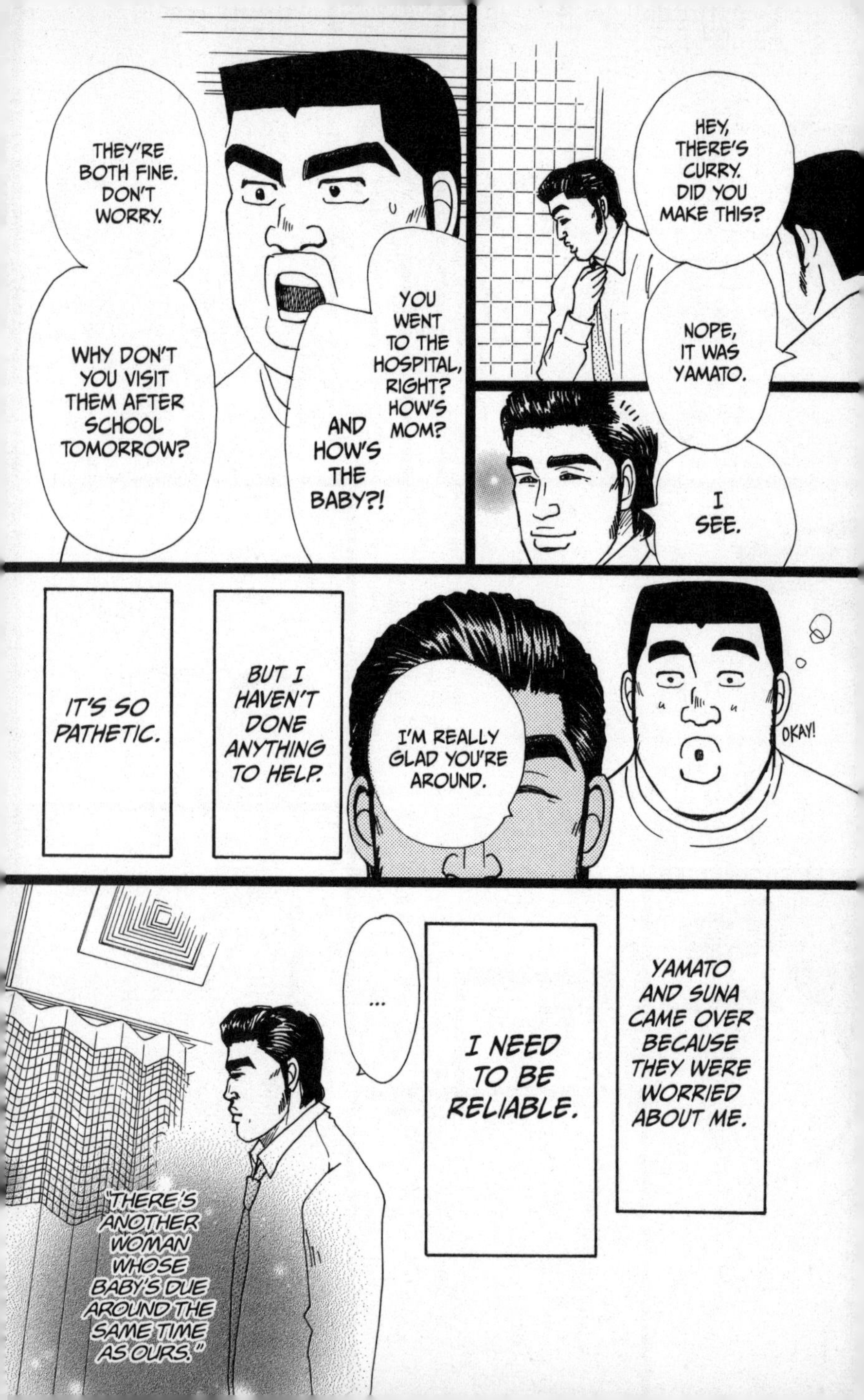
HEY, THERE'S CURRY. DID YOU MAKE THIS?
NOPE, IT WAS YAMATO.
I SEE.
YOU WENT TO THE HOSPITAL, RIGHT? HOW'S MOM?
AND HOW'S THE BABY?!
THEY'RE BOTH FINE. DON'T WORRY.
WHY DON'T YOU VISIT THEM AFTER SCHOOL TOMORROW?
OKAY!
I'M REALLY GLAD YOU'RE AROUND.
BUT I HAVEN'T DONE ANYTHING TO HELP.
IT'S SO PATHETIC.
YAMATO AND SUNA CAME OVER BECAUSE THEY WERE WORRIED ABOUT ME.
I NEED TO BE RELIABLE.
...
"THERE'S ANOTHER WOMAN WHOSE BABY'S DUE AROUND THE SAME TIME AS OURS."

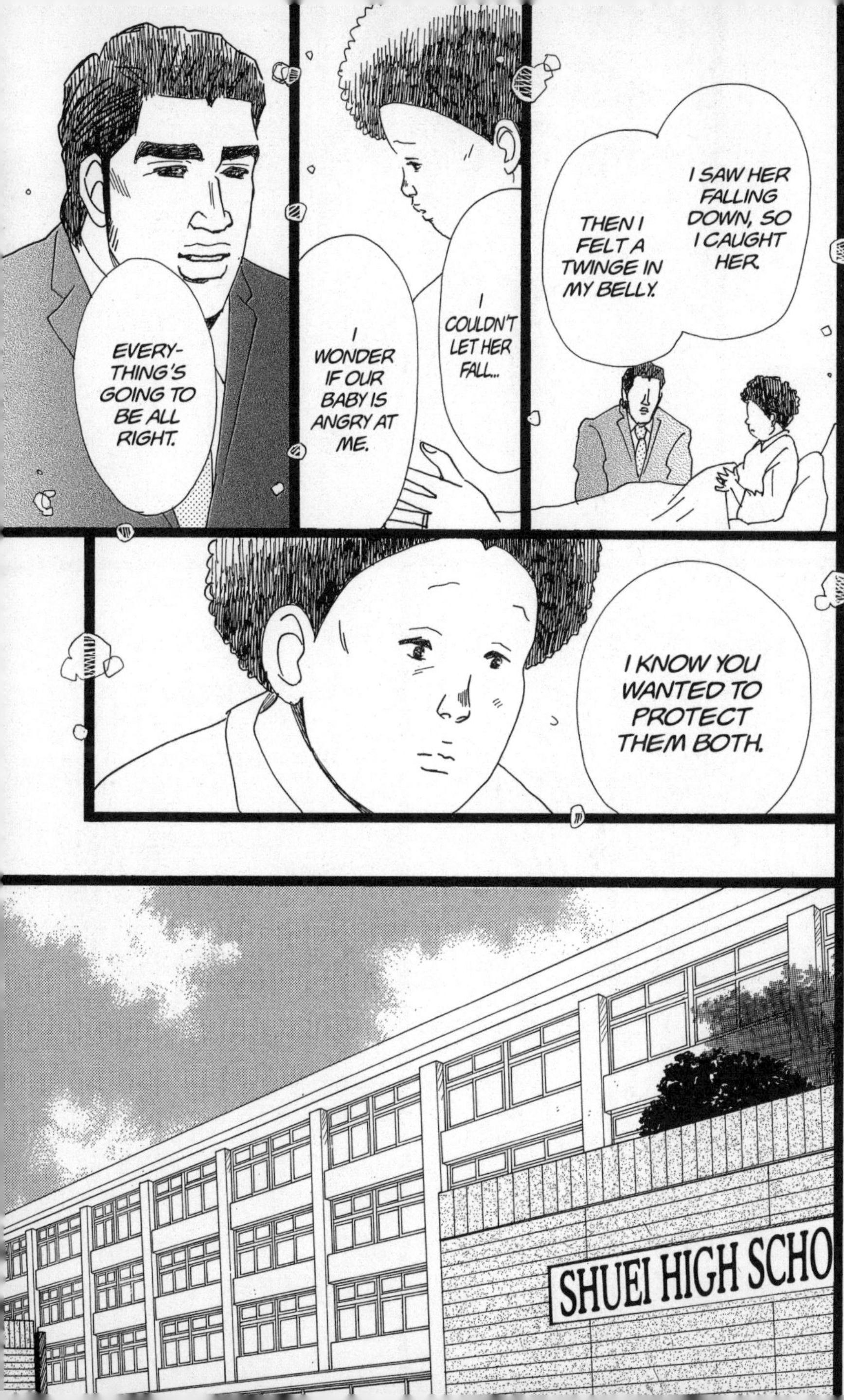
I SAW HER FALLING DOWN, SO I CAUGHT HER.
THEN I FELT A TWINGE IN MY BELLY.
I COULDN'T LET HER FALL...
I WONDER IF OUR BABY IS ANGRY AT ME.
EVERY-THING'S GOING TO BE ALL RIGHT.
I KNOW YOU WANTED TO PROTECT THEM BOTH.
SHUEI HIGH SCHO

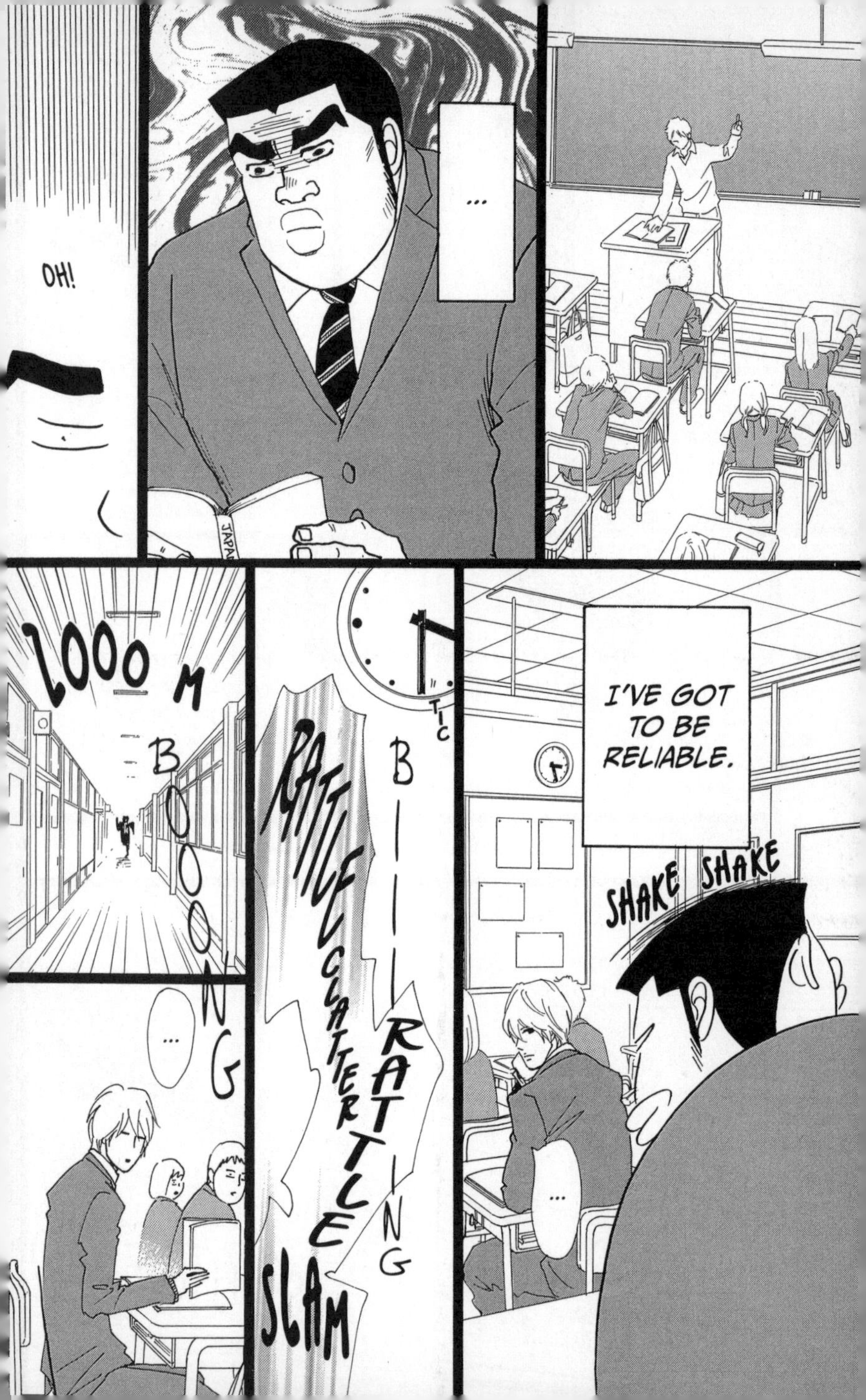
...
OH!
I'VE GOT TO BE RELIABLE.
SHAKE SHAKE
...
TIC
RATTLE
CLATTER
RATTLING
SLAM
ZOOOM
BOOOONG
...

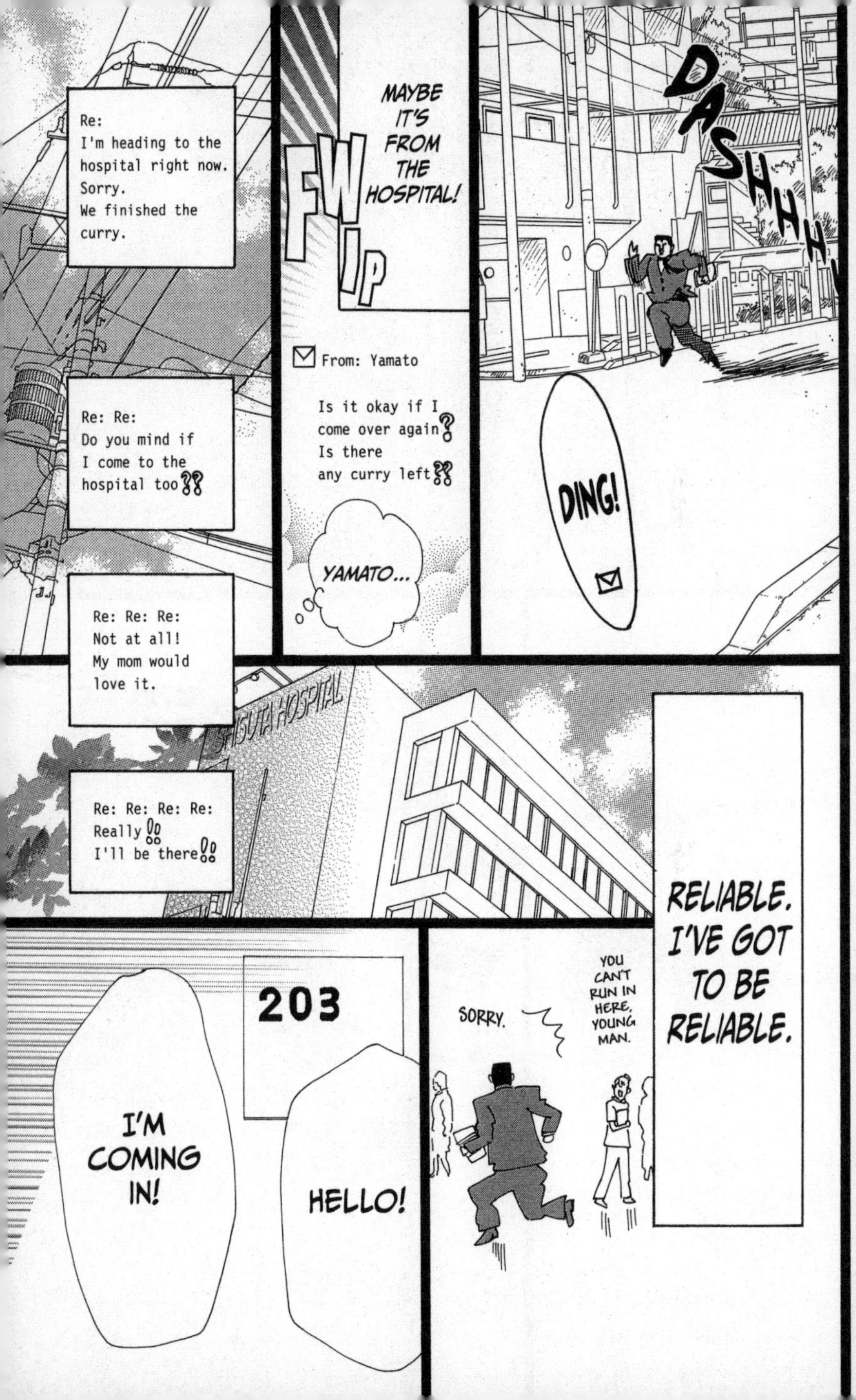
DASHHH
DING!
MAYBE IT'S FROM THE HOSPITAL!
FWIP
From: Yamato
Is it okay if I come over again? Is there any curry left??
YAMATO...
Re:
I'm heading to the hospital right now. Sorry.
We finished the curry.
Re: Re:
Do you mind if I come to the hospital too??
Re: Re: Re:
Not at all! My mom would love it.
Re: Re: Re: Re:
Really!! I'll be there!!
RELIABLE. I'VE GOT TO BE RELIABLE.
YOU CAN'T RUN IN HERE, YOUNG MAN.
SORRY.
203
HELLO!
I'M COMING IN!

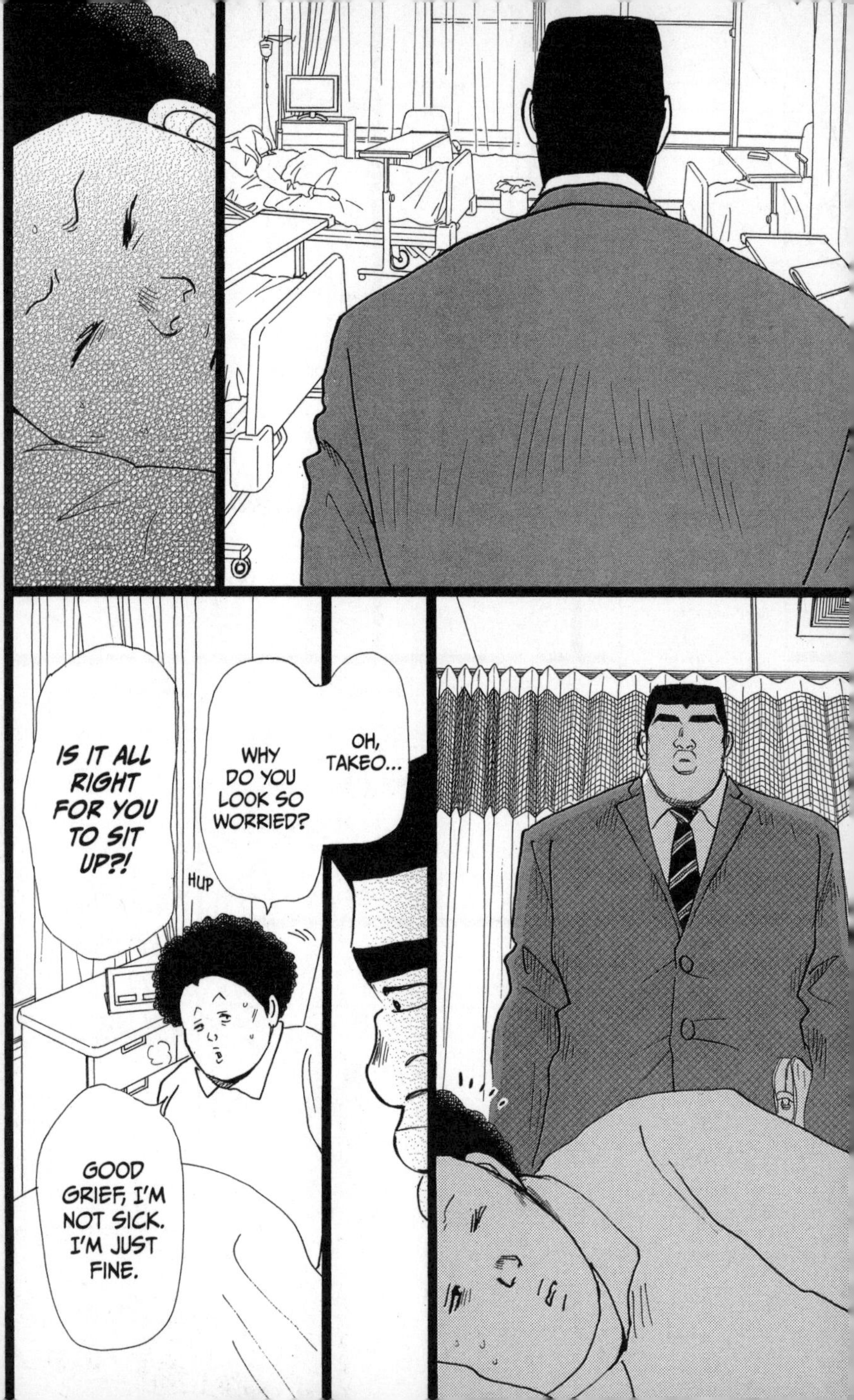
OH, TAKEO...
WHY DO YOU LOOK SO WORRIED?
IS IT ALL RIGHT FOR YOU TO SIT UP?!
HUP
GOOD GRIEF, I'M NOT SICK. I'M JUST FINE.

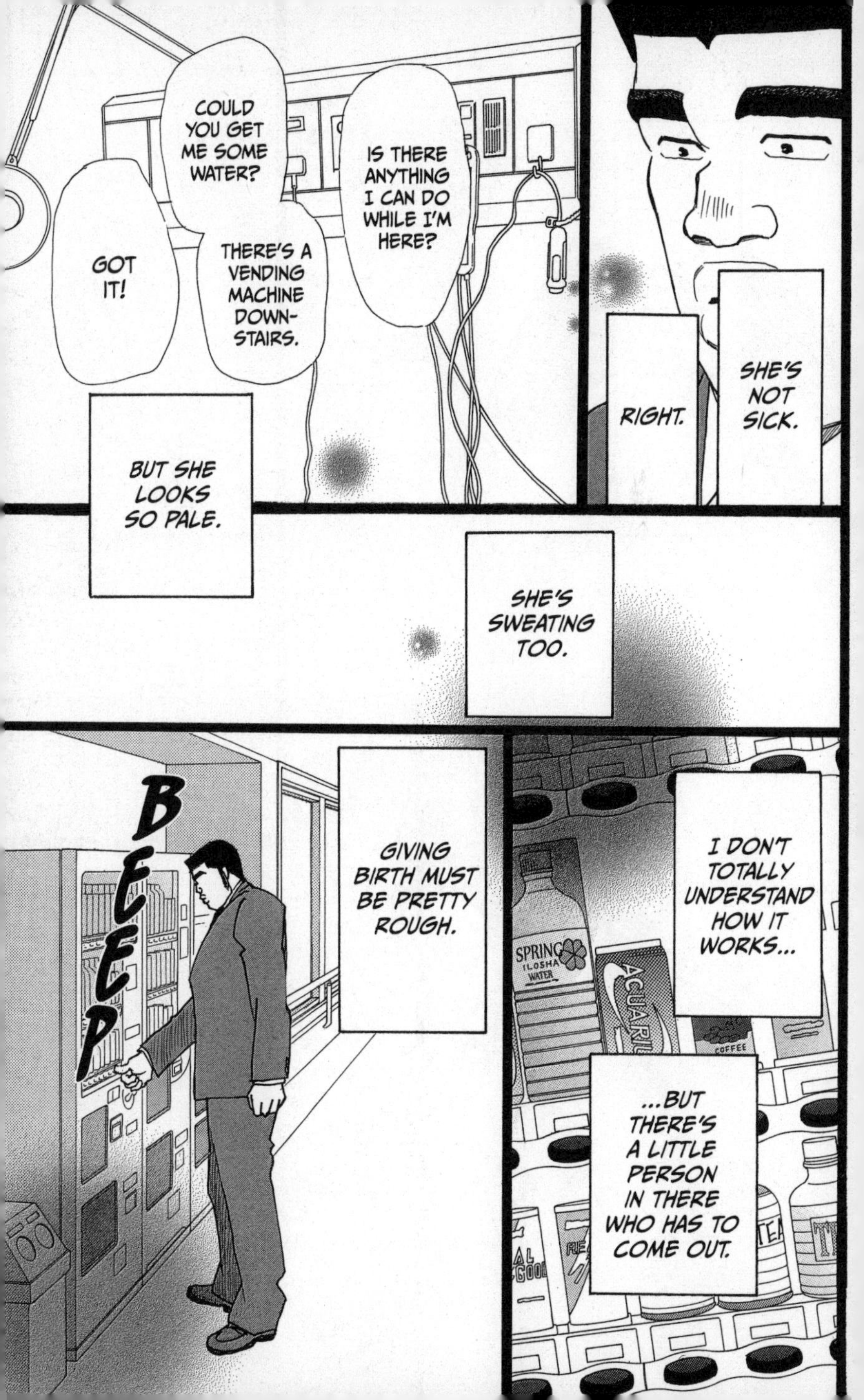
SHE'S NOT SICK.
RIGHT.
IS THERE ANYTHING I CAN DO WHILE I'M HERE?
COULD YOU GET ME SOME WATER?
THERE'S A VENDING MACHINE DOWN-STAIRS.
GOT IT!
BUT SHE LOOKS SO PALE.
SHE'S SWEATING TOO.
I DON'T TOTALLY UNDERSTAND HOW IT WORKS...
SPRING ILOSHA WATER
COFFEE
...BUT THERE'S A LITTLE PERSON IN THERE WHO HAS TO COME OUT.
GIVING BIRTH MUST BE PRETTY ROUGH.
BEEP

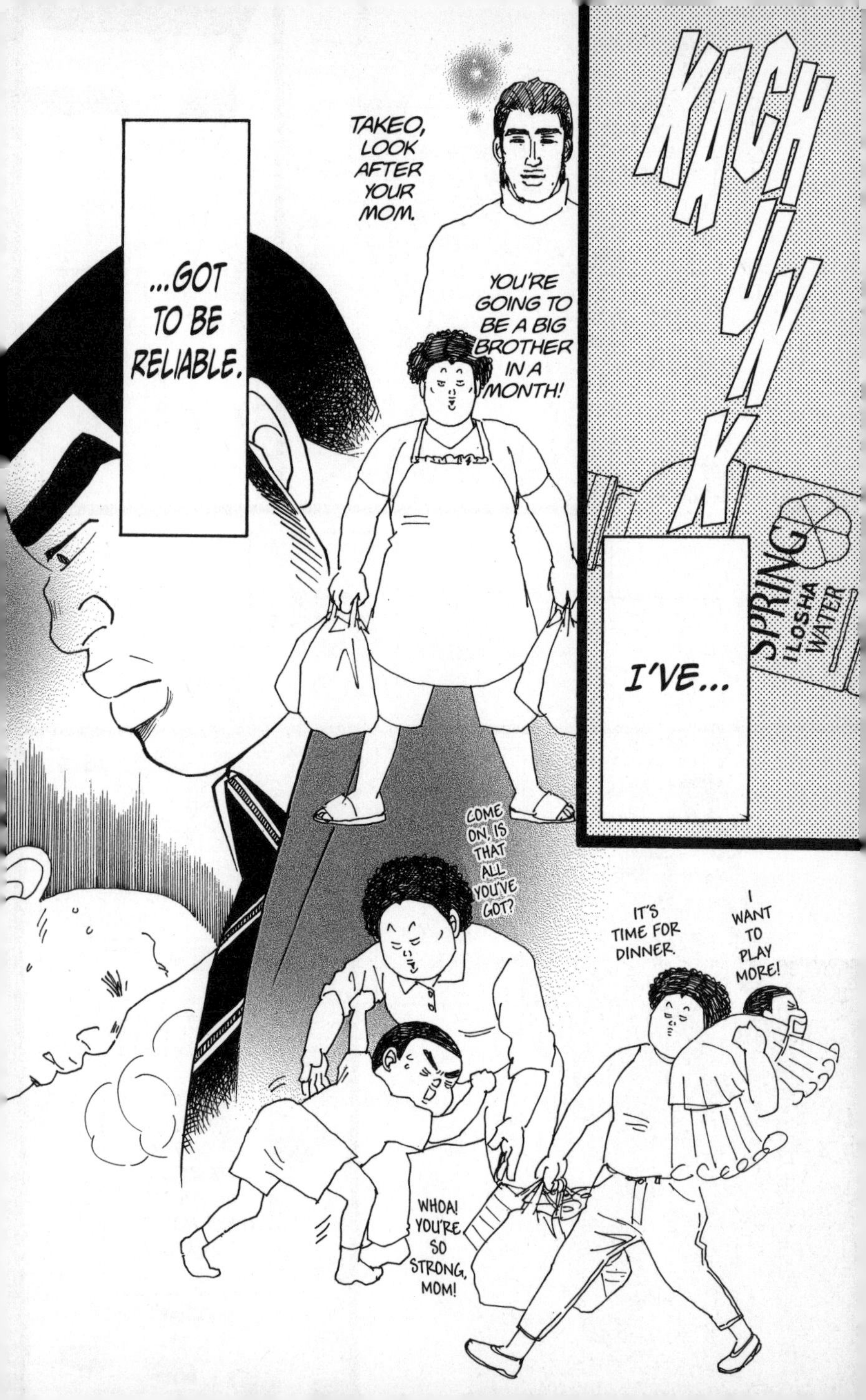
KACHUNK
SPRING ILOSHA WATER
I'VE...
...GOT TO BE RELIABLE.
TAKEO, LOOK AFTER YOUR MOM.
YOU'RE GOING TO BE A BIG BROTHER IN A MONTH!
I WANT TO PLAY MORE!
IT'S TIME FOR DINNER.
COME ON, IS THAT ALL YOU'VE GOT?
WHOA! YOU'RE SO STRONG, MOM!

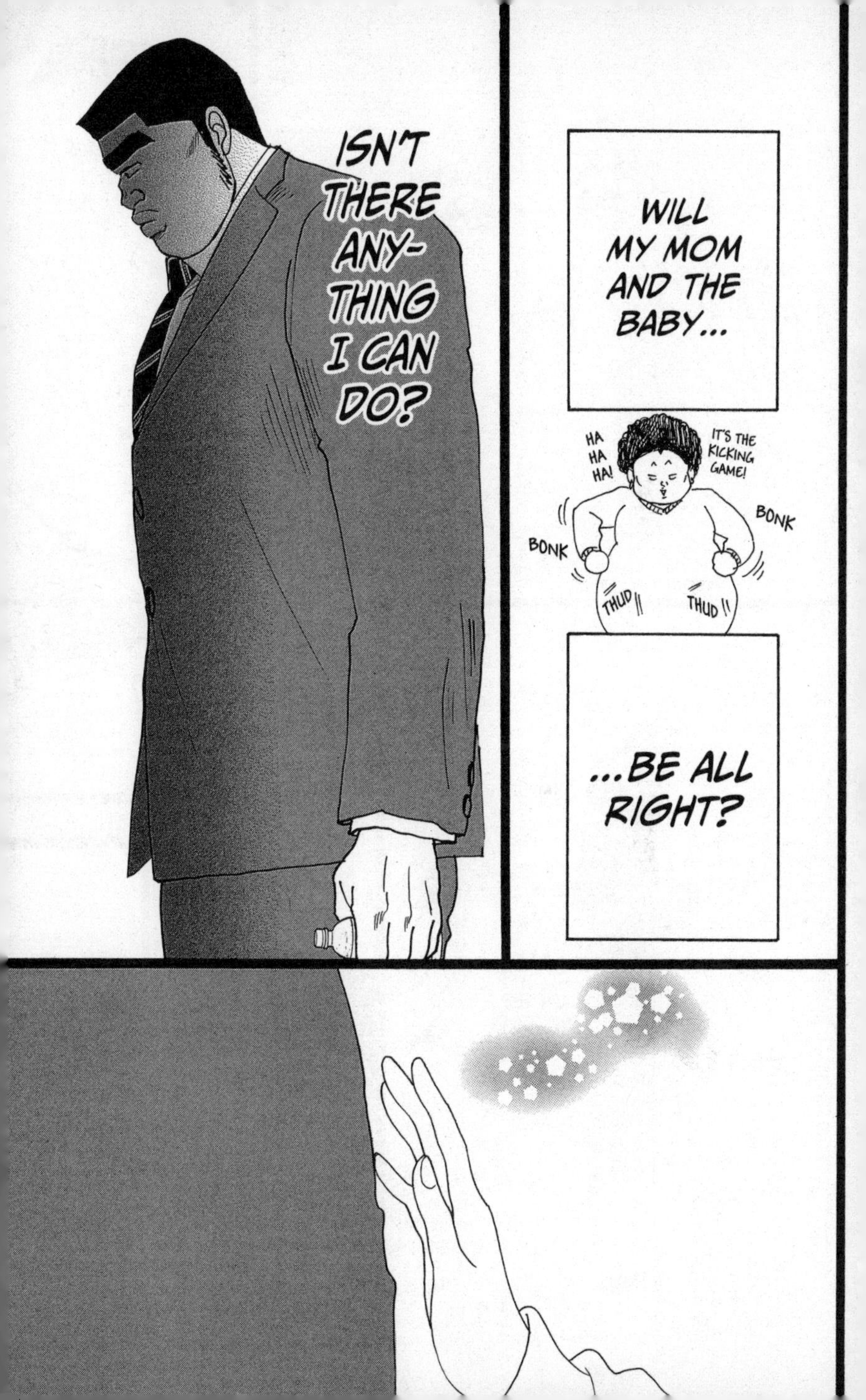
WILL MY MOM AND THE BABY...
IT'S THE KICKING GAME!
HA HA HA!
BONK
BONK
THUD
THUD
...BE ALL RIGHT?
ISN'T THERE ANY-THING I CAN DO?

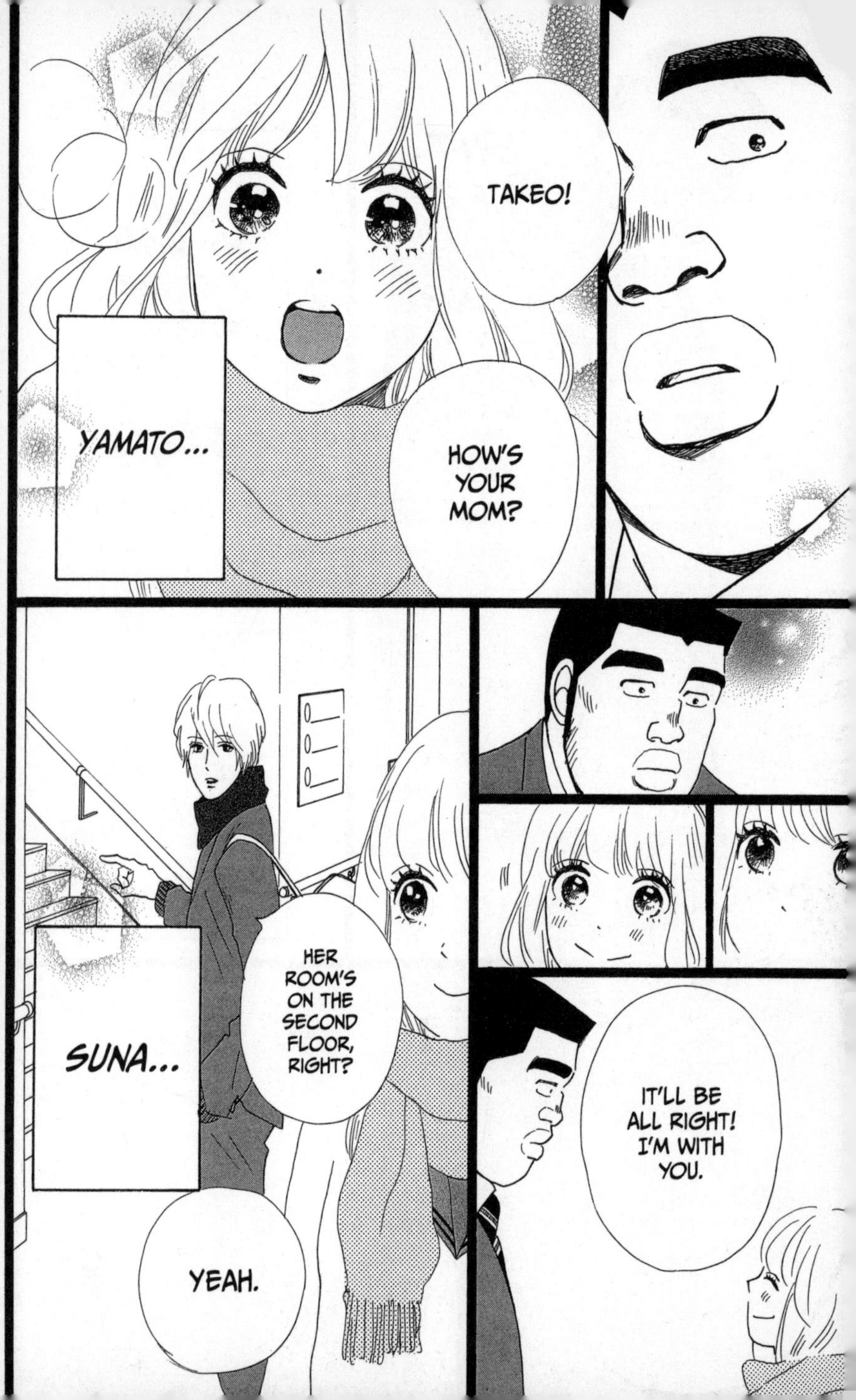
TAKEO!
YAMATO...
HOW'S YOUR MOM?
IT'LL BE ALL RIGHT! I'M WITH YOU.
HER ROOM'S ON THE SECOND FLOOR, RIGHT?
SUNA...
YEAH.

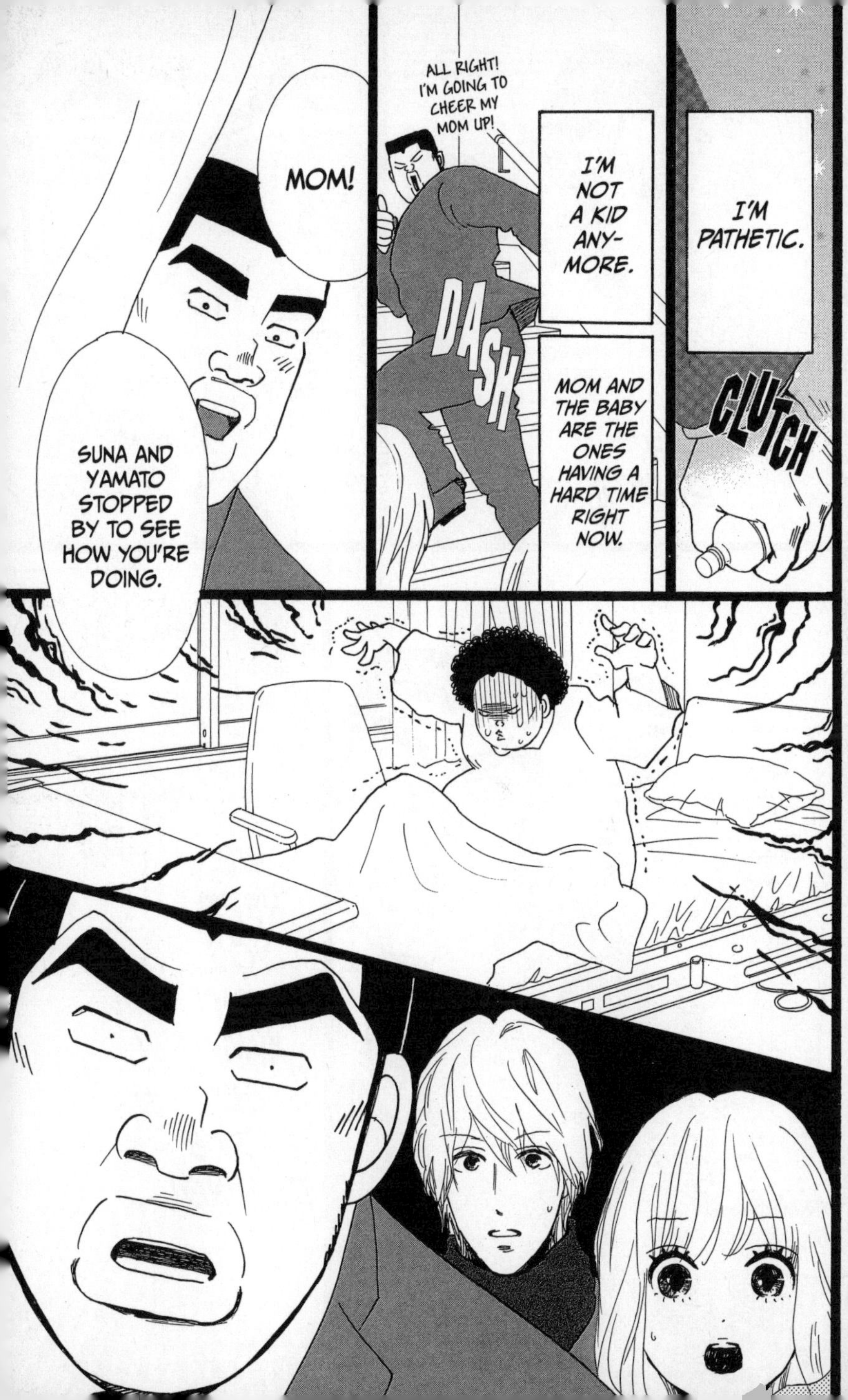
I'M PATHETIC.
CLUTCH
I'M NOT A KID ANYMORE.
MOM AND THE BABY ARE THE ONES HAVING A HARD TIME RIGHT NOW.
ALL RIGHT! I'M GOING TO CHEER MY MOM UP!
DASH
MOM!
SUNA AND YAMATO STOPPED BY TO SEE HOW YOU'RE DOING.

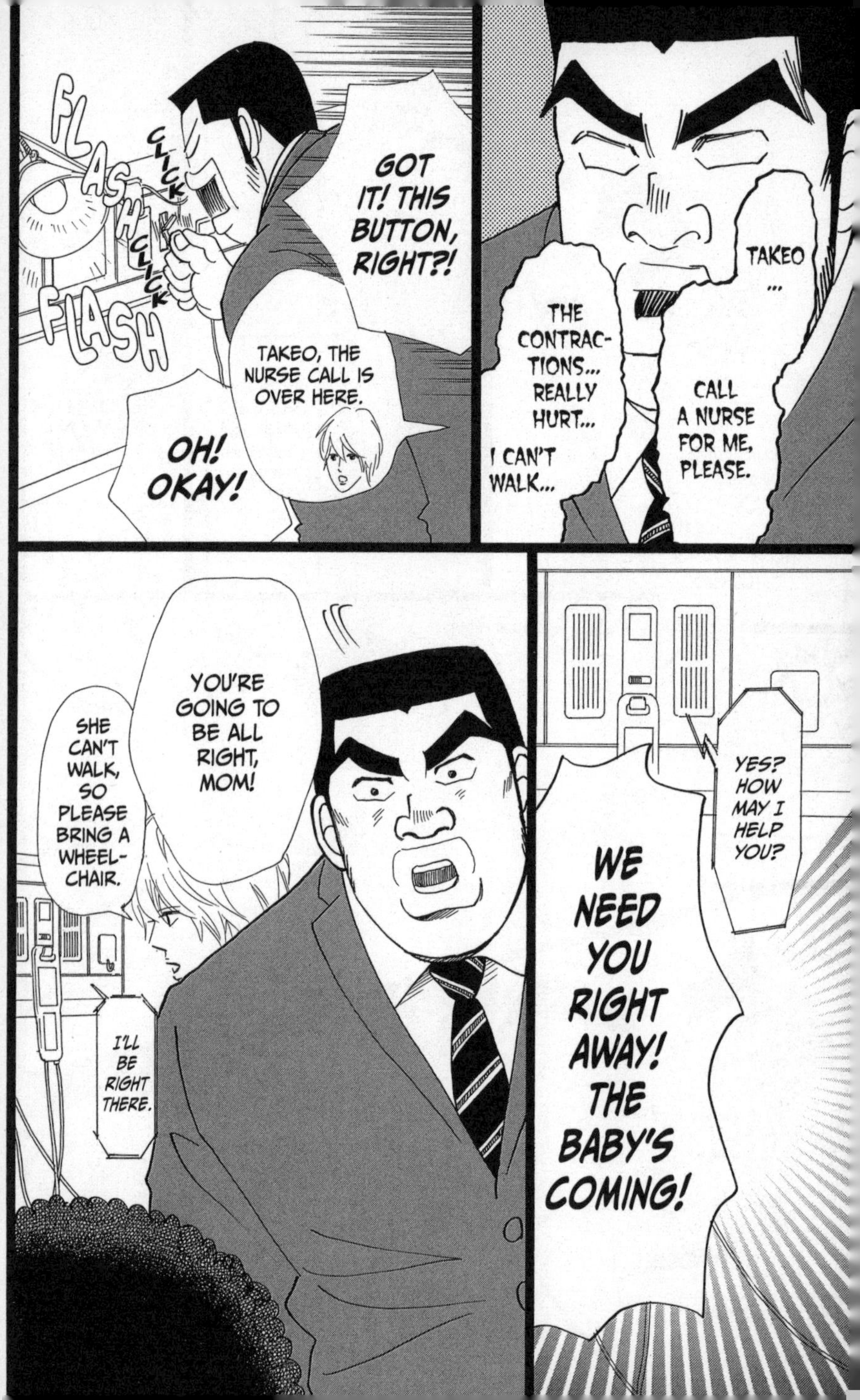
TAKEO ...
THE CONTRACTIONS... REALLY HURT...
I CAN'T WALK...
CALL A NURSE FOR ME, PLEASE.
GOT IT! THIS BUTTON, RIGHT?!
CLICK CLICK CLICK
FLASH FLASH
TAKEO, THE NURSE CALL IS OVER HERE.
OH! OKAY!
YES? HOW MAY I HELP YOU?
WE NEED YOU RIGHT AWAY! THE BABY'S COMING!
YOU'RE GOING TO BE ALL RIGHT, MOM!
SHE CAN'T WALK, SO PLEASE BRING A WHEEL-CHAIR.
I'LL BE RIGHT THERE.

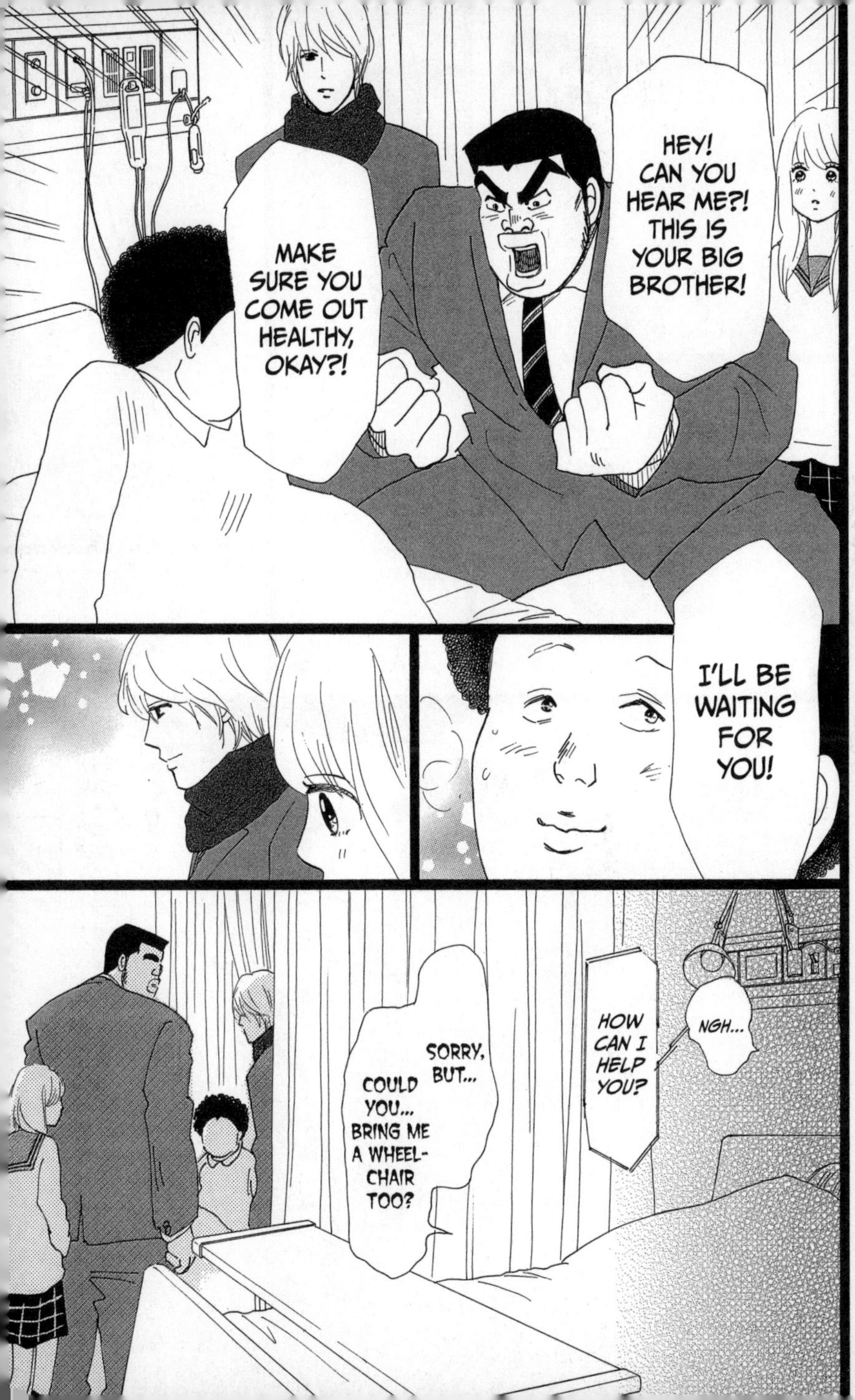
HEY! CAN YOU HEAR ME?! THIS IS YOUR BIG BROTHER!
MAKE SURE YOU COME OUT HEALTHY, OKAY?!
I'LL BE WAITING FOR YOU!
NGH...
HOW CAN I HELP YOU?
SORRY, BUT...
COULD YOU... BRING ME A WHEEL-CHAIR TOO?

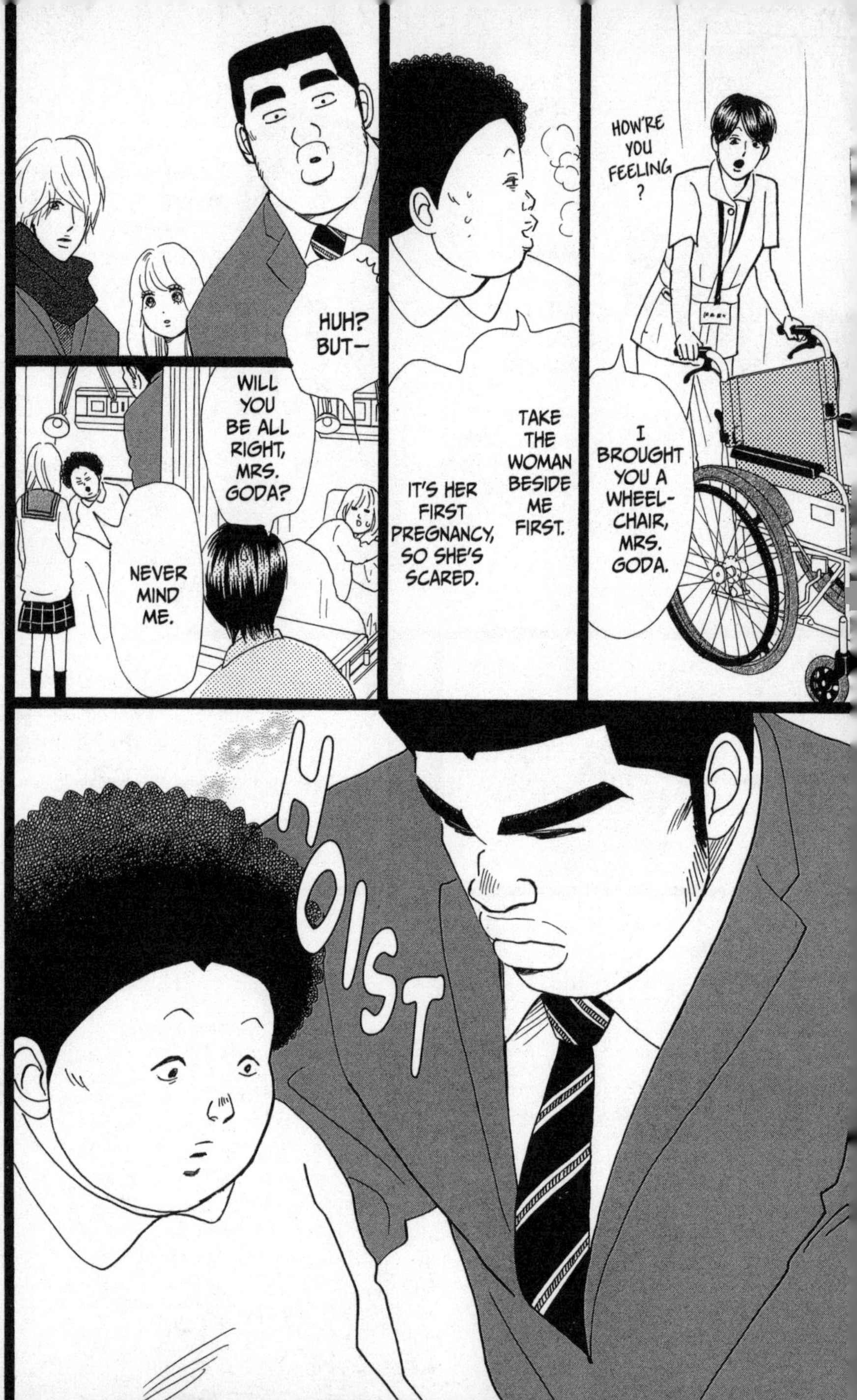
HOW'RE YOU FEELING?
I BROUGHT YOU A WHEEL-CHAIR, MRS. GODA.
TAKE THE WOMAN BESIDE ME FIRST.
IT'S HER FIRST PREGNANCY, SO SHE'S SCARED.
HUH? BUT—
WILL YOU BE ALL RIGHT, MRS. GODA?
NEVER MIND ME.
HOIST

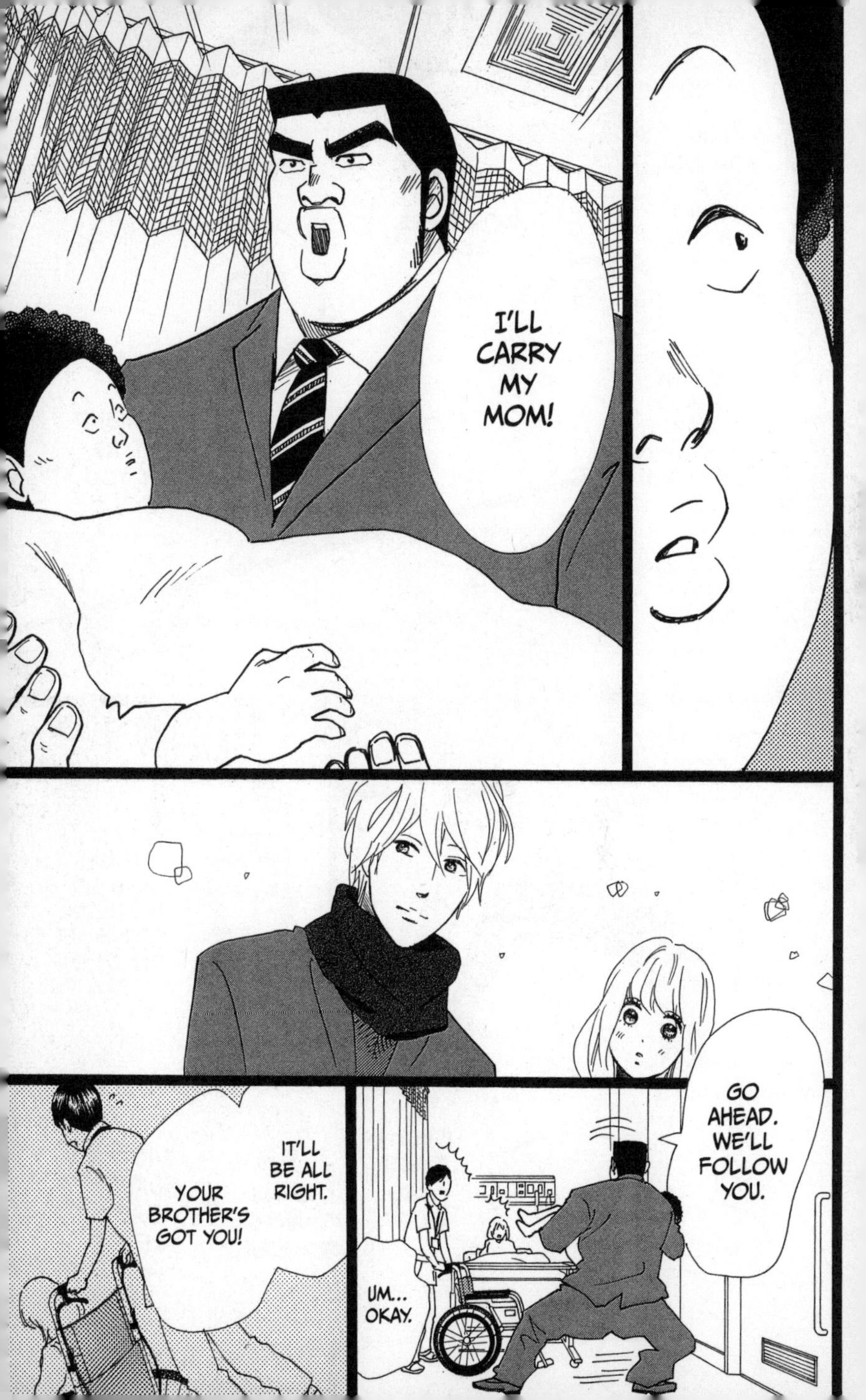
I'LL CARRY MY MOM!
GO AHEAD. WE'LL FOLLOW YOU.
UM... OKAY.
IT'LL BE ALL RIGHT.
YOUR BROTHER'S GOT YOU!

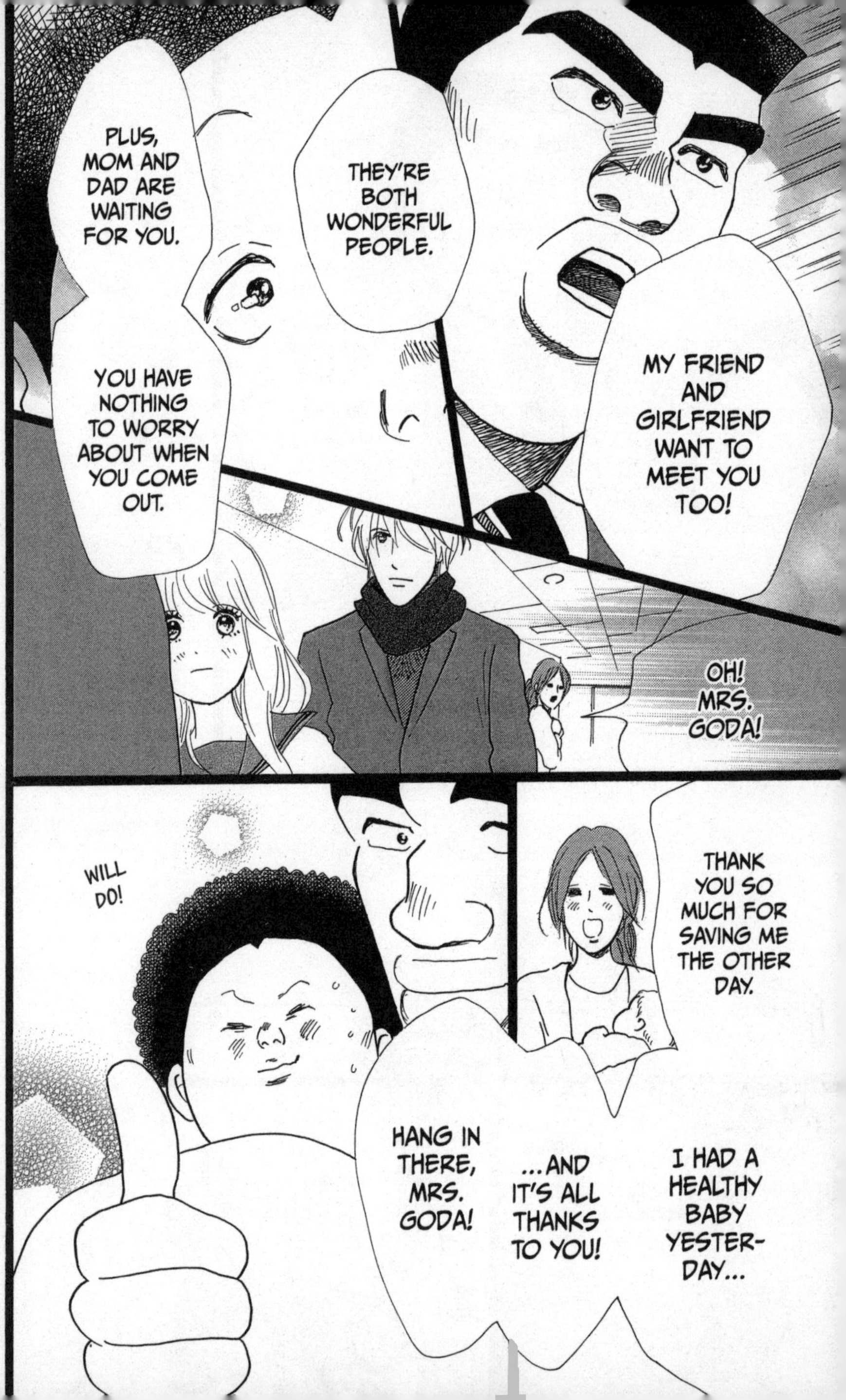
MY FRIEND AND GIRLFRIEND WANT TO MEET YOU TOO!
THEY'RE BOTH WONDERFUL PEOPLE.
PLUS, MOM AND DAD ARE WAITING FOR YOU.
YOU HAVE NOTHING TO WORRY ABOUT WHEN YOU COME OUT.
OH! MRS. GODA!
THANK YOU SO MUCH FOR SAVING ME THE OTHER DAY.
I HAD A HEALTHY BABY YESTERDAY...
...AND IT'S ALL THANKS TO YOU!
HANG IN THERE, MRS. GODA!
WILL DO!

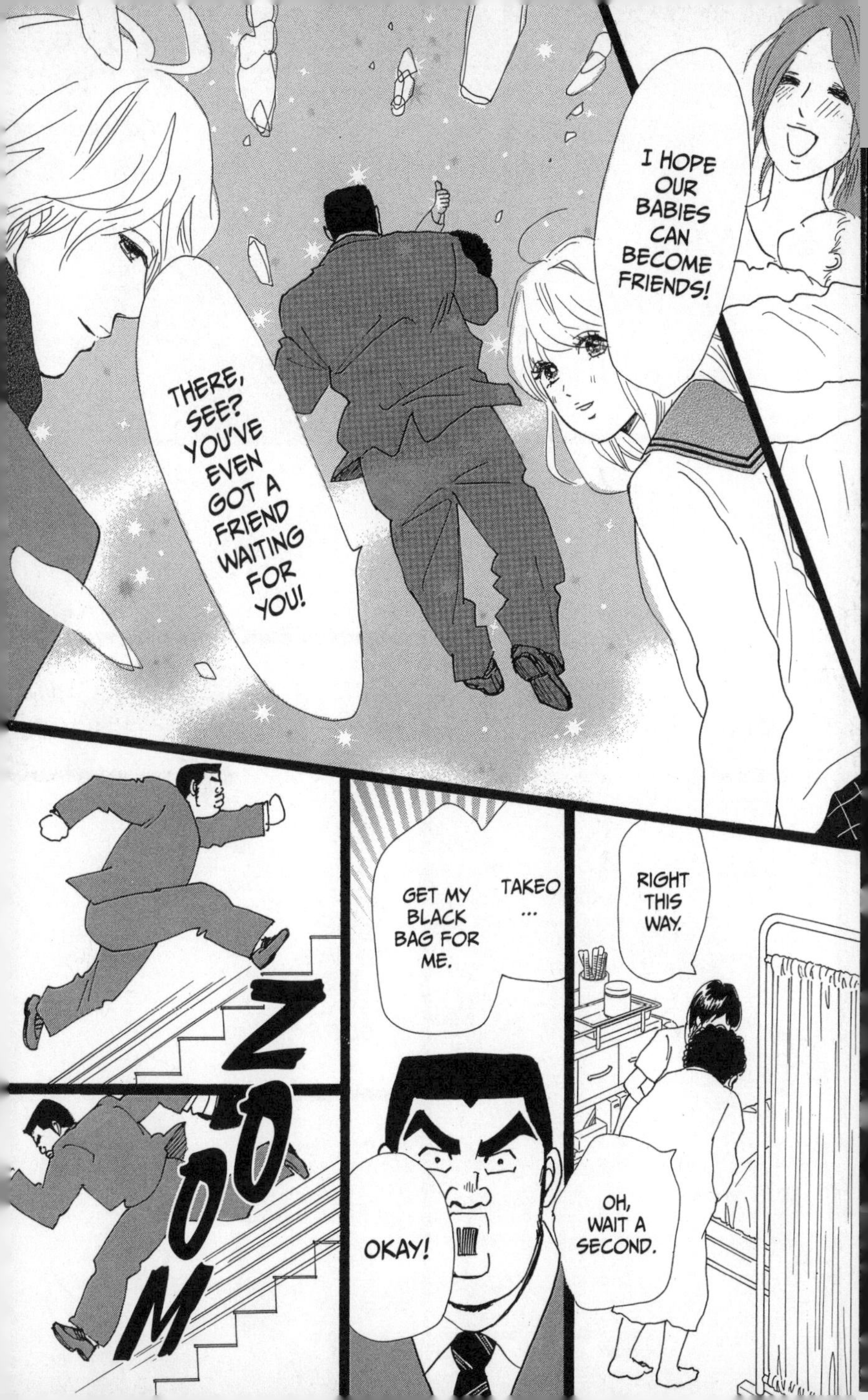
I HOPE OUR BABIES CAN BECOME FRIENDS!
THERE, SEE? YOU'VE EVEN GOT A FRIEND WAITING FOR YOU!
RIGHT THIS WAY.
OH, WAIT A SECOND.
TAKEO ...
GET MY BLACK BAG FOR ME.
OKAY!
ZOOOM

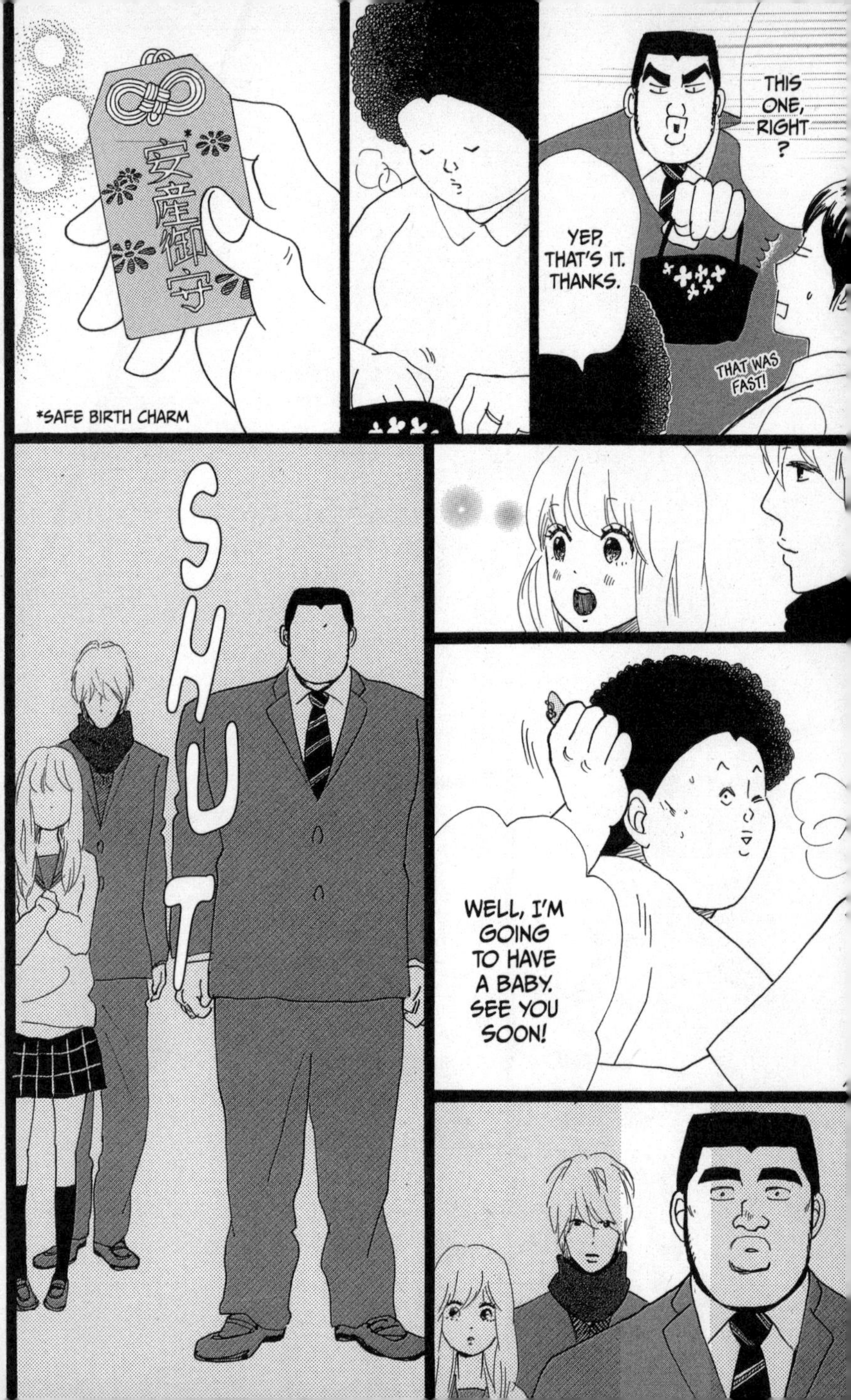
THIS ONE, RIGHT?
YEP, THAT'S IT. THANKS.
THAT WAS FAST!
安産御守*
*SAFE BIRTH CHARM
WELL, I'M GOING TO HAVE A BABY. SEE YOU SOON!
SHUT

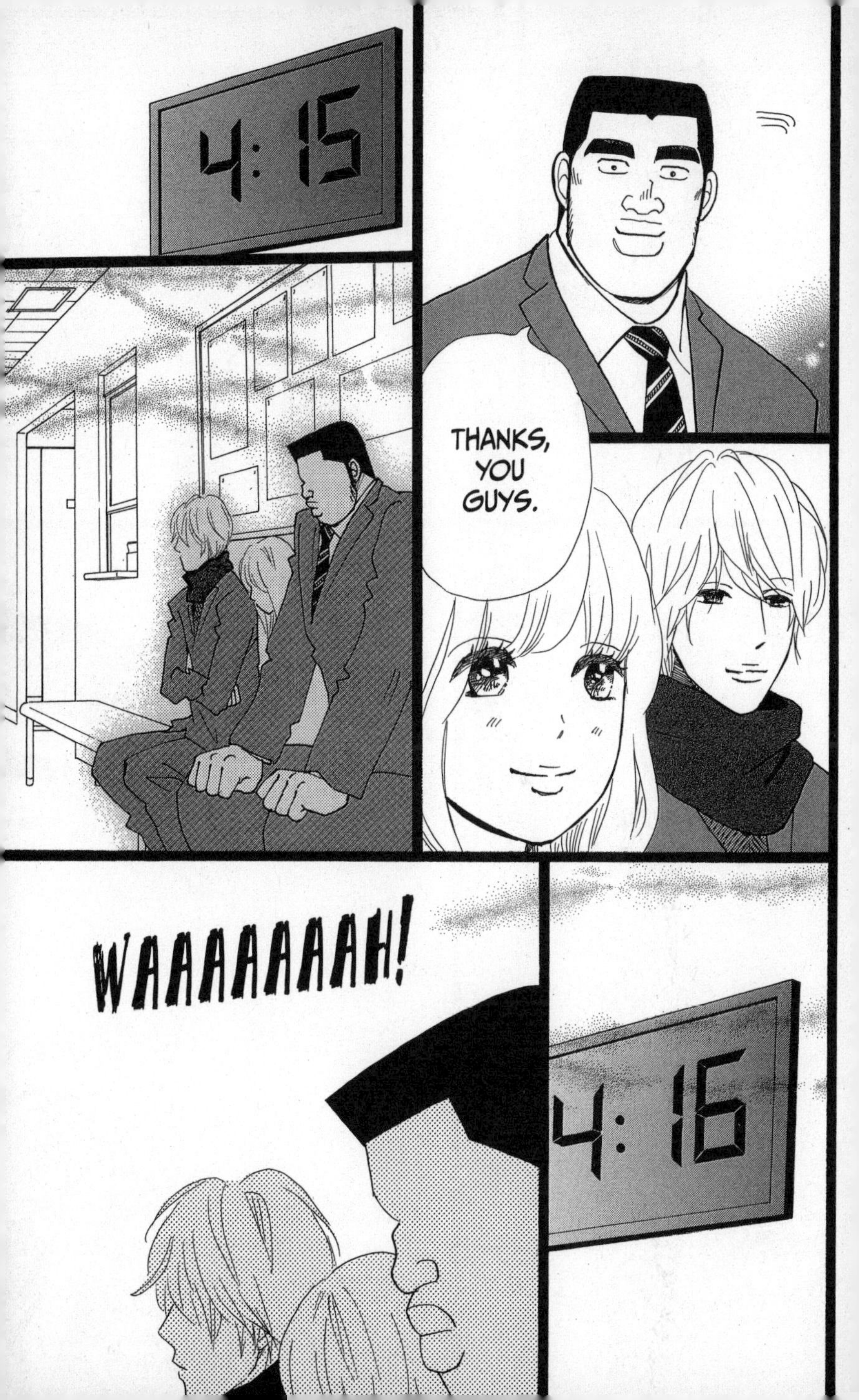
4:15
THANKS, YOU GUYS.
WAAAAAAAAH!
4:16

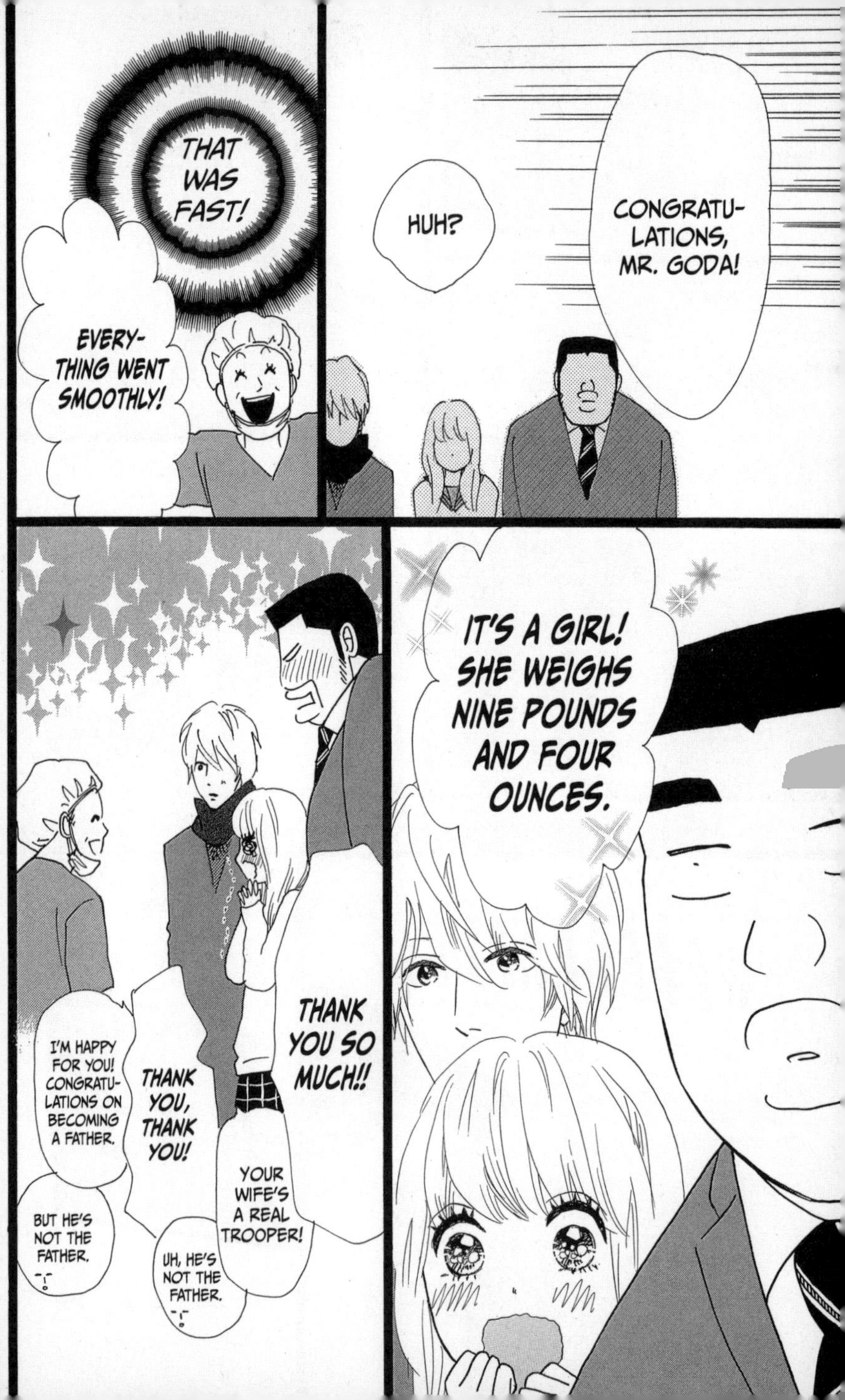
CONGRATU-LATIONS, MR. GODA!
HUH?
THAT WAS FAST!
EVERY-THING WENT SMOOTHLY!
IT'S A GIRL! SHE WEIGHS NINE POUNDS AND FOUR OUNCES.
THANK YOU SO MUCH!!
THANK YOU, THANK YOU!
I'M HAPPY FOR YOU! CONGRATU-LATIONS ON BECOMING A FATHER.
YOUR WIFE'S A REAL TROOPER!
UH, HE'S NOT THE FATHER.
BUT HE'S NOT THE FATHER.

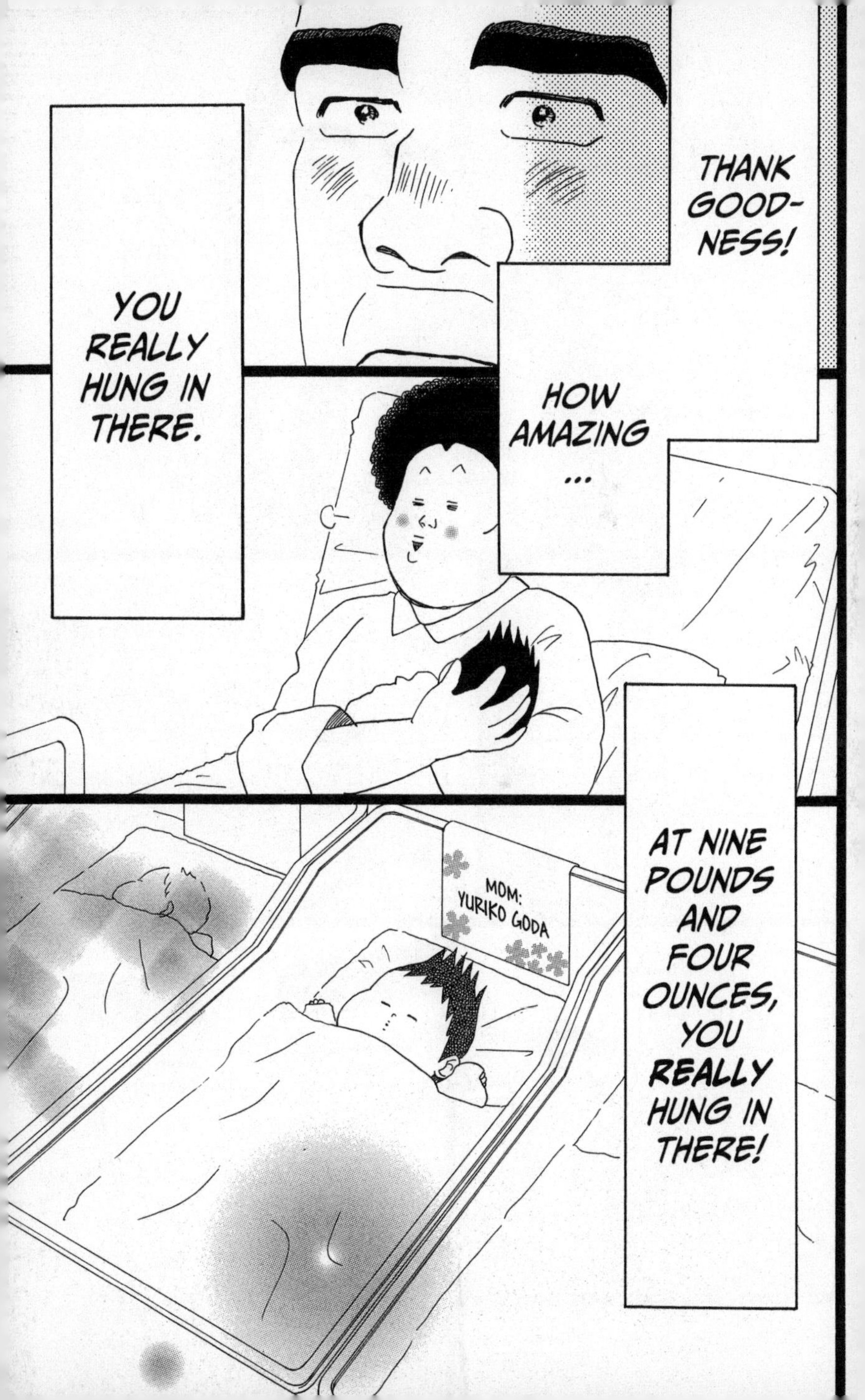
THANK GOODNESS!
HOW AMAZING ...
YOU REALLY HUNG IN THERE.
AT NINE POUNDS AND FOUR OUNCES, YOU REALLY HUNG IN THERE!
MOM: YURIKO GODA

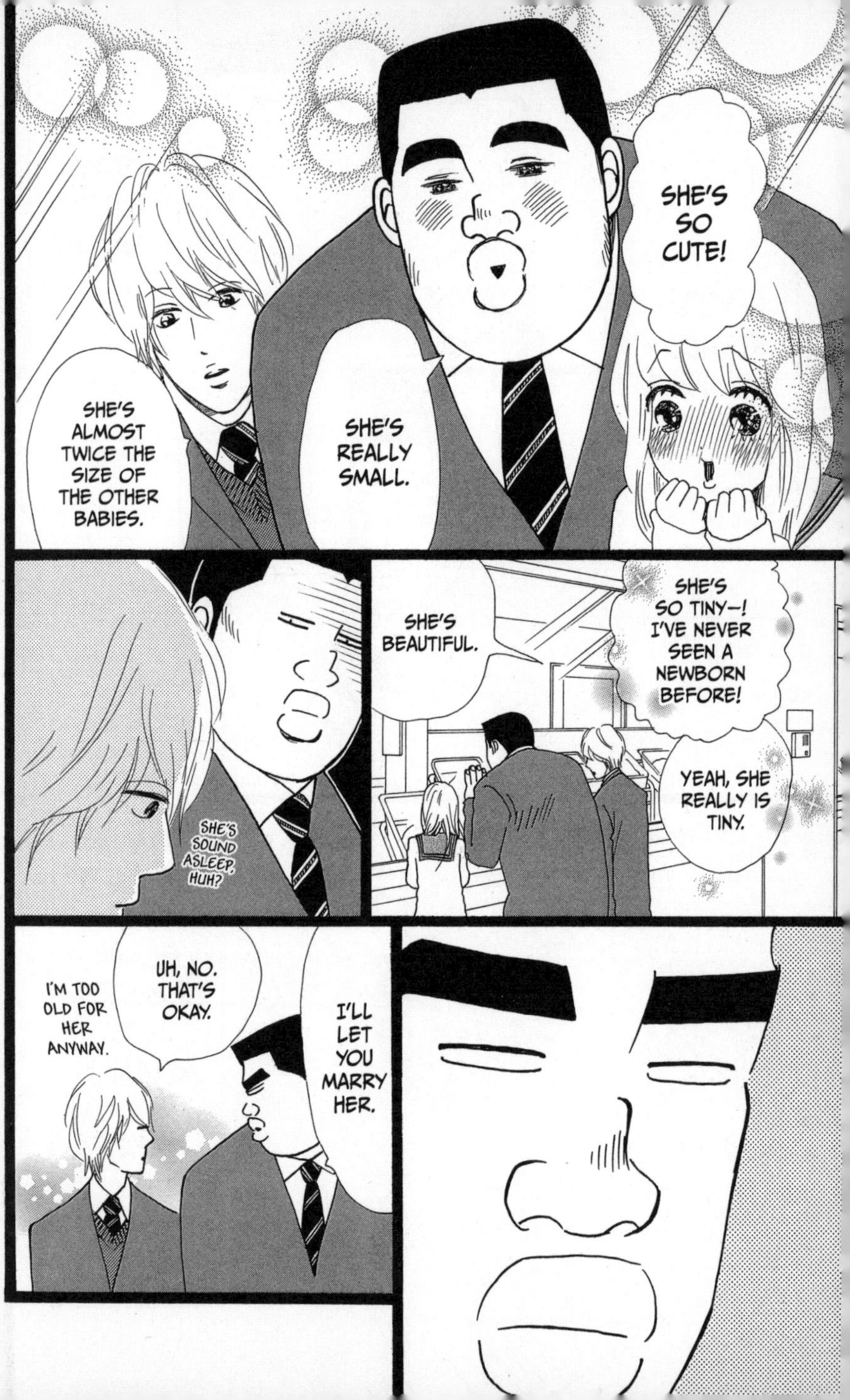
SHE'S SO CUTE!
SHE'S REALLY SMALL.
SHE'S ALMOST TWICE THE SIZE OF THE OTHER BABIES.
SHE'S SO TINY—! I'VE NEVER SEEN A NEWBORN BEFORE!
SHE'S BEAUTIFUL.
YEAH, SHE REALLY IS TINY.
SHE'S SOUND ASLEEP, HUH?
I'LL LET YOU MARRY HER.
UH, NO. THAT'S OKAY.
I'M TOO OLD FOR HER ANYWAY.

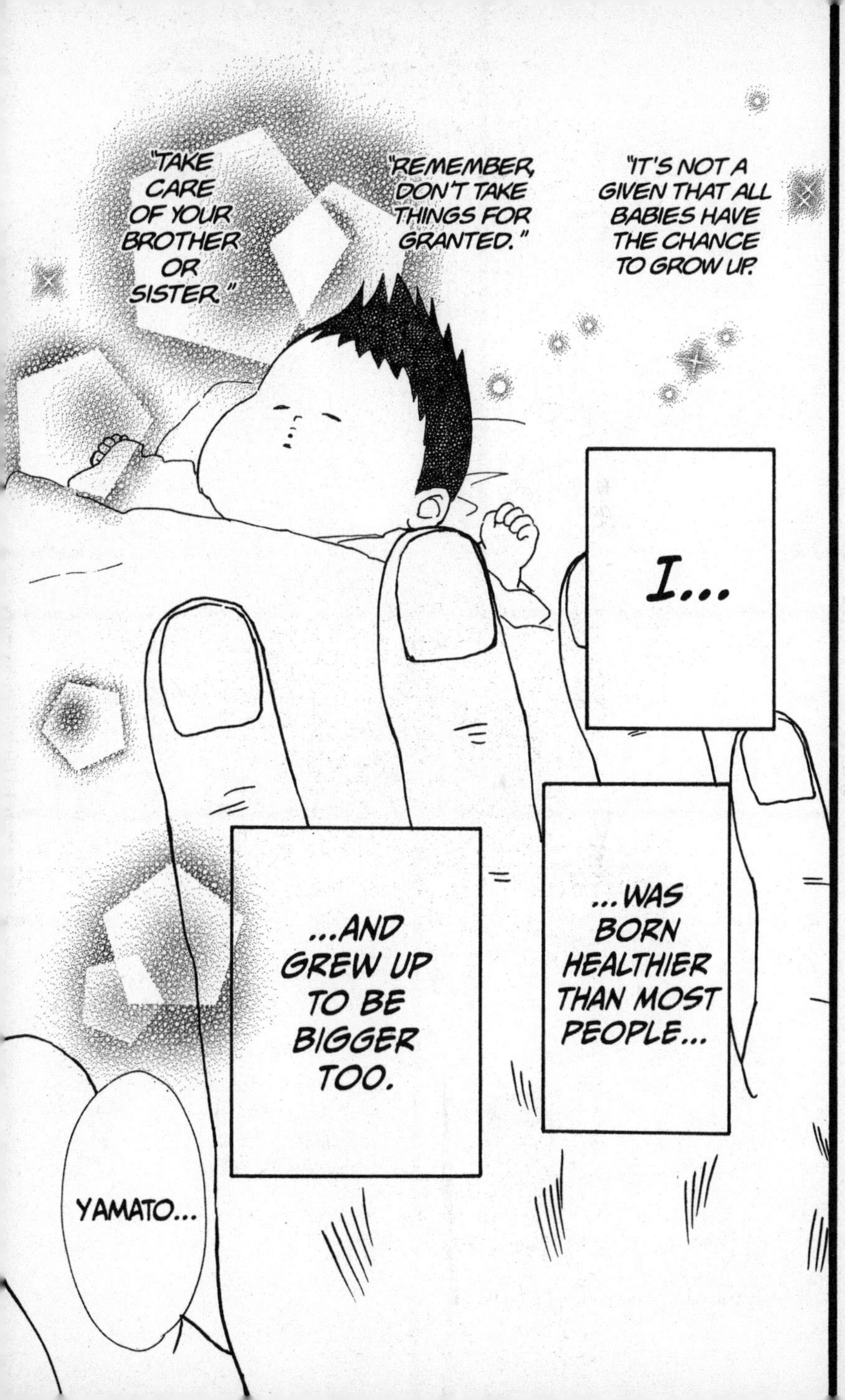
"IT'S NOT A GIVEN THAT ALL BABIES HAVE THE CHANCE TO GROW UP.
"REMEMBER, DON'T TAKE THINGS FOR GRANTED."
"TAKE CARE OF YOUR BROTHER OR SISTER."
I...
...WAS BORN HEALTHIER THAN MOST PEOPLE...
...AND GREW UP TO BE BIGGER TOO.
YAMATO...

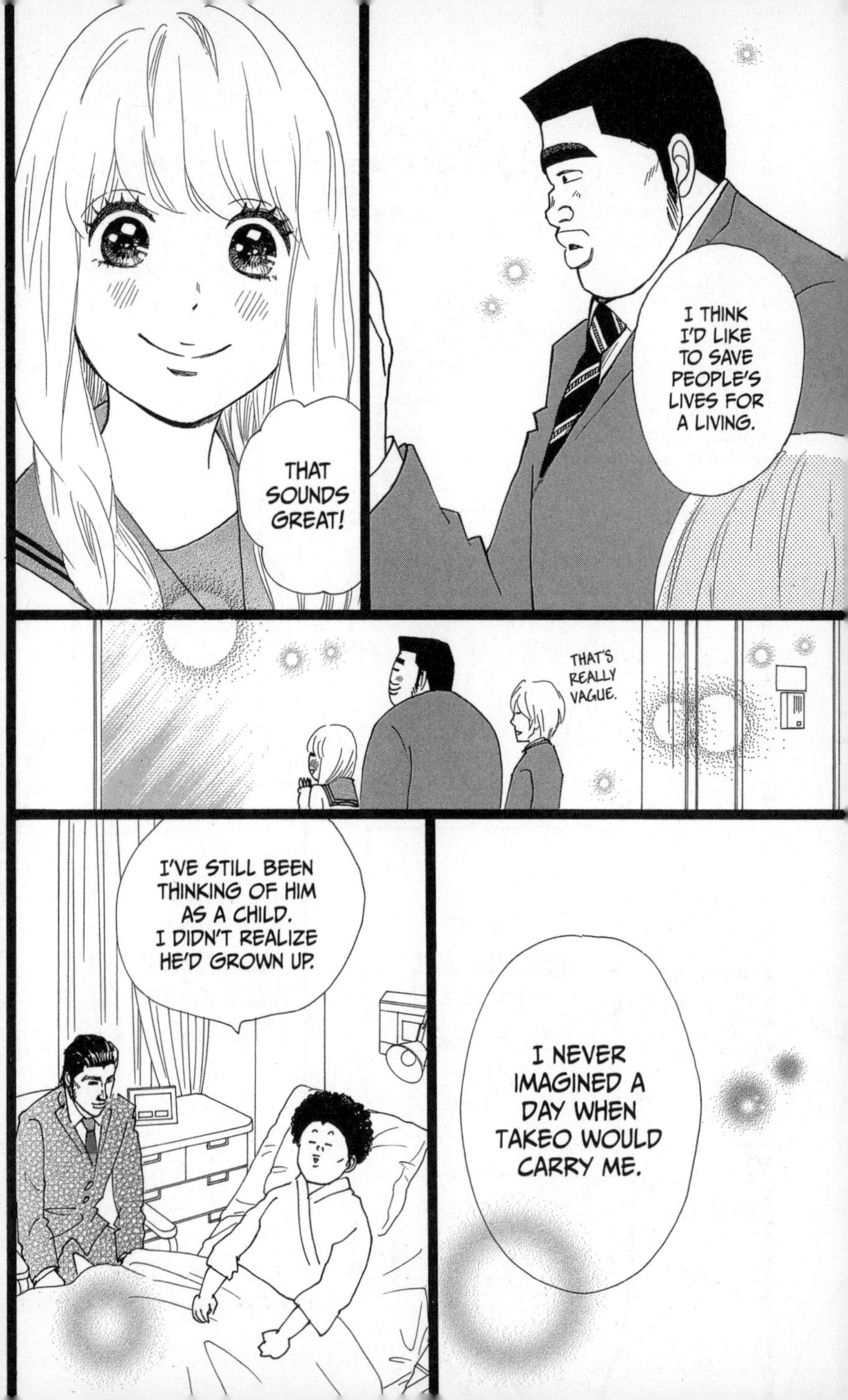
I THINK I'D LIKE TO SAVE PEOPLE'S LIVES FOR A LIVING.
THAT SOUNDS GREAT!
THAT'S REALLY VAGUE.
I NEVER IMAGINED A DAY WHEN TAKEO WOULD CARRY ME.
I'VE STILL BEEN THINKING OF HIM AS A CHILD. I DIDN'T REALIZE HE'D GROWN UP.

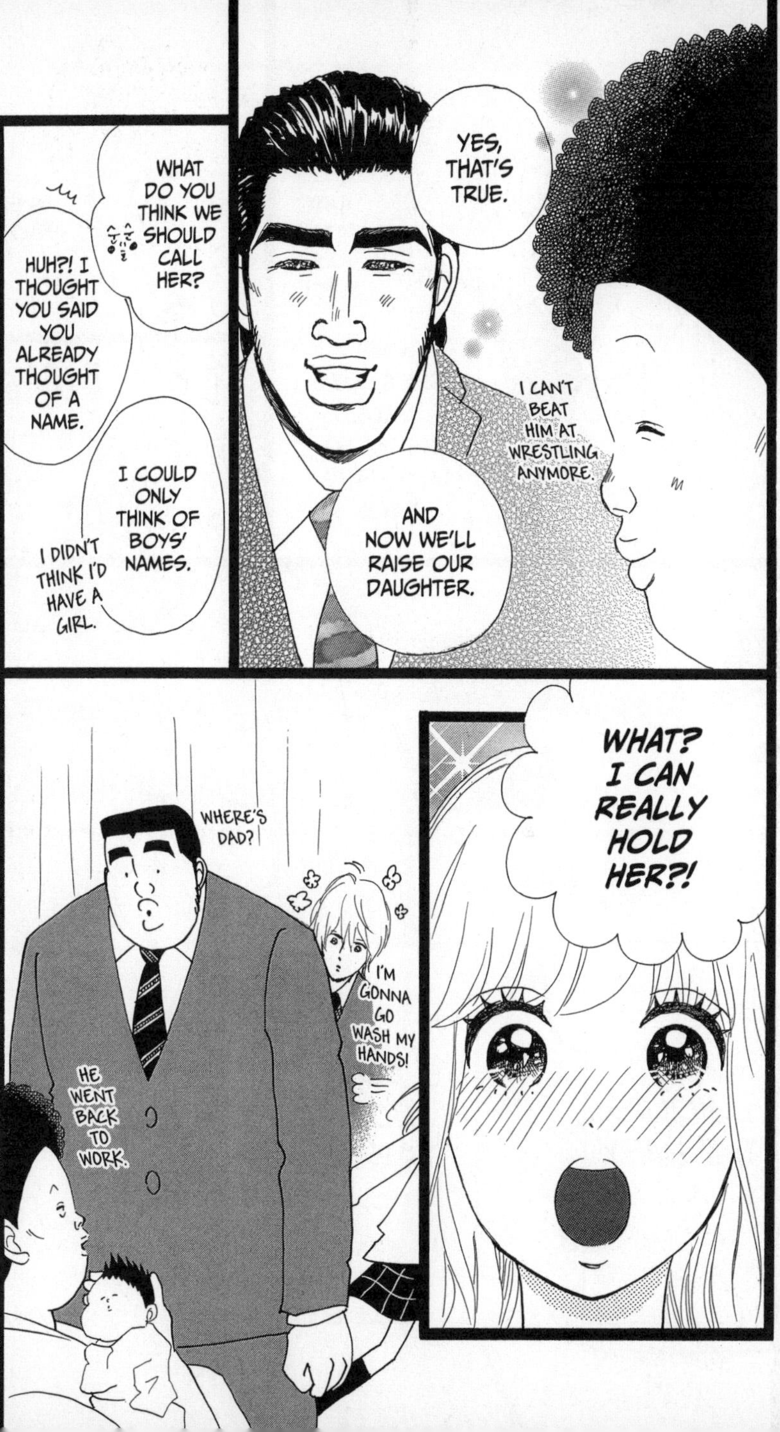

YES, THAT'S TRUE.
I CAN'T BEAT HIM AT WRESTLING ANYMORE.
AND NOW WE'LL RAISE OUR DAUGHTER.
WHAT DO YOU THINK WE SHOULD CALL HER?
HUH?! I THOUGHT YOU SAID YOU ALREADY THOUGHT OF A NAME.
I COULD ONLY THINK OF BOYS' NAMES.
I DIDN'T THINK I'D HAVE A GIRL.
WHAT? I CAN REALLY HOLD HER?!
WHERE'S DAD?
I'M GONNA GO WASH MY HANDS!
HE WENT BACK TO WORK.

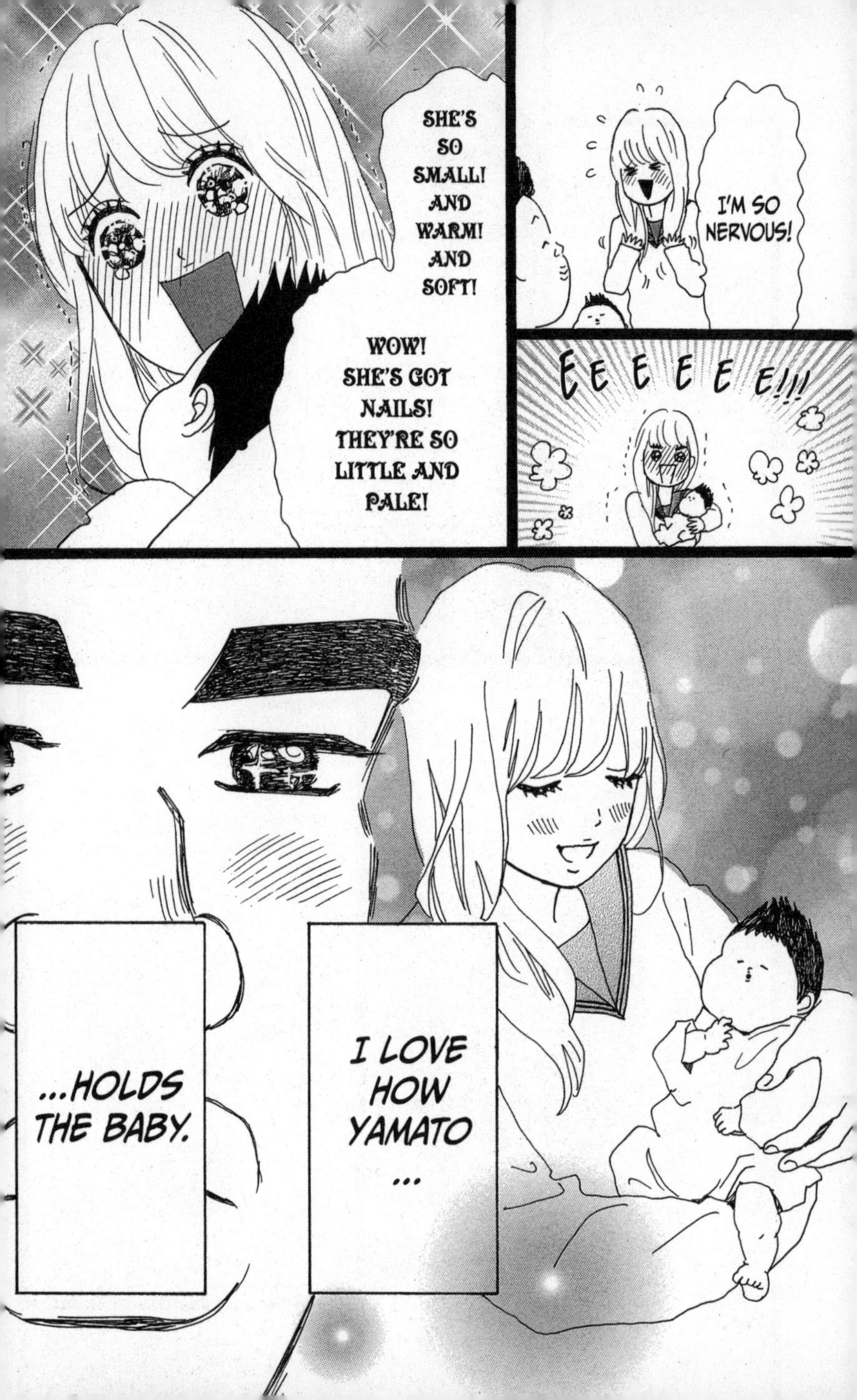
I'M SO NERVOUS!
EEEEE!!!
SHE'S SO SMALL! AND WARM! AND SOFT!
WOW! SHE'S GOT NAILS! THEY'RE SO LITTLE AND PALE!
I LOVE HOW YAMATO ...
...HOLDS THE BABY.

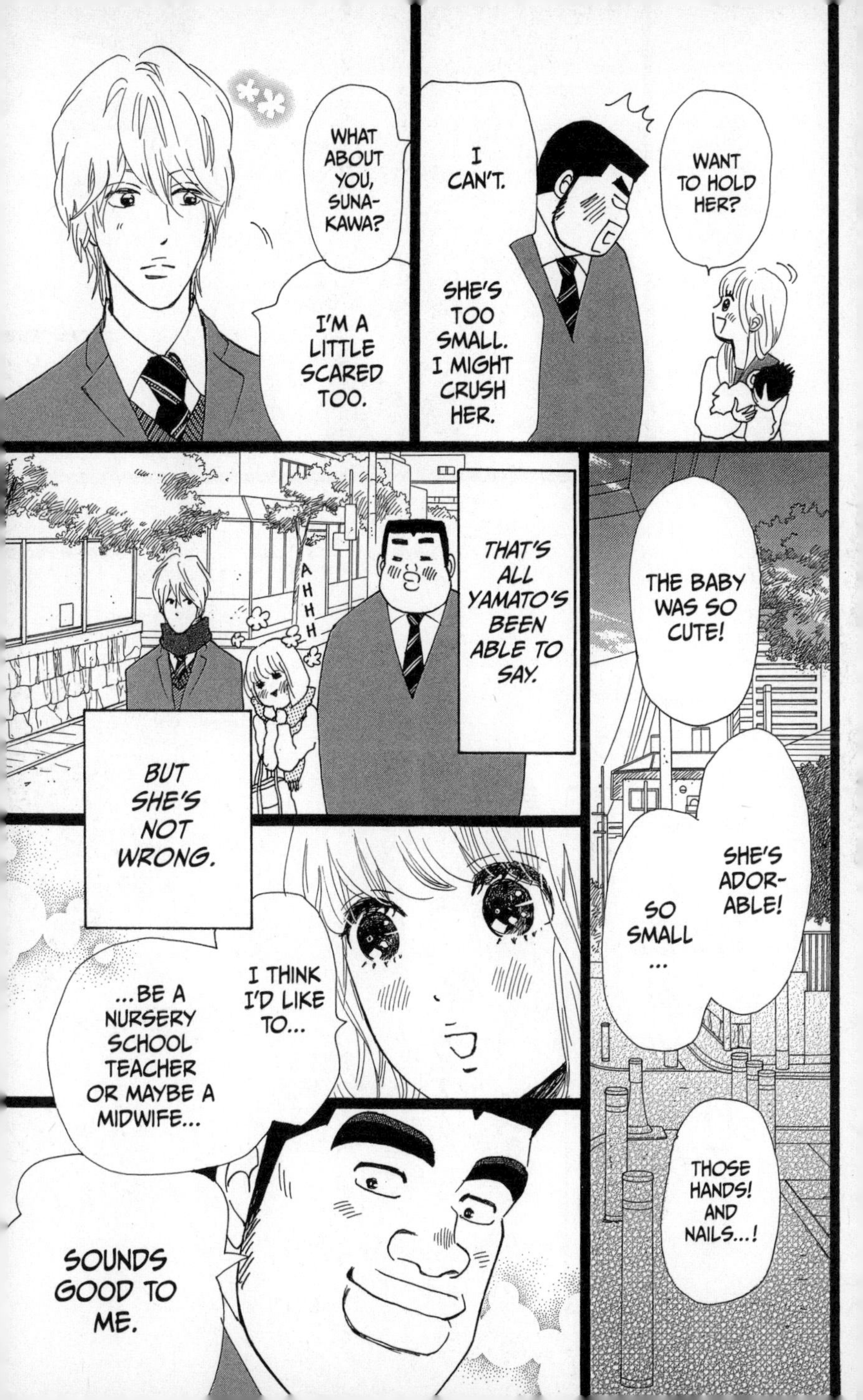

WANT TO HOLD HER?
I CAN'T.
SHE'S TOO SMALL. I MIGHT CRUSH HER.
WHAT ABOUT YOU, SUNA-KAWA?
I'M A LITTLE SCARED TOO.
THE BABY WAS SO CUTE!
SHE'S ADOR-ABLE!
SO SMALL...
THOSE HANDS! AND NAILS...!
THAT'S ALL YAMATO'S BEEN ABLE TO SAY.
AHHH
BUT SHE'S NOT WRONG.
I THINK I'D LIKE TO...
...BE A NURSERY SCHOOL TEACHER OR MAYBE A MIDWIFE...
SOUNDS GOOD TO ME.

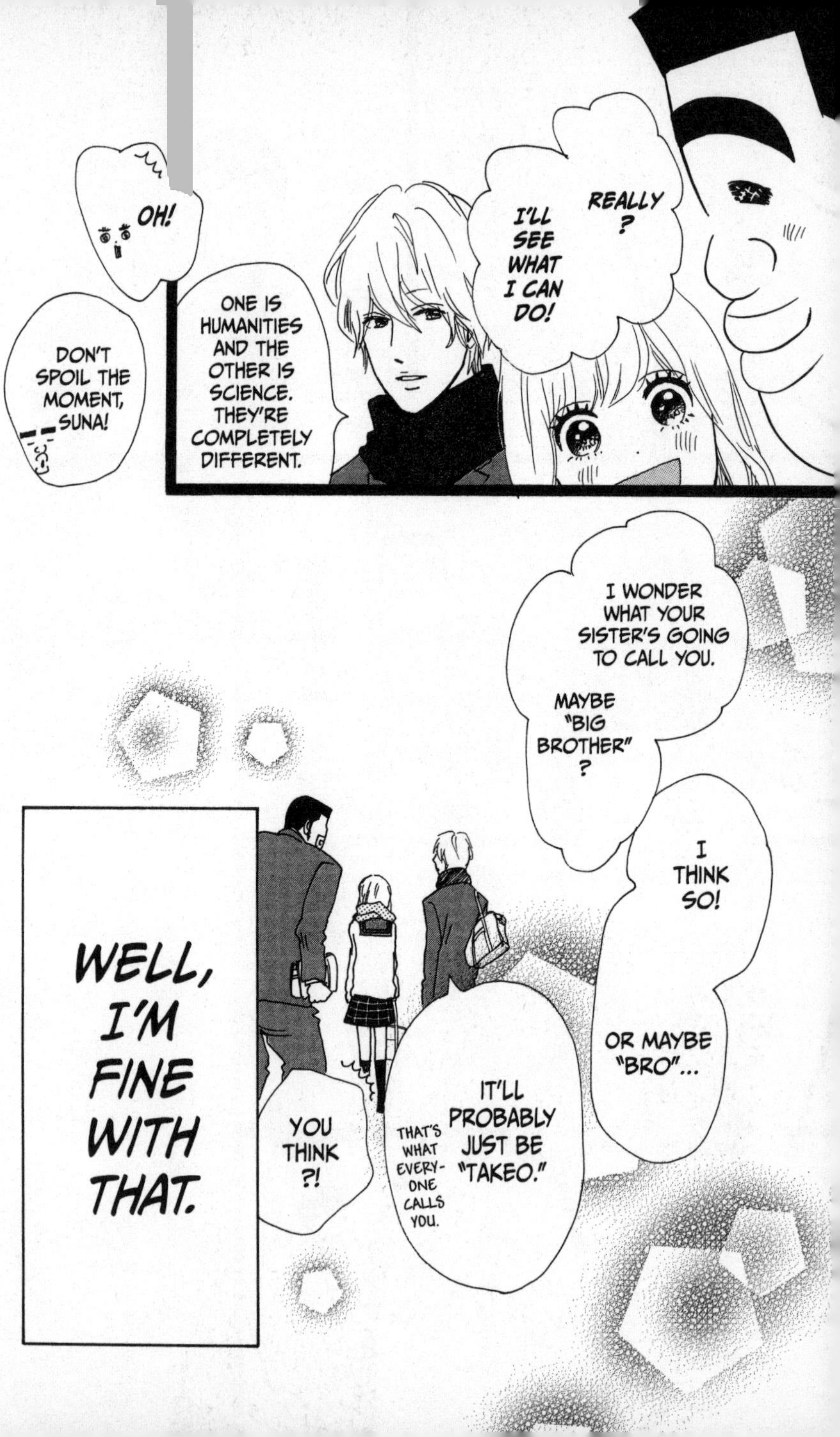
REALLY?
I'LL SEE WHAT I CAN DO!
ONE IS HUMANITIES AND THE OTHER IS SCIENCE. THEY'RE COMPLETELY DIFFERENT.
OH!
DON'T SPOIL THE MOMENT, SUNA!
I WONDER WHAT YOUR SISTER'S GOING TO CALL YOU.
MAYBE "BIG BROTHER"?
I THINK SO!
OR MAYBE "BRO"...
IT'LL PROBABLY JUST BE "TAKEO."
THAT'S WHAT EVERYONE CALLS YOU.
YOU THINK?!
WELL, I'M FINE WITH THAT.

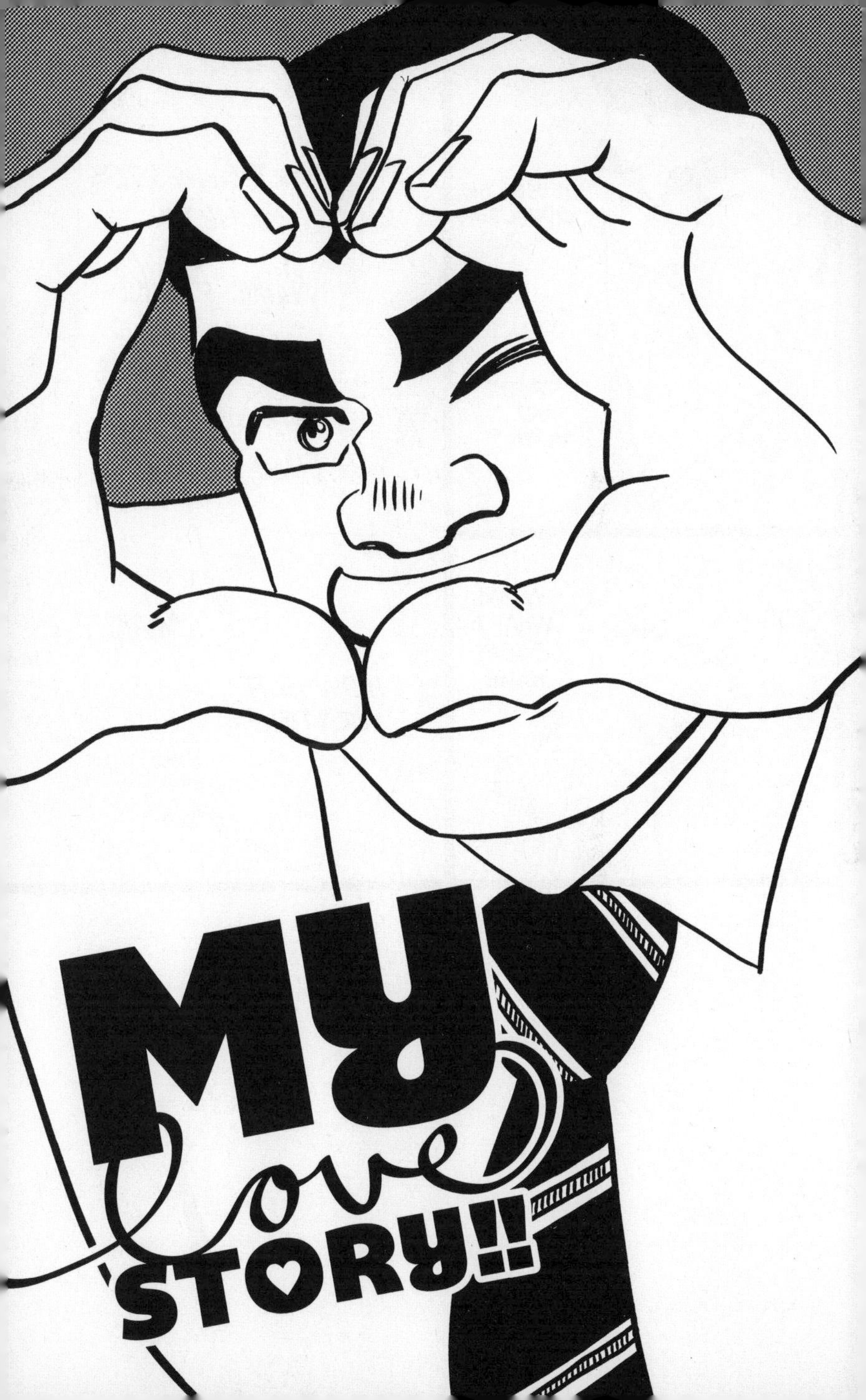
MY Love STORY!!

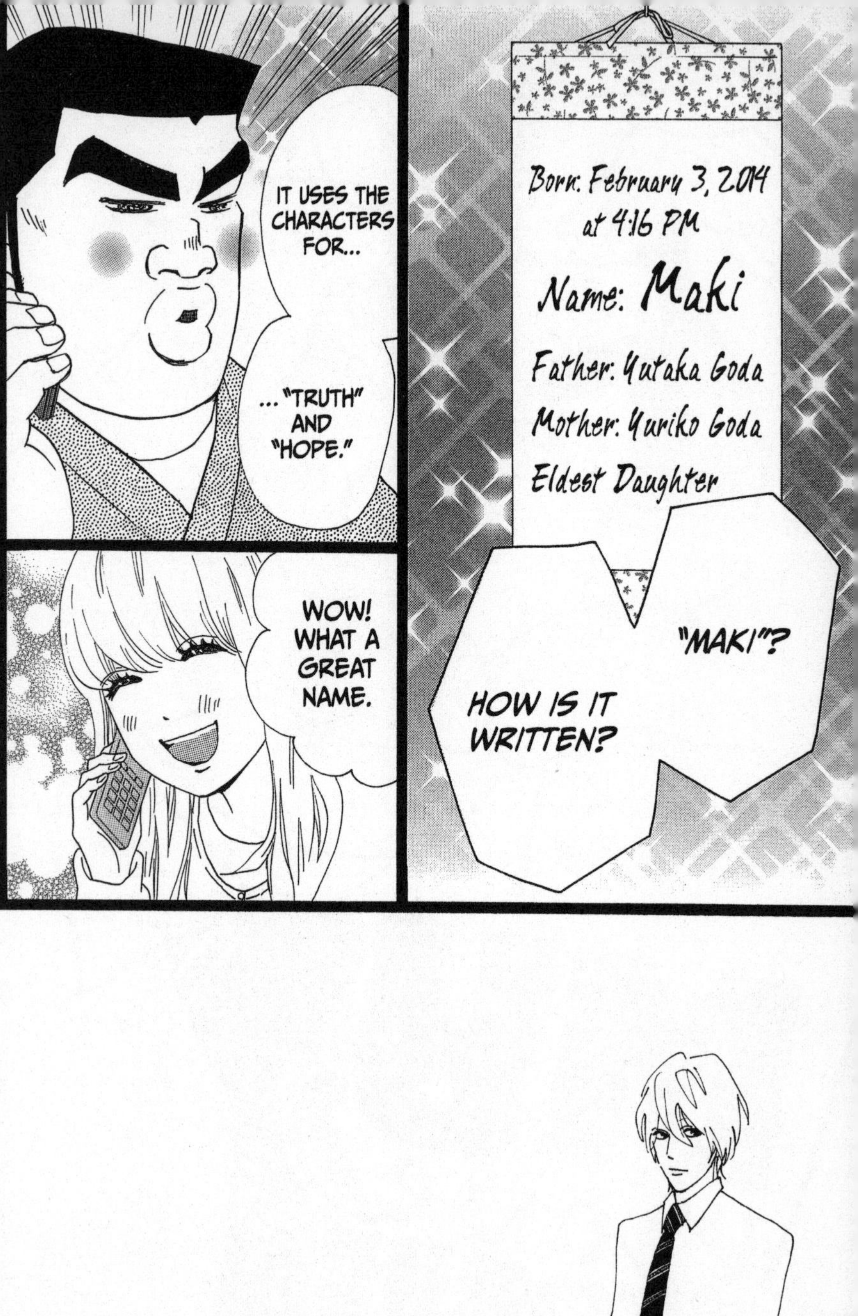
Born: February 3, 2014 at 4:16 PM
Name: Maki
Father: Yutaka Goda
Mother: Yuriko Goda
Eldest Daughter
"MAKI"?
HOW IS IT WRITTEN?
IT USES THE CHARACTERS FOR...
..."TRUTH" AND "HOPE."
WOW! WHAT A GREAT NAME.

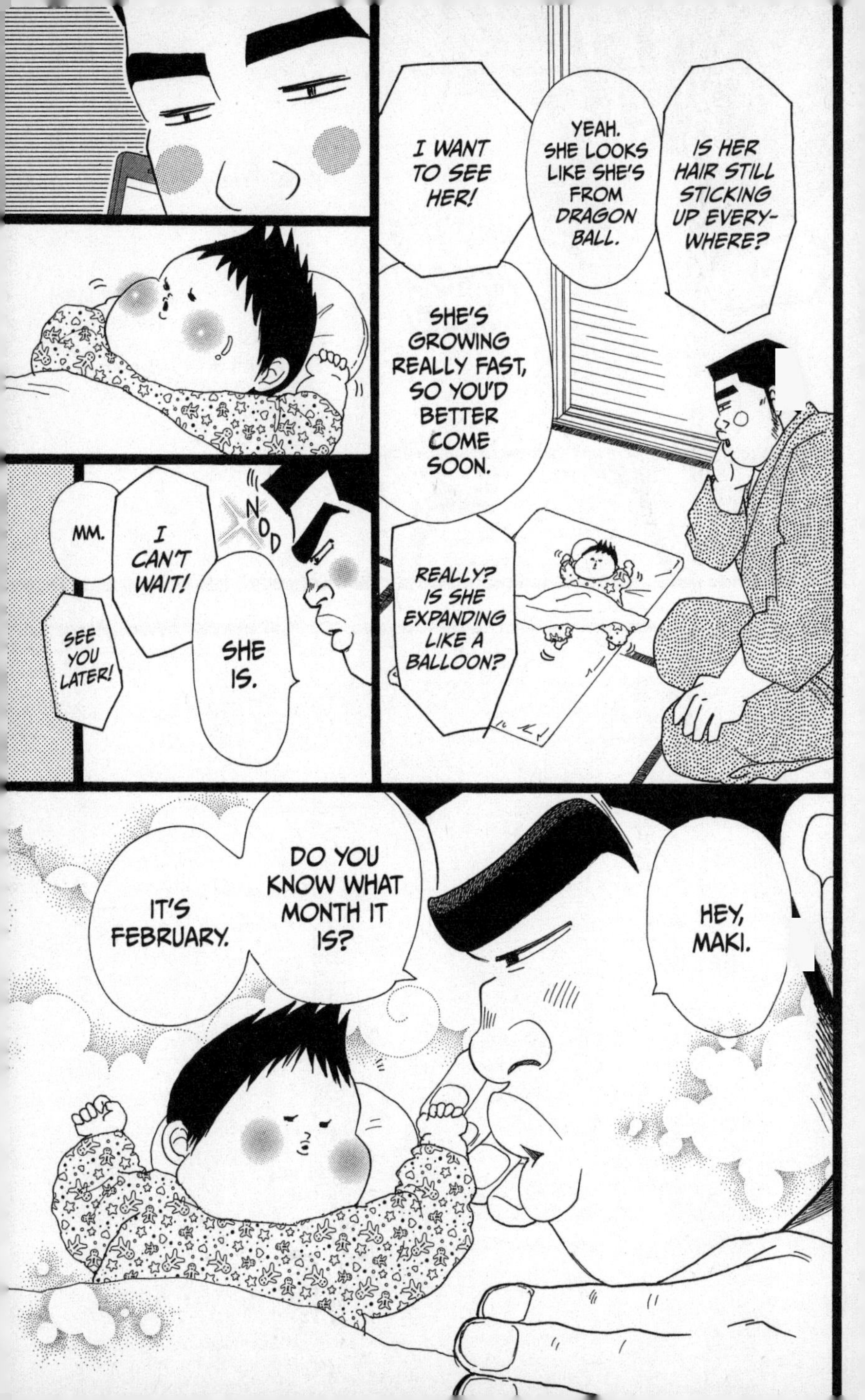
IS HER HAIR STILL STICKING UP EVERY-WHERE?
YEAH. SHE LOOKS LIKE SHE'S FROM DRAGON BALL.
I WANT TO SEE HER!
SHE'S GROWING REALLY FAST, SO YOU'D BETTER COME SOON.
REALLY? IS SHE EXPANDING LIKE A BALLOON?
NOD
SHE IS.
I CAN'T WAIT!
MM.
SEE YOU LATER!
HEY, MAKI.
DO YOU KNOW WHAT MONTH IT IS?
IT'S FEBRUARY.

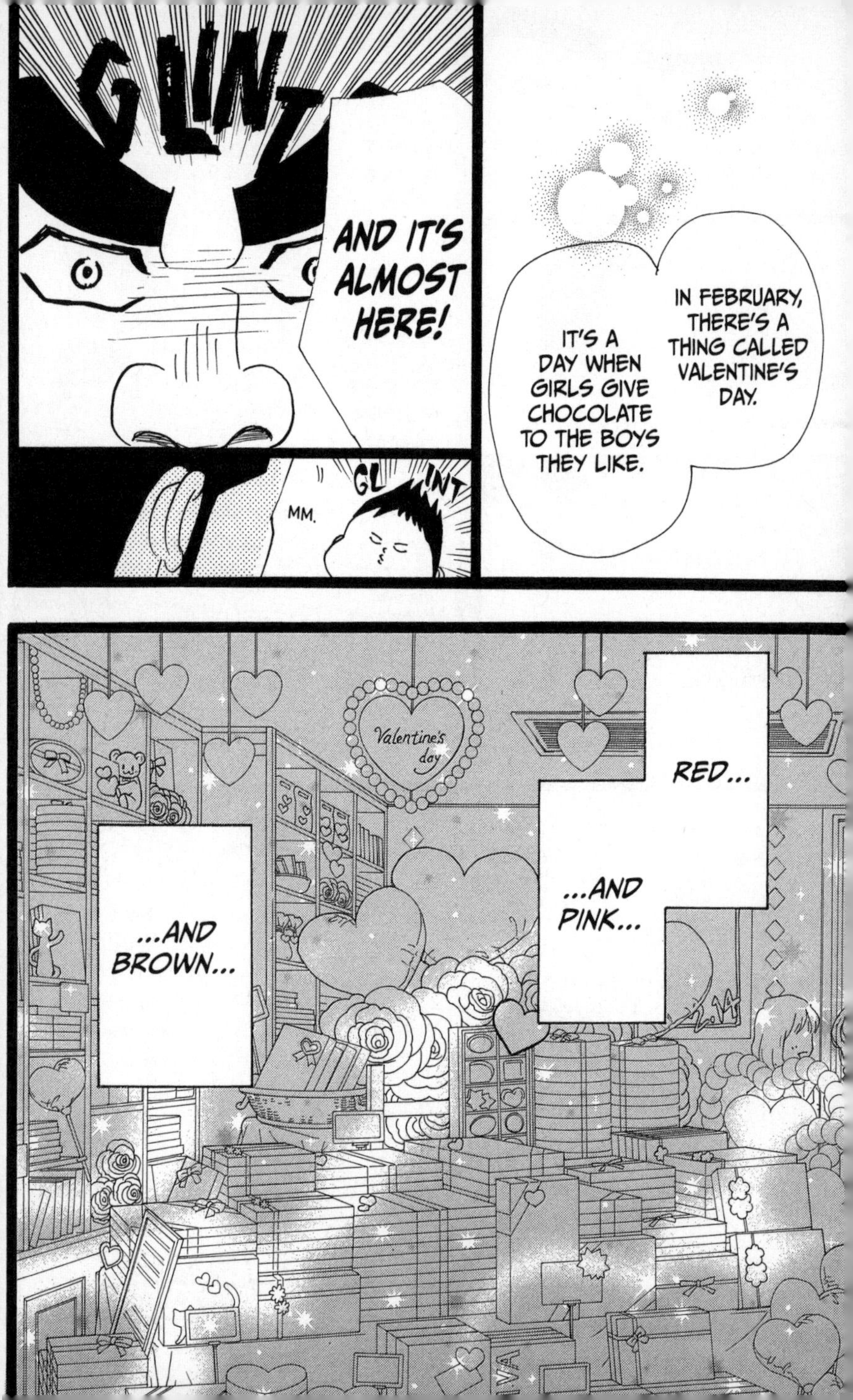
IN FEBRUARY, THERE'S A THING CALLED VALENTINE'S DAY.
IT'S A DAY WHEN GIRLS GIVE CHOCOLATE TO THE BOYS THEY LIKE.
GLINT
AND IT'S ALMOST HERE!
GLINT
MM.
Valentine's day
RED...
...AND PINK...
...AND BROWN...

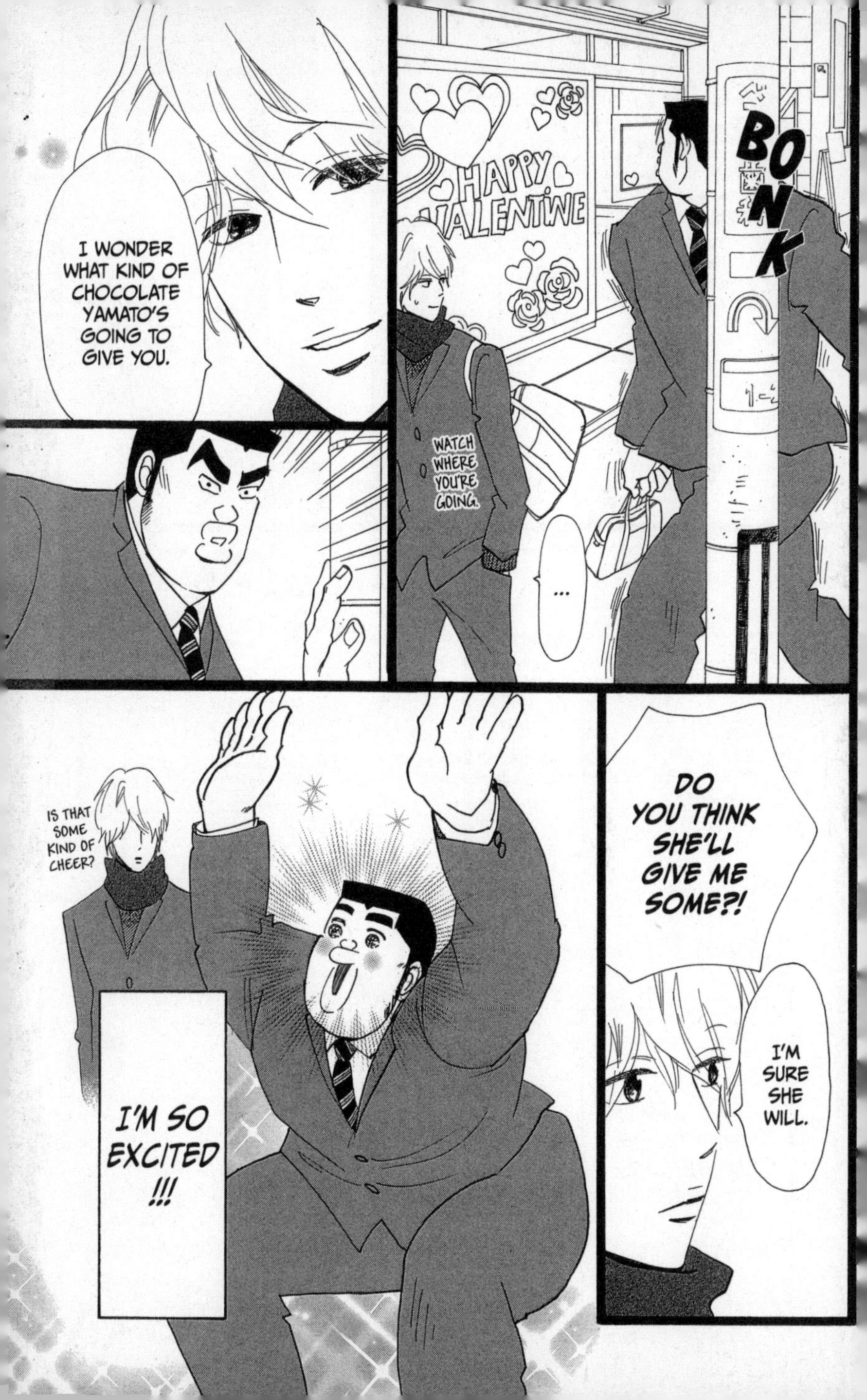
BONK
WATCH WHERE YOU'RE GOING.
...
I WONDER WHAT KIND OF CHOCOLATE YAMATO'S GOING TO GIVE YOU.
DO YOU THINK SHE'LL GIVE ME SOME?!
I'M SURE SHE WILL.
IS THAT SOME KIND OF CHEER?
I'M SO EXCITED !!!

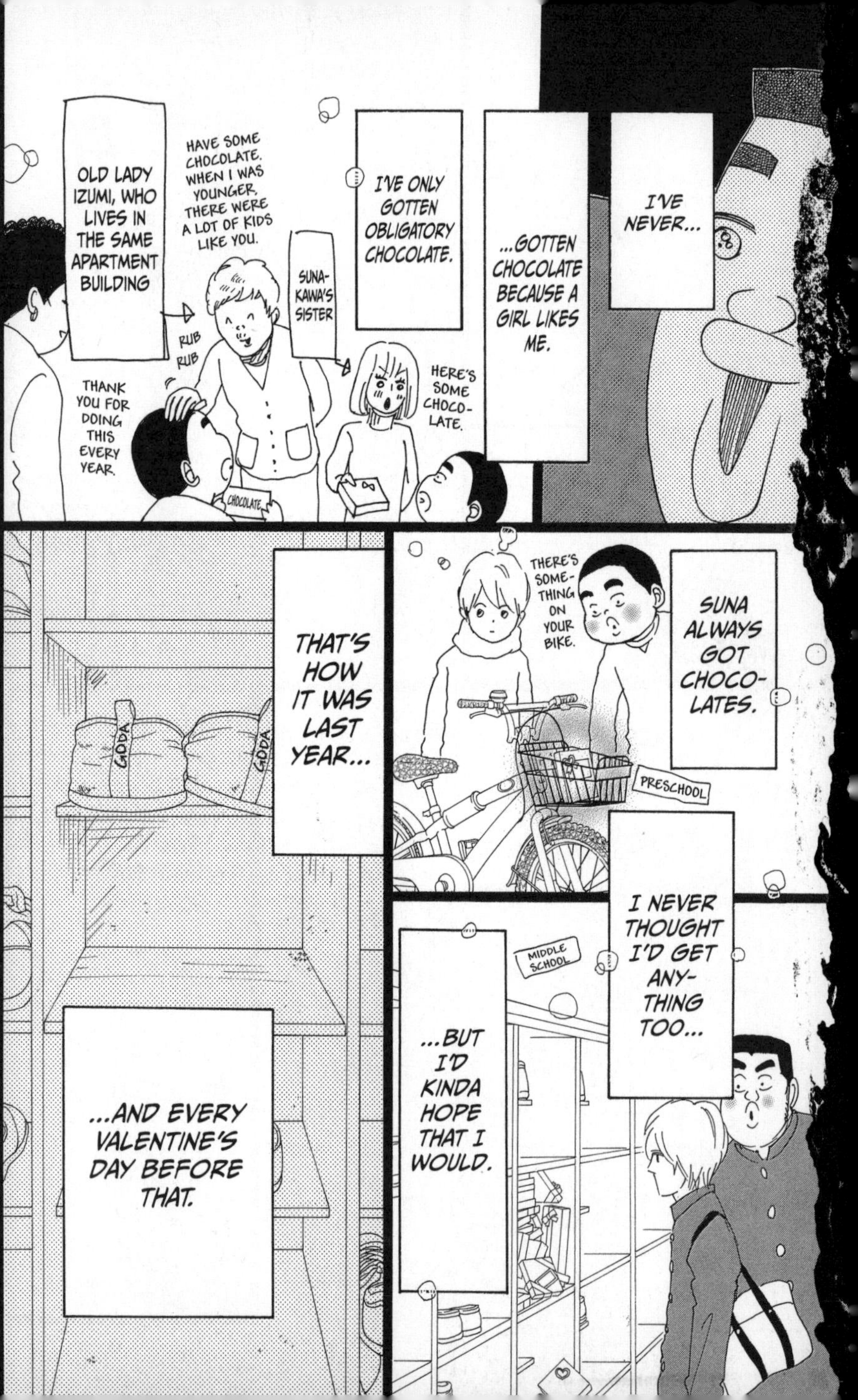
I'VE NEVER...
...GOTTEN CHOCOLATE BECAUSE A GIRL LIKES ME.
I'VE ONLY GOTTEN OBLIGATORY CHOCOLATE.
SUNA-KAWA'S SISTER
HERE'S SOME CHOCO-LATE.
HAVE SOME CHOCOLATE. WHEN I WAS YOUNGER, THERE WERE A LOT OF KIDS LIKE YOU.
OLD LADY IZUMI, WHO LIVES IN THE SAME APARTMENT BUILDING
RUB RUB
THANK YOU FOR DOING THIS EVERY YEAR.
CHOCOLATE
SUNA ALWAYS GOT CHOCO-LATES.
THERE'S SOME-THING ON YOUR BIKE.
PRESCHOOL
I NEVER THOUGHT I'D GET ANY-THING TOO...
...BUT I'D KINDA HOPE THAT I WOULD.
MIDDLE SCHOOL
THAT'S HOW IT WAS LAST YEAR...
GODA
GODA
...AND EVERY VALENTINE'S DAY BEFORE THAT.

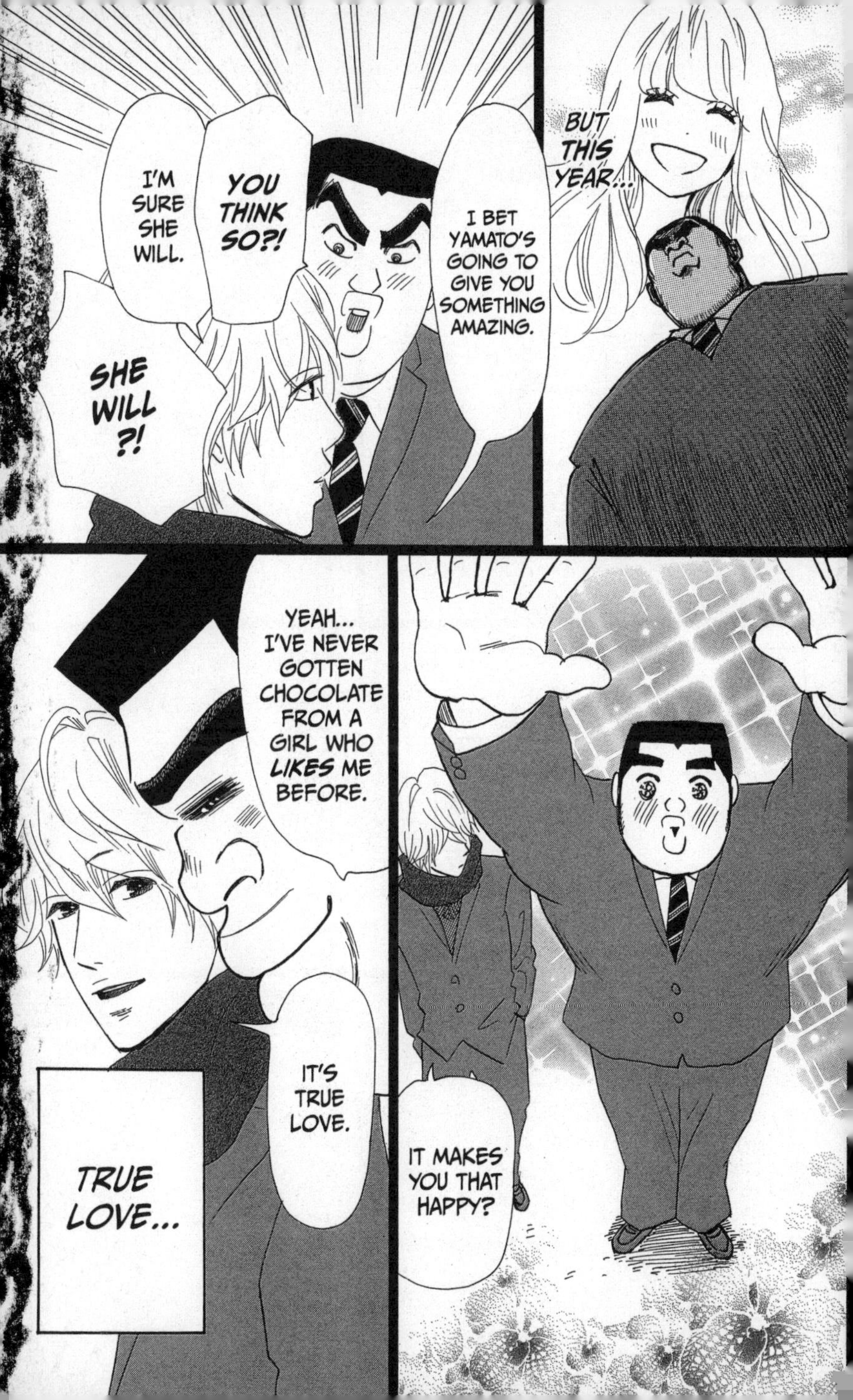
BUT THIS YEAR...
I BET YAMATO'S GOING TO GIVE YOU SOMETHING AMAZING.
YOU THINK SO?!
I'M SURE SHE WILL.
SHE WILL?!
IT MAKES YOU THAT HAPPY?
YEAH... I'VE NEVER GOTTEN CHOCOLATE FROM A GIRL WHO *LIKES* ME BEFORE.
IT'S TRUE LOVE.
TRUE LOVE...

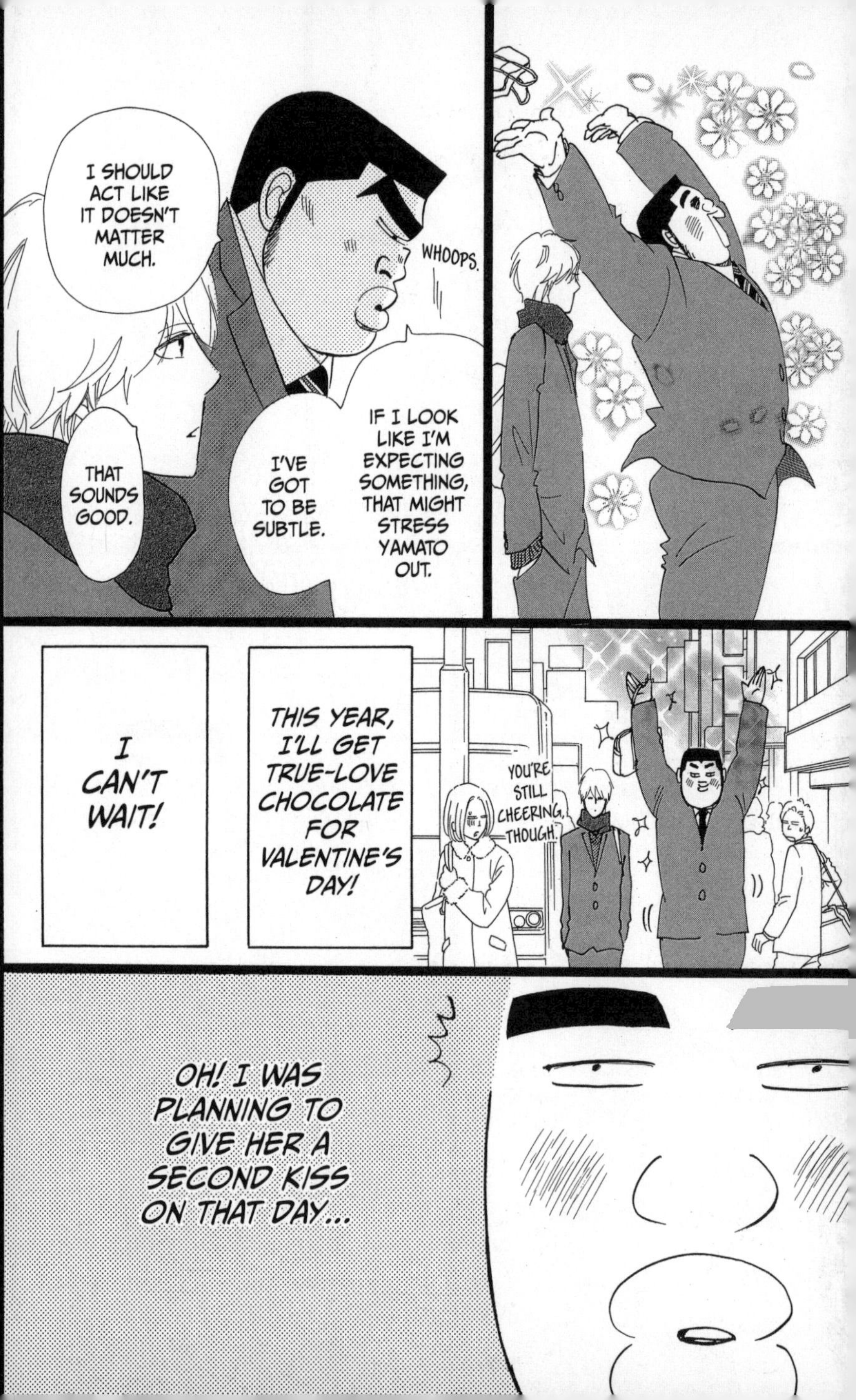
WHOOPS.
IF I LOOK LIKE I'M EXPECTING SOMETHING, THAT MIGHT STRESS YAMATO OUT.
I'VE GOT TO BE SUBTLE.
I SHOULD ACT LIKE IT DOESN'T MATTER MUCH.
THAT SOUNDS GOOD.
YOU'RE STILL CHEERING, THOUGH.
THIS YEAR, I'LL GET TRUE-LOVE CHOCOLATE FOR VALENTINE'S DAY!
I CAN'T WAIT!
OH! I WAS PLANNING TO GIVE HER A SECOND KISS ON THAT DAY...

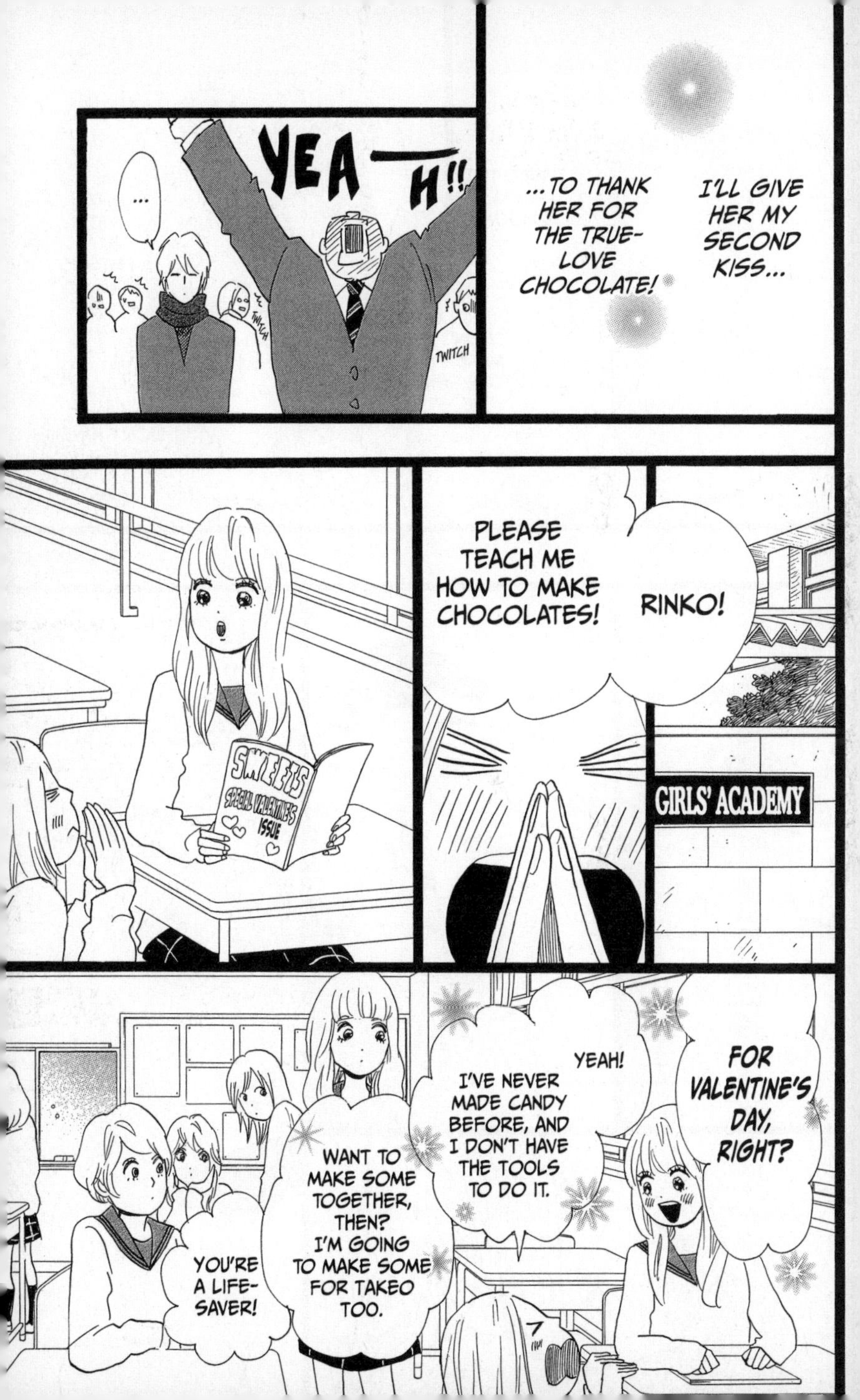
I'LL GIVE HER MY SECOND KISS...
...TO THANK HER FOR THE TRUE-LOVE CHOCOLATE!
YEA—H!!
...
TWITCH
TWITCH
GIRLS' ACADEMY
RINKO!
PLEASE TEACH ME HOW TO MAKE CHOCOLATES!
SWEETS SPECIAL VALENTINE'S ISSUE
FOR VALENTINE'S DAY, RIGHT?
YEAH!
I'VE NEVER MADE CANDY BEFORE, AND I DON'T HAVE THE TOOLS TO DO IT.
WANT TO MAKE SOME TOGETHER, THEN? I'M GOING TO MAKE SOME FOR TAKEO TOO.
YOU'RE A LIFE-SAVER!

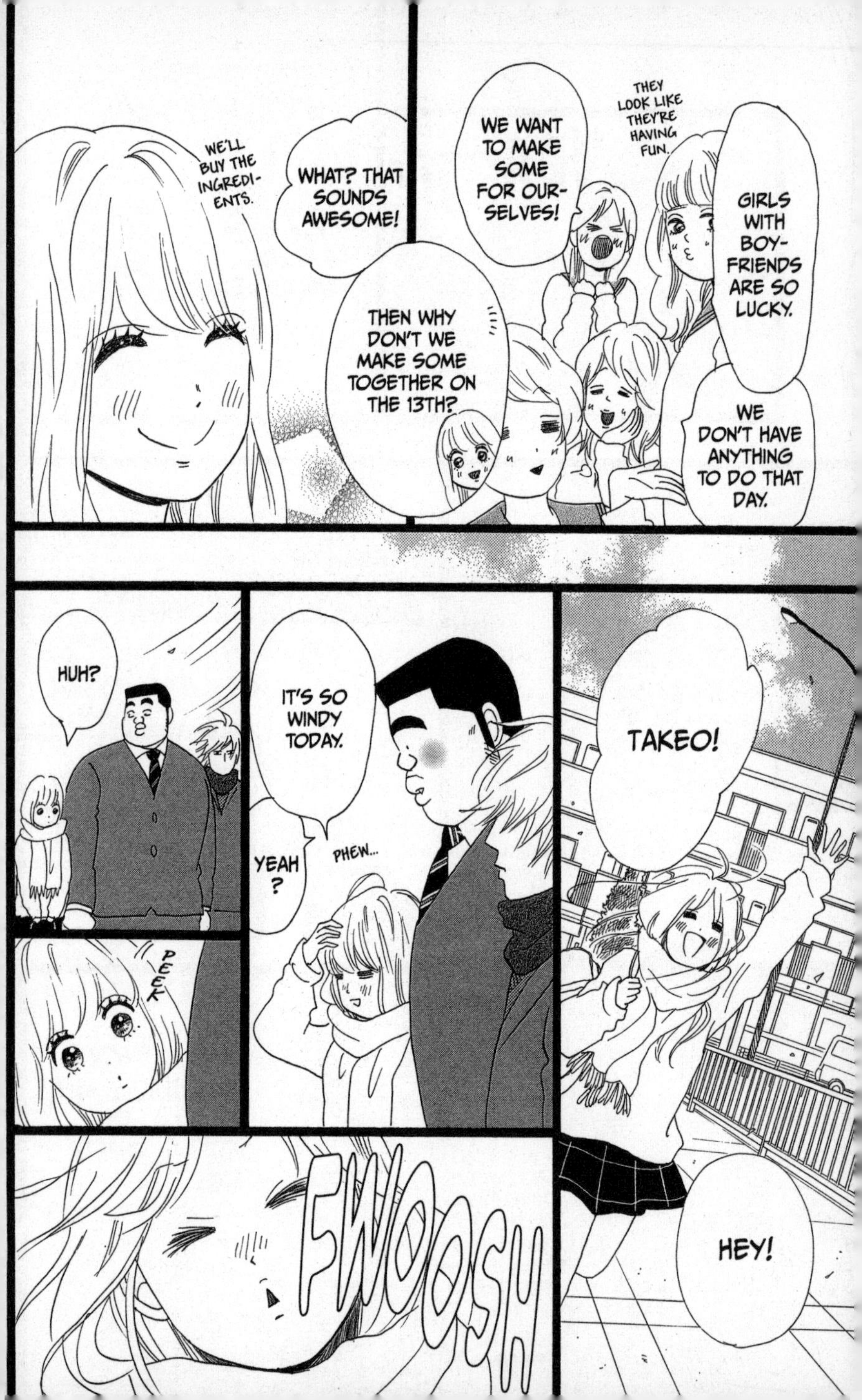
THEY LOOK LIKE THEY'RE HAVING FUN.
GIRLS WITH BOYFRIENDS ARE SO LUCKY.
WE WANT TO MAKE SOME FOR OURSELVES!
WE DON'T HAVE ANYTHING TO DO THAT DAY.
THEN WHY DON'T WE MAKE SOME TOGETHER ON THE 13TH?
WHAT? THAT SOUNDS AWESOME!
WE'LL BUY THE INGREDIENTS.
TAKEO!
HEY!
IT'S SO WINDY TODAY.
PHEW...
YEAH?
HUH?
PEEK
FWOOSH

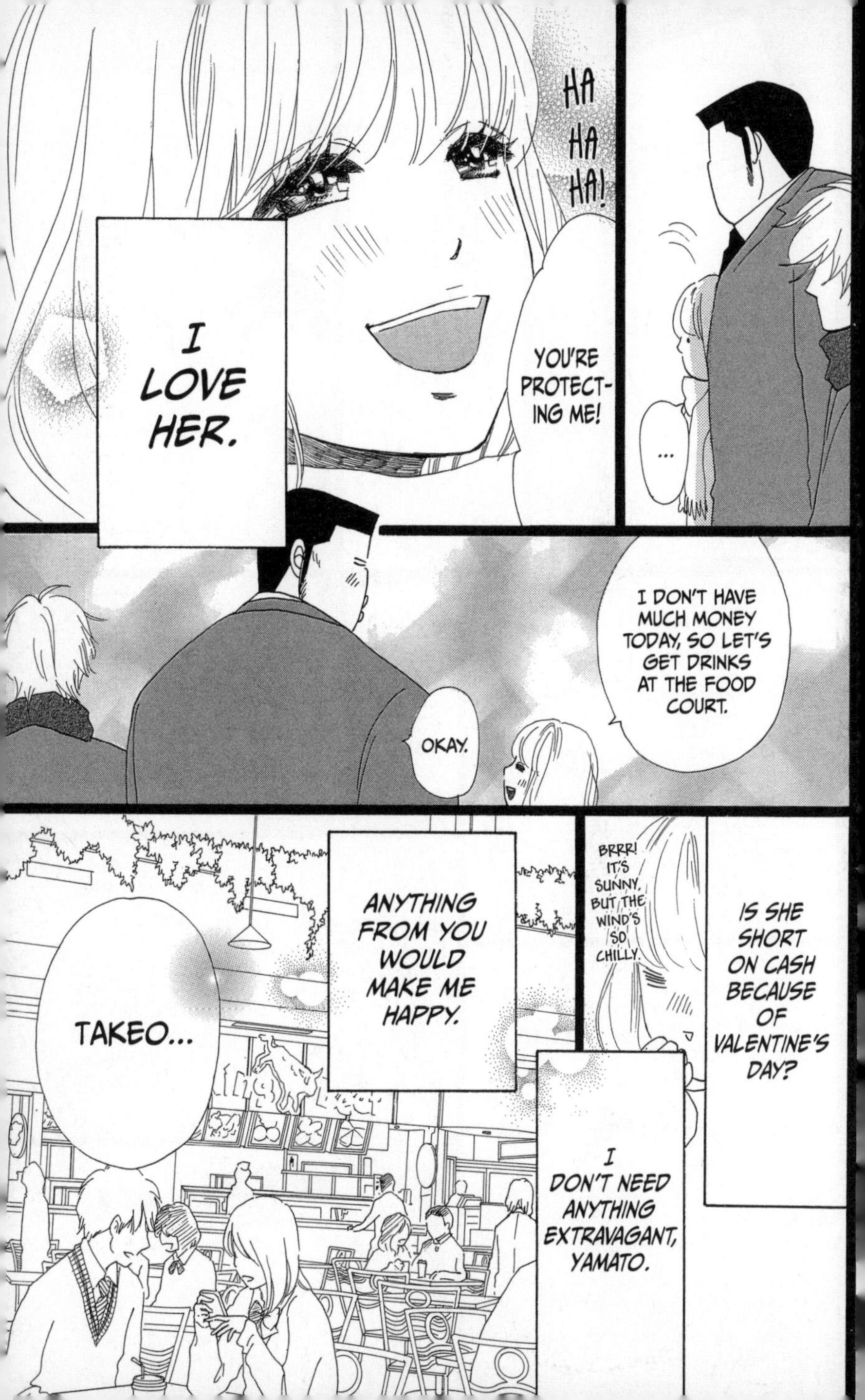
...
HA HA HA!
YOU'RE PROTECTING ME!
I LOVE HER.
I DON'T HAVE MUCH MONEY TODAY, SO LET'S GET DRINKS AT THE FOOD COURT.
OKAY.
IS SHE SHORT ON CASH BECAUSE OF VALENTINE'S DAY?
BRRR! IT'S SUNNY, BUT THE WIND'S SO CHILLY.
I DON'T NEED ANYTHING EXTRAVAGANT, YAMATO.
ANYTHING FROM YOU WOULD MAKE ME HAPPY.
TAKEO...

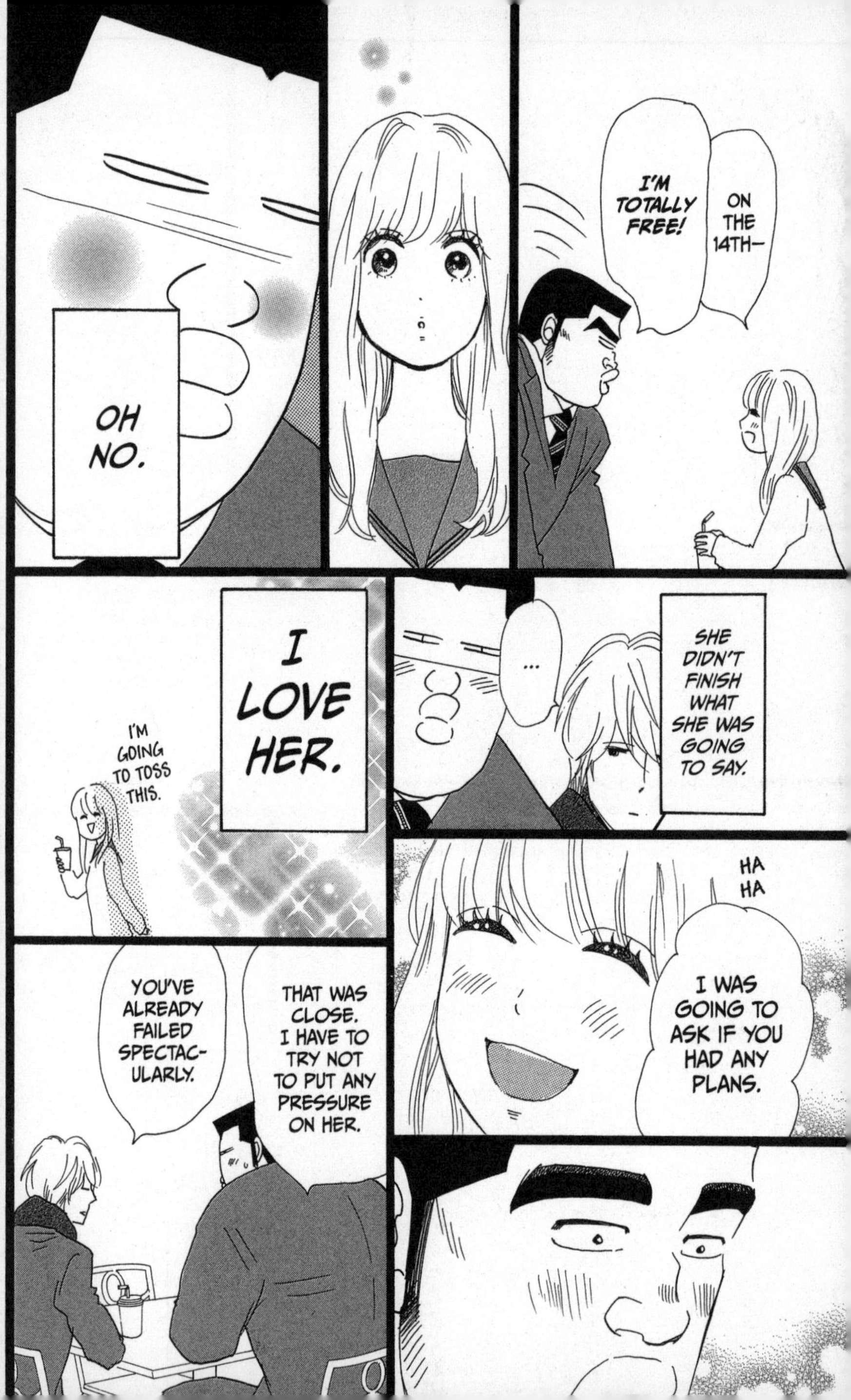
ON THE 14TH—
I'M TOTALLY FREE!
OH NO.
SHE DIDN'T FINISH WHAT SHE WAS GOING TO SAY.
...
HA HA
I WAS GOING TO ASK IF YOU HAD ANY PLANS.
I LOVE HER.
I'M GOING TO TOSS THIS.
THAT WAS CLOSE. I HAVE TO TRY NOT TO PUT ANY PRESSURE ON HER.
YOU'VE ALREADY FAILED SPECTAC-ULARLY.

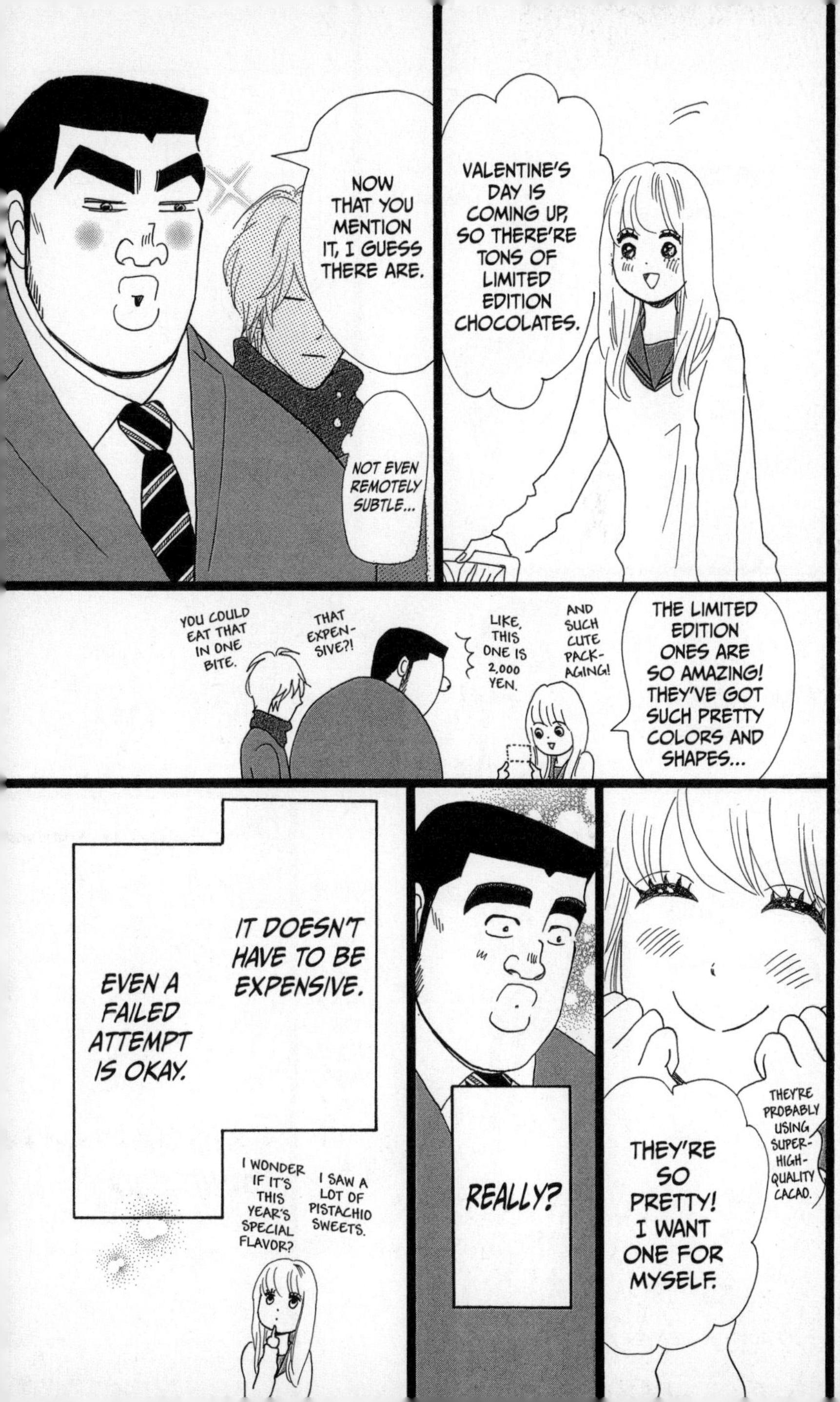
VALENTINE'S DAY IS COMING UP, SO THERE'RE TONS OF LIMITED EDITION CHOCOLATES.
NOW THAT YOU MENTION IT, I GUESS THERE ARE.
NOT EVEN REMOTELY SUBTLE...
THE LIMITED EDITION ONES ARE SO AMAZING! THEY'VE GOT SUCH PRETTY COLORS AND SHAPES...
AND SUCH CUTE PACK-AGING!
LIKE, THIS ONE IS 2,000 YEN.
THAT EXPEN-SIVE?!
YOU COULD EAT THAT IN ONE BITE.
THEY'RE PROBABLY USING SUPER-HIGH-QUALITY CACAO.
THEY'RE SO PRETTY! I WANT ONE FOR MYSELF.
REALLY?
IT DOESN'T HAVE TO BE EXPENSIVE.
EVEN A FAILED ATTEMPT IS OKAY.
I SAW A LOT OF PISTACHIO SWEETS.
I WONDER IF IT'S THIS YEAR'S SPECIAL FLAVOR?

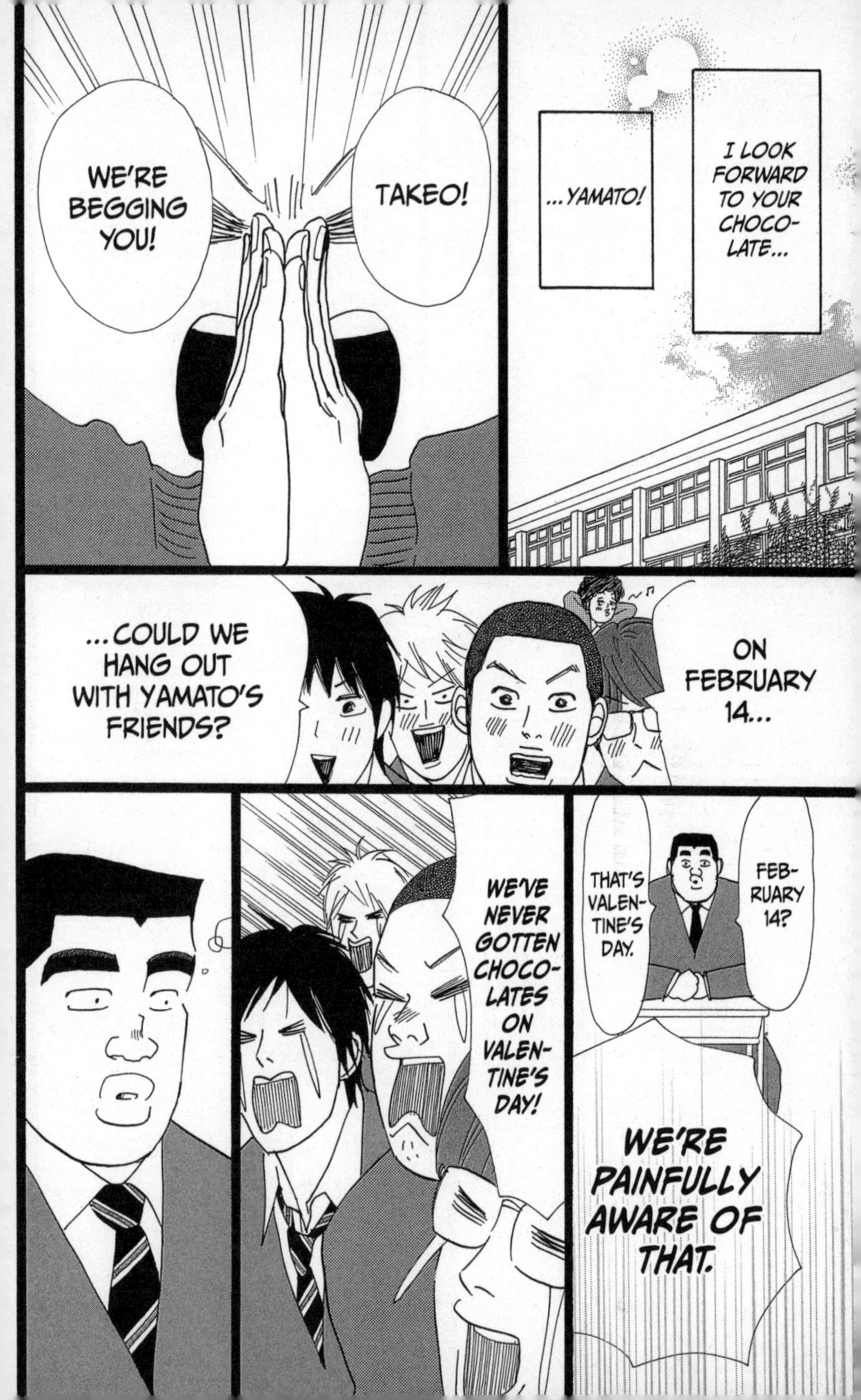

I LOOK FORWARD TO YOUR CHOCOLATE...
...YAMATO!
TAKEO!
WE'RE BEGGING YOU!
ON FEBRUARY 14...
...COULD WE HANG OUT WITH YAMATO'S FRIENDS?
FEBRUARY 14?
THAT'S VALENTINE'S DAY.
WE'RE PAINFULLY AWARE OF THAT.
WE'VE NEVER GOTTEN CHOCOLATES ON VALENTINE'S DAY!

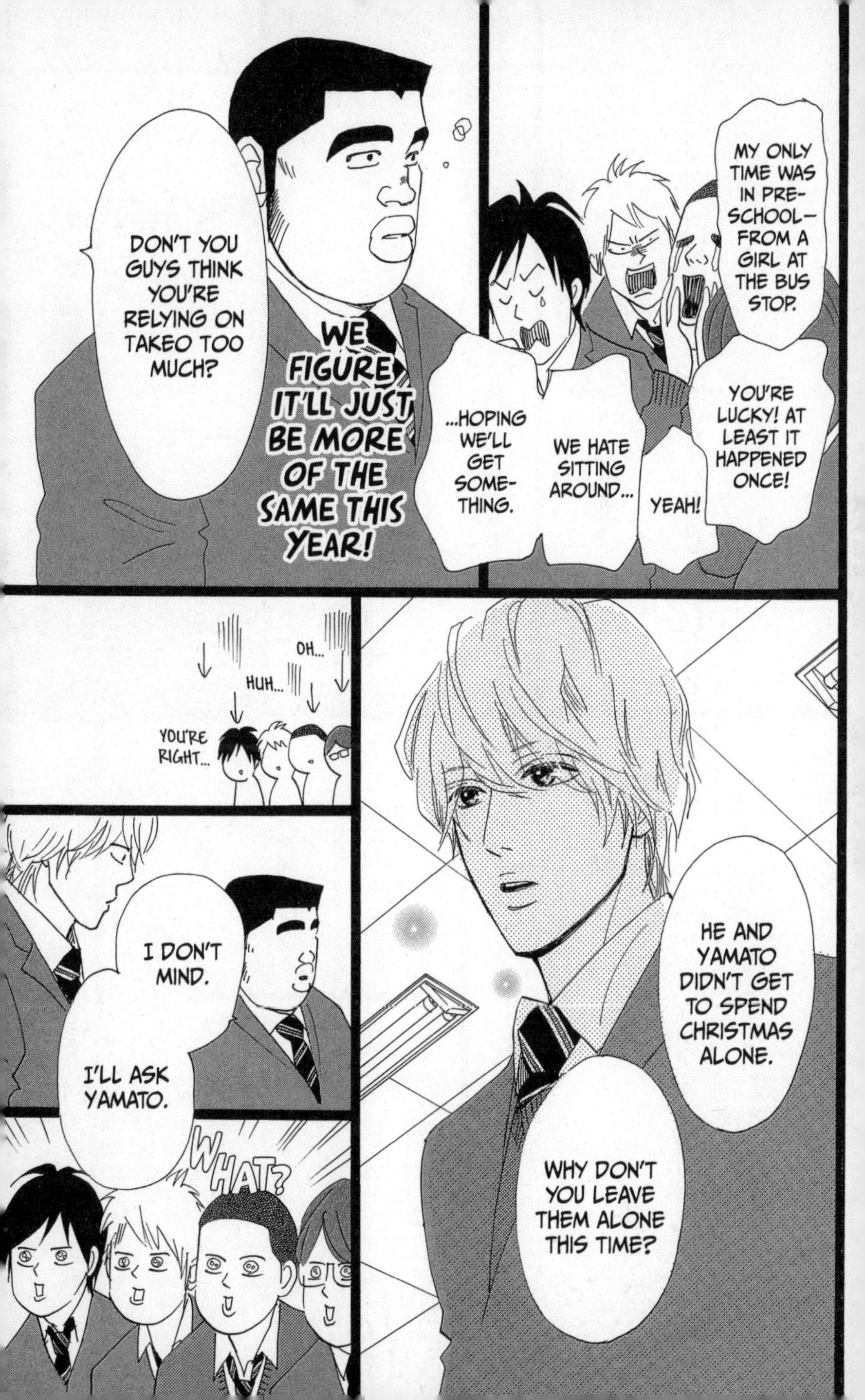

MY ONLY TIME WAS IN PRE-SCHOOL—FROM A GIRL AT THE BUS STOP.
YOU'RE LUCKY! AT LEAST IT HAPPENED ONCE!
YEAH!
WE HATE SITTING AROUND...
...HOPING WE'LL GET SOME-THING.
WE FIGURE IT'LL JUST BE MORE OF THE SAME THIS YEAR!
DON'T YOU GUYS THINK YOU'RE RELYING ON TAKEO TOO MUCH?
HE AND YAMATO DIDN'T GET TO SPEND CHRISTMAS ALONE.
WHY DON'T YOU LEAVE THEM ALONE THIS TIME?
OH...
HUH...
YOU'RE RIGHT...
I DON'T MIND.
I'LL ASK YAMATO.
WHAT?

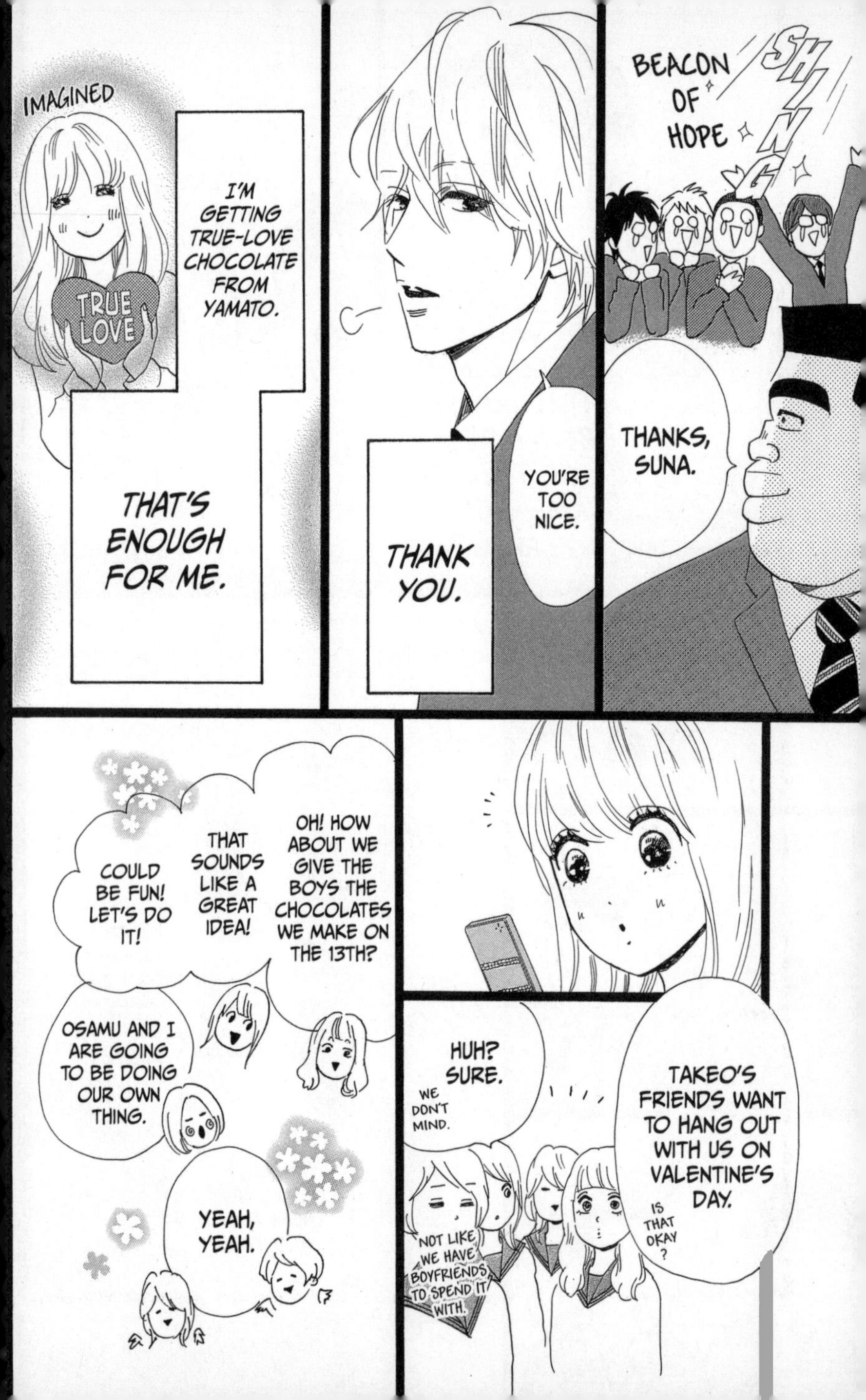
BEACON OF HOPE
SHING
THANKS, SUNA.
YOU'RE TOO NICE.
THANK YOU.
IMAGINED
I'M GETTING TRUE-LOVE CHOCOLATE FROM YAMATO.
TRUE LOVE
THAT'S ENOUGH FOR ME.
TAKEO'S FRIENDS WANT TO HANG OUT WITH US ON VALENTINE'S DAY.
IS THAT OKAY?
HUH? SURE.
WE DON'T MIND.
NOT LIKE WE HAVE BOYFRIENDS TO SPEND IT WITH.
OH! HOW ABOUT WE GIVE THE BOYS THE CHOCOLATES WE MAKE ON THE 13TH?
THAT SOUNDS LIKE A GREAT IDEA!
COULD BE FUN! LET'S DO IT!
OSAMU AND I ARE GOING TO BE DOING OUR OWN THING.
YEAH, YEAH.

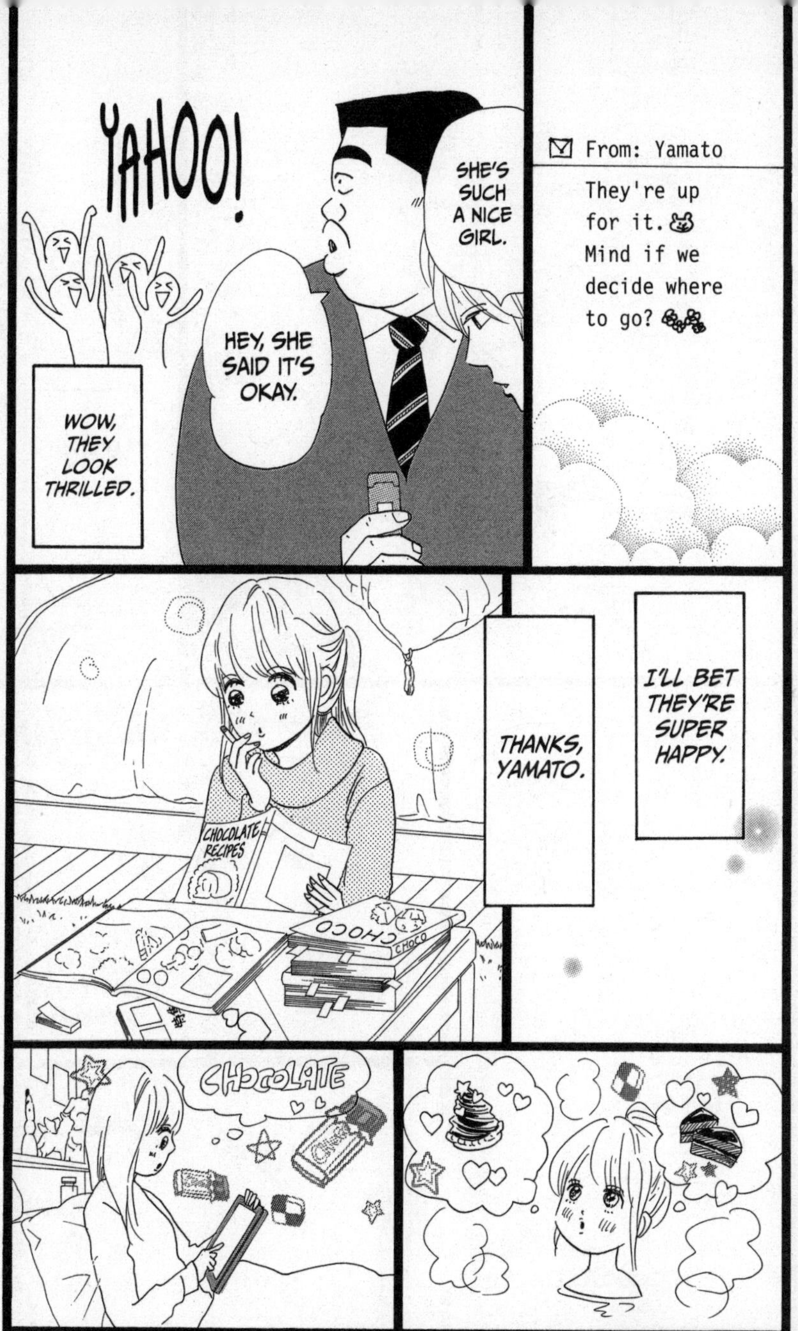
From: Yamato
They're up for it. Mind if we decide where to go?
SHE'S SUCH A NICE GIRL.
YAHOO!
HEY, SHE SAID IT'S OKAY.
WOW, THEY LOOK THRILLED.
I'LL BET THEY'RE SUPER HAPPY.
THANKS, YAMATO.
CHOCOLATE RECIPES
CHOCO
CHOCO
CHOCOLATE

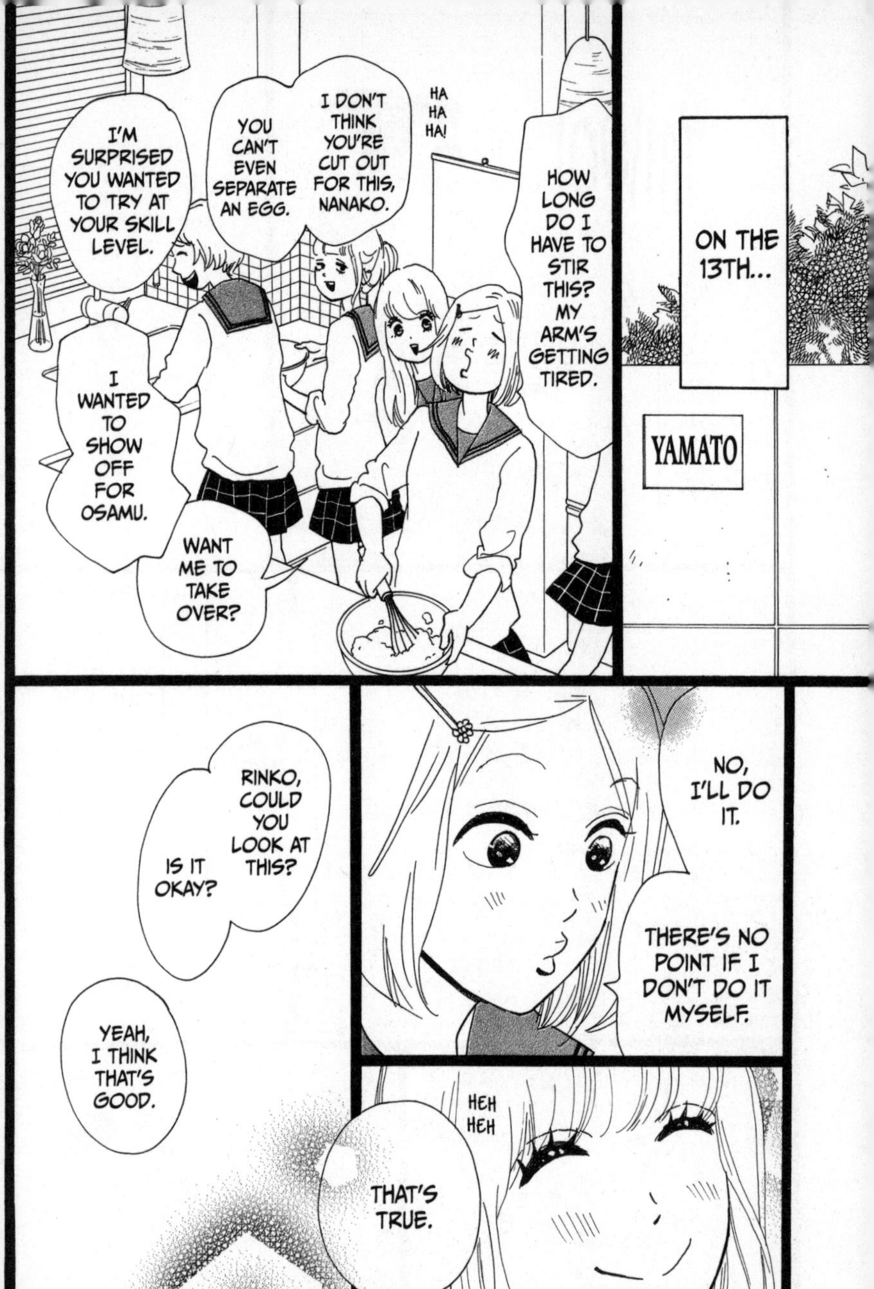
ON THE 13TH...
YAMATO
HOW LONG DO I HAVE TO STIR THIS? MY ARM'S GETTING TIRED.
HA HA HA!
I DON'T THINK YOU'RE CUT OUT FOR THIS, NANAKO.
YOU CAN'T EVEN SEPARATE AN EGG.
I'M SURPRISED YOU WANTED TO TRY AT YOUR SKILL LEVEL.
I WANTED TO SHOW OFF FOR OSAMU.
WANT ME TO TAKE OVER?
NO, I'LL DO IT.
THERE'S NO POINT IF I DON'T DO IT MYSELF.
HEH HEH
THAT'S TRUE.
RINKO, COULD YOU LOOK AT THIS?
IS IT OKAY?
YEAH, I THINK THAT'S GOOD.

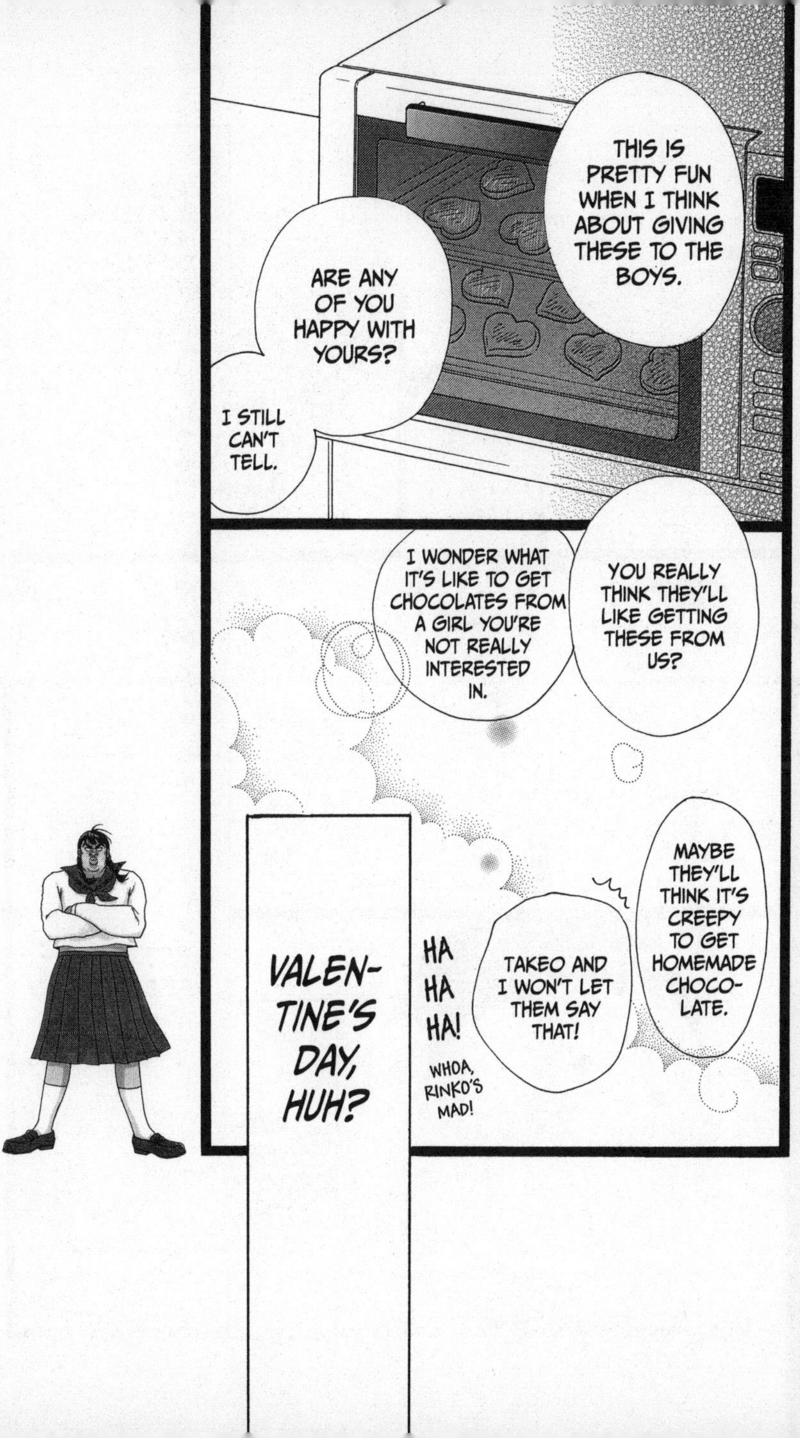
THIS IS PRETTY FUN WHEN I THINK ABOUT GIVING THESE TO THE BOYS.
ARE ANY OF YOU HAPPY WITH YOURS?
I STILL CAN'T TELL.
YOU REALLY THINK THEY'LL LIKE GETTING THESE FROM US?
I WONDER WHAT IT'S LIKE TO GET CHOCOLATES FROM A GIRL YOU'RE NOT REALLY INTERESTED IN.
MAYBE THEY'LL THINK IT'S CREEPY TO GET HOMEMADE CHOCO-LATE.
TAKEO AND I WON'T LET THEM SAY THAT!
HA HA HA!
WHOA, RINKO'S MAD!
VALEN-TINE'S DAY, HUH?

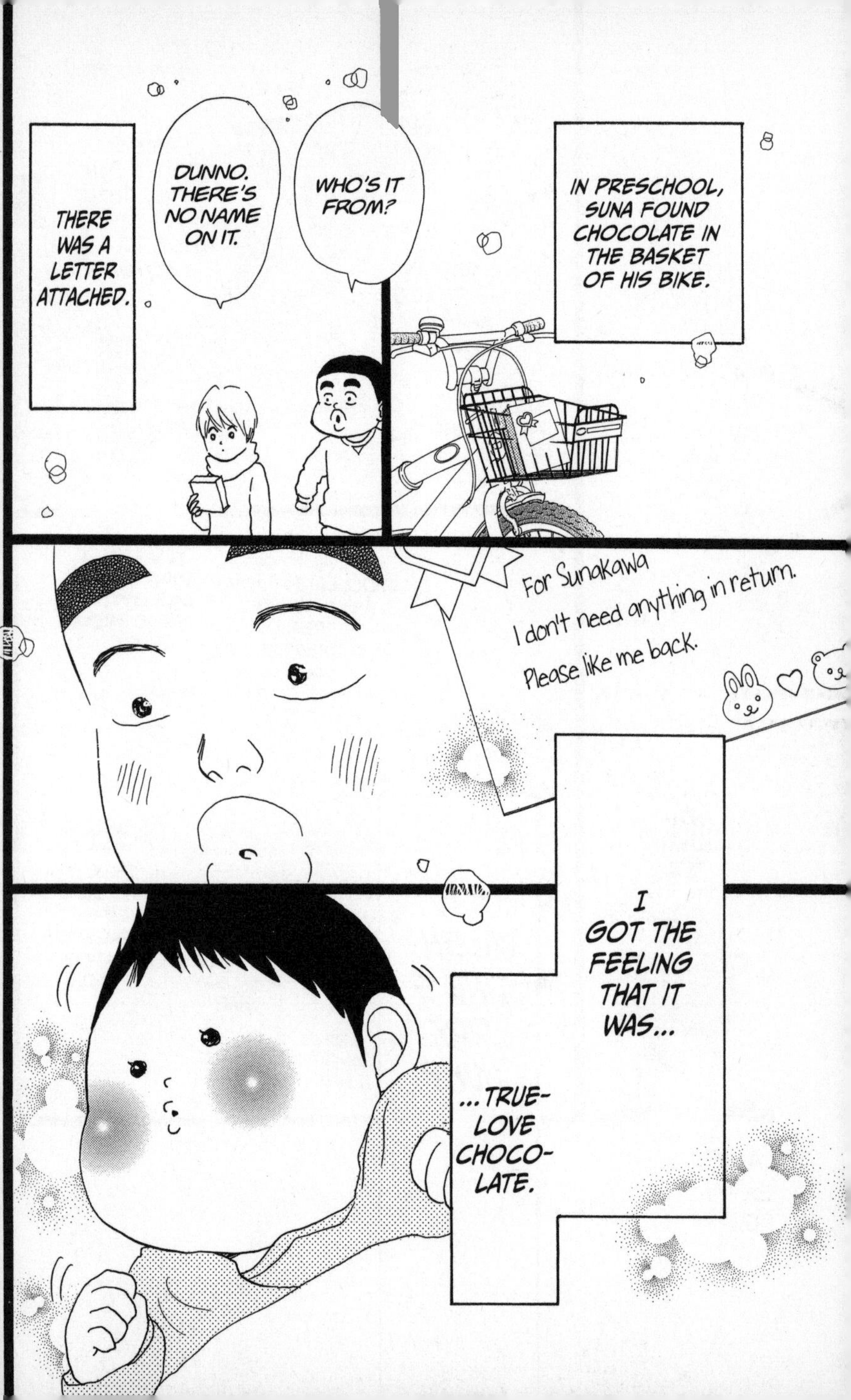

IN PRESCHOOL, SUNA FOUND CHOCOLATE IN THE BASKET OF HIS BIKE.
WHO'S IT FROM?
DUNNO. THERE'S NO NAME ON IT.
THERE WAS A LETTER ATTACHED.
For Sunakawa
I don't need anything in return.
Please like me back.
I GOT THE FEELING THAT IT WAS...
...TRUE-LOVE CHOCO-LATE.

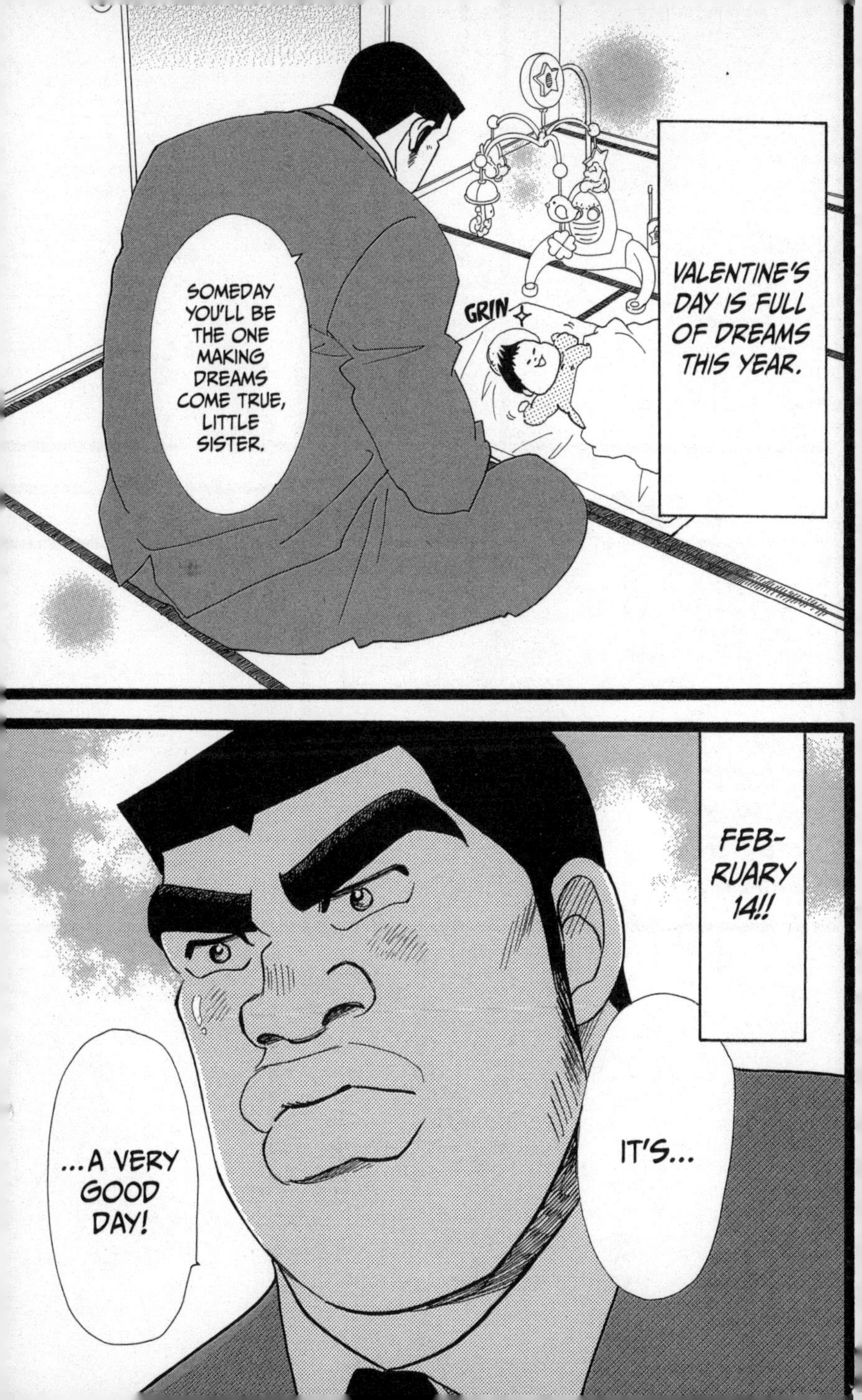
VALENTINE'S DAY IS FULL OF DREAMS THIS YEAR.
GRIN
SOMEDAY YOU'LL BE THE ONE MAKING DREAMS COME TRUE, LITTLE SISTER.
FEB-RUARY 14!!
IT'S...
...A VERY GOOD DAY!

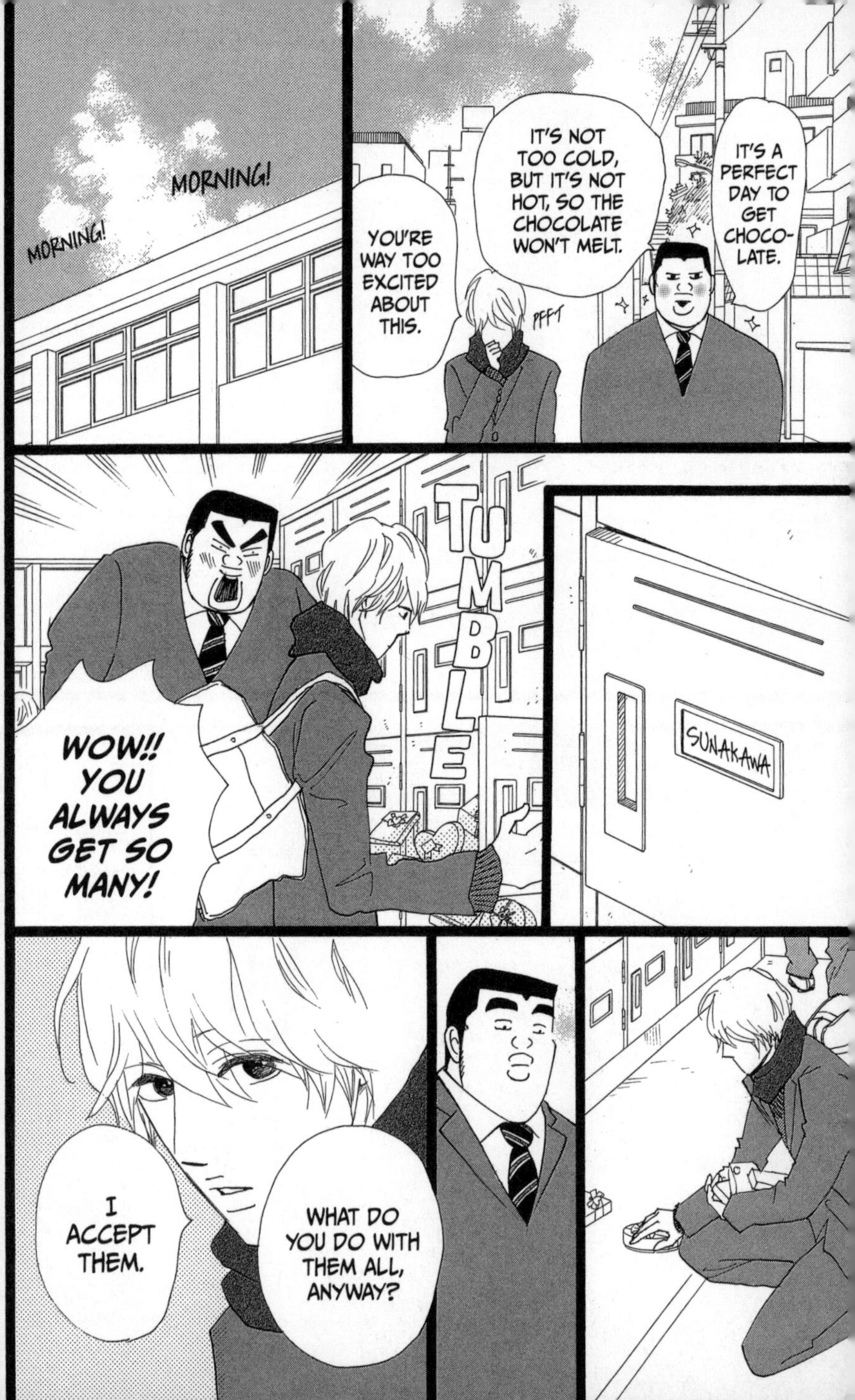
IT'S A PERFECT DAY TO GET CHOCO-LATE.
IT'S NOT TOO COLD, BUT IT'S NOT HOT, SO THE CHOCOLATE WON'T MELT.
PFFT
YOU'RE WAY TOO EXCITED ABOUT THIS.
MORNING!
MORNING!
SUNAKAWA
TUMBLE
WOW!! YOU ALWAYS GET SO MANY!
WHAT DO YOU DO WITH THEM ALL, ANYWAY?
I ACCEPT THEM.

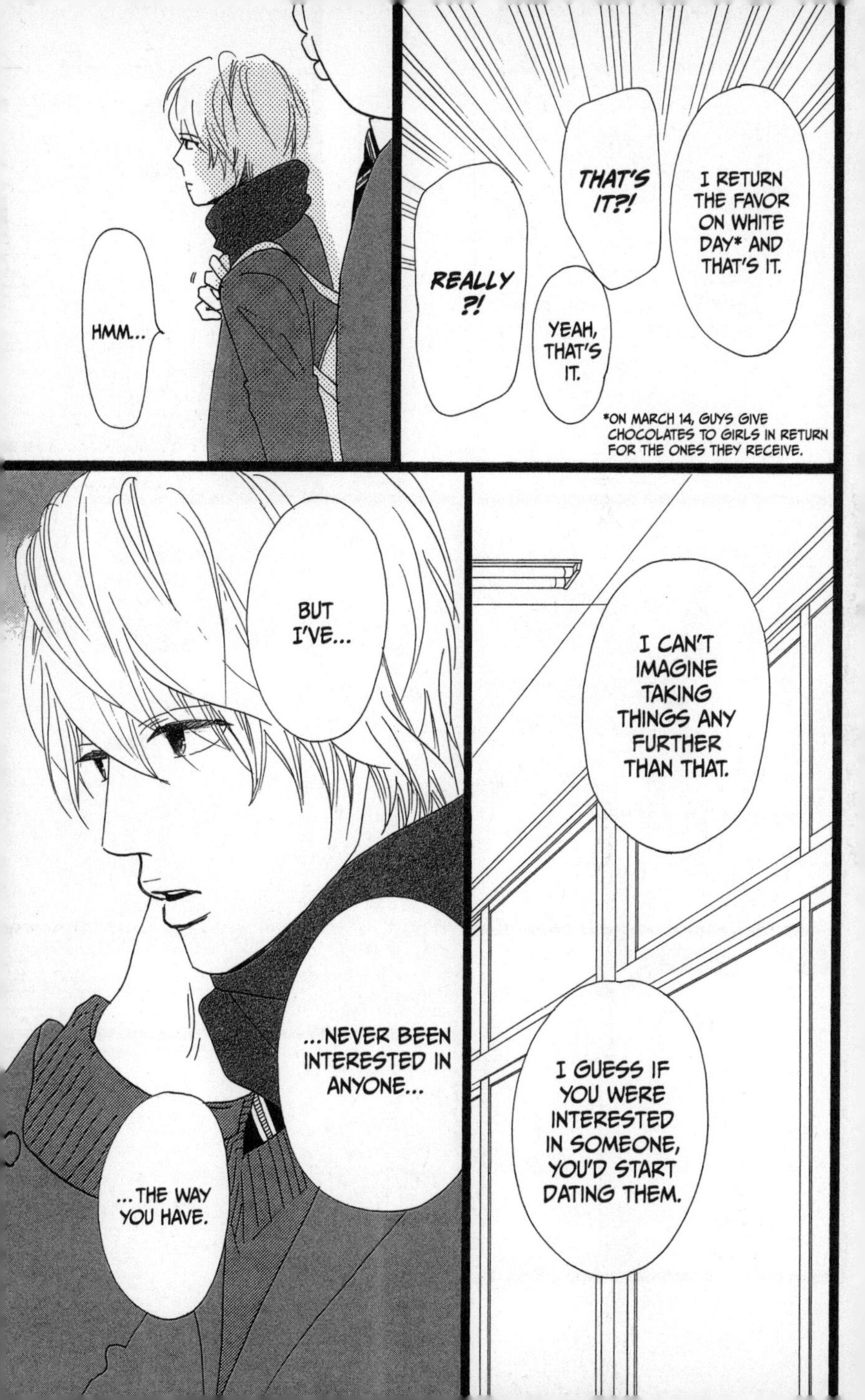

I RETURN THE FAVOR ON WHITE DAY* AND THAT'S IT.
THAT'S IT?!
YEAH, THAT'S IT.
REALLY ?!
*ON MARCH 14, GUYS GIVE CHOCOLATES TO GIRLS IN RETURN FOR THE ONES THEY RECEIVE.
HMM...
I CAN'T IMAGINE TAKING THINGS ANY FURTHER THAN THAT.
I GUESS IF YOU WERE INTERESTED IN SOMEONE, YOU'D START DATING THEM.
BUT I'VE...
...NEVER BEEN INTERESTED IN ANYONE...
...THE WAY YOU HAVE.

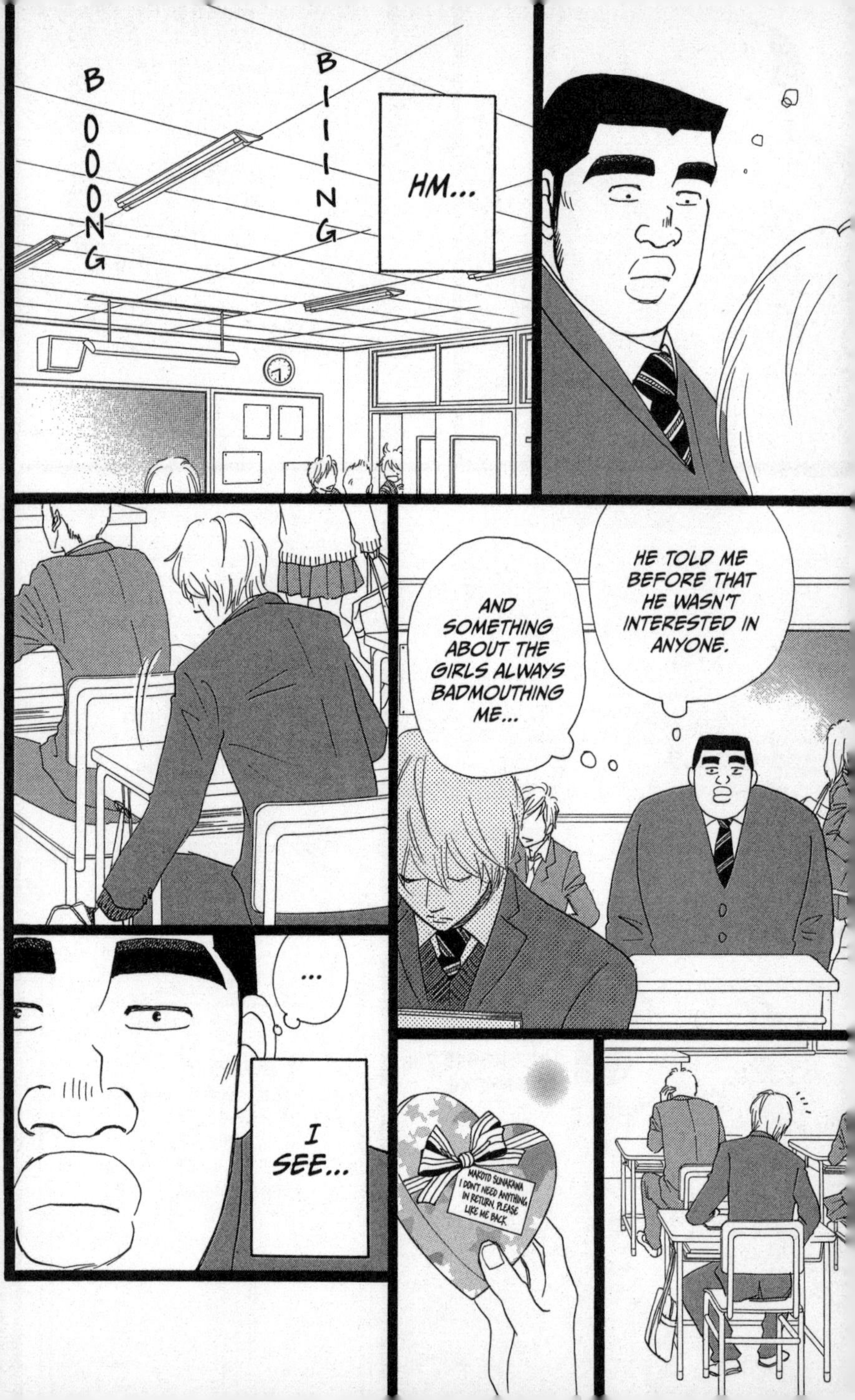
HM...
BIIING
BOOOONG
HE TOLD ME BEFORE THAT HE WASN'T INTERESTED IN ANYONE.
AND SOMETHING ABOUT THE GIRLS ALWAYS BADMOUTHING ME...
MAKOTO SUNAKAWA I DON'T NEED ANYTHING IN RETURN. PLEASE LIKE ME BACK.
...
I SEE...

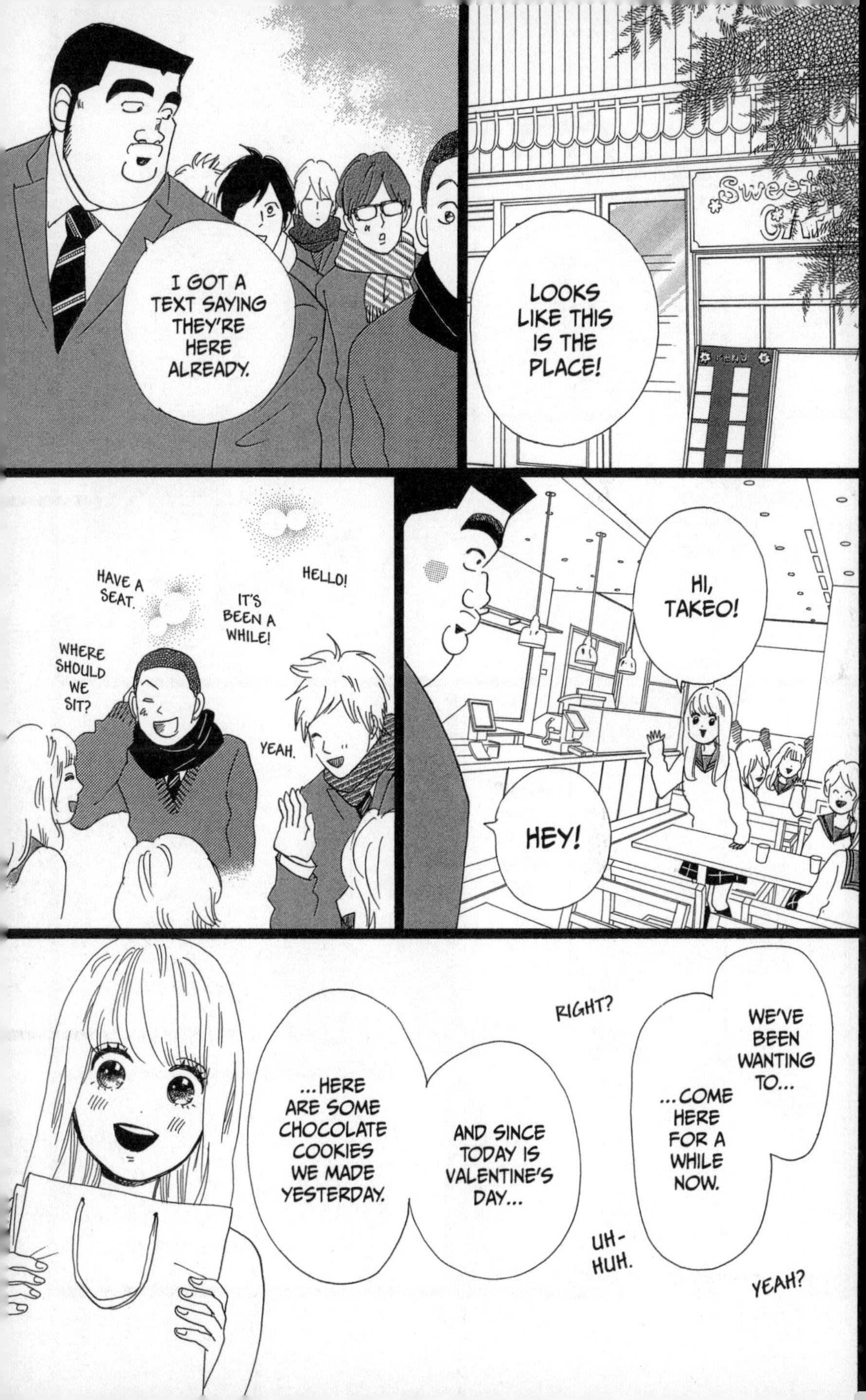
LOOKS LIKE THIS IS THE PLACE!
I GOT A TEXT SAYING THEY'RE HERE ALREADY.
HI, TAKEO!
HEY!
HELLO!
IT'S BEEN A WHILE!
HAVE A SEAT.
YEAH.
WHERE SHOULD WE SIT?
WE'VE BEEN WANTING TO...
RIGHT?
...COME HERE FOR A WHILE NOW.
YEAH?
UH-HUH.
AND SINCE TODAY IS VALENTINE'S DAY...
...HERE ARE SOME CHOCOLATE COOKIES WE MADE YESTERDAY.

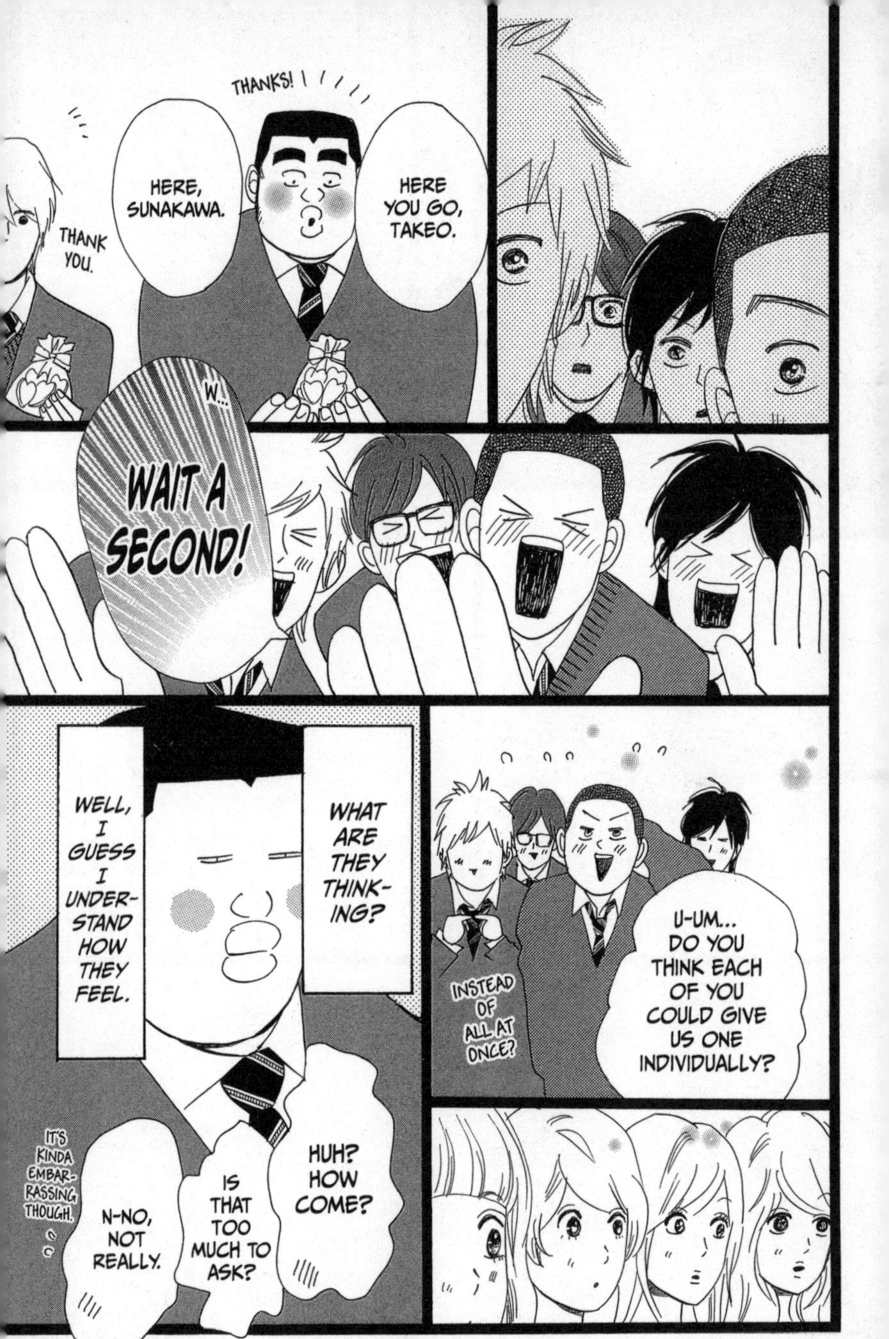
THANKS!
HERE YOU GO, TAKEO.
HERE, SUNAKAWA.
THANK YOU.
W...
WAIT A SECOND!
U-UM... DO YOU THINK EACH OF YOU COULD GIVE US ONE INDIVIDUALLY?
INSTEAD OF ALL AT ONCE?
WHAT ARE THEY THINKING?
WELL, I GUESS I UNDERSTAND HOW THEY FEEL.
HUH? HOW COME?
IS THAT TOO MUCH TO ASK?
N-NO, NOT REALLY.
IT'S KINDA EMBARRASSING THOUGH.

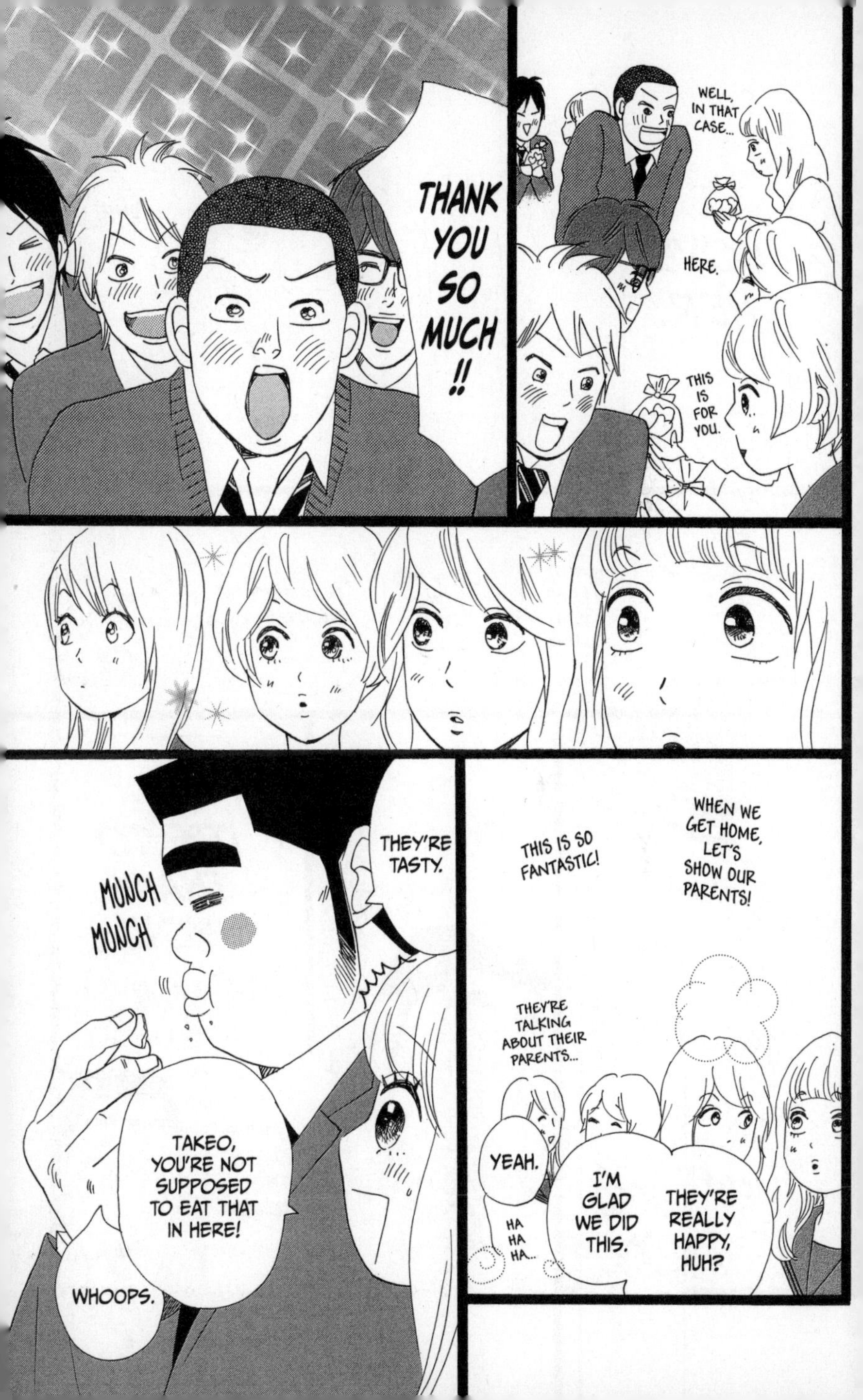
WELL, IN THAT CASE...
HERE.
THIS IS FOR YOU.
THANK YOU SO MUCH!!
WHEN WE GET HOME, LET'S SHOW OUR PARENTS!
THIS IS SO FANTASTIC!
THEY'RE TALKING ABOUT THEIR PARENTS...
THEY'RE REALLY HAPPY, HUH?
I'M GLAD WE DID THIS.
YEAH.
HA HA HA...
THEY'RE TASTY.
MUNCH MUNCH
TAKEO, YOU'RE NOT SUPPOSED TO EAT THAT IN HERE!
WHOOPS.

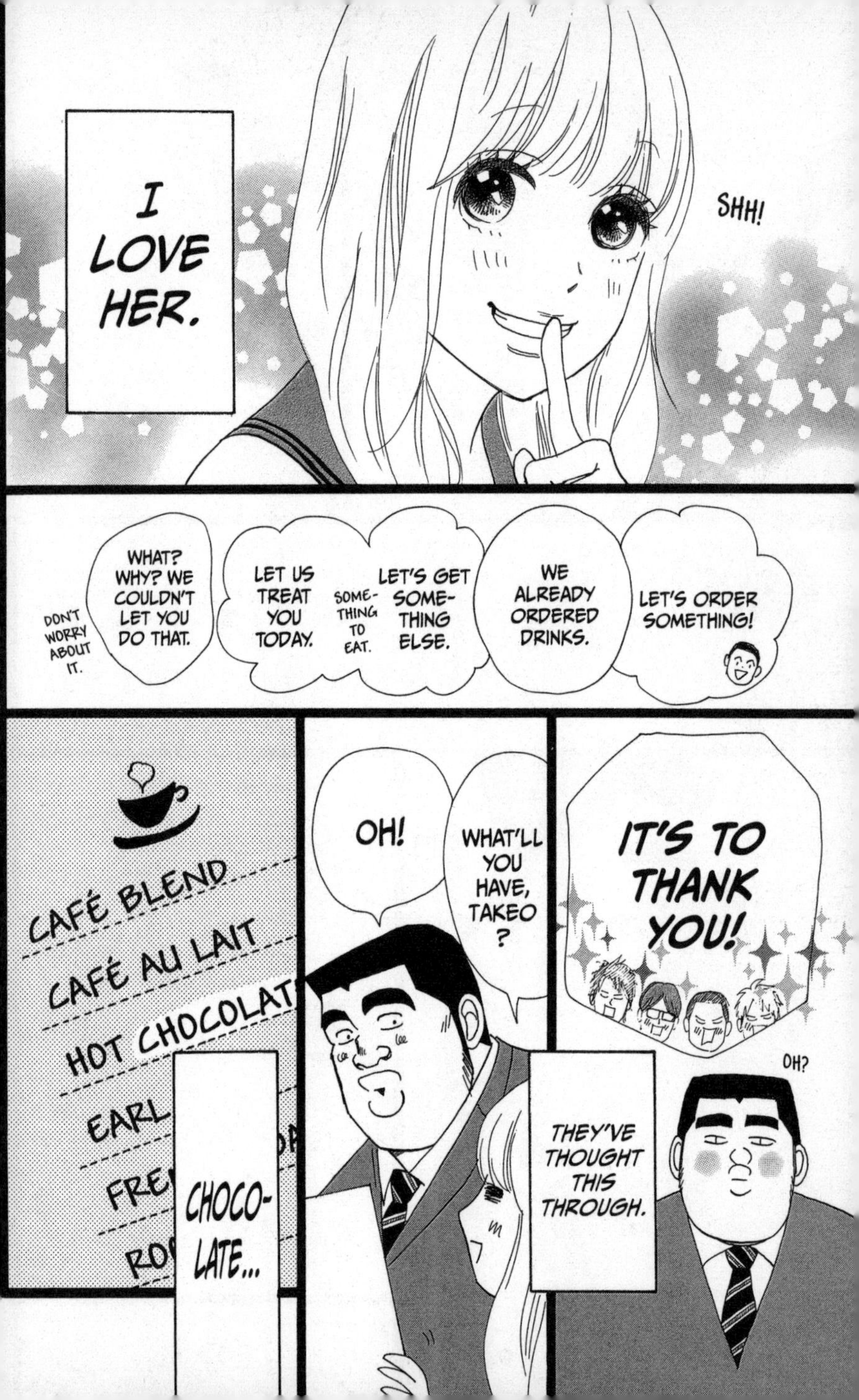
SHH!
I LOVE HER.
LET'S ORDER SOMETHING!
WE ALREADY ORDERED DRINKS.
LET'S GET SOME-THING ELSE.
SOME-THING TO EAT.
LET US TREAT YOU TODAY.
WHAT? WHY? WE COULDN'T LET YOU DO THAT.
DON'T WORRY ABOUT IT.
IT'S TO THANK YOU!
OH?
THEY'VE THOUGHT THIS THROUGH.
WHAT'LL YOU HAVE, TAKEO?
OH!
CAFÉ BLEND
CAFÉ AU LAIT
HOT CHOCOLAT
EARL
FRE
RO
CHOCO-LATE...

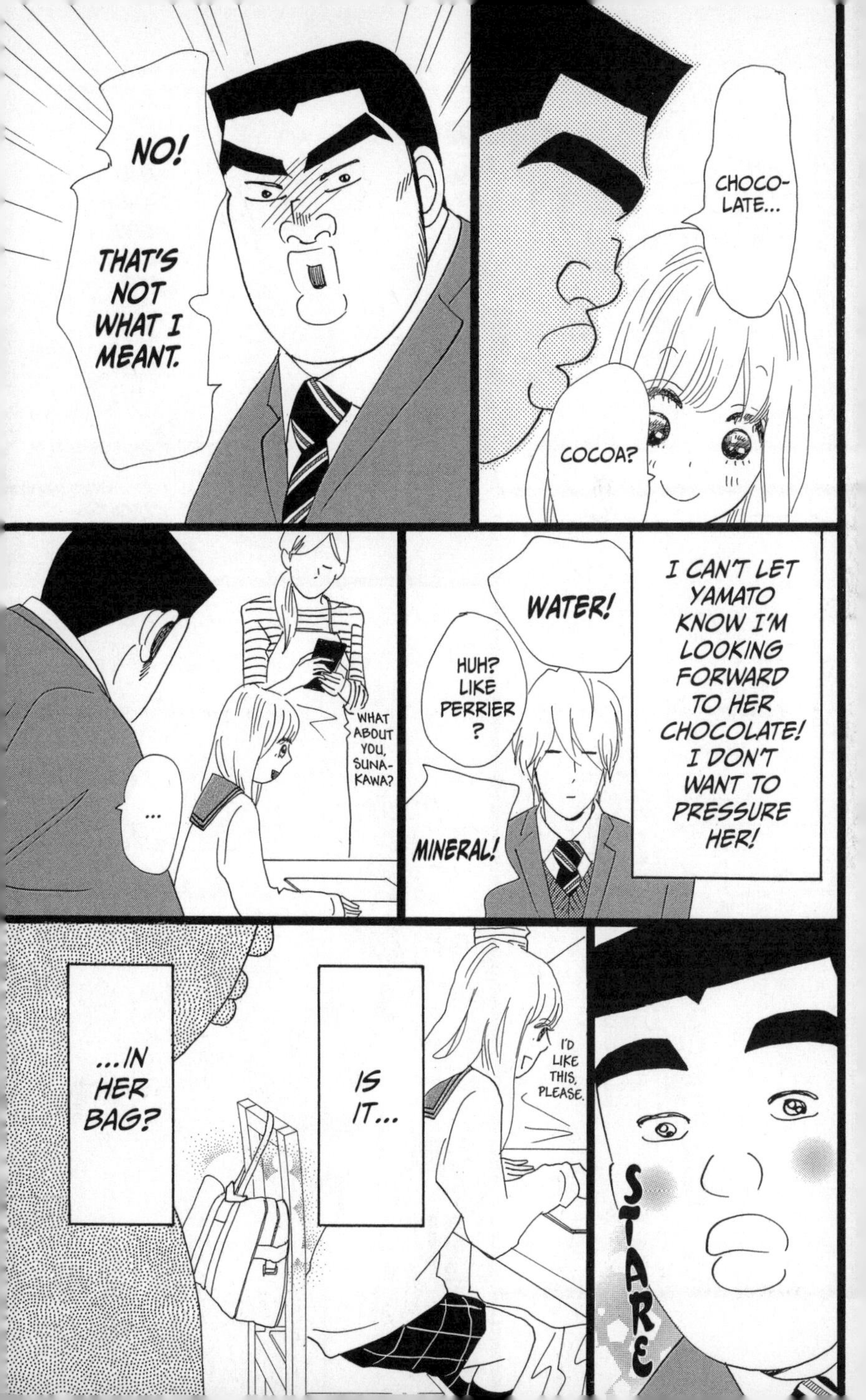
CHOCO-LATE...
COCOA?
NO!
THAT'S NOT WHAT I MEANT.
I CAN'T LET YAMATO KNOW I'M LOOKING FORWARD TO HER CHOCOLATE! I DON'T WANT TO PRESSURE HER!
WATER!
HUH? LIKE PERRIER?
MINERAL!
WHAT ABOUT YOU, SUNA-KAWA?
...
STARE
I'D LIKE THIS, PLEASE.
IS IT...
...IN HER BAG?

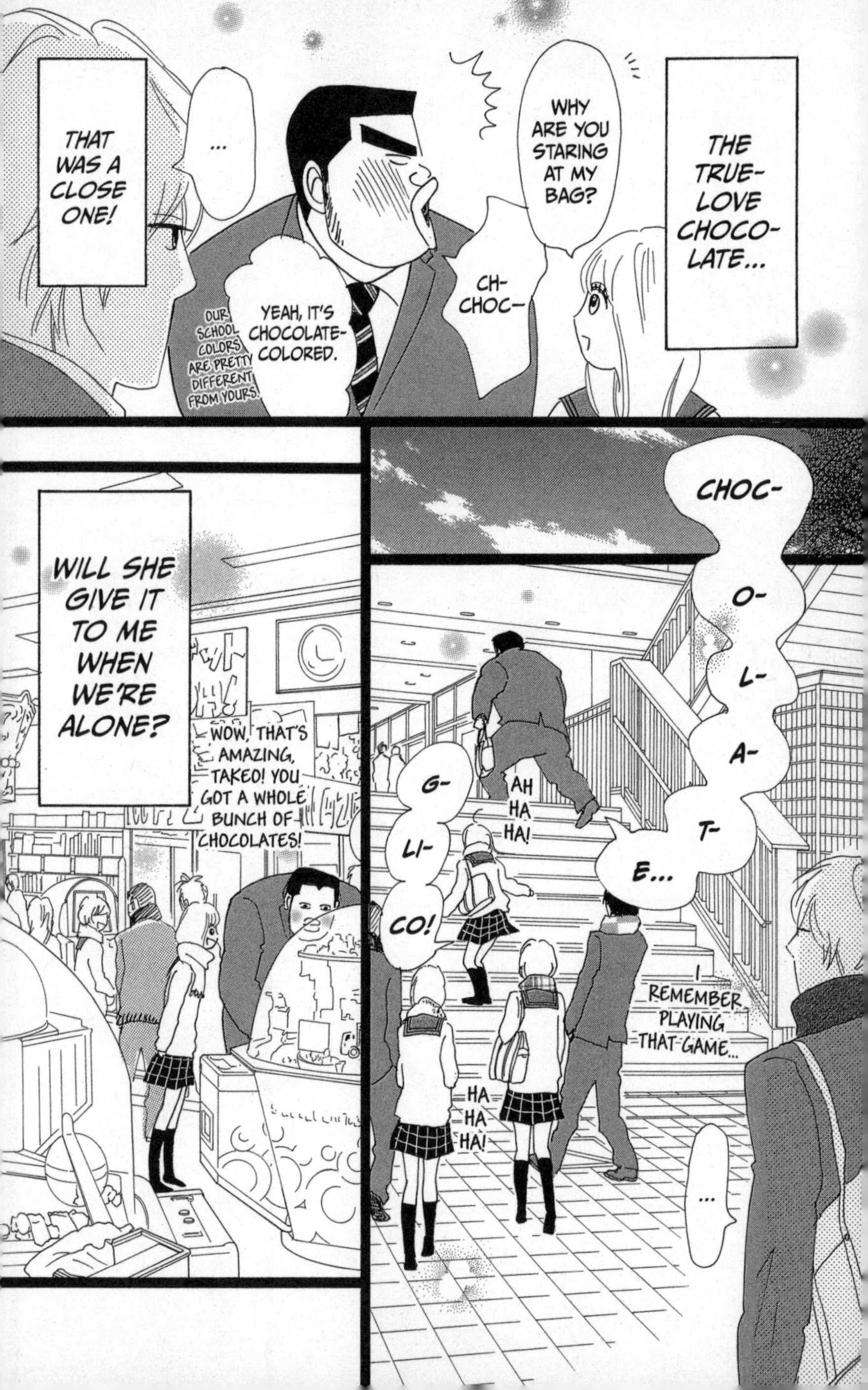
THE TRUE-LOVE CHOCOLATE...
WHY ARE YOU STARING AT MY BAG?
CH-CHOC-
YEAH, IT'S CHOCOLATE-COLORED.
OUR SCHOOL COLORS ARE PRETTY DIFFERENT FROM YOURS.
...
THAT WAS A CLOSE ONE!
CHOC-O-L-A-T-E...
G-LI-CO!
AH HA HA!
I REMEMBER PLAYING THAT GAME...
HA HA HA!
...
WILL SHE GIVE IT TO ME WHEN WE'RE ALONE?
WOW, THAT'S AMAZING, TAKEO! YOU GOT A WHOLE BUNCH OF CHOCOLATES!

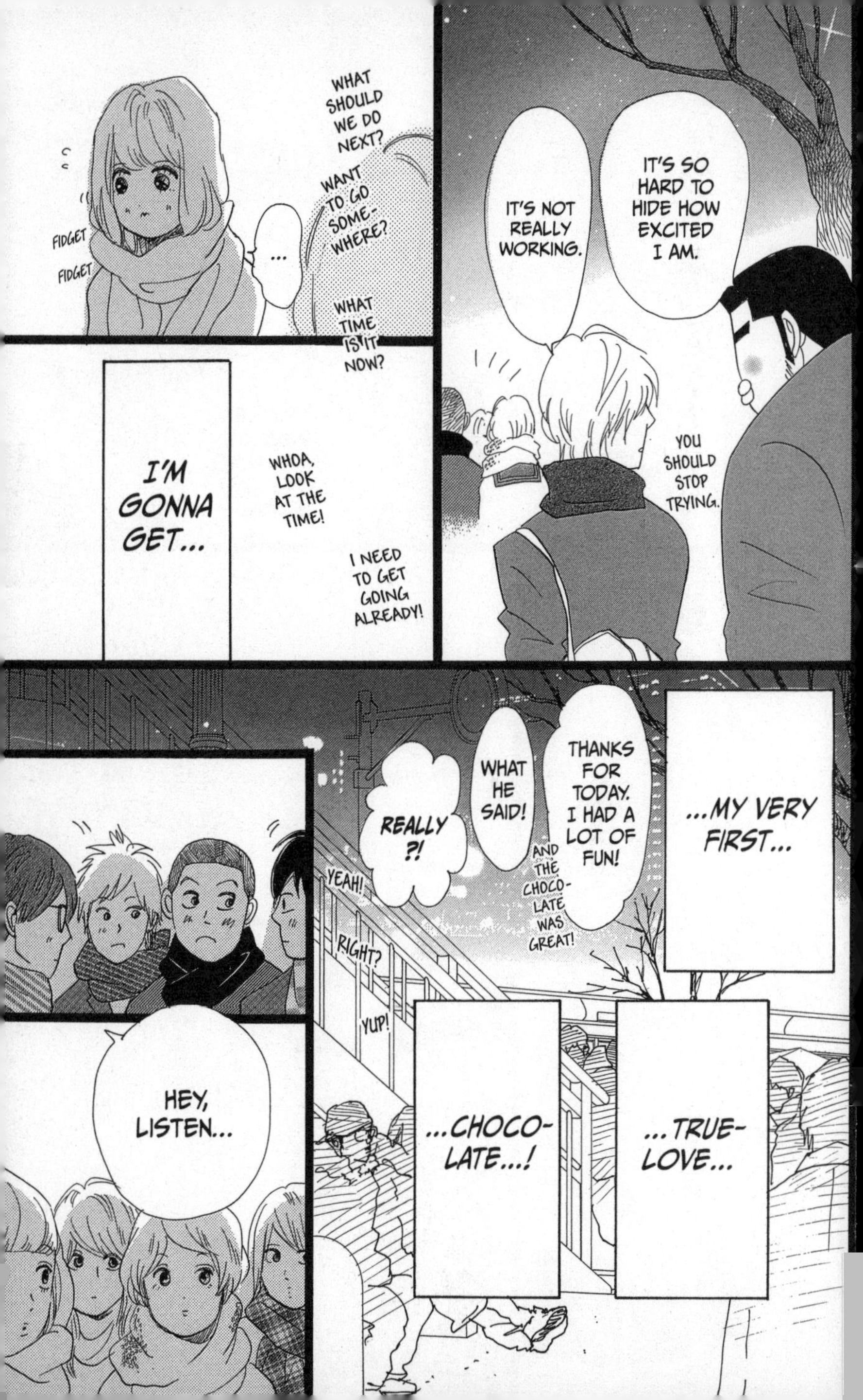
IT'S SO HARD TO HIDE HOW EXCITED I AM.
IT'S NOT REALLY WORKING.
YOU SHOULD STOP TRYING.
WHAT SHOULD WE DO NEXT?
WANT TO GO SOME-WHERE?
...
FIDGET
FIDGET
WHAT TIME IS IT NOW?
WHOA, LOOK AT THE TIME!
I NEED TO GET GOING ALREADY!
I'M GONNA GET...
...MY VERY FIRST...
THANKS FOR TODAY. I HAD A LOT OF FUN!
AND THE CHOCO-LATE WAS GREAT!
WHAT HE SAID!
REALLY?!
YEAH!
RIGHT?
YUP!
...TRUE-LOVE...
...CHOCO-LATE...!
HEY, LISTEN...

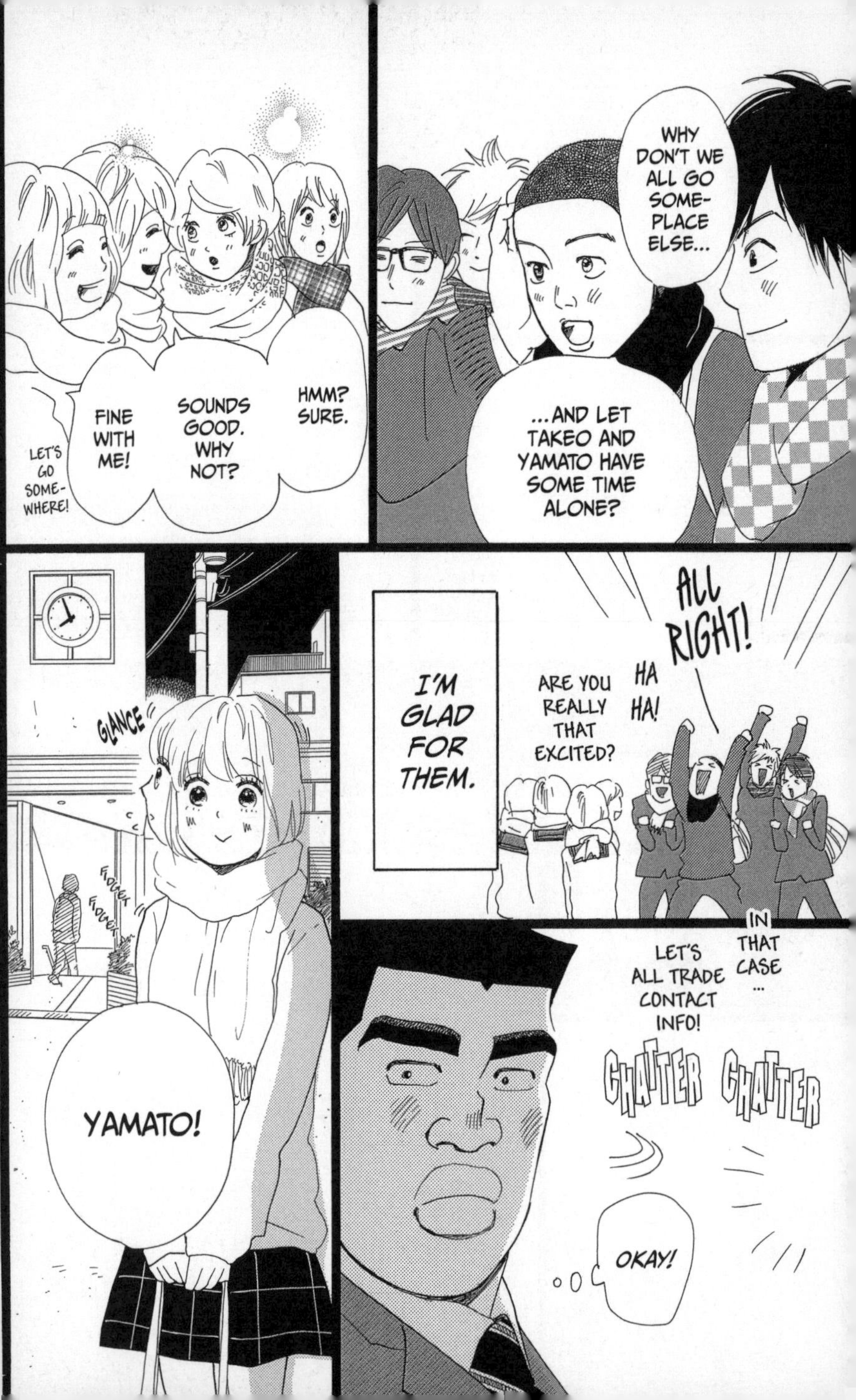
WHY DON'T WE ALL GO SOME-PLACE ELSE...
...AND LET TAKEO AND YAMATO HAVE SOME TIME ALONE?
HMM? SURE.
SOUNDS GOOD. WHY NOT?
FINE WITH ME!
LET'S GO SOME-WHERE!
ALL RIGHT!
HA HA!
ARE YOU REALLY THAT EXCITED?
I'M GLAD FOR THEM.
IN THAT CASE ...
LET'S ALL TRADE CONTACT INFO!
CHATTER CHATTER
OKAY!
GLANCE
FIDGET FIDGET
YAMATO!

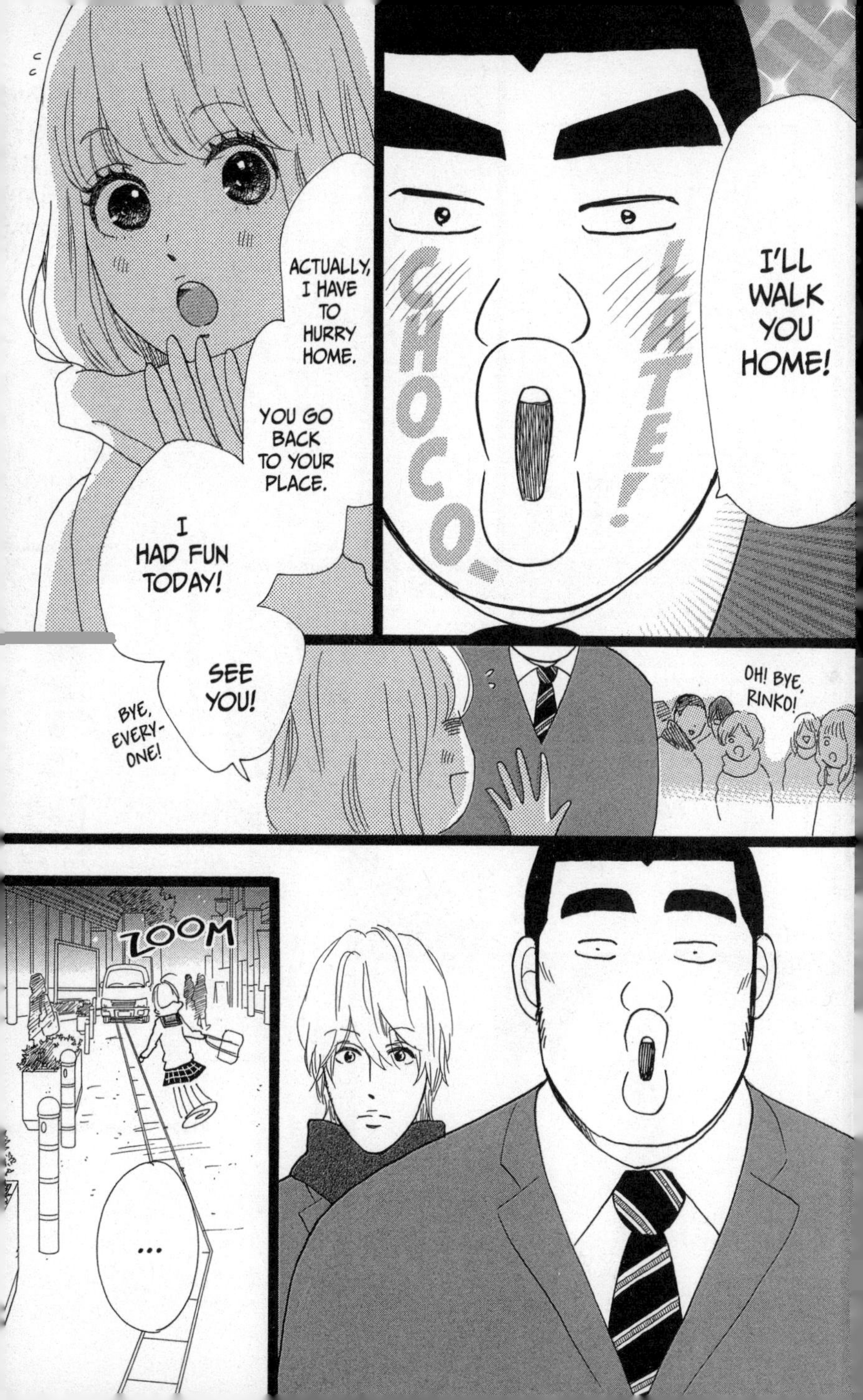
I'LL WALK YOU HOME!
CHOCO-LATE!
ACTUALLY, I HAVE TO HURRY HOME.
YOU GO BACK TO YOUR PLACE.
I HAD FUN TODAY!
OH! BYE, RINKO!
SEE YOU!
BYE, EVERY-ONE!
ZOOM
...

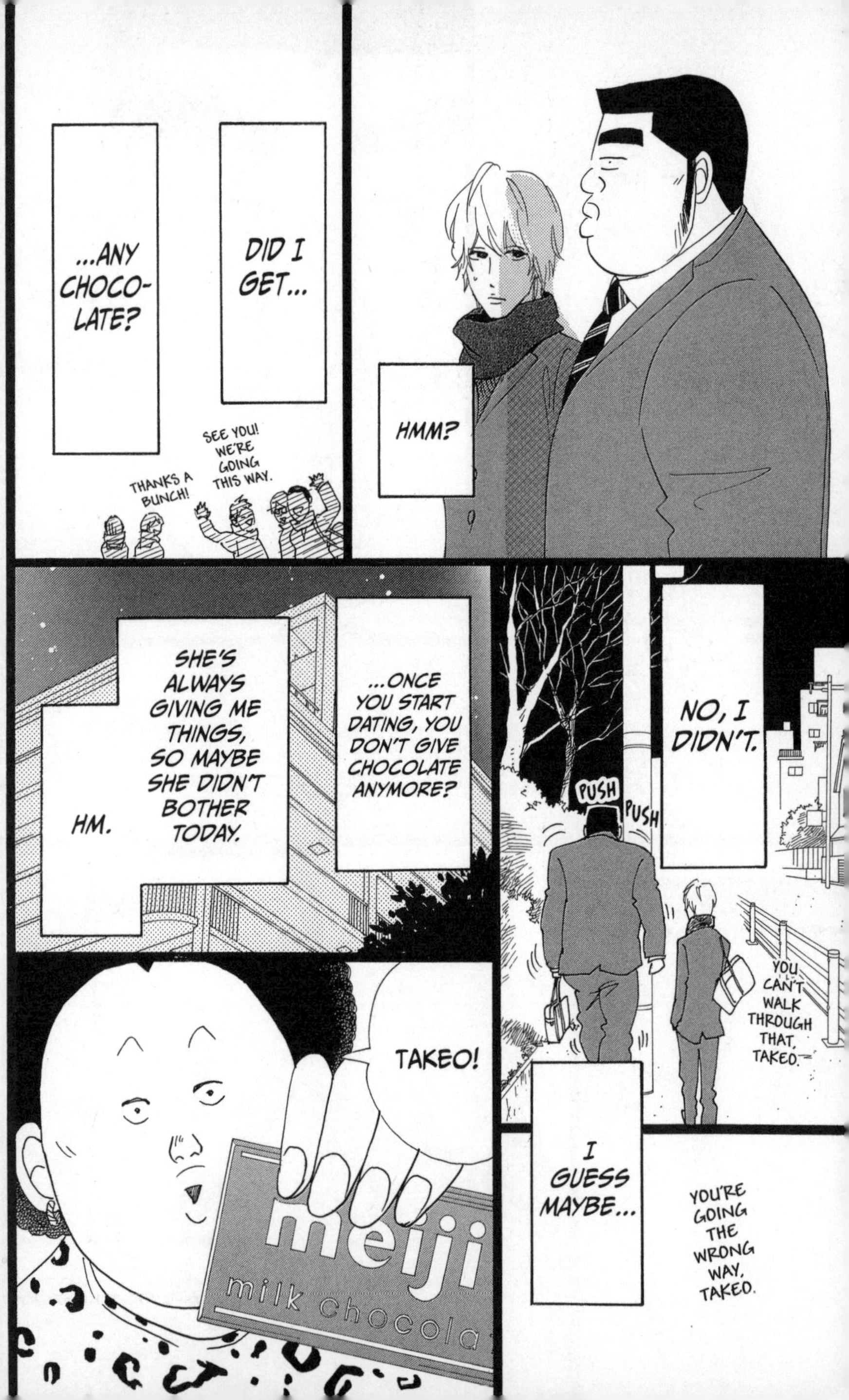
HMM?
DID I GET...
...ANY CHOCOLATE?
SEE YOU! WE'RE GOING THIS WAY.
THANKS A BUNCH!
NO, I DIDN'T.
PUSH
PUSH
YOU CAN'T WALK THROUGH THAT, TAKEO.
...ONCE YOU START DATING, YOU DON'T GIVE CHOCOLATE ANYMORE?
SHE'S ALWAYS GIVING ME THINGS, SO MAYBE SHE DIDN'T BOTHER TODAY.
HM.
TAKEO!
meiji
milk chocola
I GUESS MAYBE...
YOU'RE GOING THE WRONG WAY, TAKEO.

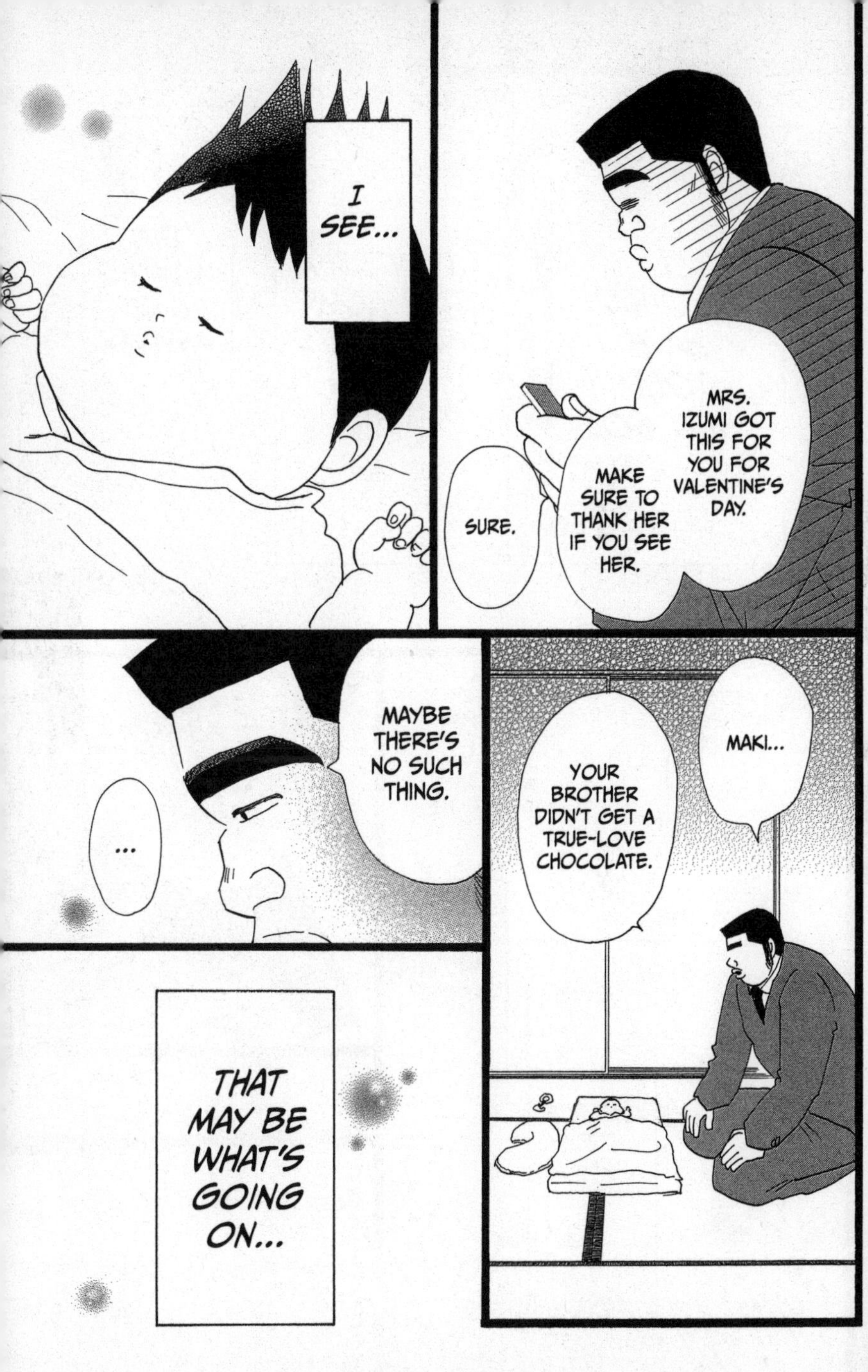
MRS. IZUMI GOT THIS FOR YOU FOR VALENTINE'S DAY.
MAKE SURE TO THANK HER IF YOU SEE HER.
SURE.
I SEE...
MAKI...
YOUR BROTHER DIDN'T GET A TRUE-LOVE CHOCOLATE.
MAYBE THERE'S NO SUCH THING.
...
THAT MAY BE WHAT'S GOING ON...

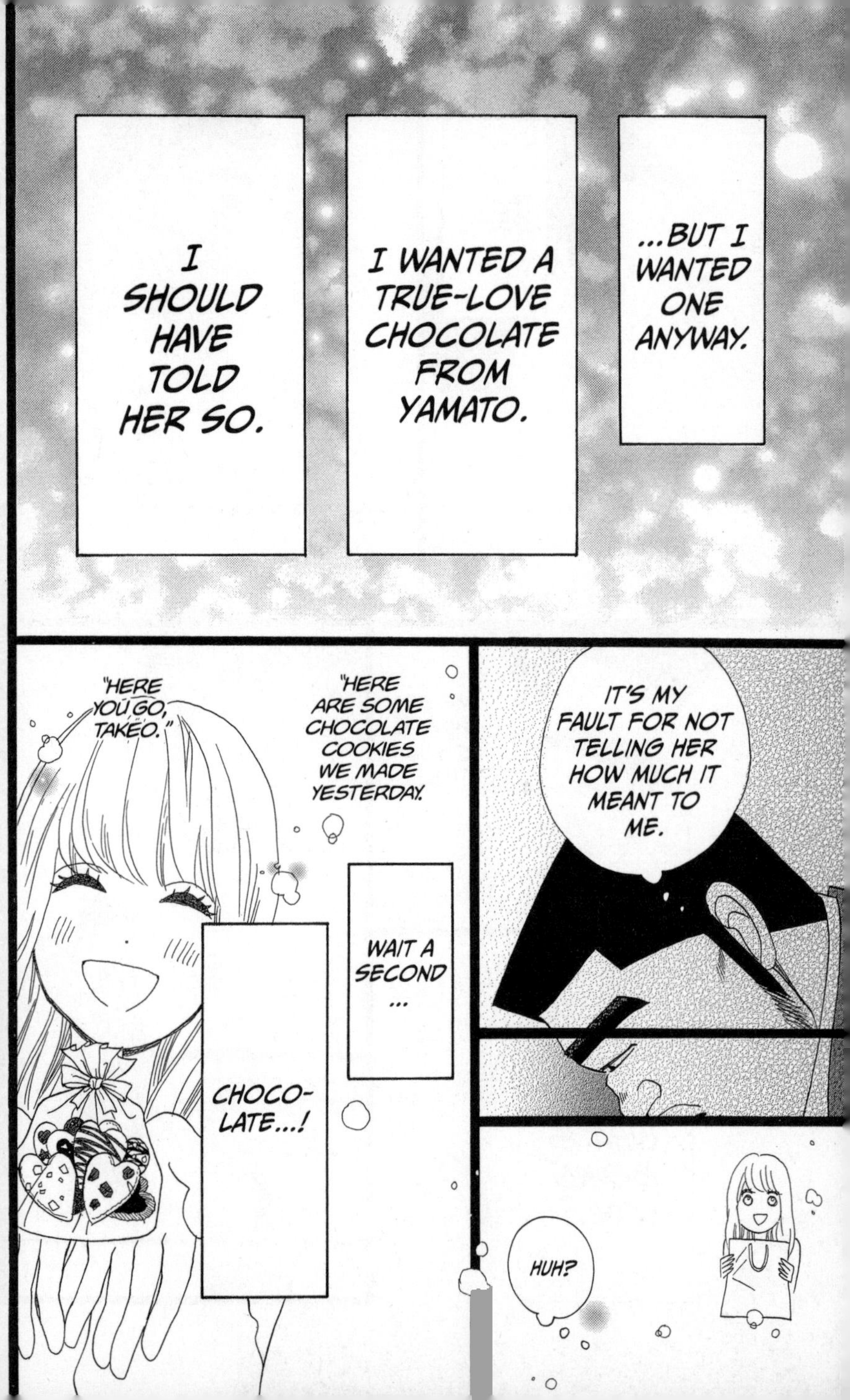

...BUT I WANTED ONE ANYWAY.
I WANTED A TRUE-LOVE CHOCOLATE FROM YAMATO.
I SHOULD HAVE TOLD HER SO.
IT'S MY FAULT FOR NOT TELLING HER HOW MUCH IT MEANT TO ME.
HUH?
"HERE ARE SOME CHOCOLATE COOKIES WE MADE YESTERDAY.
"HERE YOU GO, TAKEO."
WAIT A SECOND ...
CHOCO-LATE...!

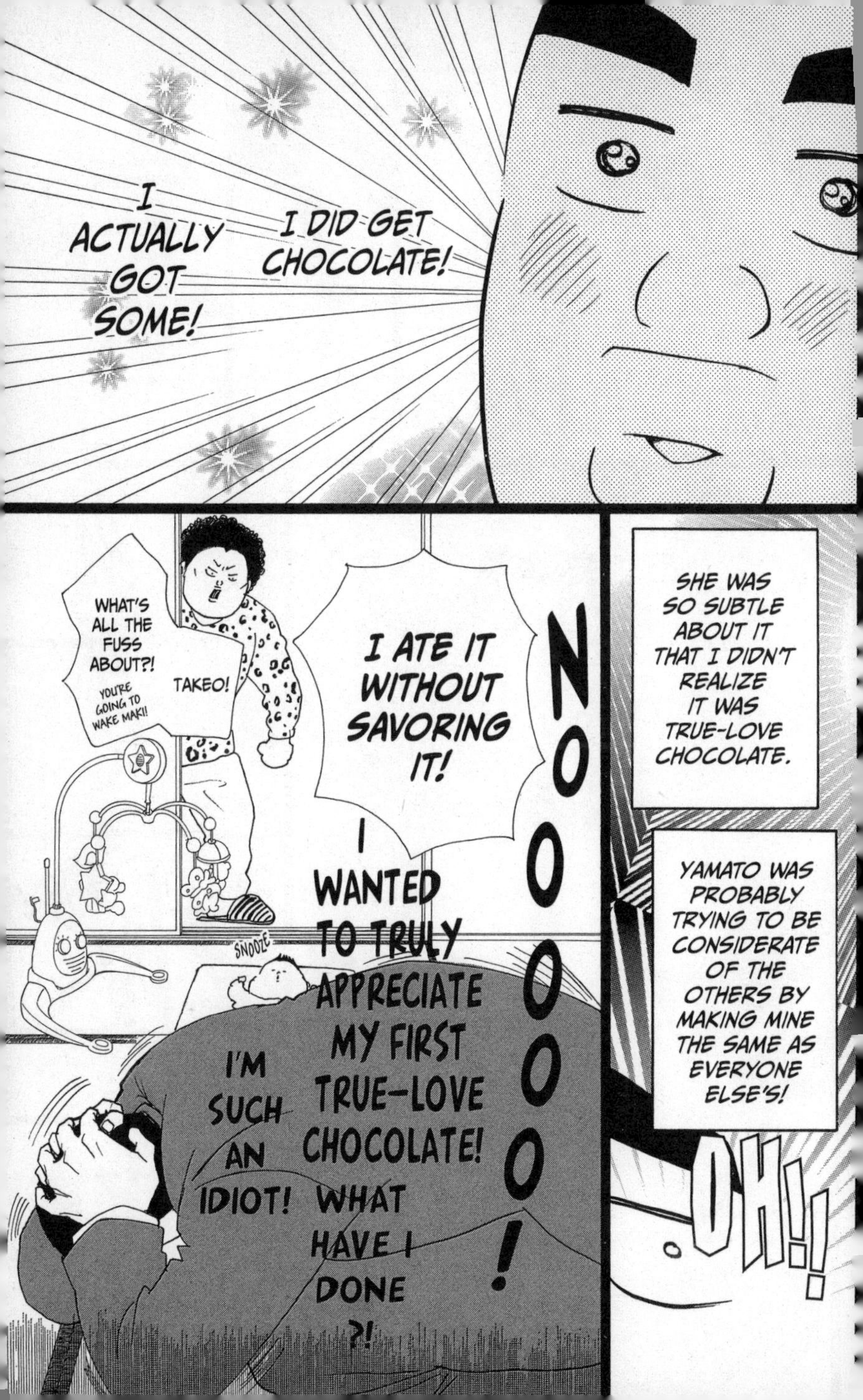
I DID GET CHOCOLATE!
I ACTUALLY GOT SOME!
SHE WAS SO SUBTLE ABOUT IT THAT I DIDN'T REALIZE IT WAS TRUE-LOVE CHOCOLATE.
YAMATO WAS PROBABLY TRYING TO BE CONSIDERATE OF THE OTHERS BY MAKING MINE THE SAME AS EVERYONE ELSE'S!
OH!!
NOOOOO!
I ATE IT WITHOUT SAVORING IT!
I WANTED TO TRULY APPRECIATE MY FIRST TRUE-LOVE CHOCOLATE! WHAT HAVE I DONE?!
I'M SUCH AN IDIOT!
TAKEO!
WHAT'S ALL THE FUSS ABOUT?!
YOU'RE GOING TO WAKE MAKI!
SNOOZE

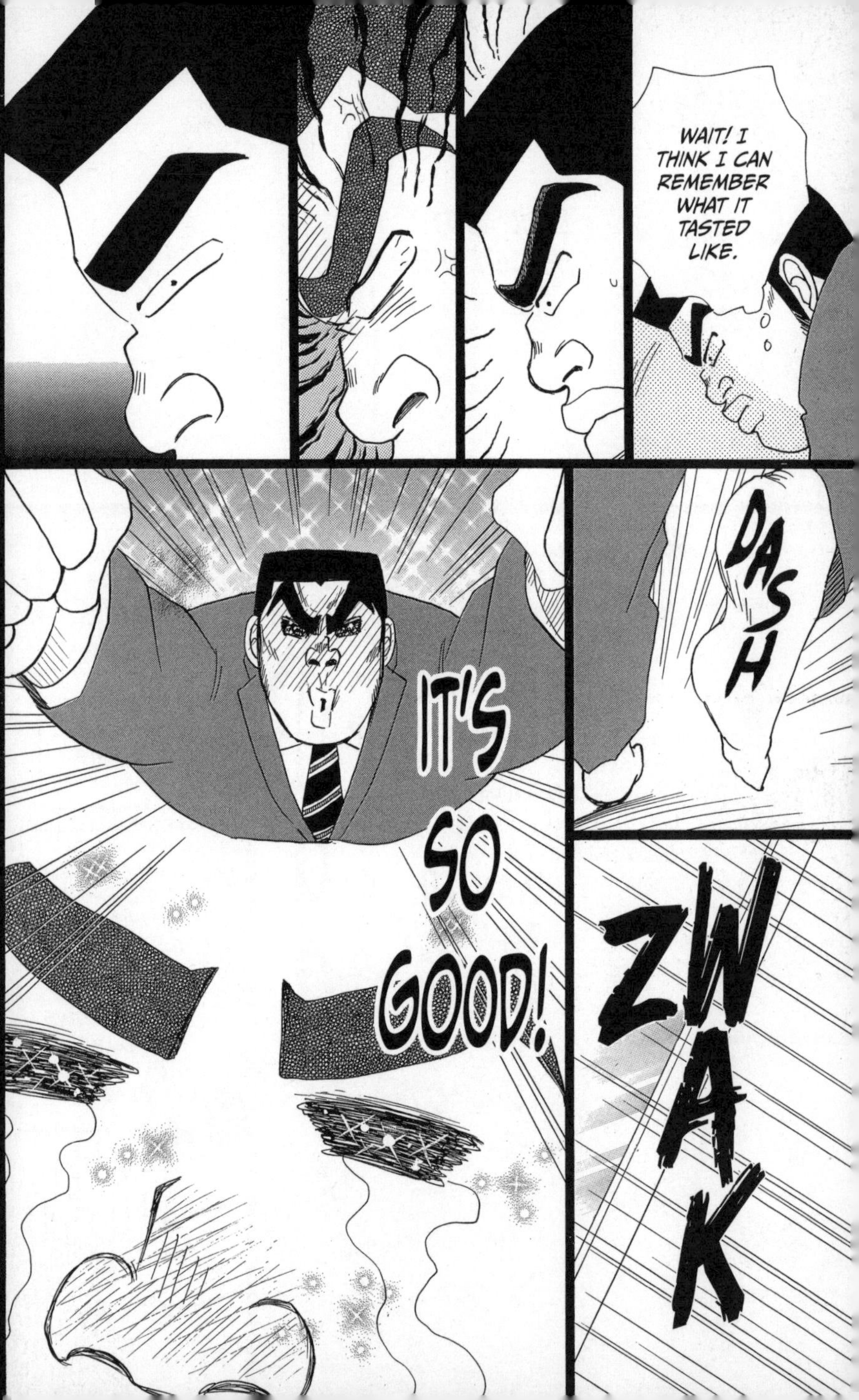
WAIT! I THINK I CAN REMEMBER WHAT IT TASTED LIKE.
DASH
ZWAK
IT'S SO GOOD!

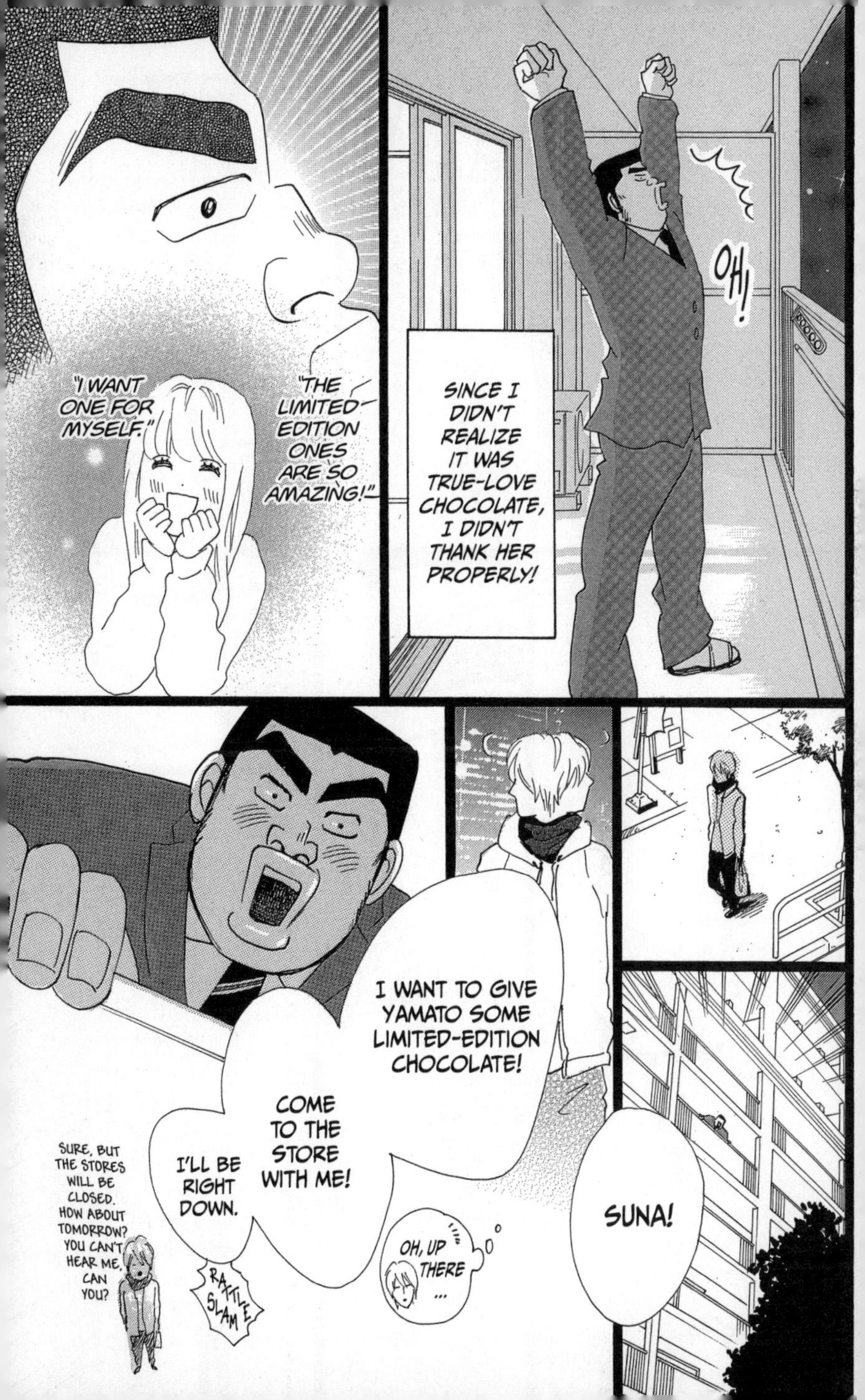
OH!
SINCE I DIDN'T REALIZE IT WAS TRUE-LOVE CHOCOLATE, I DIDN'T THANK HER PROPERLY!
"THE LIMITED EDITION ONES ARE SO AMAZING!"
"I WANT ONE FOR MYSELF."
SUNA!
OH, UP THERE ...
I WANT TO GIVE YAMATO SOME LIMITED-EDITION CHOCOLATE!
COME TO THE STORE WITH ME!
I'LL BE RIGHT DOWN.
RATTLE SLAM
SURE, BUT THE STORES WILL BE CLOSED. HOW ABOUT TOMORROW? YOU CAN'T HEAR ME, CAN YOU?

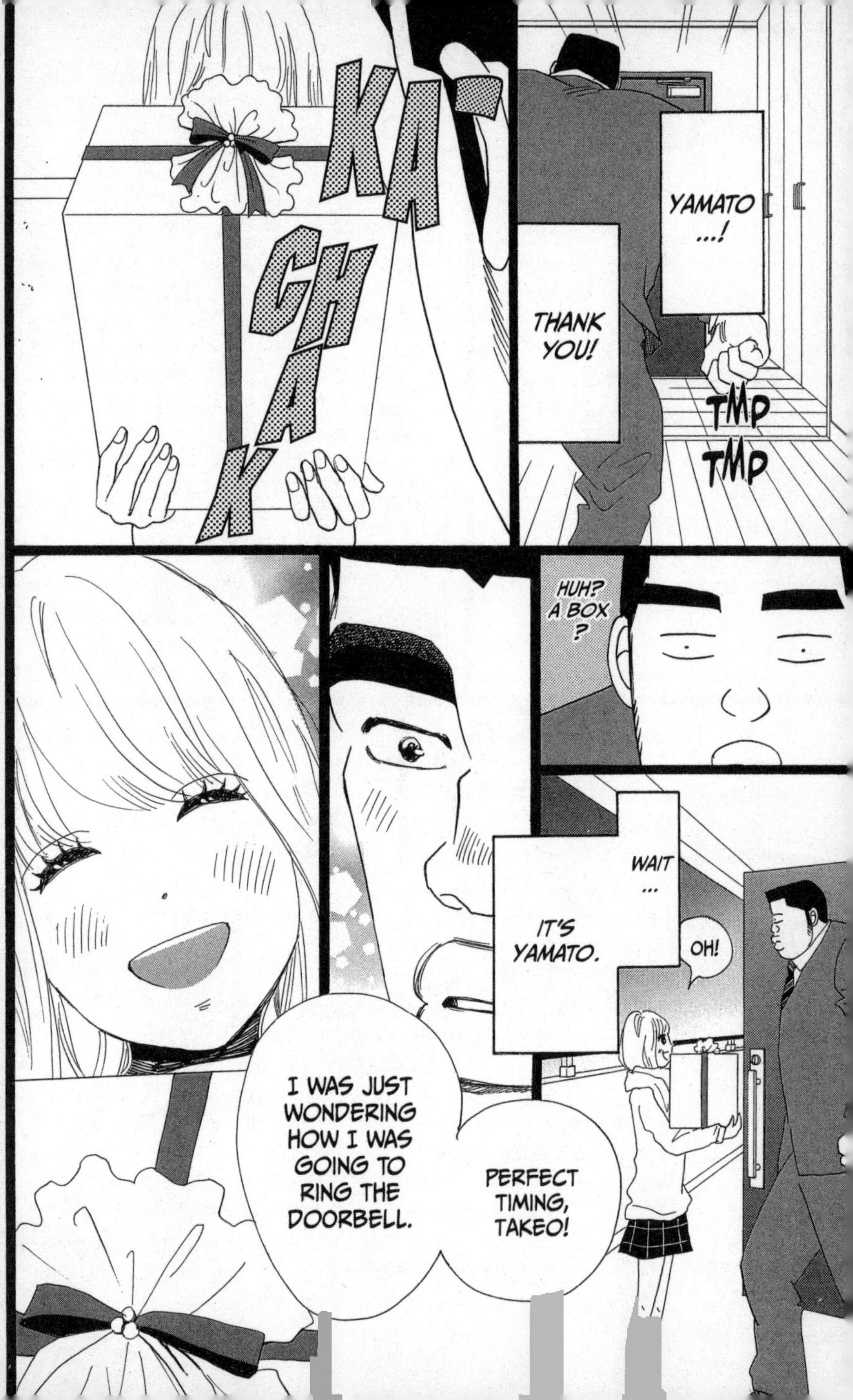

YAMATO ...!
THANK YOU!
TMP TMP
KA-CHAK
HUH? A BOX ?
OH!
WAIT ...
IT'S YAMATO.
PERFECT TIMING, TAKEO!
I WAS JUST WONDERING HOW I WAS GOING TO RING THE DOORBELL.

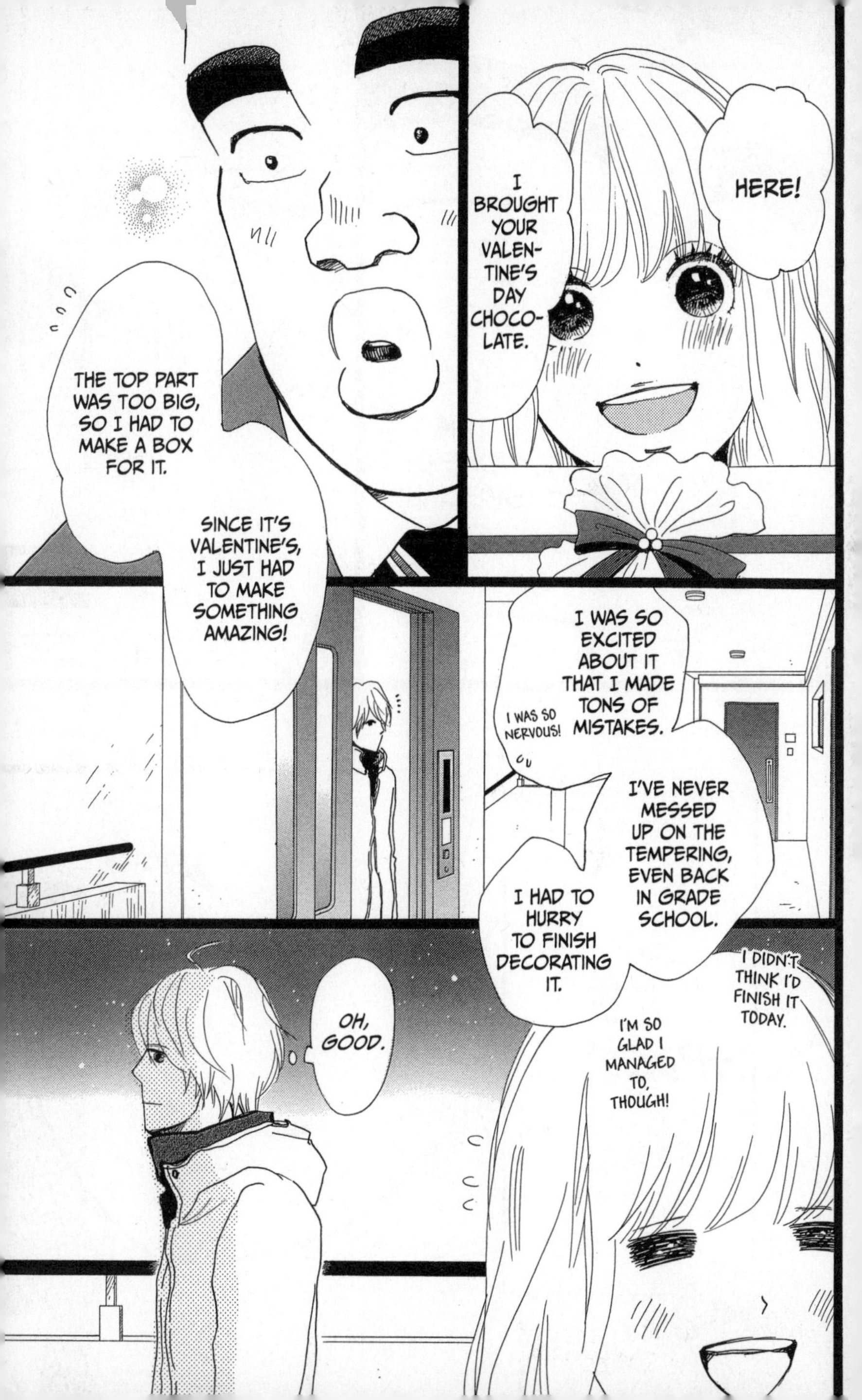
HERE!
I BROUGHT YOUR VALENTINE'S DAY CHOCOLATE.
THE TOP PART WAS TOO BIG, SO I HAD TO MAKE A BOX FOR IT.
SINCE IT'S VALENTINE'S, I JUST HAD TO MAKE SOMETHING AMAZING!
I WAS SO EXCITED ABOUT IT THAT I MADE TONS OF MISTAKES.
I WAS SO NERVOUS!
I'VE NEVER MESSED UP ON THE TEMPERING, EVEN BACK IN GRADE SCHOOL.
I HAD TO HURRY TO FINISH DECORATING IT.
I DIDN'T THINK I'D FINISH IT TODAY.
I'M SO GLAD I MANAGED TO, THOUGH!
OH, GOOD.

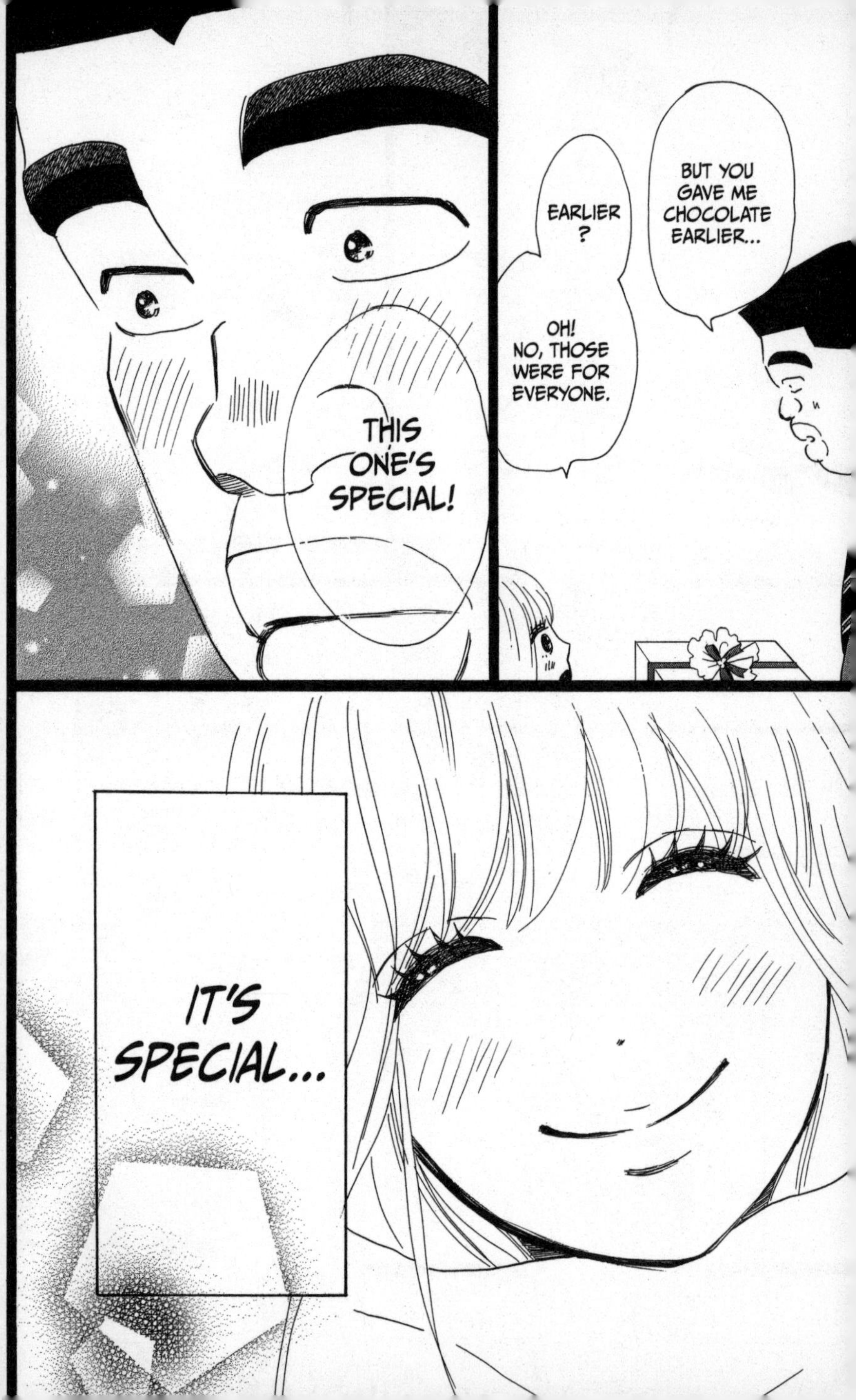
BUT YOU GAVE ME CHOCOLATE EARLIER...
EARLIER?
OH! NO, THOSE WERE FOR EVERYONE.
THIS ONE'S SPECIAL!
IT'S SPECIAL...

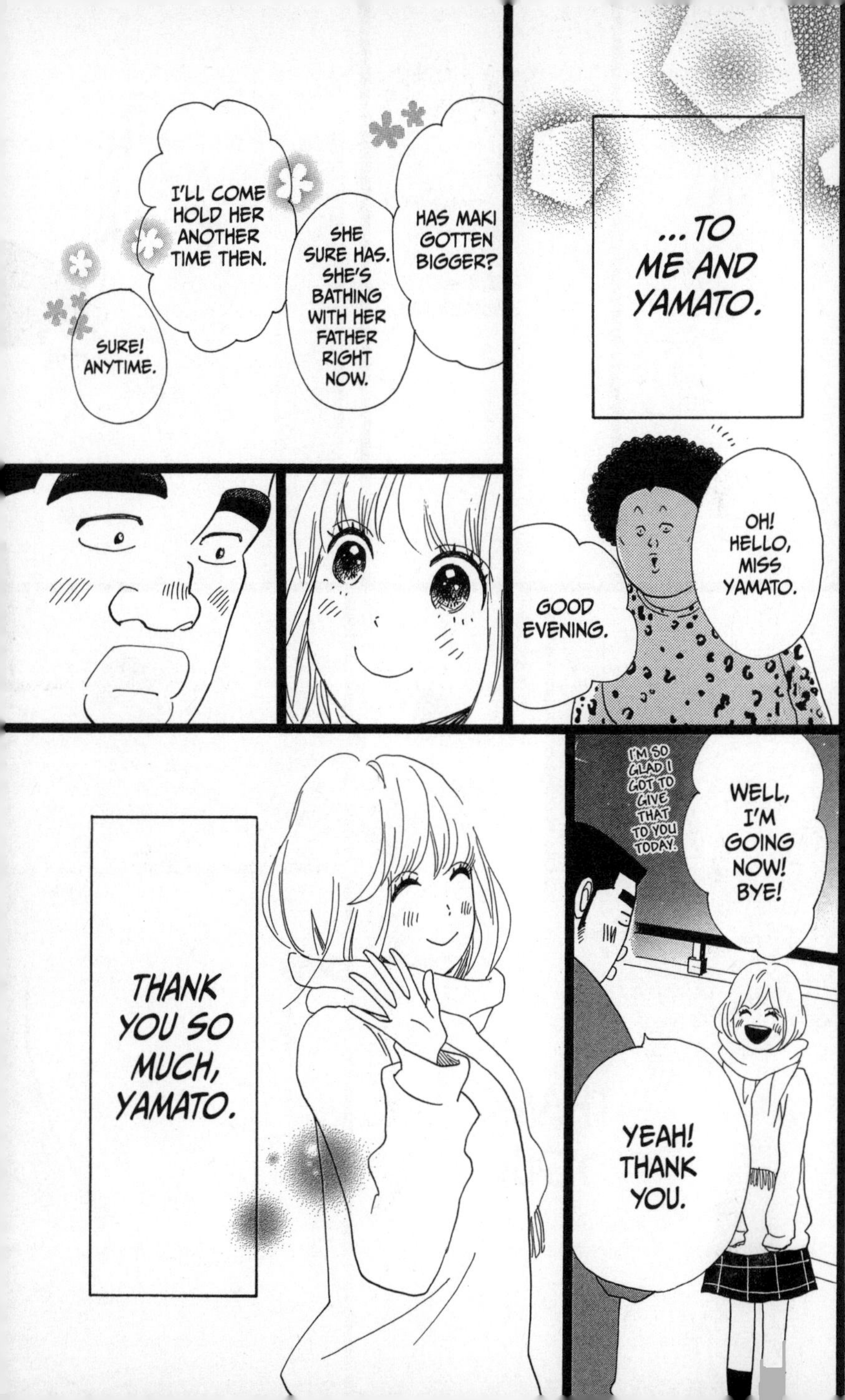
...TO ME AND YAMATO.
HAS MAKI GOTTEN BIGGER?
SHE SURE HAS. SHE'S BATHING WITH HER FATHER RIGHT NOW.
I'LL COME HOLD HER ANOTHER TIME THEN.
SURE! ANYTIME.
OH! HELLO, MISS YAMATO.
GOOD EVENING.
WELL, I'M GOING NOW! BYE!
I'M SO GLAD I GOT TO GIVE THAT TO YOU TODAY.
YEAH! THANK YOU.
THANK YOU SO MUCH, YAMATO.

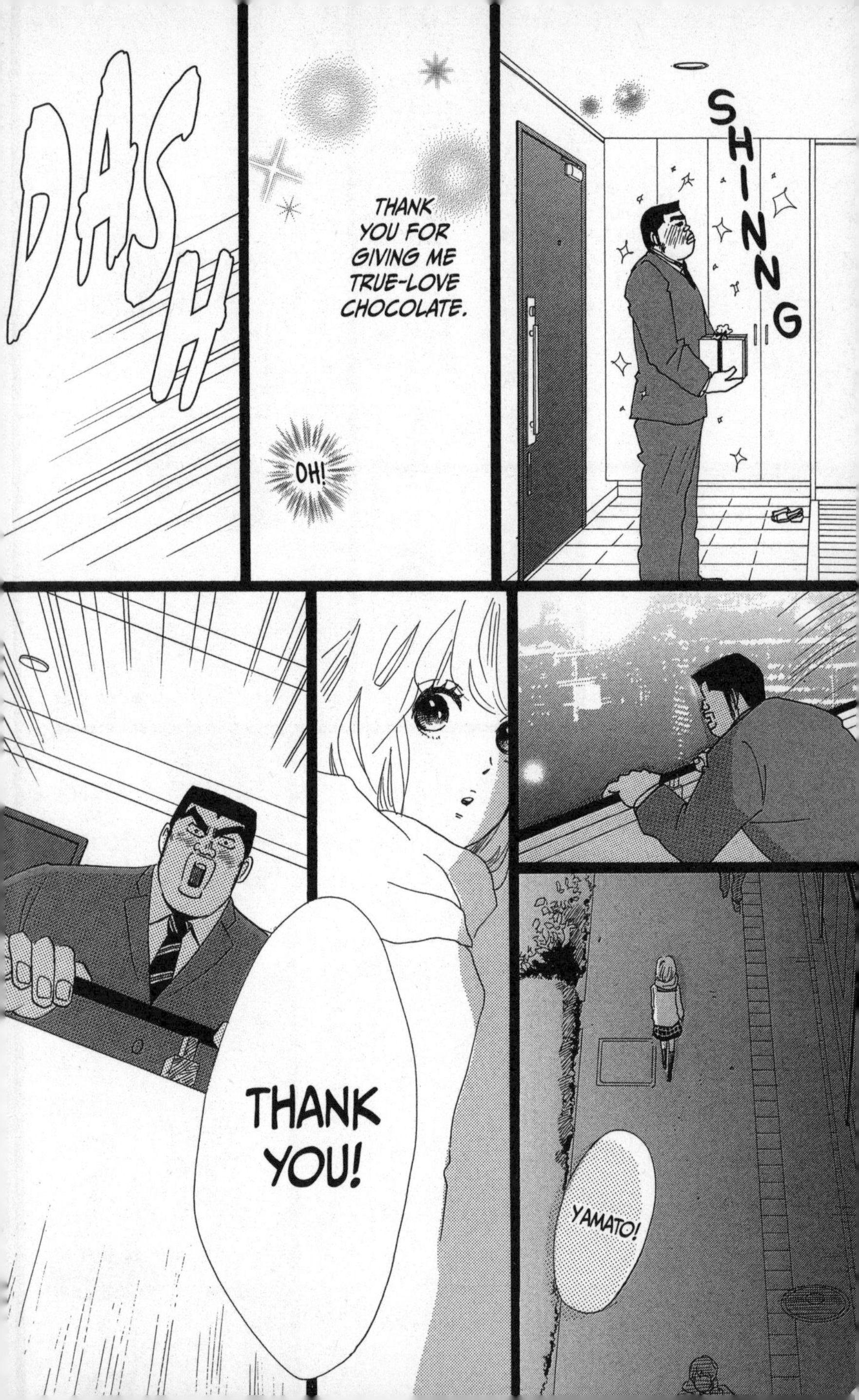
SHINNG
THANK YOU FOR GIVING ME TRUE-LOVE CHOCOLATE.
OH!
DASH
YAMATO!
THANK YOU!

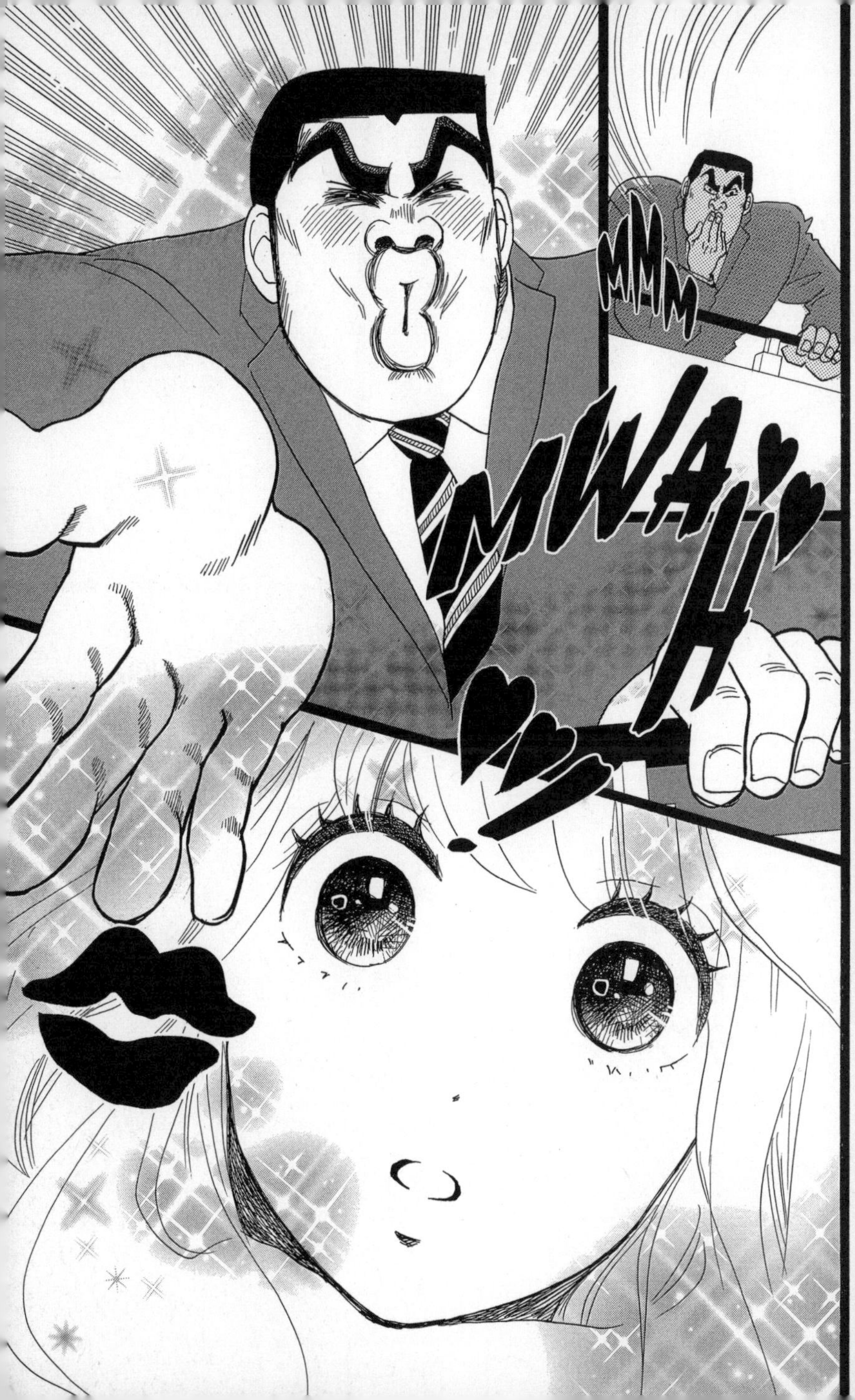
MMM
MWAH

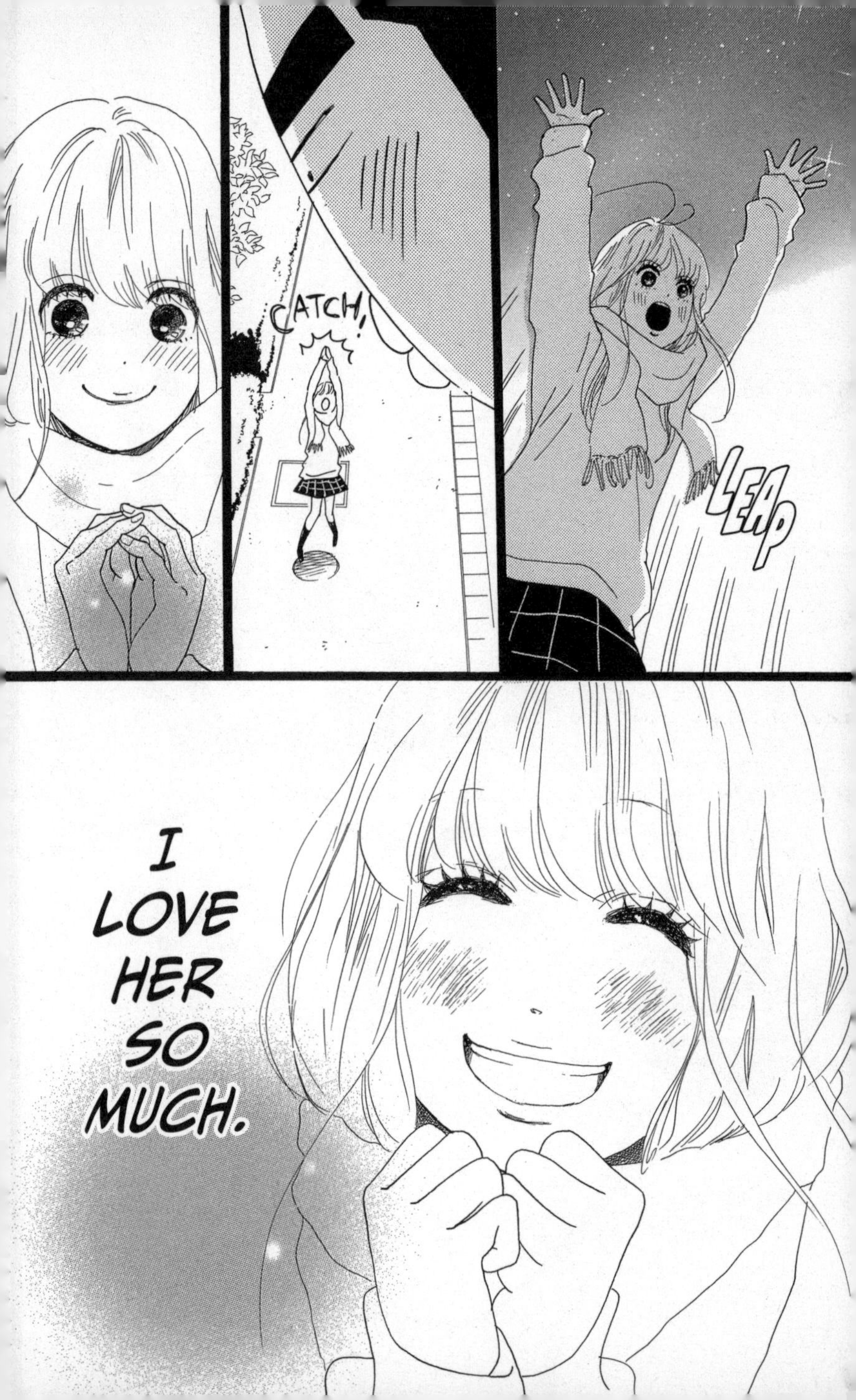
LEAP
CATCH!
I LOVE HER SO MUCH.

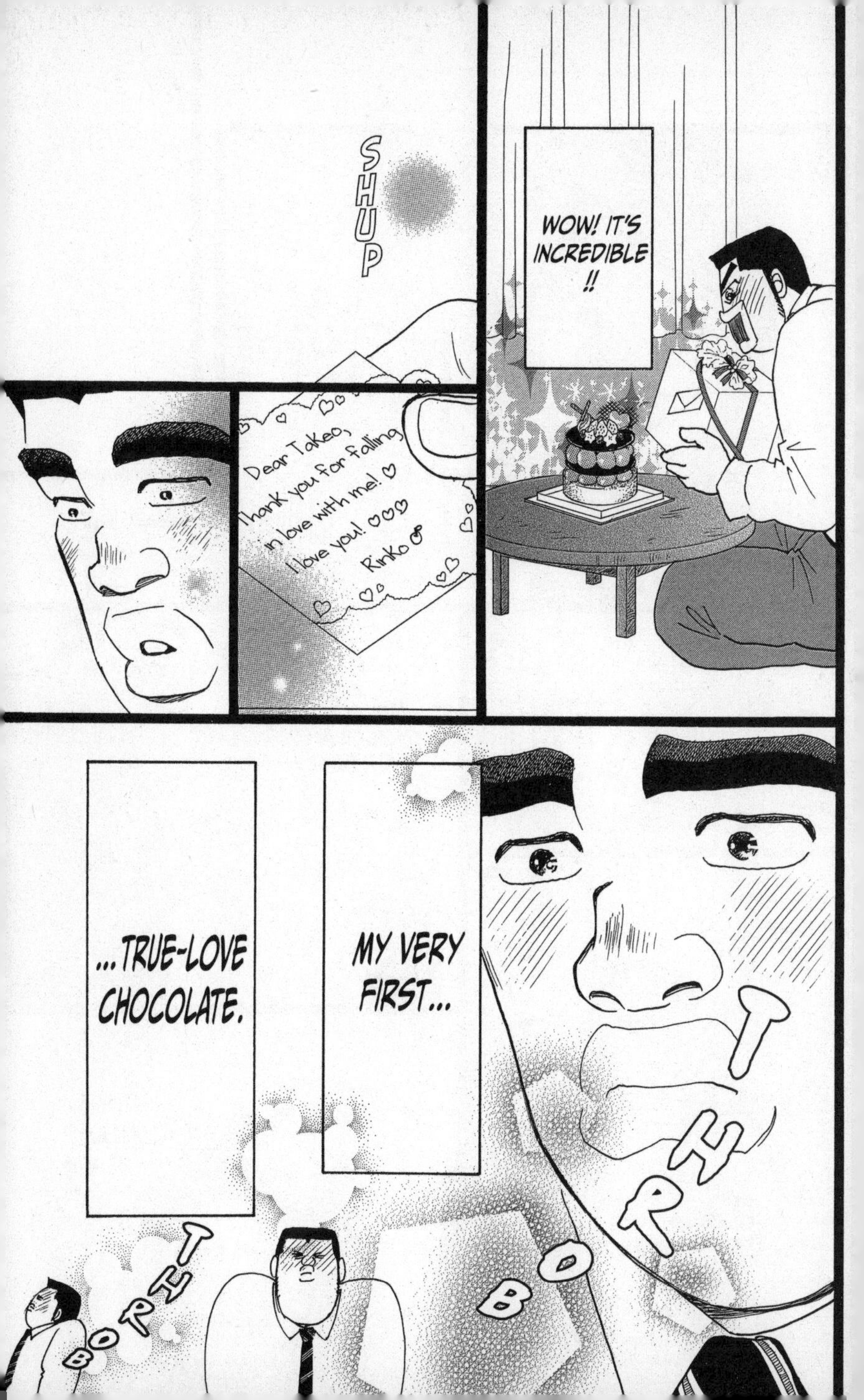
WOW! IT'S INCREDIBLE !!
SHUP
Dear Takeo,
Thank you for falling in love with me! ♡
I love you! ♡♡♡
Rinko
MY VERY FIRST...
...TRUE-LOVE CHOCOLATE.
BORHT
BORHT

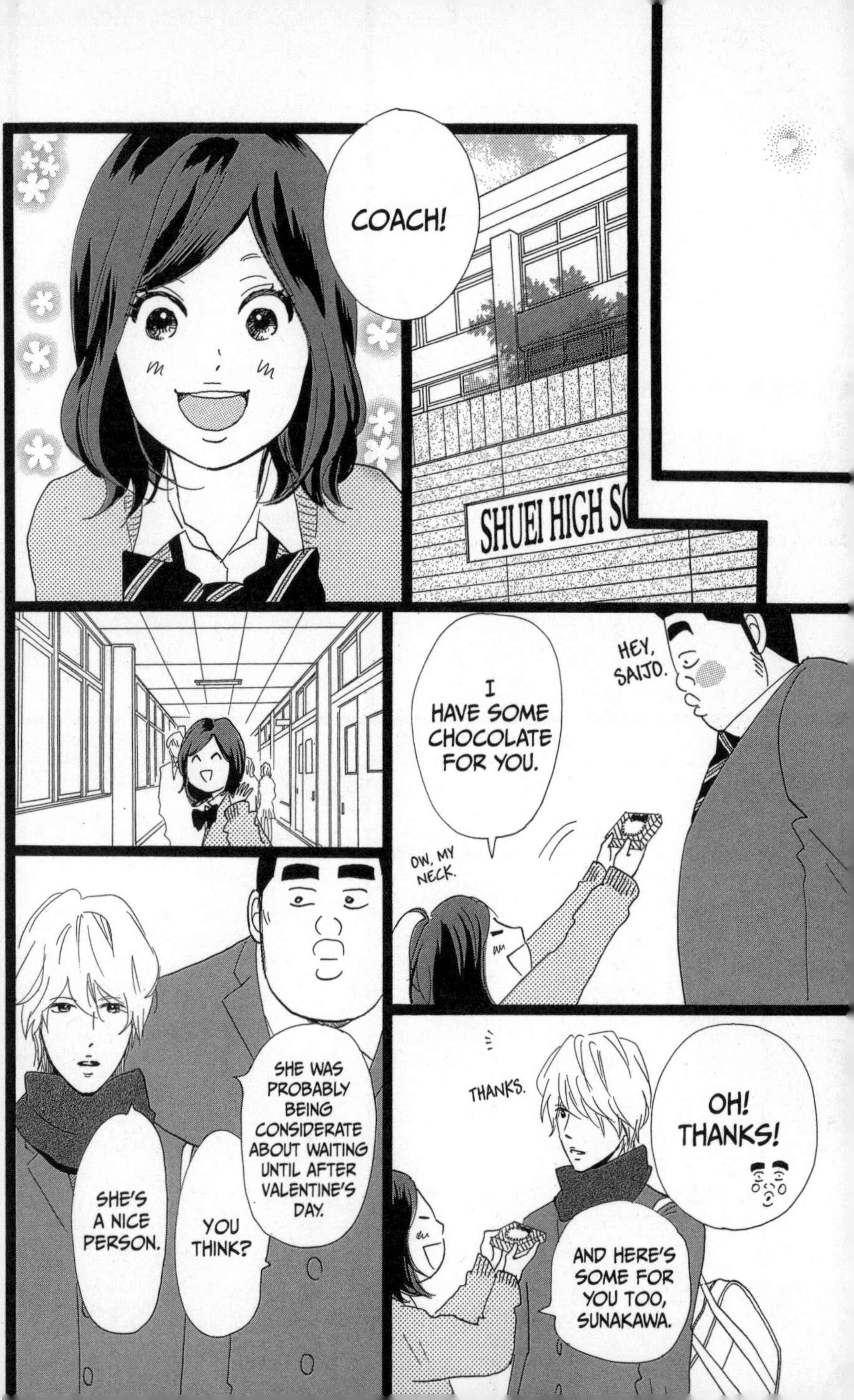
SHUEI HIGH SC
COACH!
HEY, SAIJO.
I HAVE SOME CHOCOLATE FOR YOU.
OW, MY NECK.
OH! THANKS!
THANKS.
AND HERE'S SOME FOR YOU TOO, SUNAKAWA.
SHE WAS PROBABLY BEING CONSIDERATE ABOUT WAITING UNTIL AFTER VALENTINE'S DAY.
YOU THINK?
SHE'S A NICE PERSON.

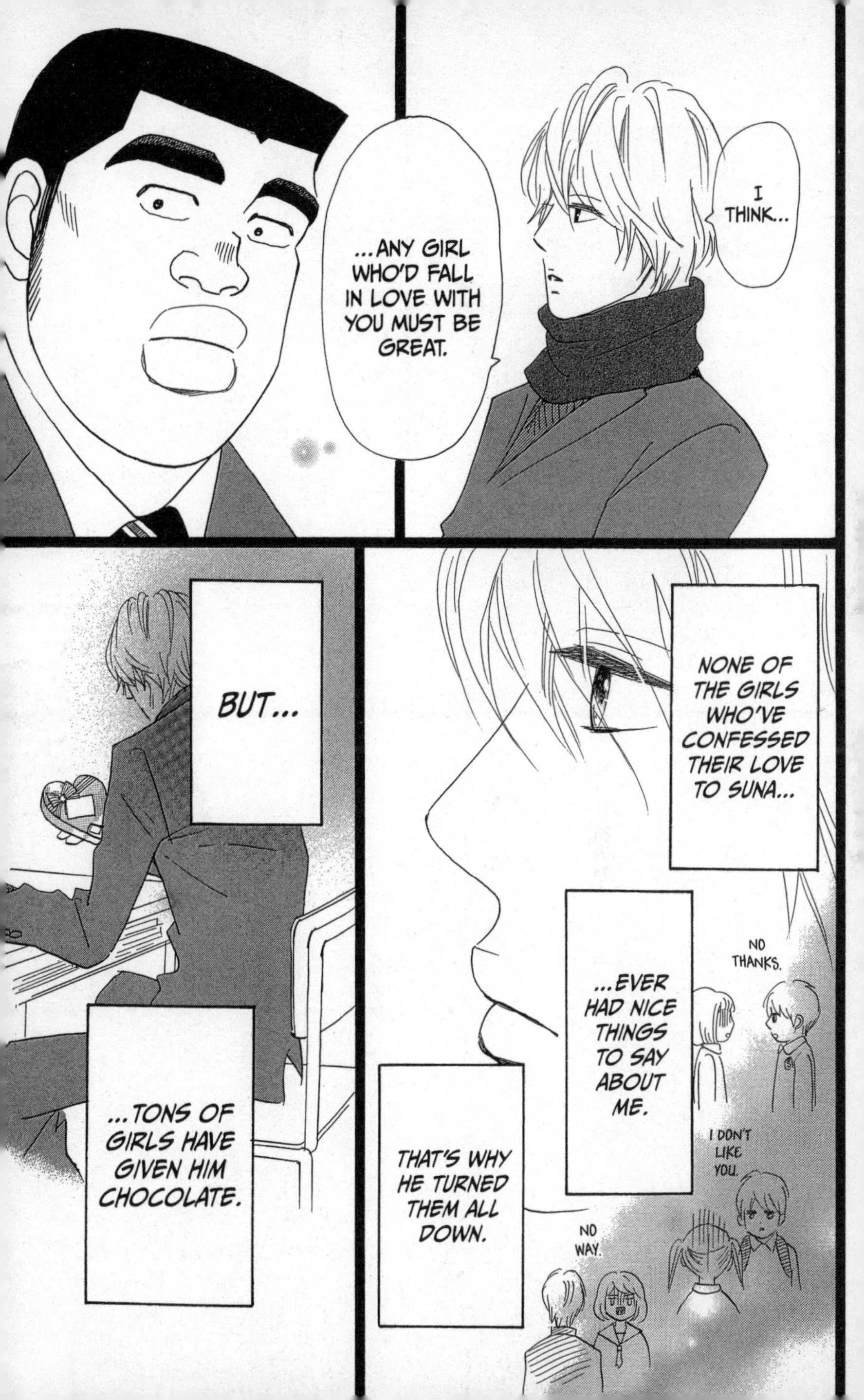
I THINK...
...ANY GIRL WHO'D FALL IN LOVE WITH YOU MUST BE GREAT.
NONE OF THE GIRLS WHO'VE CONFESSED THEIR LOVE TO SUNA...
NO THANKS.
...EVER HAD NICE THINGS TO SAY ABOUT ME.
I DON'T LIKE YOU.
THAT'S WHY HE TURNED THEM ALL DOWN.
NO WAY.
BUT...
...TONS OF GIRLS HAVE GIVEN HIM CHOCOLATE.

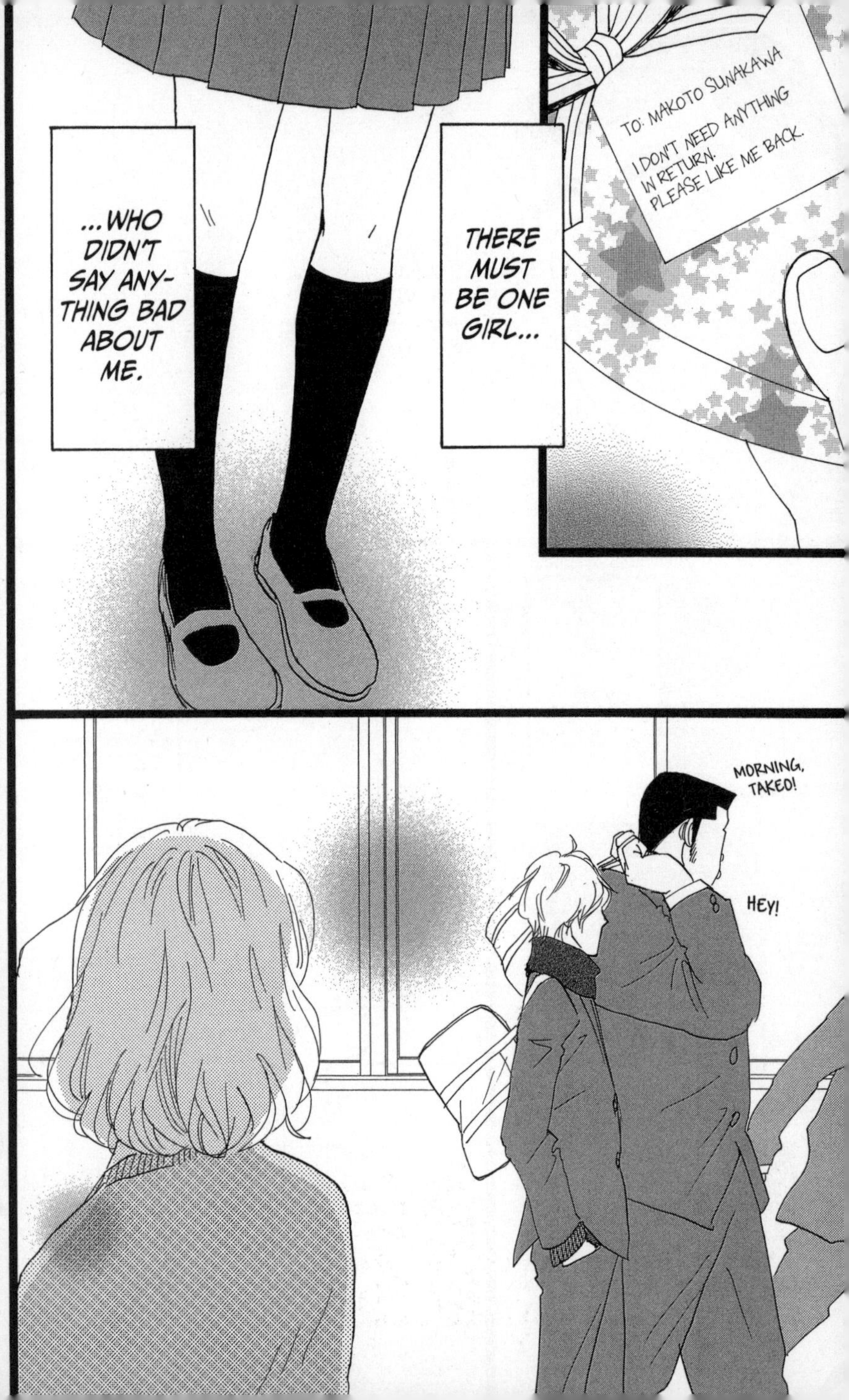
TO: MAKOTO SUNAKAWA
I DON'T NEED ANYTHING IN RETURN. PLEASE LIKE ME BACK.
THERE MUST BE ONE GIRL...
...WHO DIDN'T SAY ANY-THING BAD ABOUT ME.
MORNING, TAKEO!
HEY!

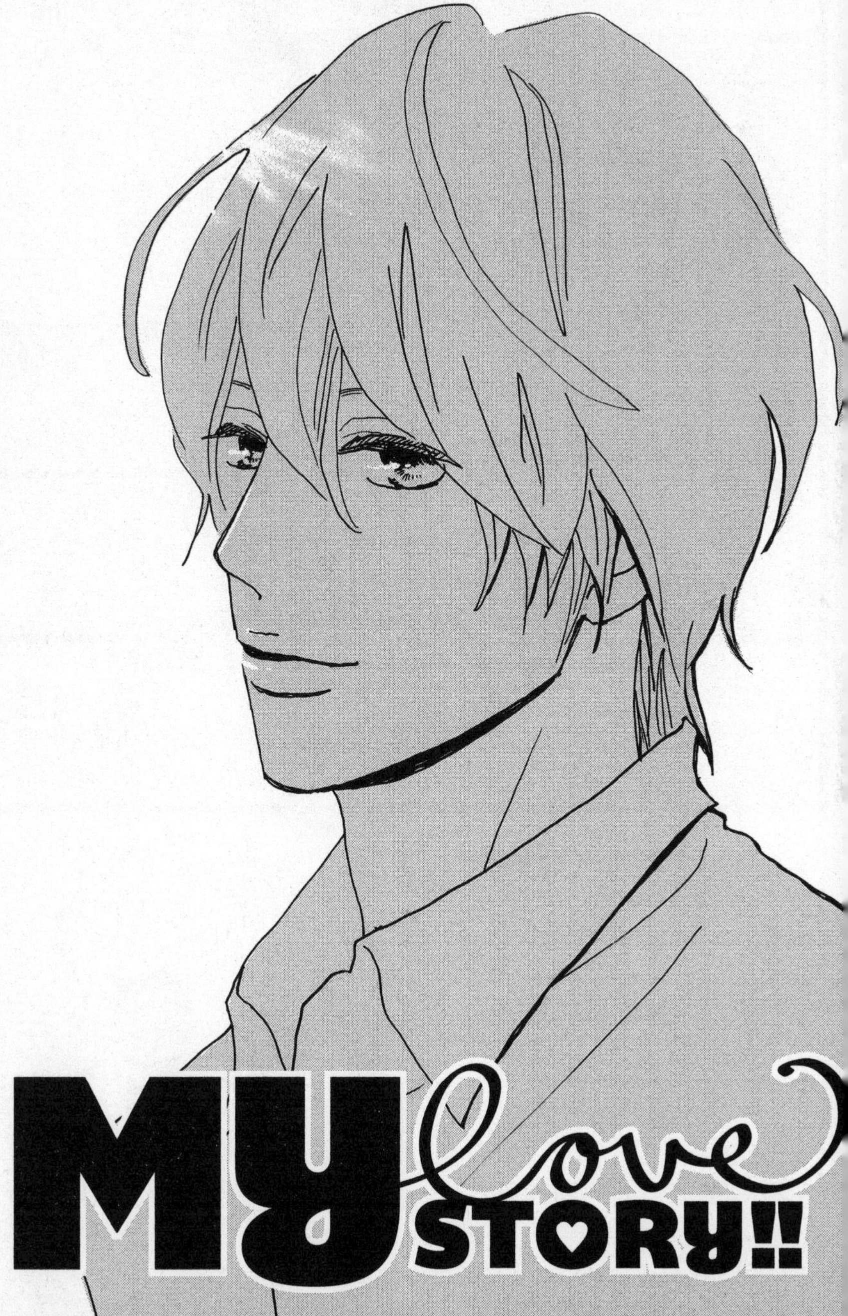
MY love STORY!!

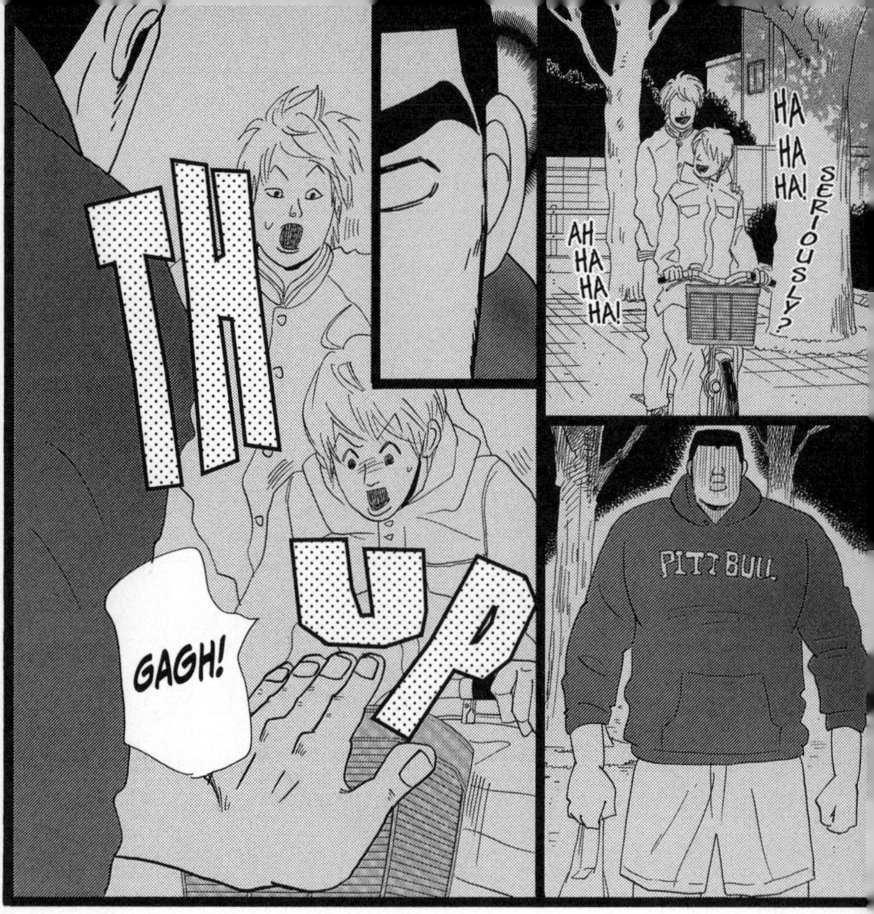
HA HA HA!
SERIOUSLY?
AH HA HA HA HA!
PITTBULL
THUP
GAGH!

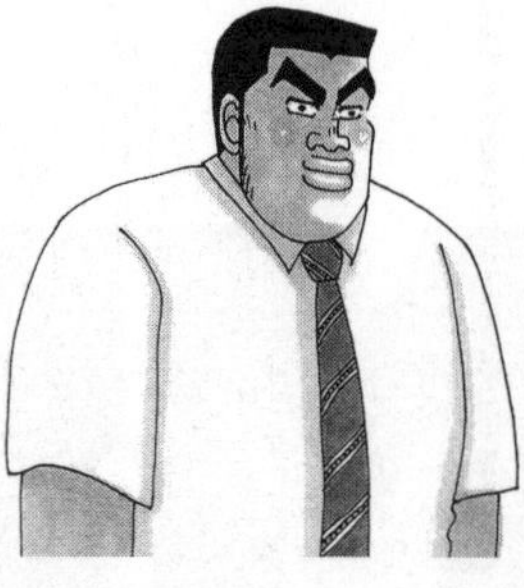

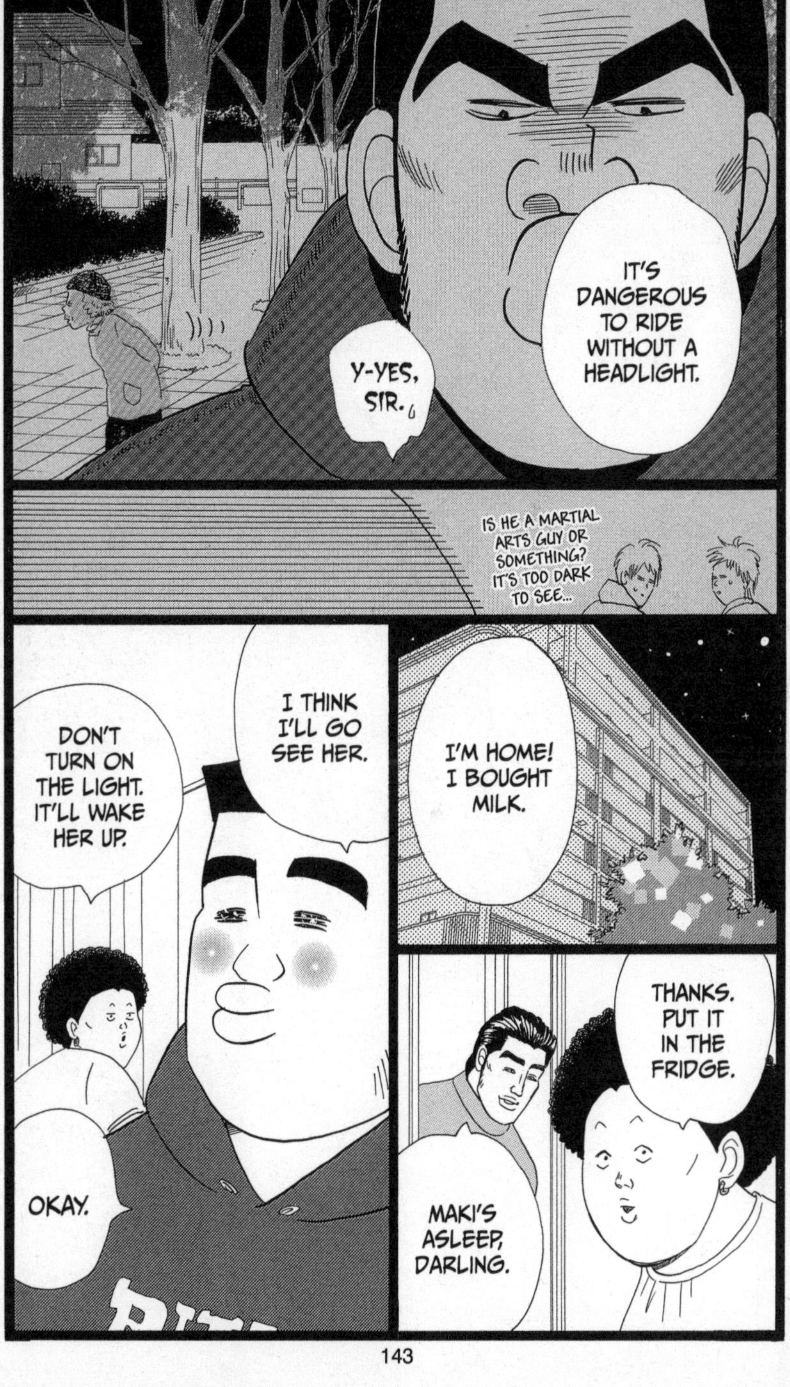
IT'S DANGEROUS TO RIDE WITHOUT A HEADLIGHT.
Y-YES, SIR.
IS HE A MARTIAL ARTS GUY OR SOMETHING? IT'S TOO DARK TO SEE...
I'M HOME! I BOUGHT MILK.
THANKS. PUT IT IN THE FRIDGE.
MAKI'S ASLEEP, DARLING.
I THINK I'LL GO SEE HER.
DON'T TURN ON THE LIGHT. IT'LL WAKE HER UP.
OKAY.

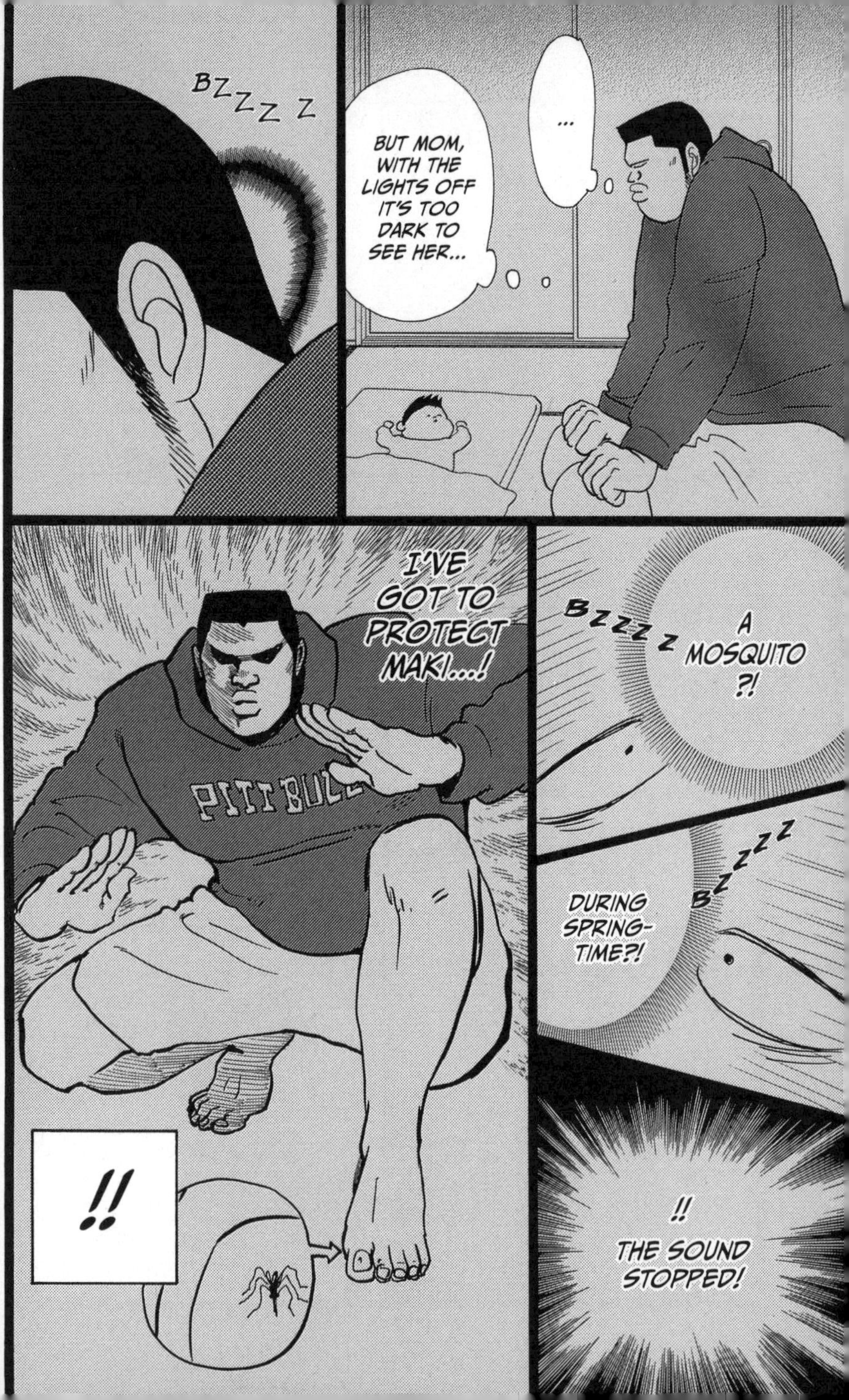
...
BUT MOM, WITH THE LIGHTS OFF IT'S TOO DARK TO SEE HER...
BZZZZ Z
A MOSQUITO?!
BZZZZ Z
BZZZZZ
DURING SPRING-TIME?!
!! THE SOUND STOPPED!
I'VE GOT TO PROTECT MAKI...!
PIT BULL
!!

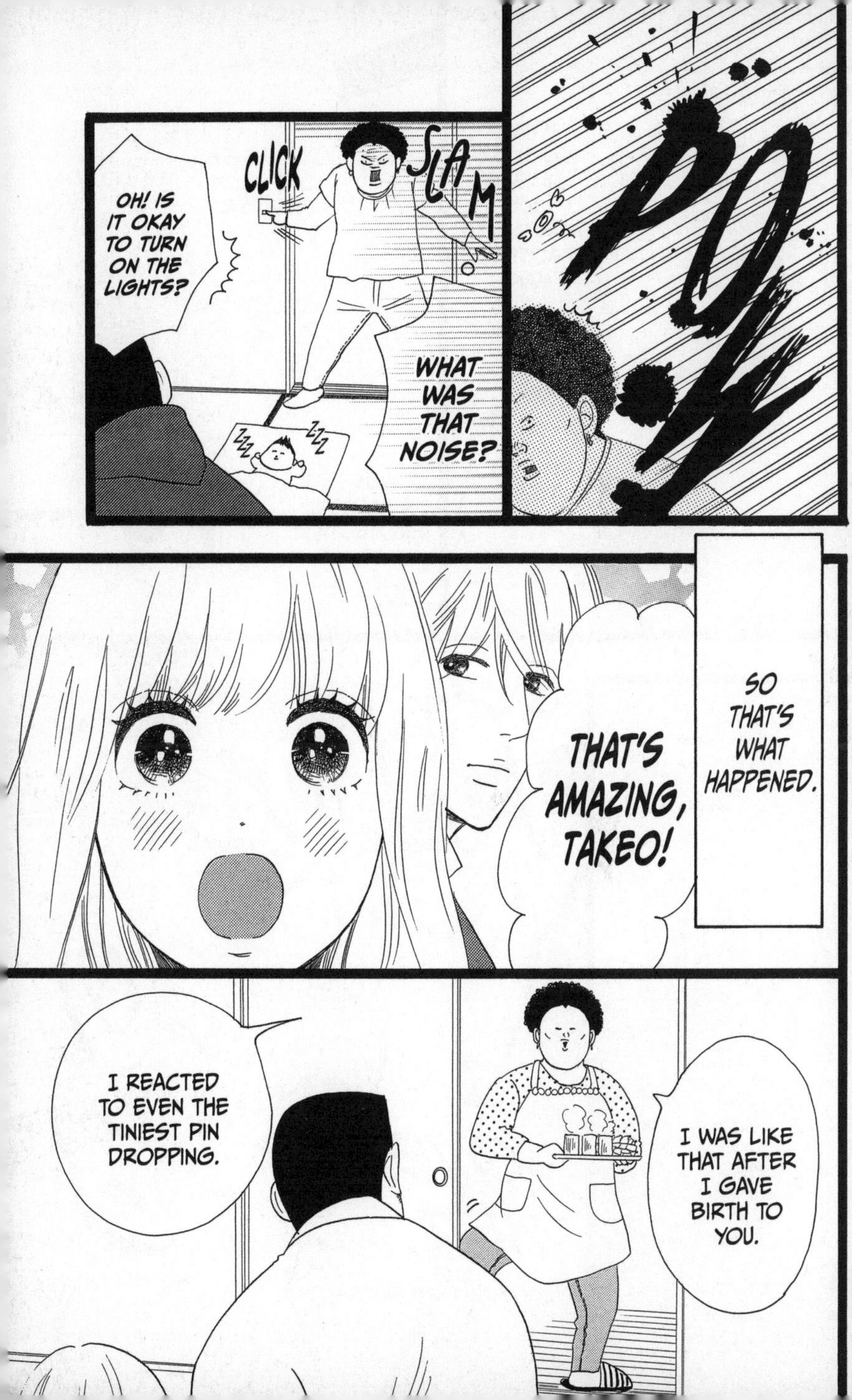
POW
SLAM
CLICK
OH! IS IT OKAY TO TURN ON THE LIGHTS?
WHAT WAS THAT NOISE?
SO THAT'S WHAT HAPPENED.
THAT'S AMAZING, TAKEO!
I WAS LIKE THAT AFTER I GAVE BIRTH TO YOU.
I REACTED TO EVEN THE TINIEST PIN DROPPING.

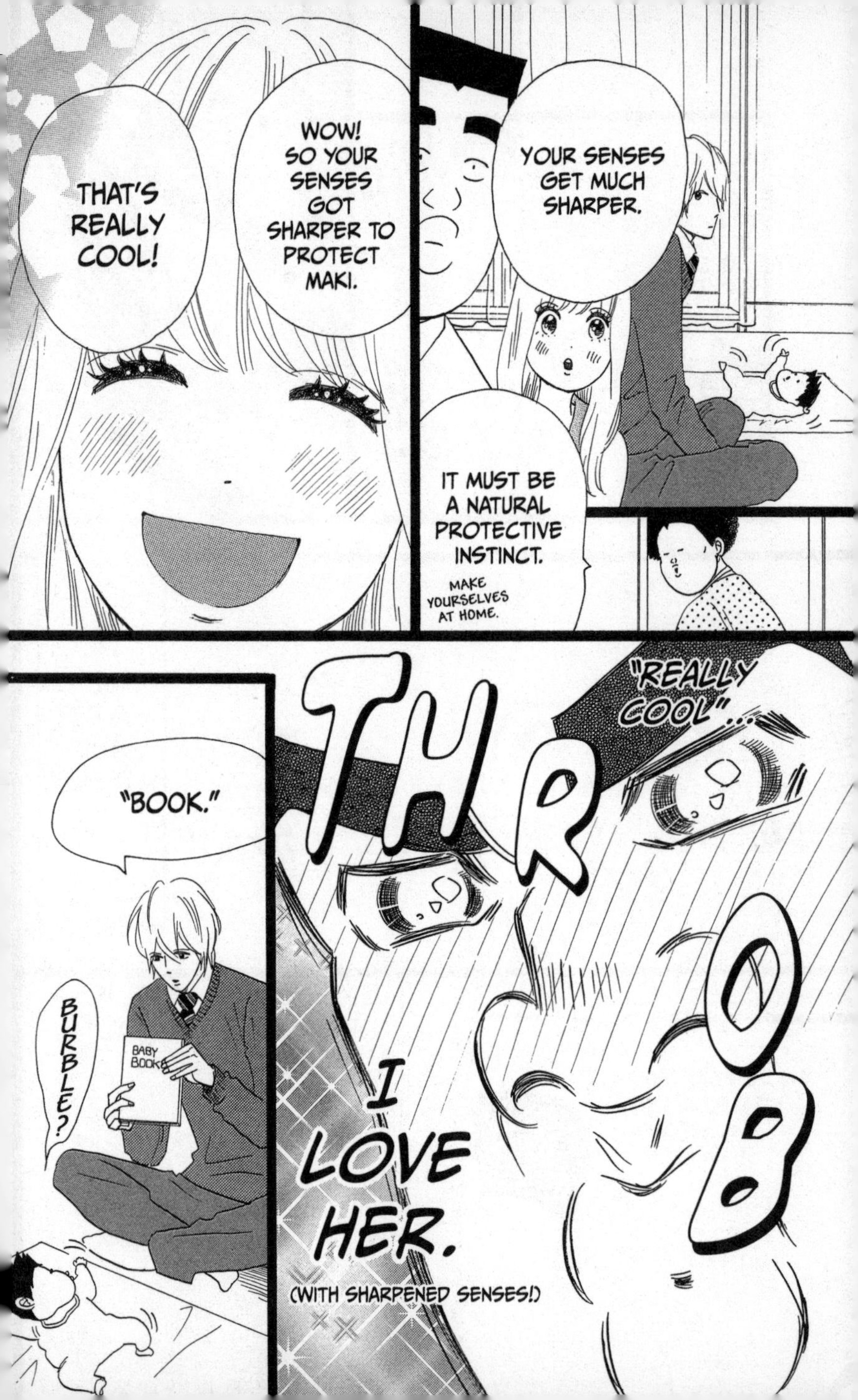
YOUR SENSES GET MUCH SHARPER.
IT MUST BE A NATURAL PROTECTIVE INSTINCT.
MAKE YOURSELVES AT HOME.
WOW! SO YOUR SENSES GOT SHARPER TO PROTECT MAKI.
THAT'S REALLY COOL!
"REALLY COOL"...
THROB
I LOVE HER.
(WITH SHARPENED SENSES!)
"BOOK."
BABY BOOK
BURBLE?

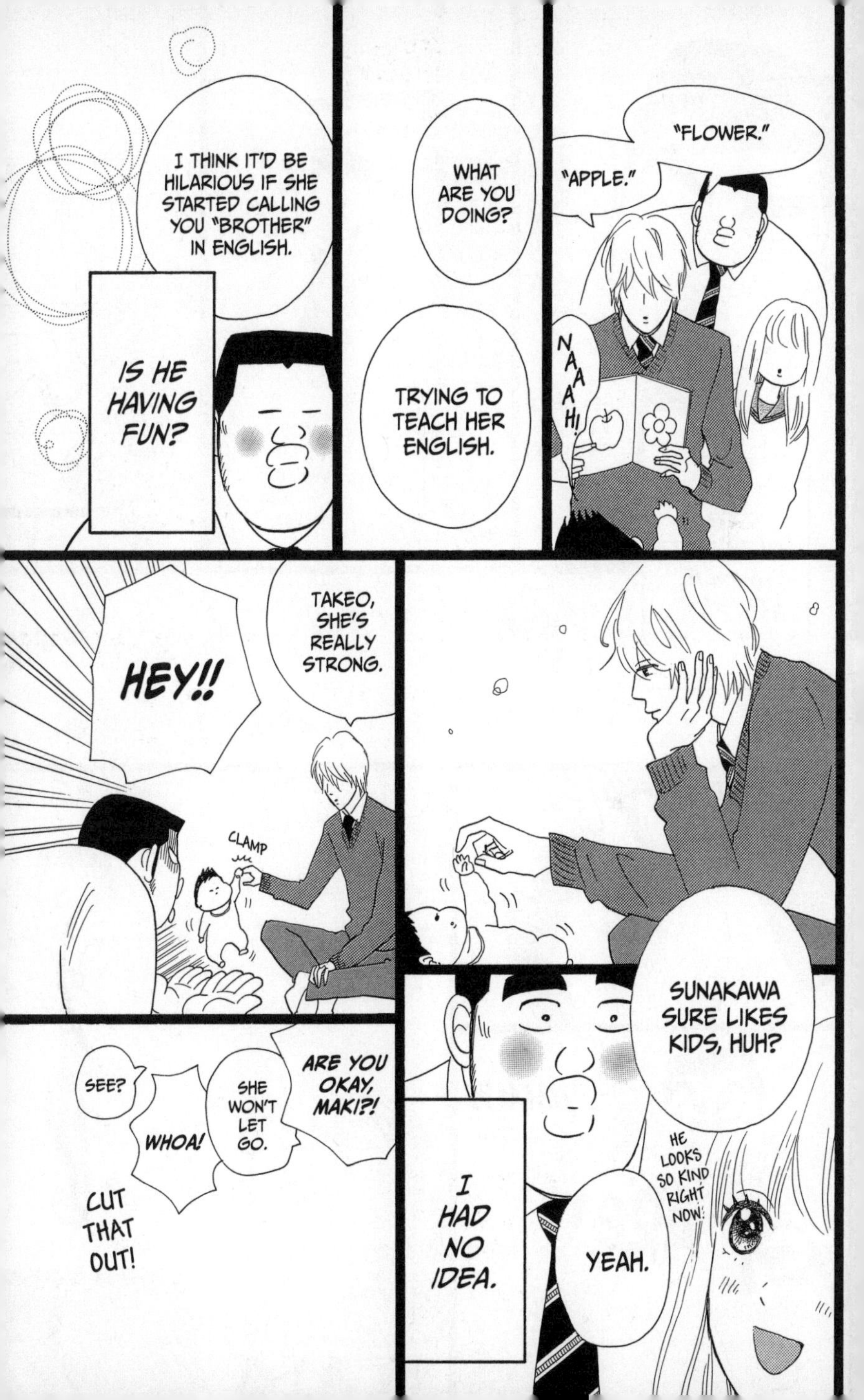
"FLOWER."
"APPLE."
NAAAAH!
WHAT ARE YOU DOING?
TRYING TO TEACH HER ENGLISH.
I THINK IT'D BE HILARIOUS IF SHE STARTED CALLING YOU "BROTHER" IN ENGLISH.
IS HE HAVING FUN?
TAKEO, SHE'S REALLY STRONG.
HEY!!
CLAMP
SUNAKAWA SURE LIKES KIDS, HUH?
HE LOOKS SO KIND RIGHT NOW!
YEAH.
I HAD NO IDEA.
ARE YOU OKAY, MAKI?!
SHE WON'T LET GO.
SEE?
WHOA!
CUT THAT OUT!

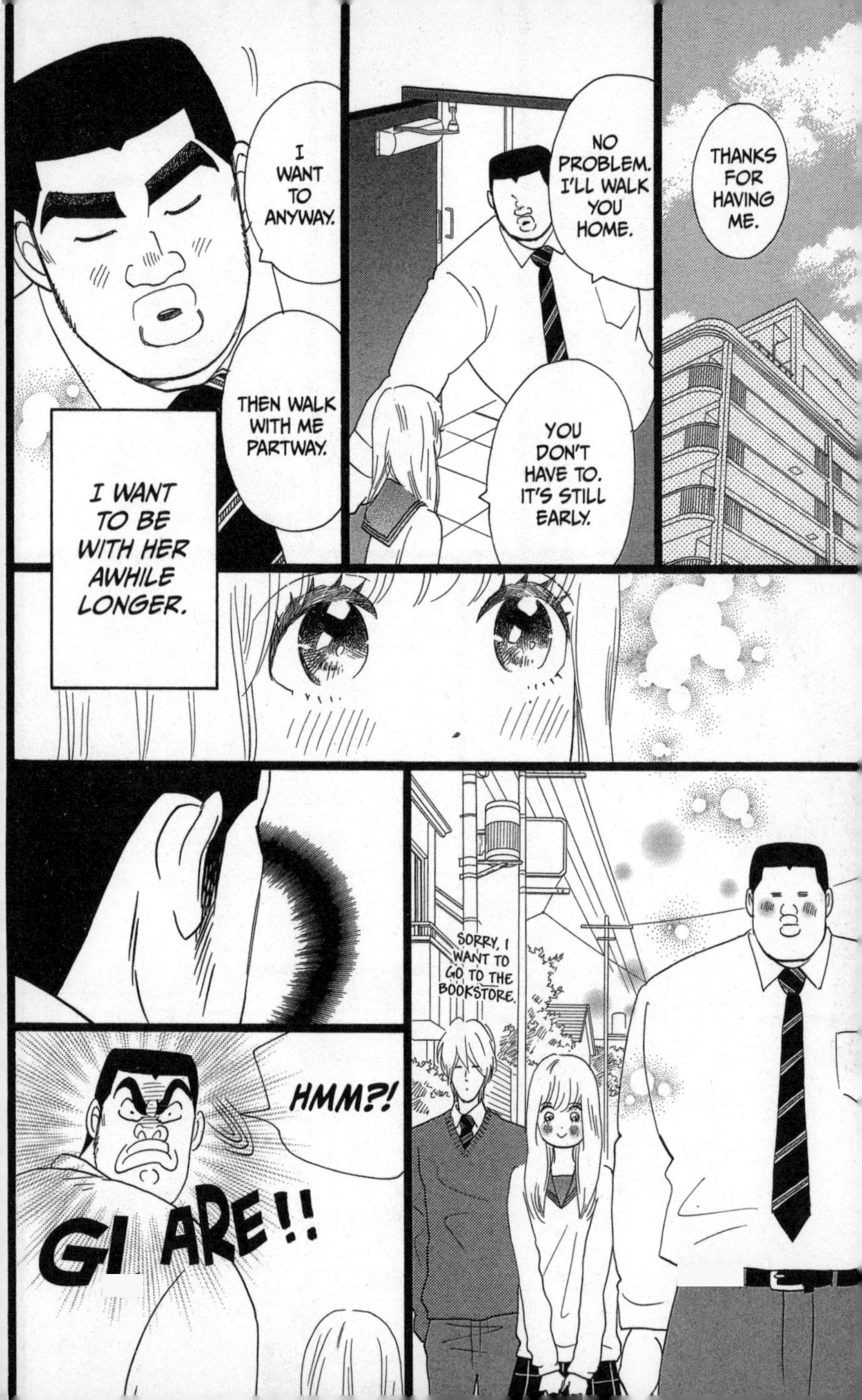
THANKS FOR HAVING ME.
NO PROBLEM. I'LL WALK YOU HOME.
YOU DON'T HAVE TO. IT'S STILL EARLY.
I WANT TO ANYWAY.
THEN WALK WITH ME PARTWAY.
I WANT TO BE WITH HER AWHILE LONGER.
SORRY, I WANT TO GO TO THE BOOKSTORE.
HMM?!
GLARE!!

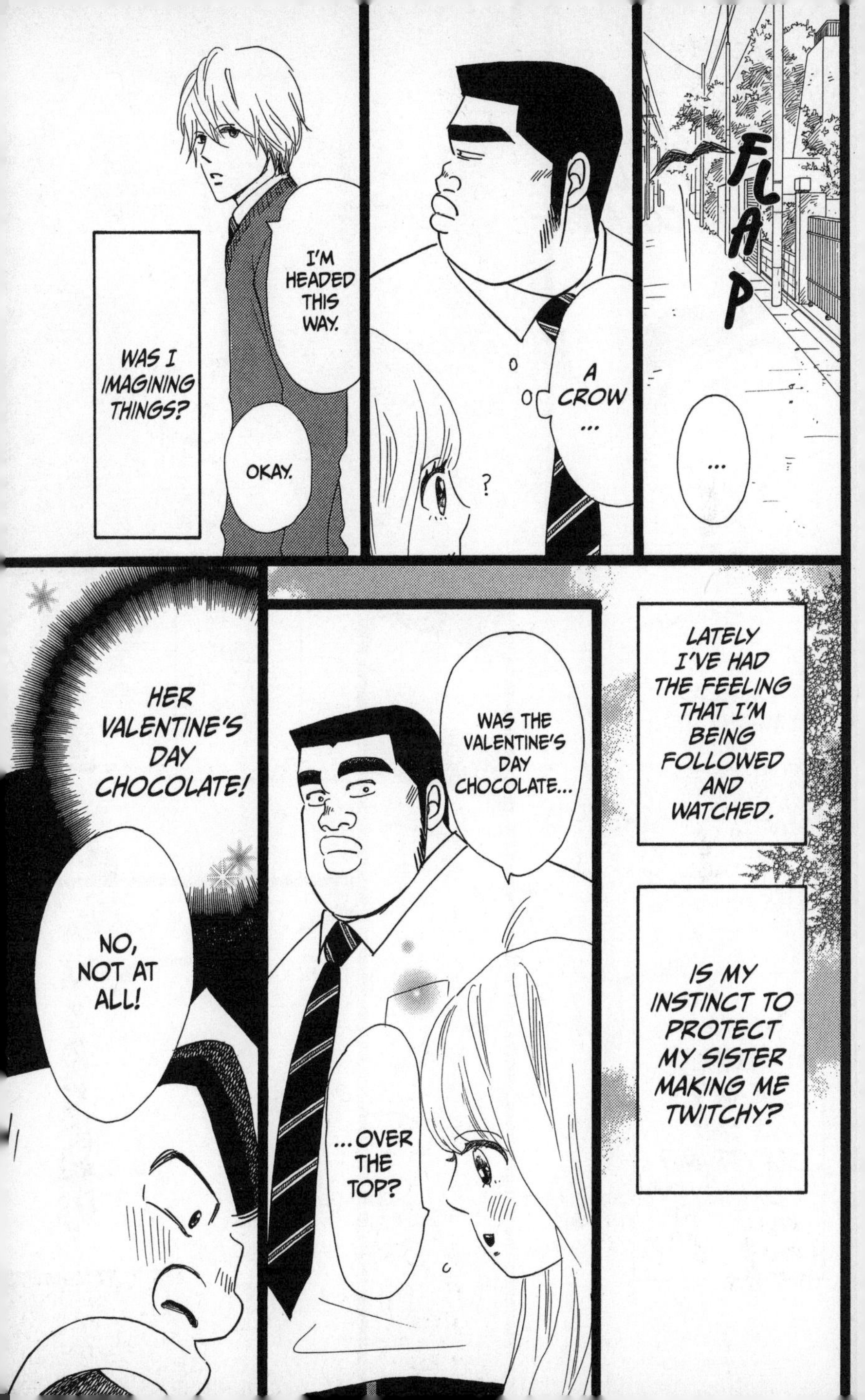
FLAP
...
A CROW ...
?
I'M HEADED THIS WAY.
OKAY.
WAS I IMAGINING THINGS?
LATELY I'VE HAD THE FEELING THAT I'M BEING FOLLOWED AND WATCHED.
IS MY INSTINCT TO PROTECT MY SISTER MAKING ME TWITCHY?
WAS THE VALENTINE'S DAY CHOCOLATE...
...OVER THE TOP?
HER VALENTINE'S DAY CHOCOLATE!
NO, NOT AT ALL!

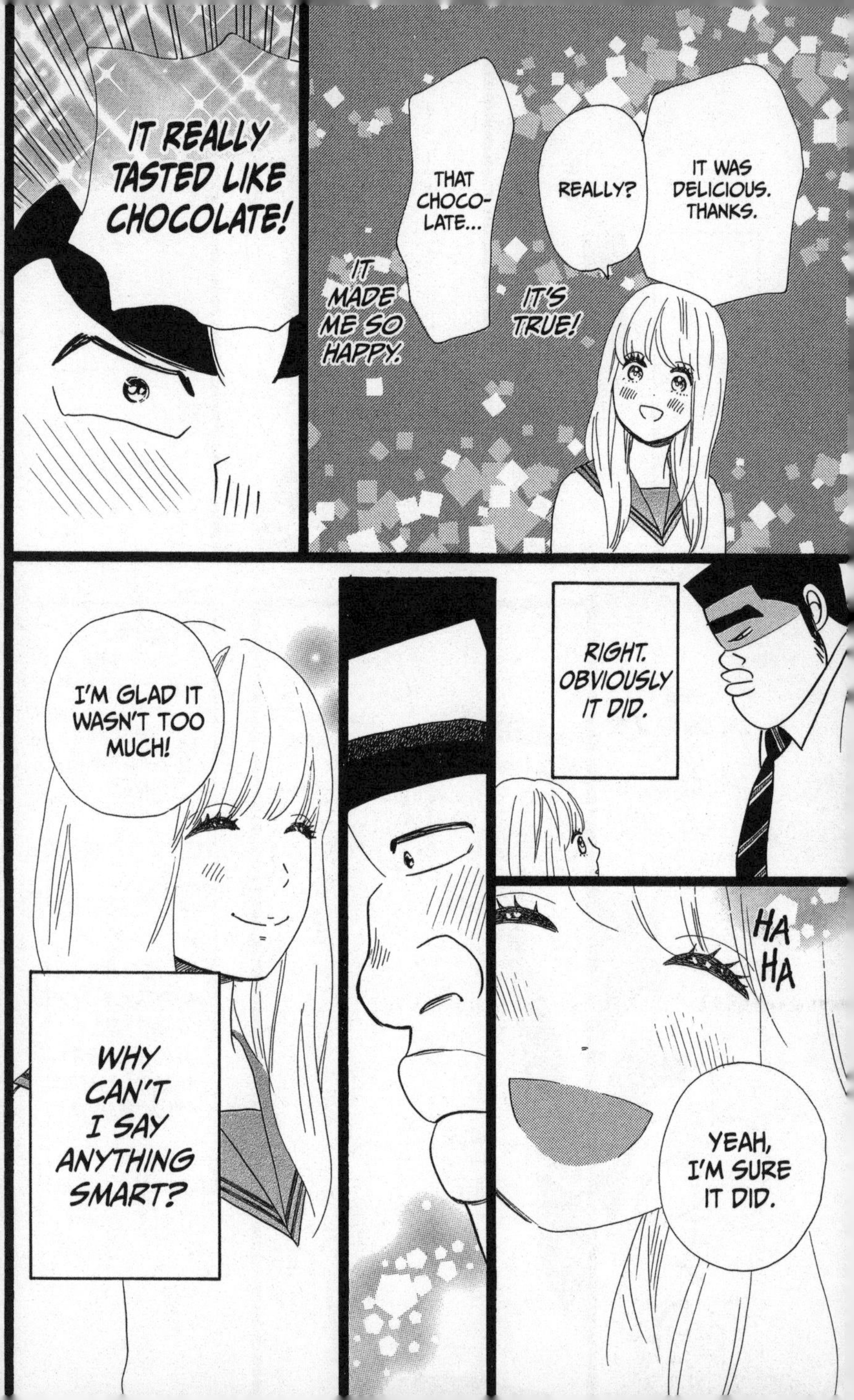
IT WAS DELICIOUS. THANKS.
REALLY?
THAT CHOCO-LATE...
IT'S TRUE!
IT MADE ME SO HAPPY.
IT REALLY TASTED LIKE CHOCOLATE!
RIGHT. OBVIOUSLY IT DID.
HA HA
YEAH, I'M SURE IT DID.
I'M GLAD IT WASN'T TOO MUCH!
WHY CAN'T I SAY ANYTHING SMART?

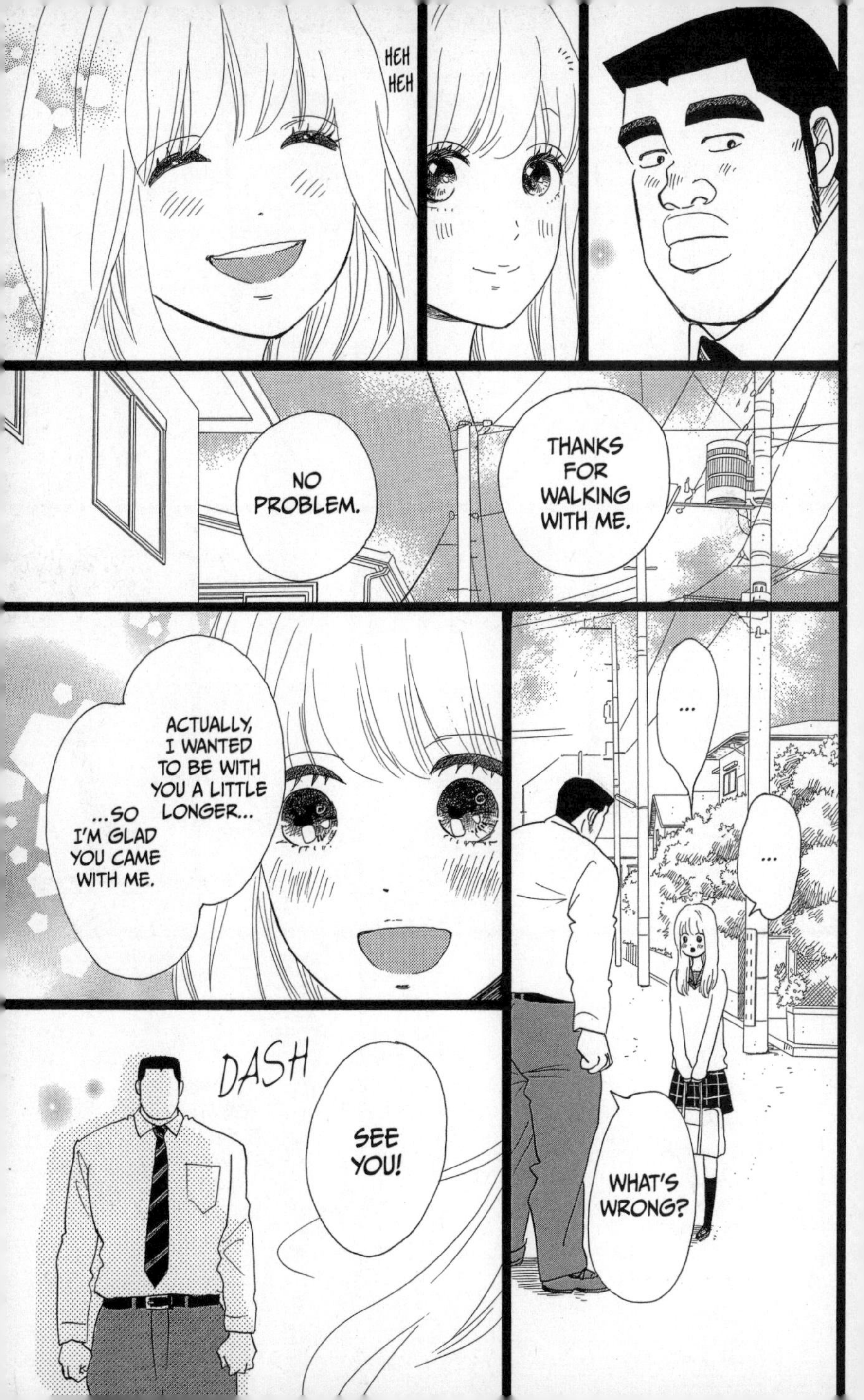
HEH HEH
THANKS FOR WALKING WITH ME.
NO PROBLEM.
...
...
WHAT'S WRONG?
ACTUALLY, I WANTED TO BE WITH YOU A LITTLE LONGER...
...SO I'M GLAD YOU CAME WITH ME.
SEE YOU!
DASH

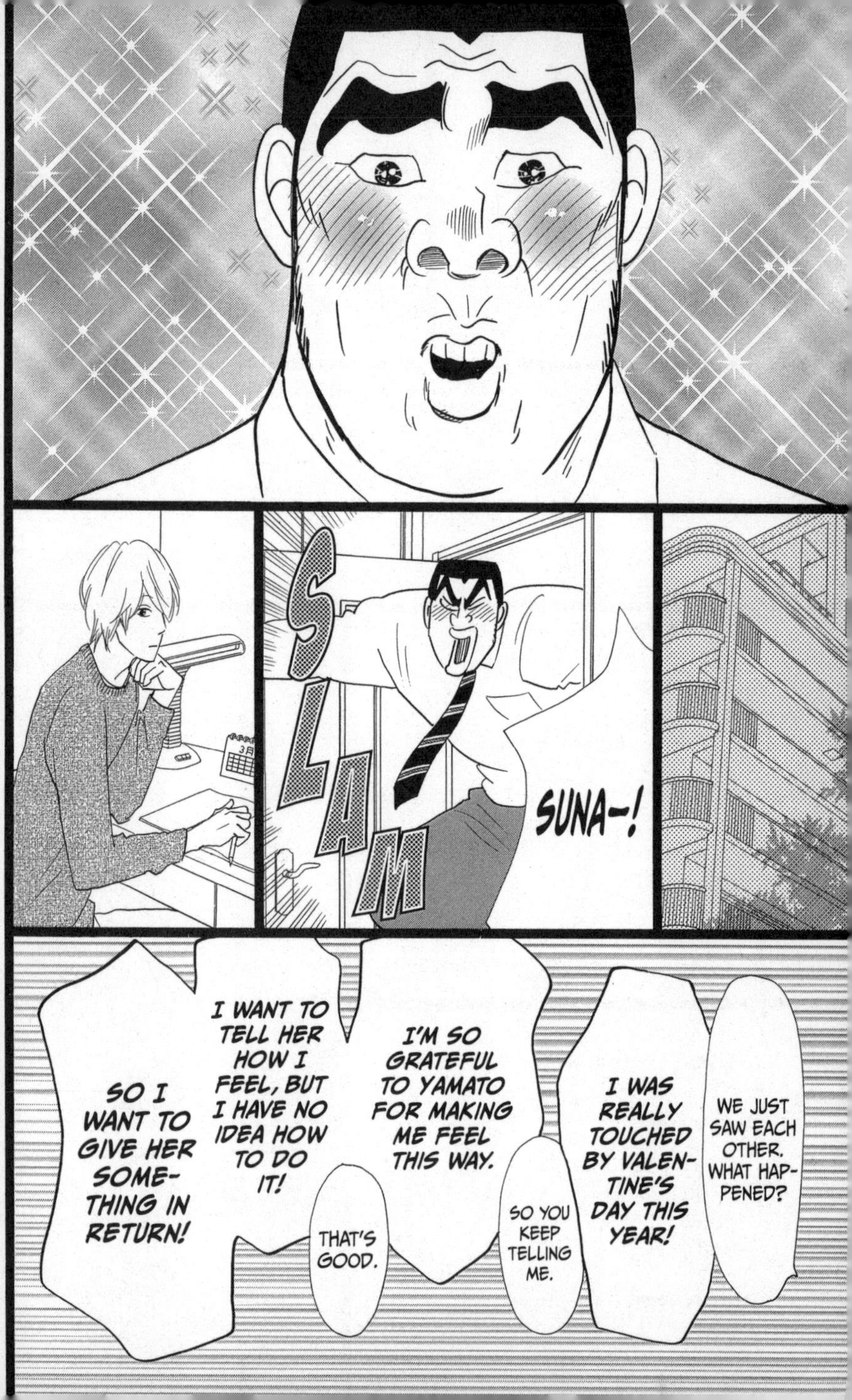
SLAM
SUNA-!
3月
WE JUST SAW EACH OTHER. WHAT HAPPENED?
I WAS REALLY TOUCHED BY VALENTINE'S DAY THIS YEAR!
SO YOU KEEP TELLING ME.
I'M SO GRATEFUL TO YAMATO FOR MAKING ME FEEL THIS WAY.
THAT'S GOOD.
I WANT TO TELL HER HOW I FEEL, BUT I HAVE NO IDEA HOW TO DO IT!
SO I WANT TO GIVE HER SOMETHING IN RETURN!

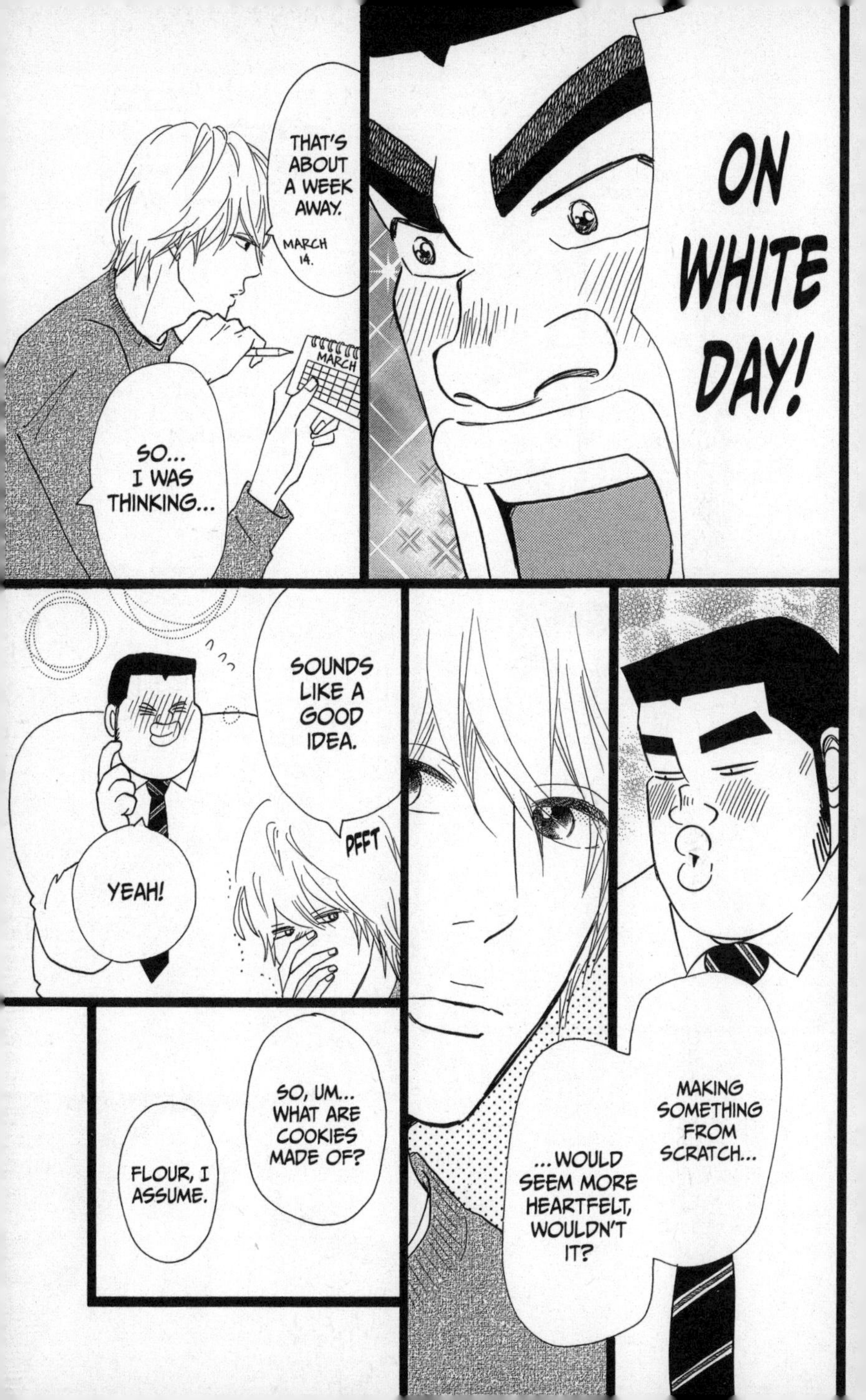
ON WHITE DAY!
THAT'S ABOUT A WEEK AWAY.
MARCH 14.
MARCH
SO... I WAS THINKING...
MAKING SOMETHING FROM SCRATCH...
...WOULD SEEM MORE HEARTFELT, WOULDN'T IT?
SOUNDS LIKE A GOOD IDEA.
PFFT
YEAH!
SO, UM... WHAT ARE COOKIES MADE OF?
FLOUR, I ASSUME.

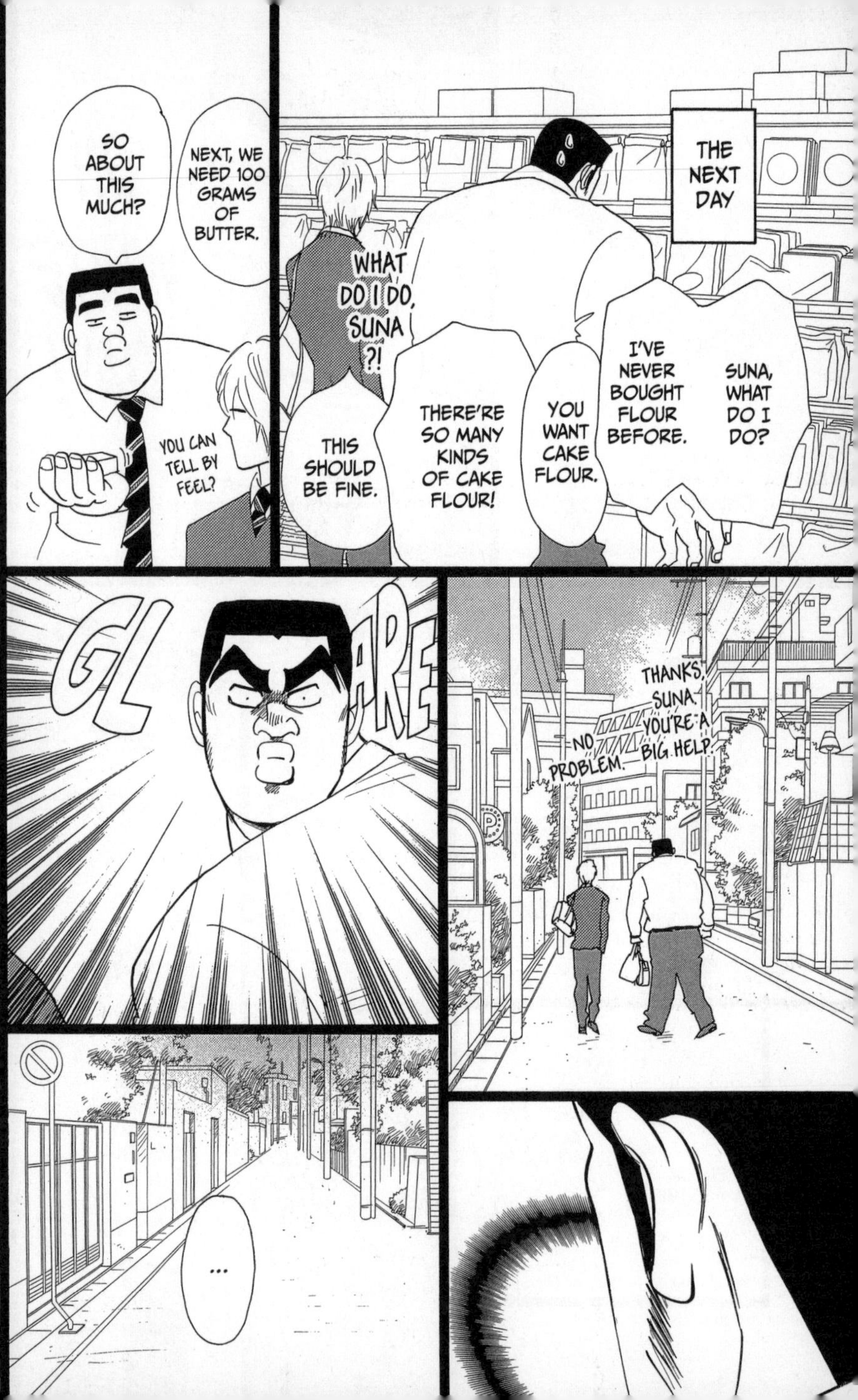
THE NEXT DAY
SUNA, WHAT DO I DO?
I'VE NEVER BOUGHT FLOUR BEFORE.
YOU WANT CAKE FLOUR.
THERE'RE SO MANY KINDS OF CAKE FLOUR!
THIS SHOULD BE FINE.
WHAT DO I DO, SUNA ?!
NEXT, WE NEED 100 GRAMS OF BUTTER.
SO ABOUT THIS MUCH?
YOU CAN TELL BY FEEL?
THANKS, SUNA. YOU'RE A BIG HELP.
NO PROBLEM.
GLARE
...

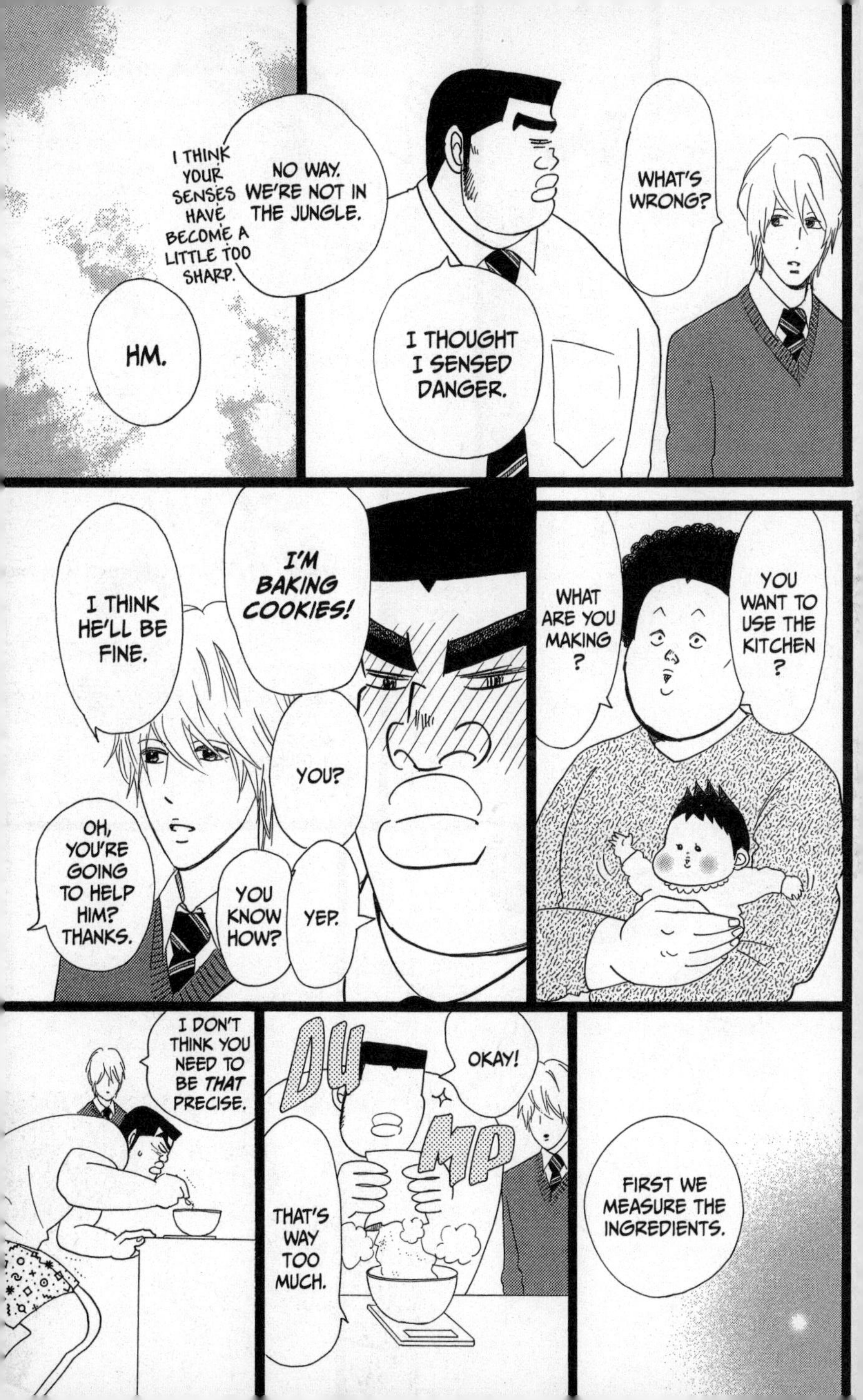
WHAT'S WRONG?
I THOUGHT I SENSED DANGER.
NO WAY. WE'RE NOT IN THE JUNGLE.
I THINK YOUR SENSES HAVE BECOME A LITTLE TOO SHARP.
HM.
YOU WANT TO USE THE KITCHEN?
WHAT ARE YOU MAKING?
I'M BAKING COOKIES!
YOU?
YEP.
YOU KNOW HOW?
I THINK HE'LL BE FINE.
OH, YOU'RE GOING TO HELP HIM? THANKS.
FIRST WE MEASURE THE INGREDIENTS.
OKAY!
DUMP
THAT'S WAY TOO MUCH.
I DON'T THINK YOU NEED TO BE *THAT* PRECISE.

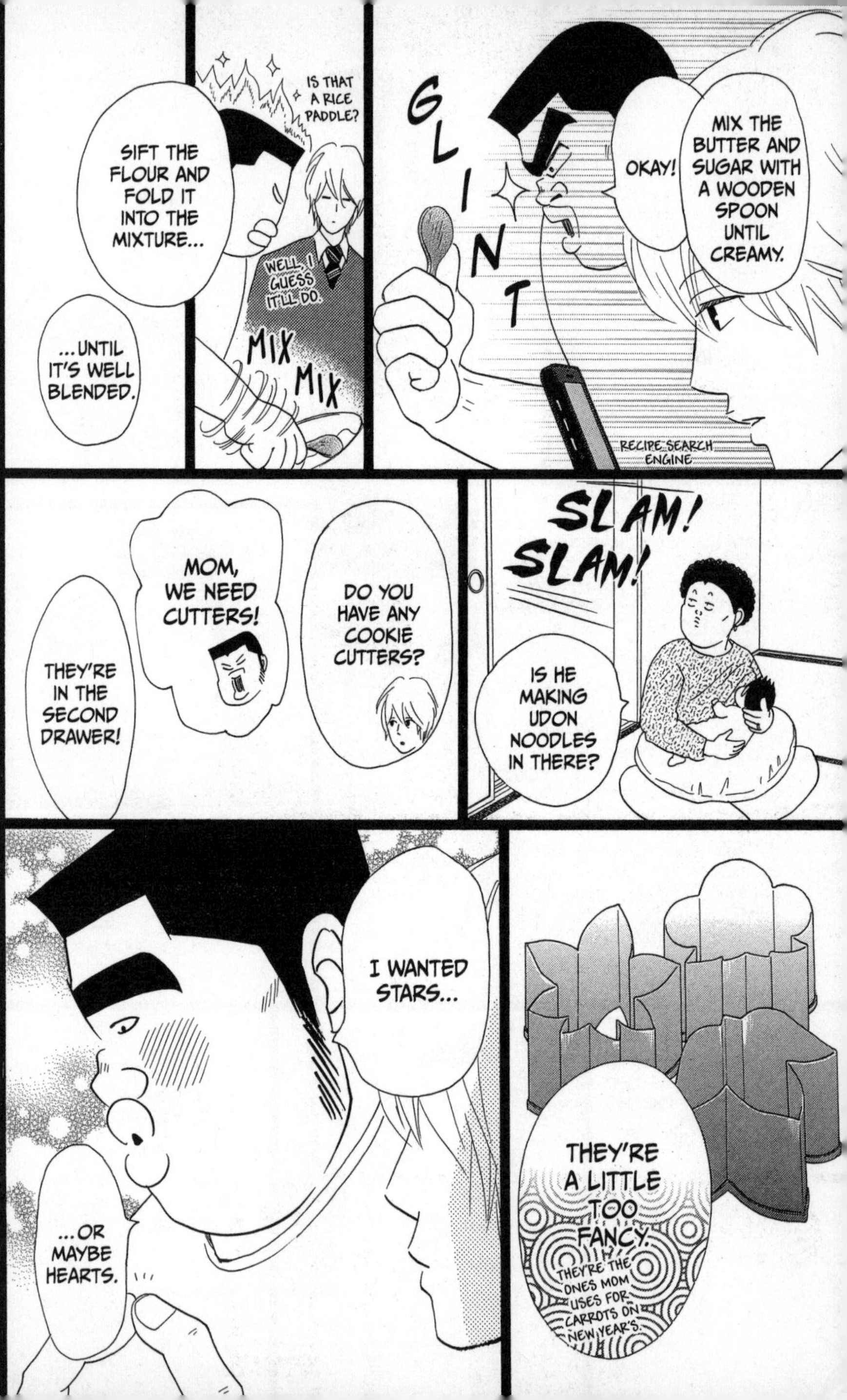
MIX THE BUTTER AND SUGAR WITH A WOODEN SPOON UNTIL CREAMY.
OKAY!
GLINT
RECIPE SEARCH ENGINE
IS THAT A RICE PADDLE?
WELL, I GUESS IT'LL DO.
MIX MIX
SIFT THE FLOUR AND FOLD IT INTO THE MIXTURE...
...UNTIL IT'S WELL BLENDED.
SLAM! SLAM!
IS HE MAKING UDON NOODLES IN THERE?
DO YOU HAVE ANY COOKIE CUTTERS?
MOM, WE NEED CUTTERS!
THEY'RE IN THE SECOND DRAWER!
THEY'RE A LITTLE TOO FANCY.
THEY'RE THE ONES MOM USES FOR CARROTS ON NEW YEAR'S.
I WANTED STARS...
...OR MAYBE HEARTS.

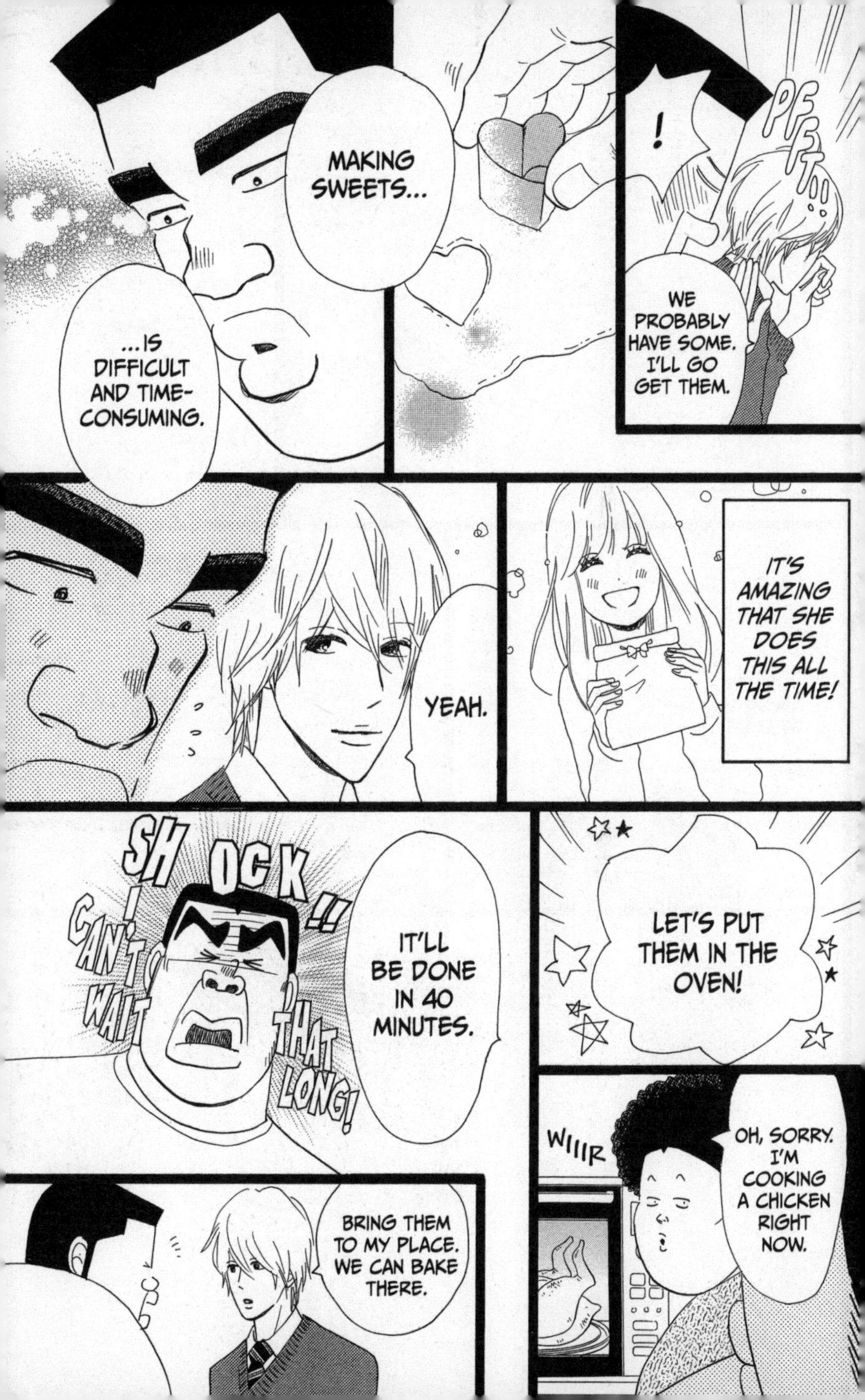
!
PFFT!!
WE PROBABLY HAVE SOME. I'LL GO GET THEM.
MAKING SWEETS...
...IS DIFFICULT AND TIME-CONSUMING.
IT'S AMAZING THAT SHE DOES THIS ALL THE TIME!
YEAH.
LET'S PUT THEM IN THE OVEN!
WIIIR
OH, SORRY. I'M COOKING A CHICKEN RIGHT NOW.
IT'LL BE DONE IN 40 MINUTES.
SHOCK!!
I CAN'T WAIT THAT LONG!
BRING THEM TO MY PLACE. WE CAN BAKE THERE.

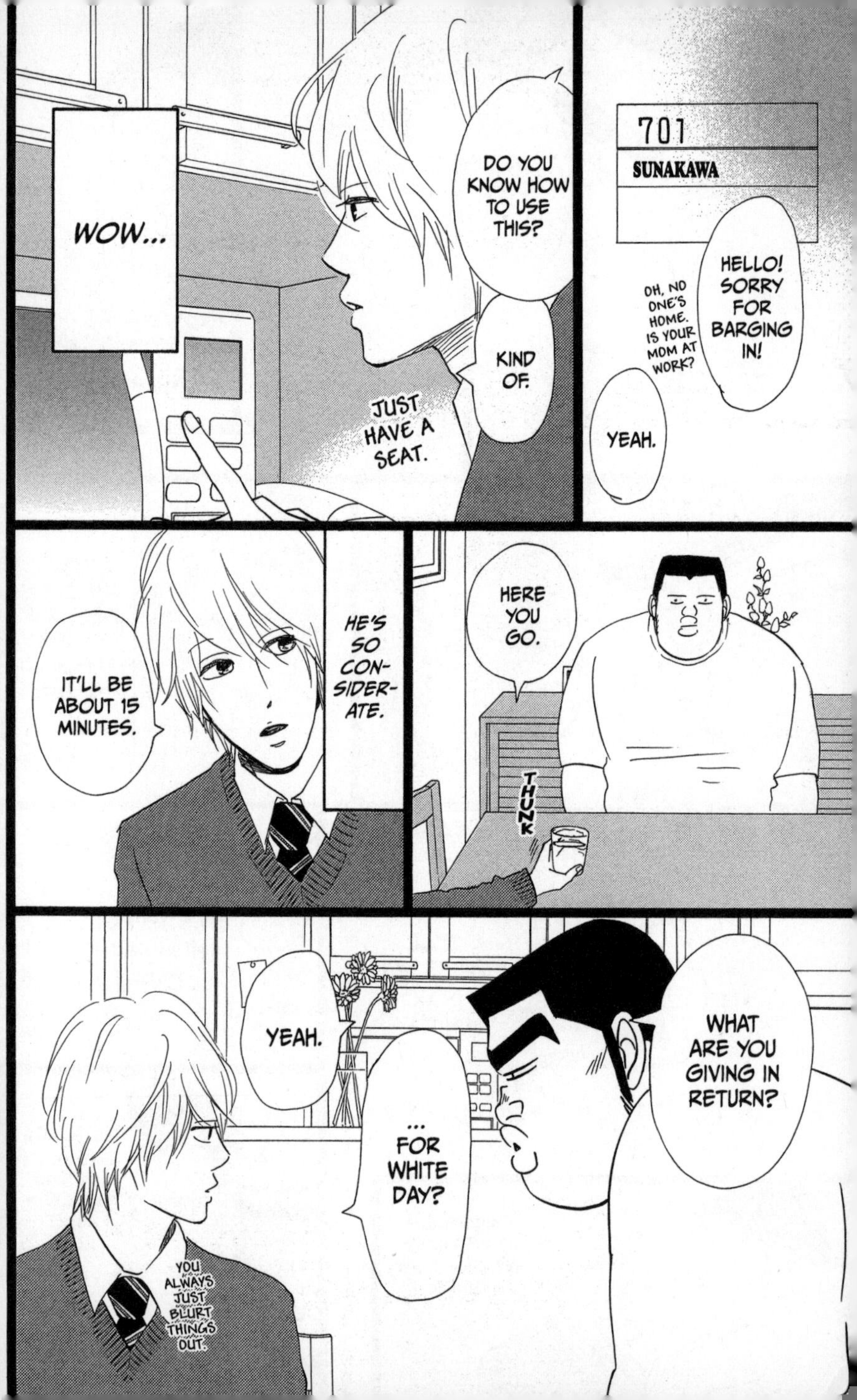
701
SUNAKAWA
HELLO! SORRY FOR BARGING IN!
OH, NO ONE'S HOME. IS YOUR MOM AT WORK?
YEAH.
DO YOU KNOW HOW TO USE THIS?
KIND OF.
JUST HAVE A SEAT.
WOW...
HERE YOU GO.
THUNK
HE'S SO CON-SIDER-ATE.
IT'LL BE ABOUT 15 MINUTES.
WHAT ARE YOU GIVING IN RETURN?
...FOR WHITE DAY?
YEAH.
YOU ALWAYS JUST BLURT THINGS OUT.

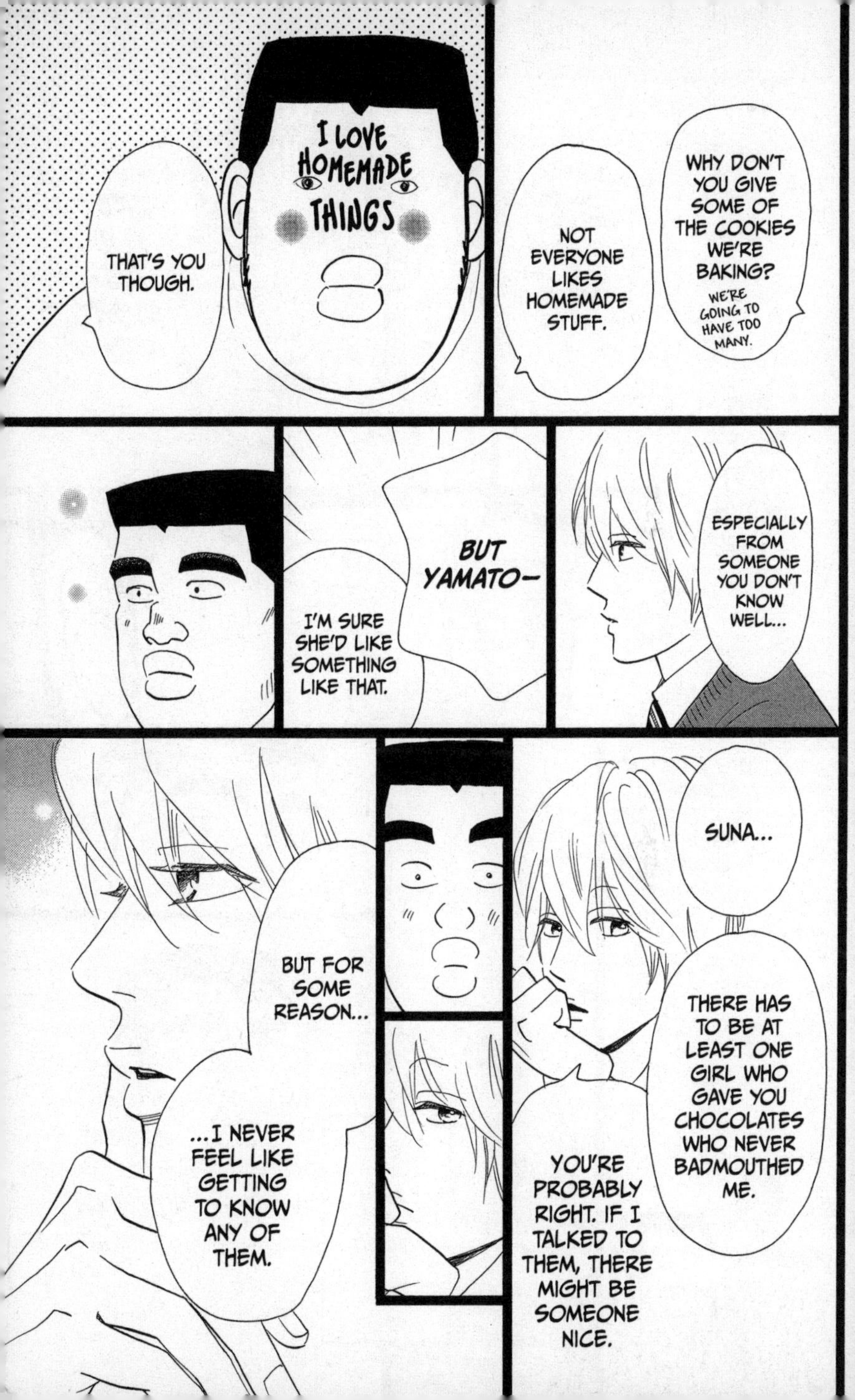
WHY DON'T YOU GIVE SOME OF THE COOKIES WE'RE BAKING?
WE'RE GOING TO HAVE TOO MANY.
NOT EVERYONE LIKES HOMEMADE STUFF.
I LOVE HOMEMADE THINGS
THAT'S YOU THOUGH.
ESPECIALLY FROM SOMEONE YOU DON'T KNOW WELL...
BUT YAMATO—
I'M SURE SHE'D LIKE SOMETHING LIKE THAT.
SUNA...
THERE HAS TO BE AT LEAST ONE GIRL WHO GAVE YOU CHOCOLATES WHO NEVER BADMOUTHED ME.
YOU'RE PROBABLY RIGHT. IF I TALKED TO THEM, THERE MIGHT BE SOMEONE NICE.
BUT FOR SOME REASON...
...I NEVER FEEL LIKE GETTING TO KNOW ANY OF THEM.

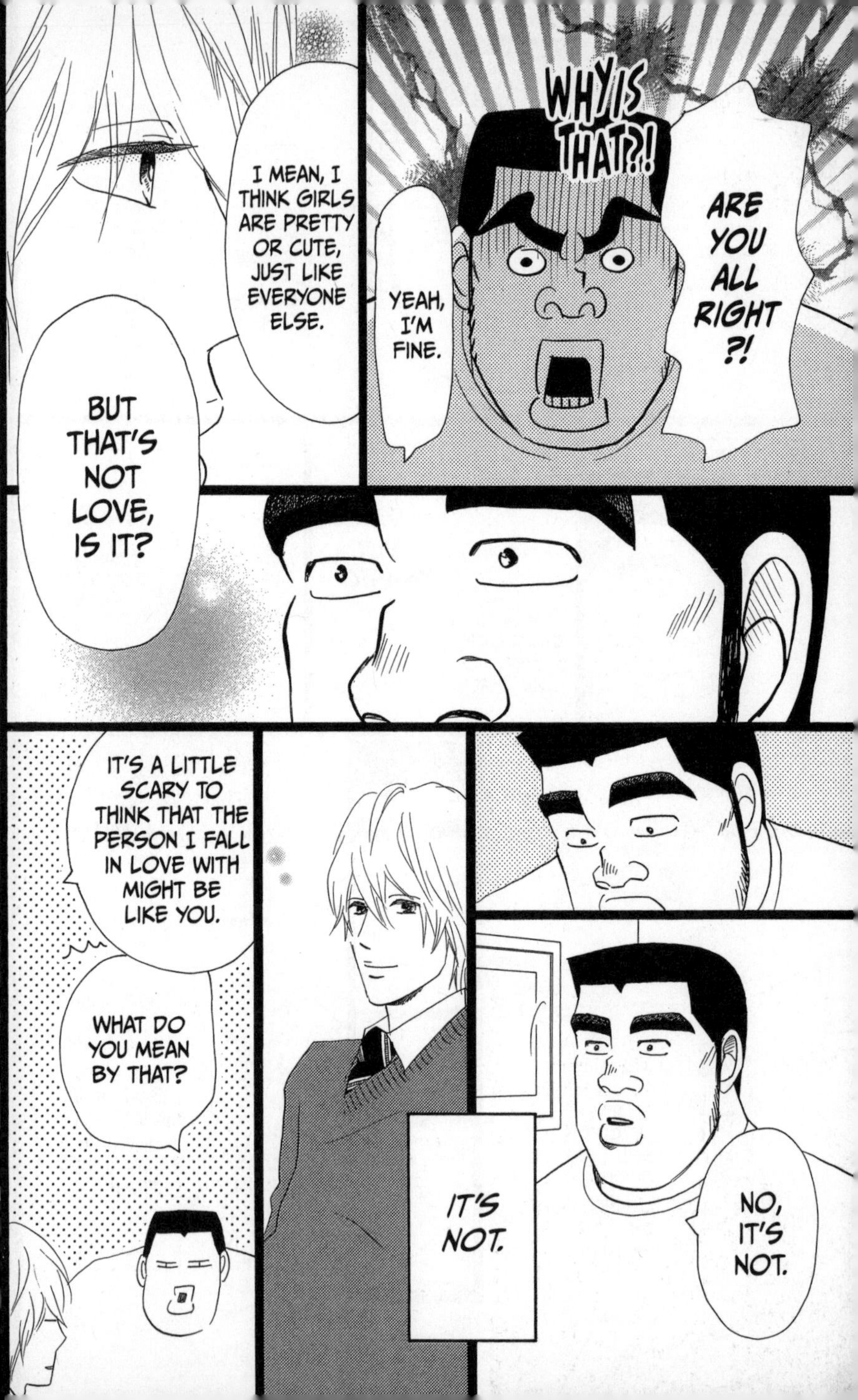
WHY IS THAT?!
ARE YOU ALL RIGHT?!
YEAH, I'M FINE.
I MEAN, I THINK GIRLS ARE PRETTY OR CUTE, JUST LIKE EVERYONE ELSE.
BUT THAT'S NOT LOVE, IS IT?
NO, IT'S NOT.
IT'S NOT.
IT'S A LITTLE SCARY TO THINK THAT THE PERSON I FALL IN LOVE WITH MIGHT BE LIKE YOU.
WHAT DO YOU MEAN BY THAT?

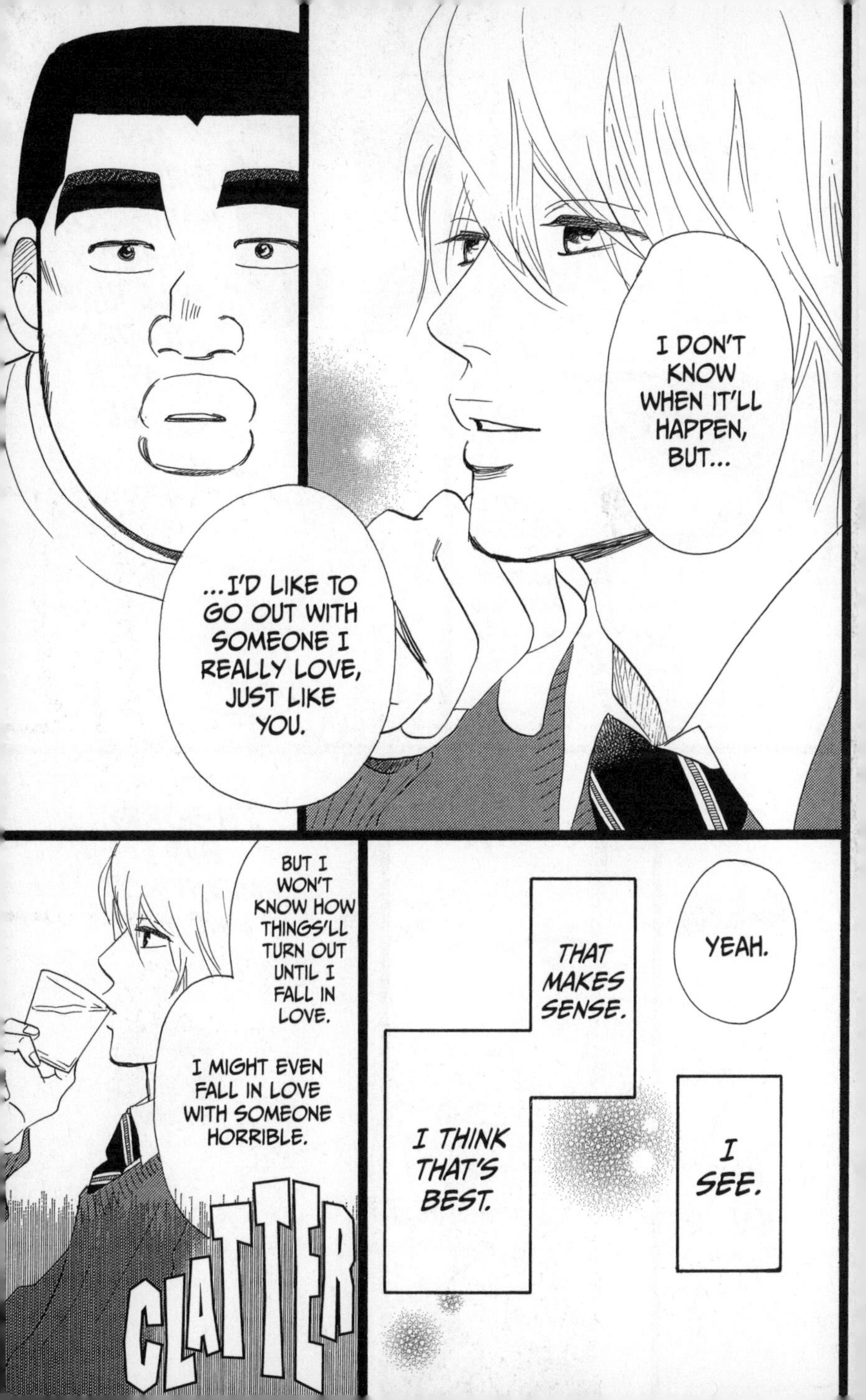
I DON'T KNOW WHEN IT'LL HAPPEN, BUT...
...I'D LIKE TO GO OUT WITH SOMEONE I REALLY LOVE, JUST LIKE YOU.
YEAH.
THAT MAKES SENSE.
I SEE.
I THINK THAT'S BEST.
BUT I WON'T KNOW HOW THINGS'LL TURN OUT UNTIL I FALL IN LOVE.
I MIGHT EVEN FALL IN LOVE WITH SOMEONE HORRIBLE.
CLATTER

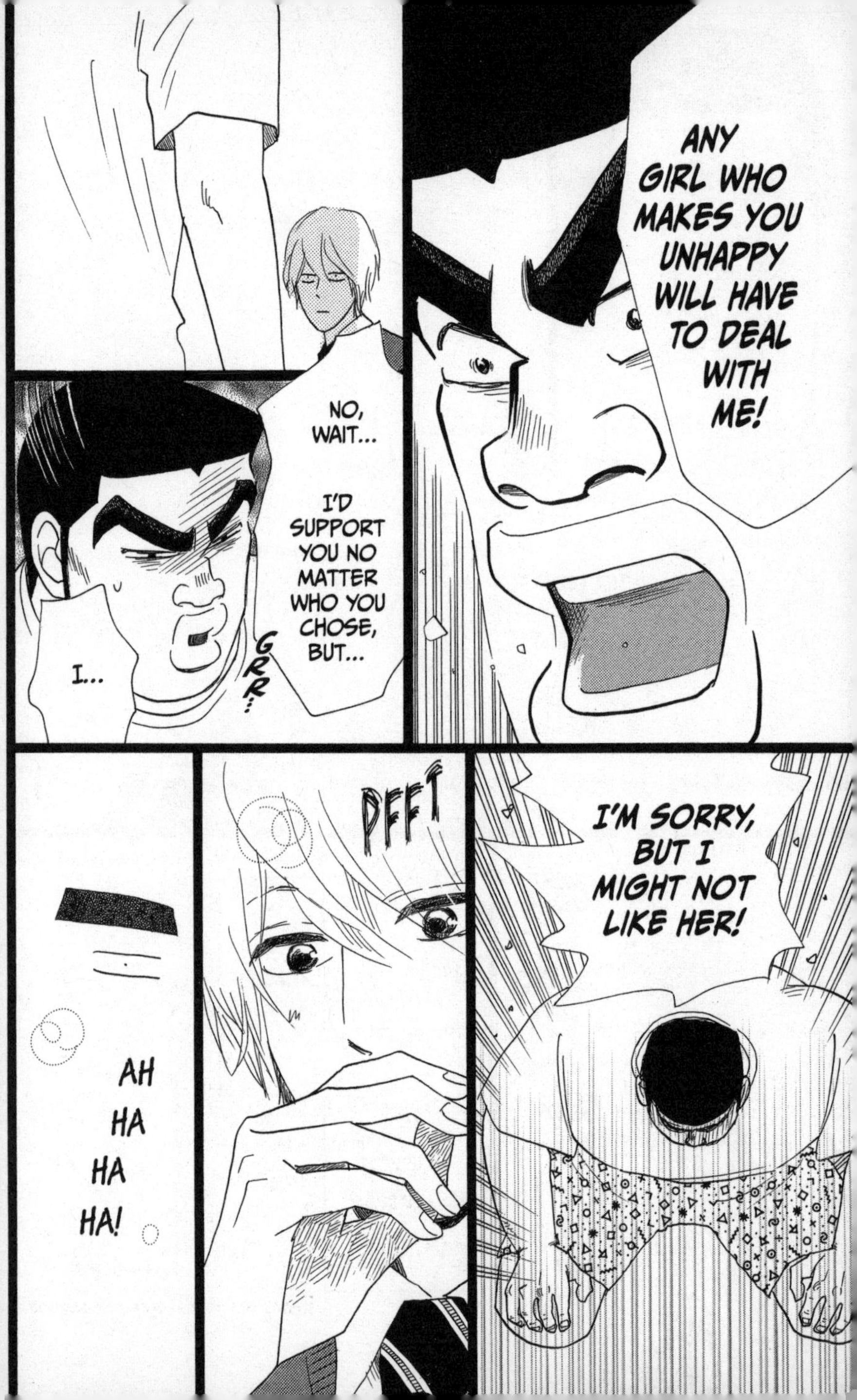
ANY GIRL WHO MAKES YOU UNHAPPY WILL HAVE TO DEAL WITH ME!
NO, WAIT...
I'D SUPPORT YOU NO MATTER WHO YOU CHOSE, BUT...
GRR...
I...
I'M SORRY, BUT I MIGHT NOT LIKE HER!
PFFT
AH HA HA HA!

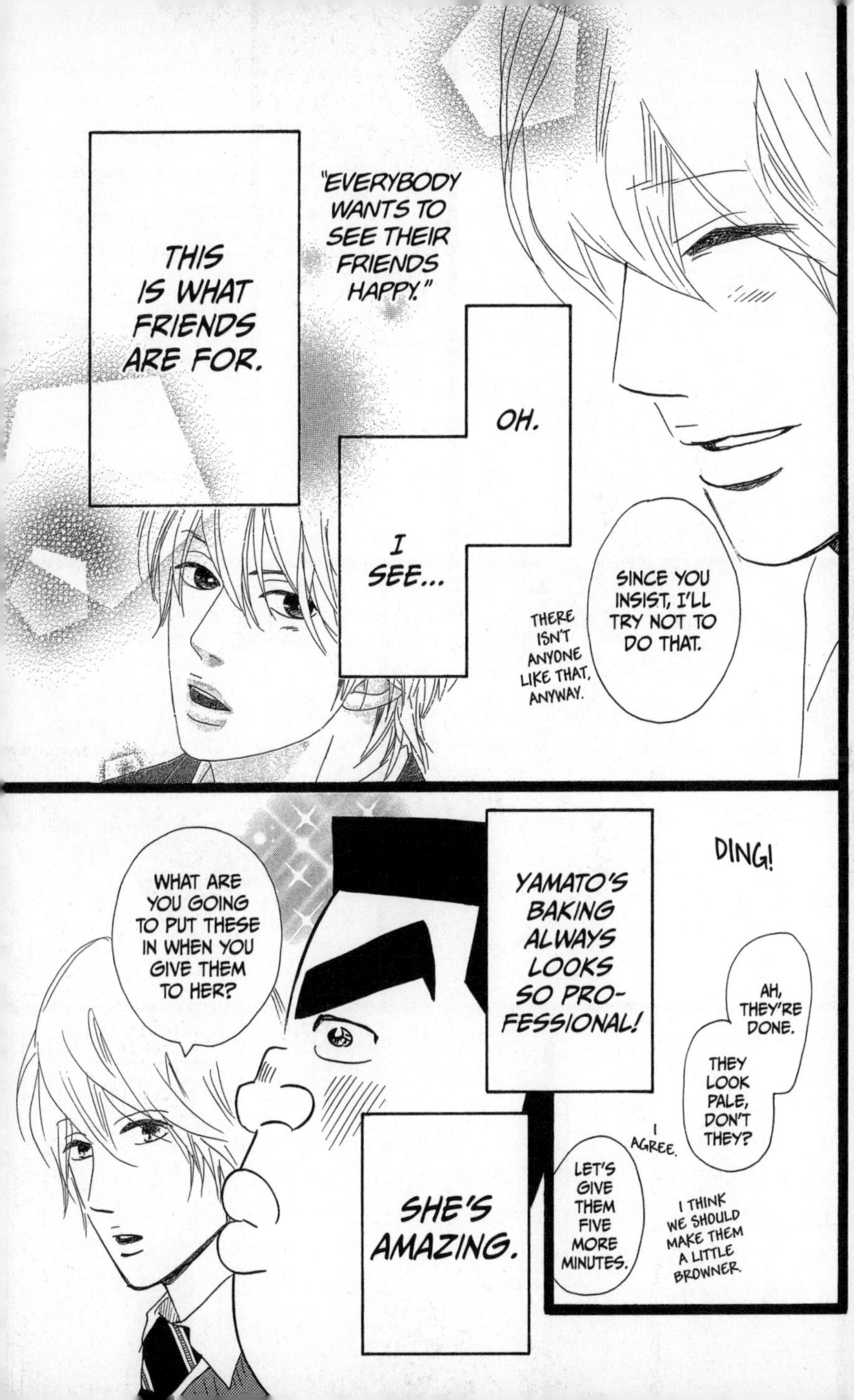
SINCE YOU INSIST, I'LL TRY NOT TO DO THAT.
THERE ISN'T ANYONE LIKE THAT, ANYWAY.
OH.
I SEE...
"EVERYBODY WANTS TO SEE THEIR FRIENDS HAPPY."
THIS IS WHAT FRIENDS ARE FOR.
DING!
AH, THEY'RE DONE.
THEY LOOK PALE, DON'T THEY?
I AGREE.
I THINK WE SHOULD MAKE THEM A LITTLE BROWNER.
LET'S GIVE THEM FIVE MORE MINUTES.
YAMATO'S BAKING ALWAYS LOOKS SO PRO-FESSIONAL!
WHAT ARE YOU GOING TO PUT THESE IN WHEN YOU GIVE THEM TO HER?
SHE'S AMAZING.

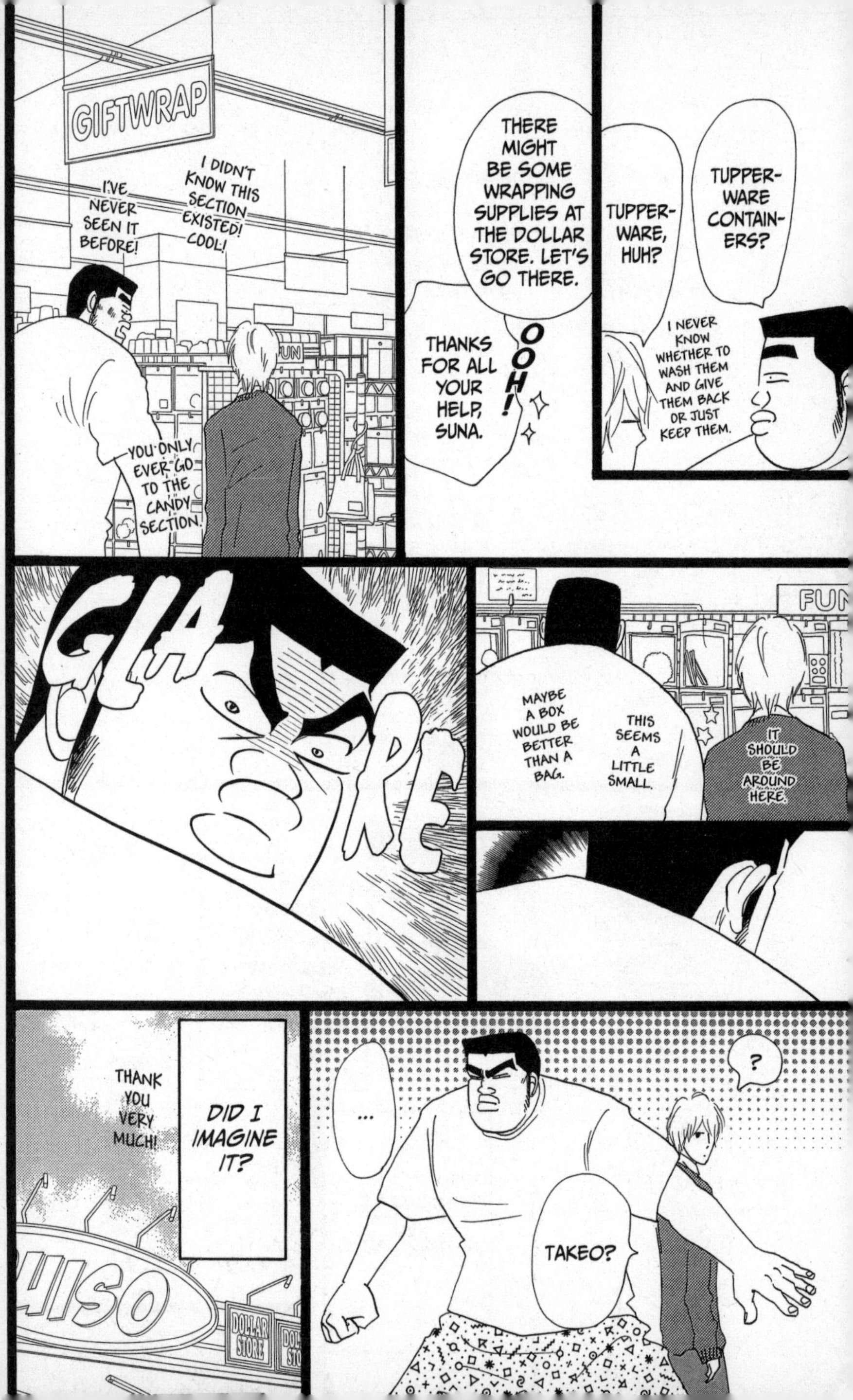
TUPPER-WARE CONTAINERS?
TUPPER-WARE, HUH?
I NEVER KNOW WHETHER TO WASH THEM AND GIVE THEM BACK OR JUST KEEP THEM.
THERE MIGHT BE SOME WRAPPING SUPPLIES AT THE DOLLAR STORE. LET'S GO THERE.
OOH!
THANKS FOR ALL YOUR HELP, SUNA.
GIFTWRAP
I DIDN'T KNOW THIS SECTION EXISTED! COOL!
I'VE NEVER SEEN IT BEFORE!
YOU ONLY EVER GO TO THE CANDY SECTION.
FUN
IT SHOULD BE AROUND HERE.
THIS SEEMS A LITTLE SMALL.
MAYBE A BOX WOULD BE BETTER THAN A BAG.
GLARE
?
TAKEO?
...
DID I IMAGINE IT?
THANK YOU VERY MUCH!
DOLLAR STORE

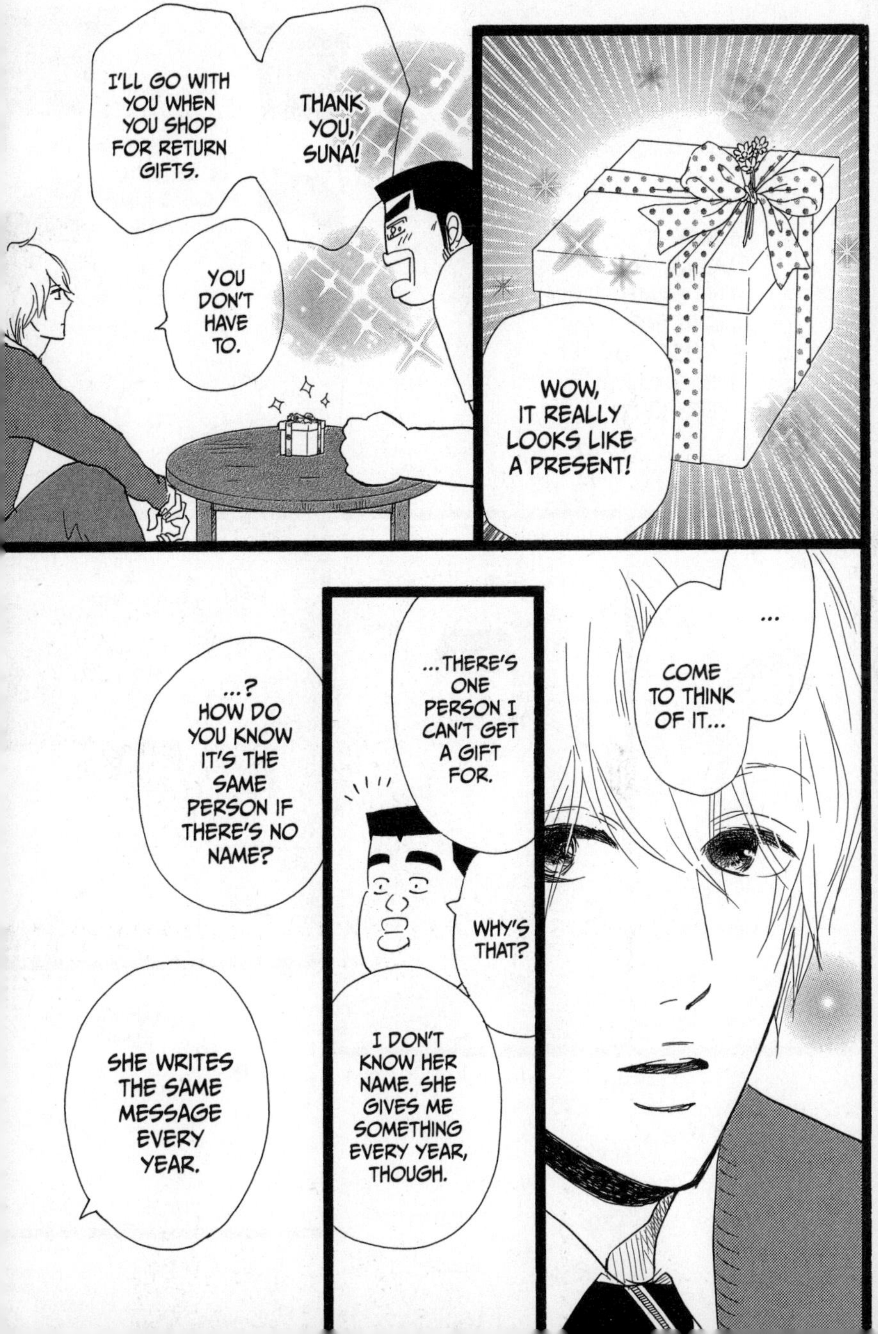
WOW, IT REALLY LOOKS LIKE A PRESENT!
THANK YOU, SUNA!
I'LL GO WITH YOU WHEN YOU SHOP FOR RETURN GIFTS.
YOU DON'T HAVE TO.
...
COME TO THINK OF IT...
...THERE'S ONE PERSON I CAN'T GET A GIFT FOR.
WHY'S THAT?
I DON'T KNOW HER NAME. SHE GIVES ME SOMETHING EVERY YEAR, THOUGH.
...? HOW DO YOU KNOW IT'S THE SAME PERSON IF THERE'S NO NAME?
SHE WRITES THE SAME MESSAGE EVERY YEAR.

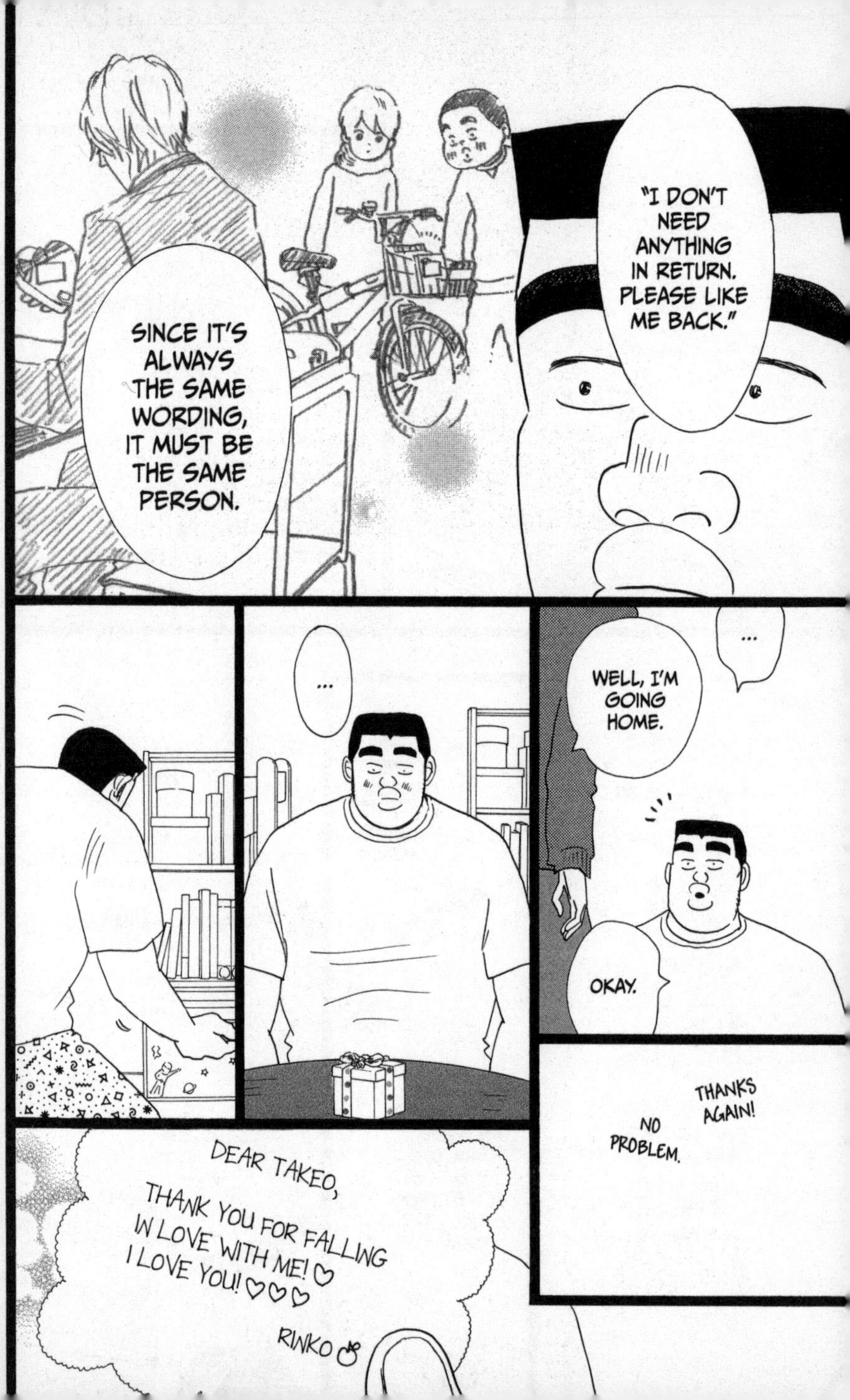
"I DON'T NEED ANYTHING IN RETURN. PLEASE LIKE ME BACK."
SINCE IT'S ALWAYS THE SAME WORDING, IT MUST BE THE SAME PERSON.
...
WELL, I'M GOING HOME.
OKAY.
...
THANKS AGAIN!
NO PROBLEM.
DEAR TAKEO,
THANK YOU FOR FALLING IN LOVE WITH ME! ♡
I LOVE YOU! ♡♡♡
RINKO

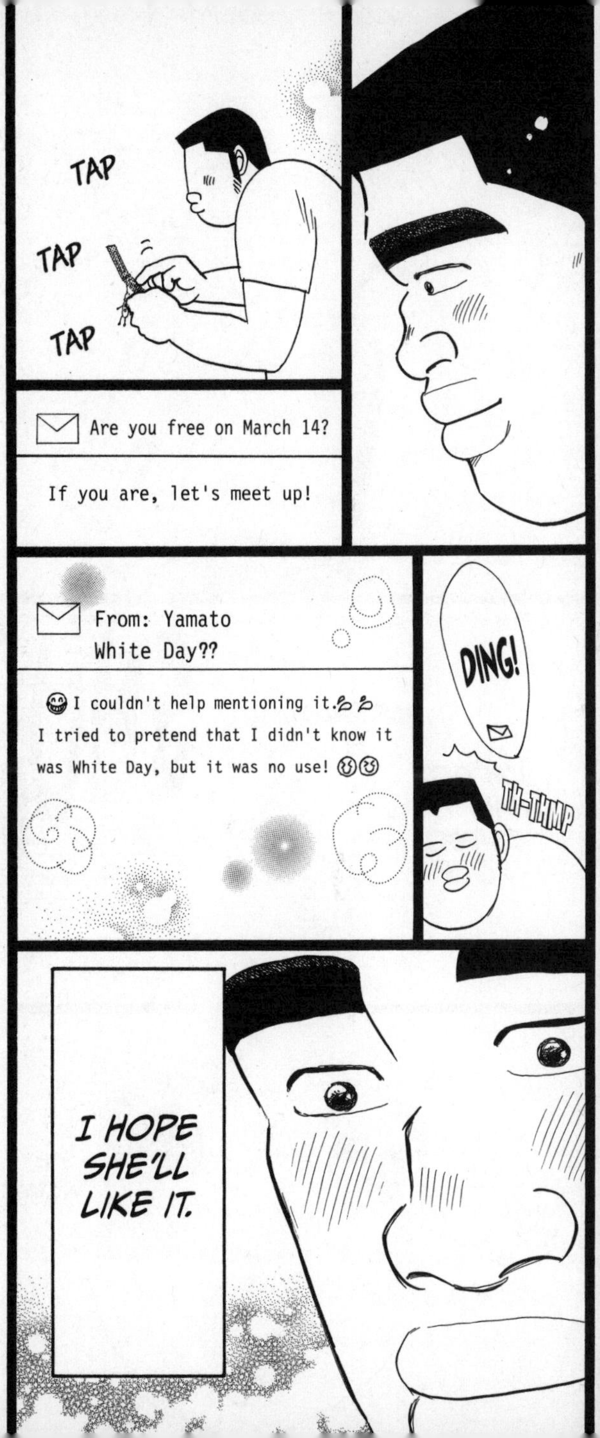
TAP
TAP
TAP
Are you free on March 14?
If you are, let's meet up!
DING!
TH-THMP
From: Yamato
White Day??
I couldn't help mentioning it.
I tried to pretend that I didn't know it was White Day, but it was no use!
I HOPE SHE'LL LIKE IT.

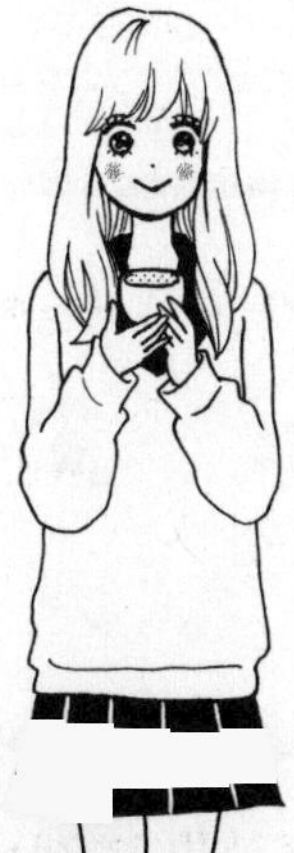

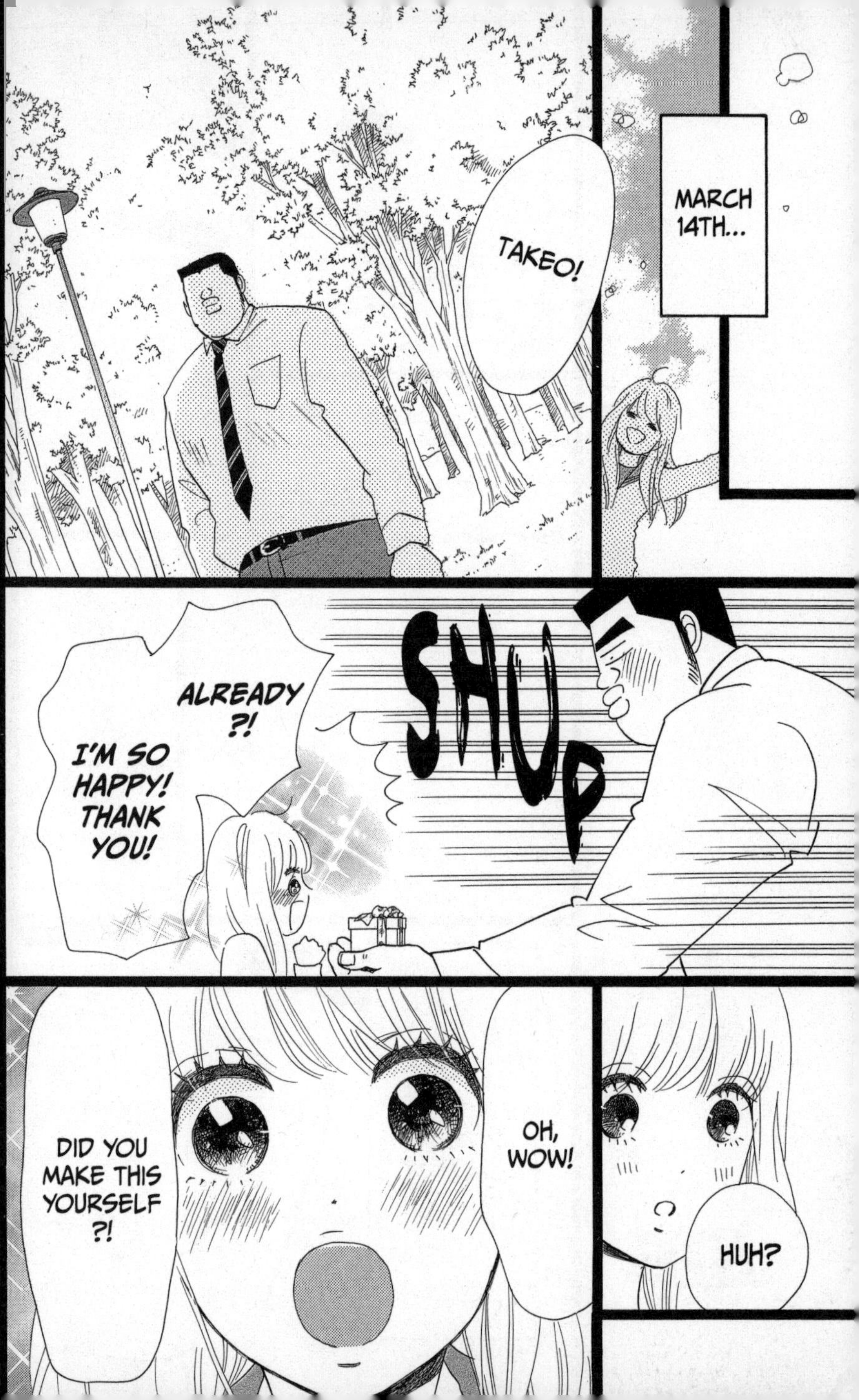
MARCH 14TH...
TAKEO!
SHUP
ALREADY ?!
I'M SO HAPPY! THANK YOU!
HUH?
OH, WOW!
DID YOU MAKE THIS YOURSELF ?!

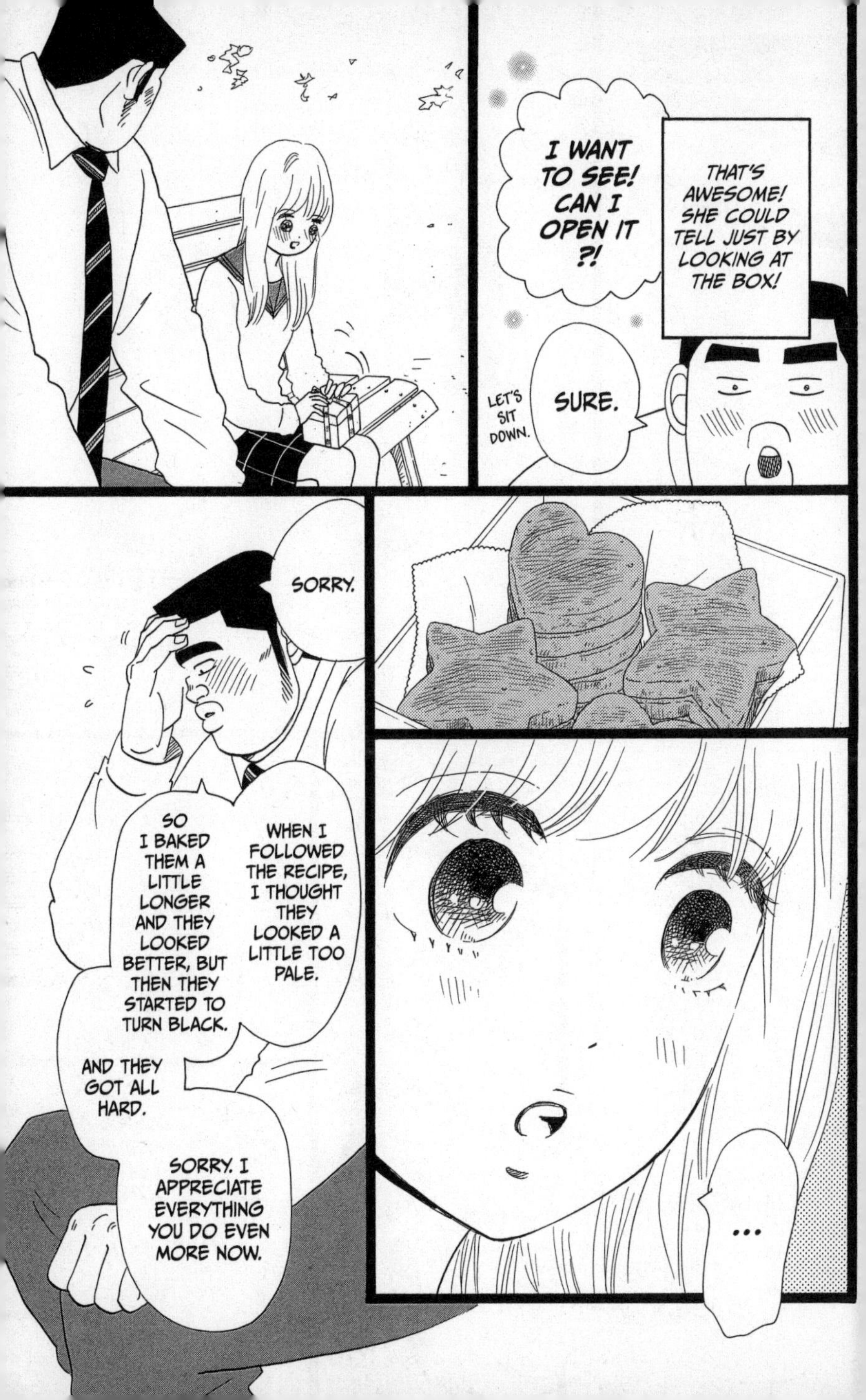
THAT'S AWESOME! SHE COULD TELL JUST BY LOOKING AT THE BOX!
I WANT TO SEE! CAN I OPEN IT ?!
SURE.
LET'S SIT DOWN.
...
SORRY.
WHEN I FOLLOWED THE RECIPE, I THOUGHT THEY LOOKED A LITTLE TOO PALE.
SO I BAKED THEM A LITTLE LONGER AND THEY LOOKED BETTER, BUT THEN THEY STARTED TO TURN BLACK.
AND THEY GOT ALL HARD.
SORRY. I APPRECIATE EVERYTHING YOU DO EVEN MORE NOW.

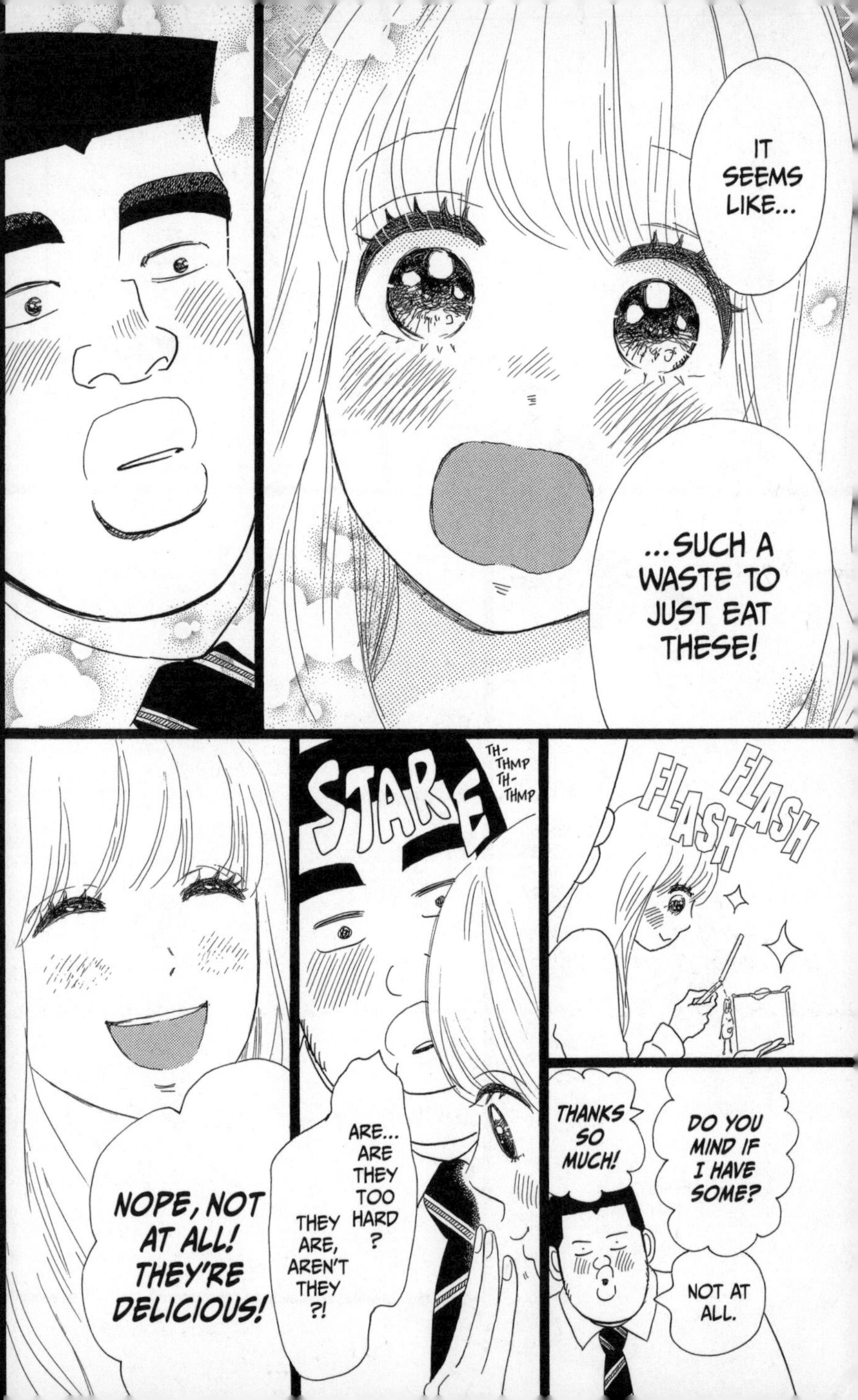
IT SEEMS LIKE...
...SUCH A WASTE TO JUST EAT THESE!
FLASH FLASH
DO YOU MIND IF I HAVE SOME?
THANKS SO MUCH!
NOT AT ALL.
TH-THMP TH-THMP
STARE
ARE... ARE THEY TOO HARD?
THEY ARE, AREN'T THEY?!
NOPE, NOT AT ALL! THEY'RE DELICIOUS!

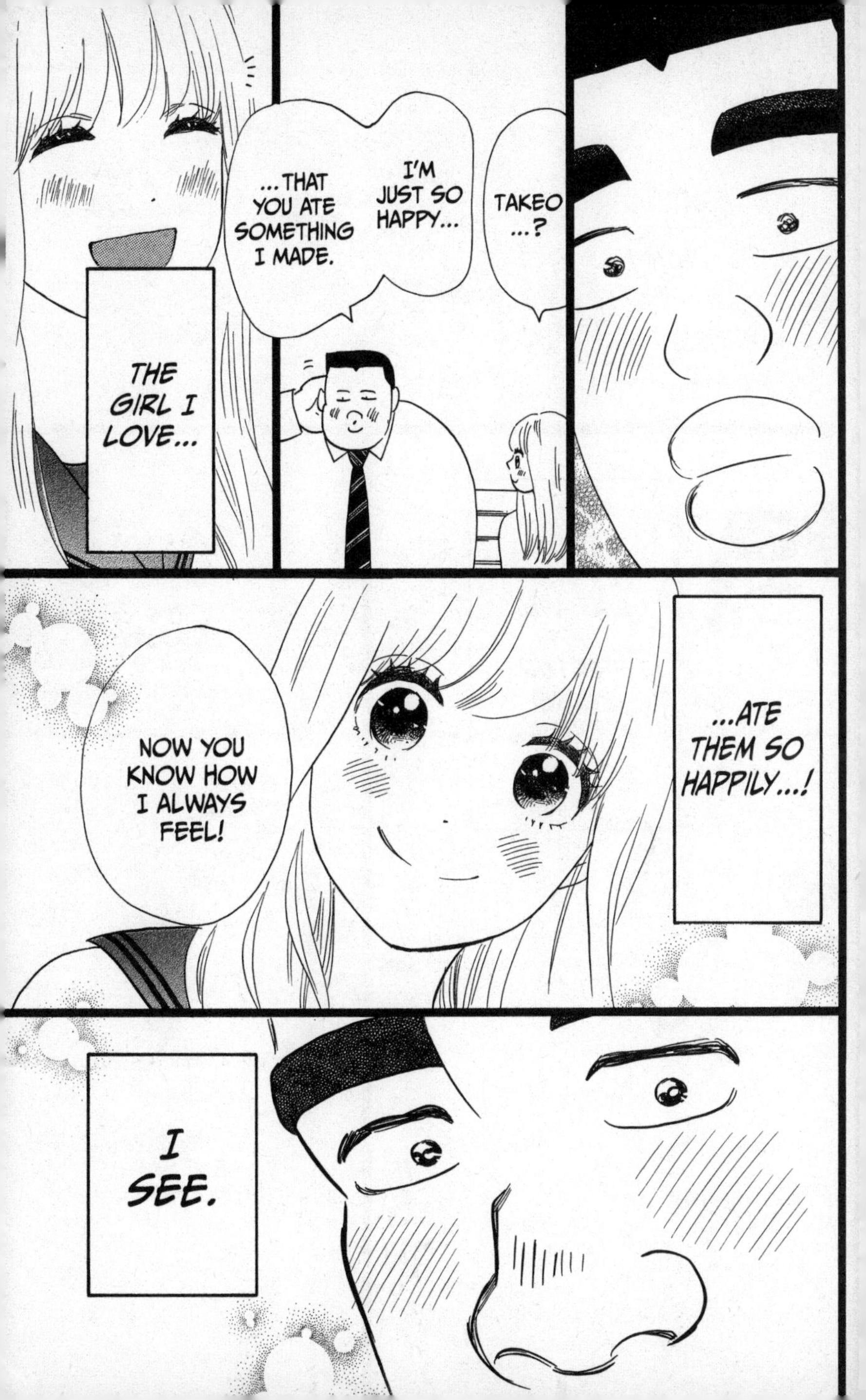
TAKEO ...?
I'M JUST SO HAPPY...
...THAT YOU ATE SOMETHING I MADE.
THE GIRL I LOVE...
...ATE THEM SO HAPPILY...!
NOW YOU KNOW HOW I ALWAYS FEEL!
I SEE.

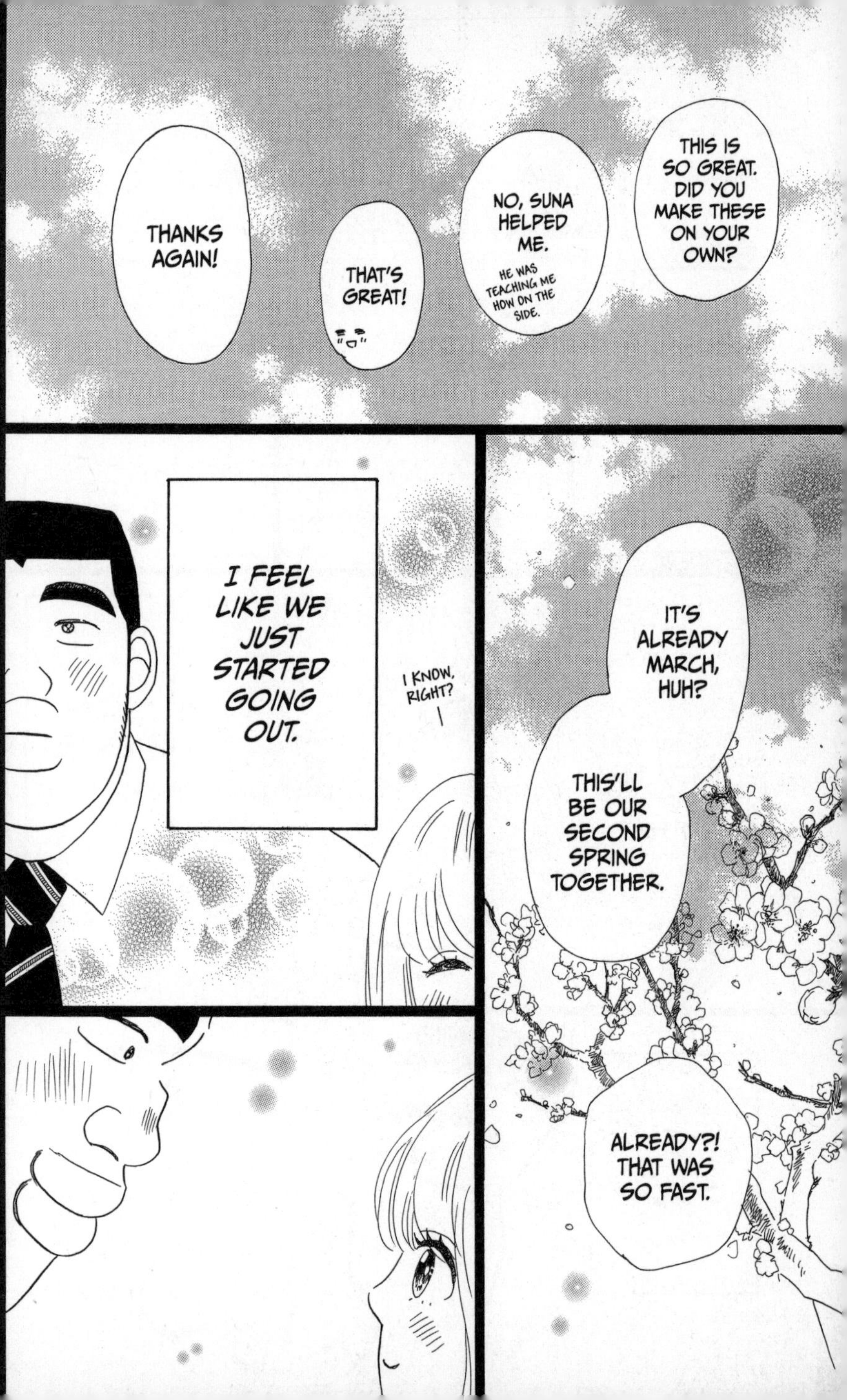
THIS IS SO GREAT. DID YOU MAKE THESE ON YOUR OWN?
NO, SUNA HELPED ME.
HE WAS TEACHING ME HOW ON THE SIDE.
THAT'S GREAT!
THANKS AGAIN!
IT'S ALREADY MARCH, HUH?
THIS'LL BE OUR SECOND SPRING TOGETHER.
ALREADY?! THAT WAS SO FAST.
I FEEL LIKE WE JUST STARTED GOING OUT.
I KNOW, RIGHT?

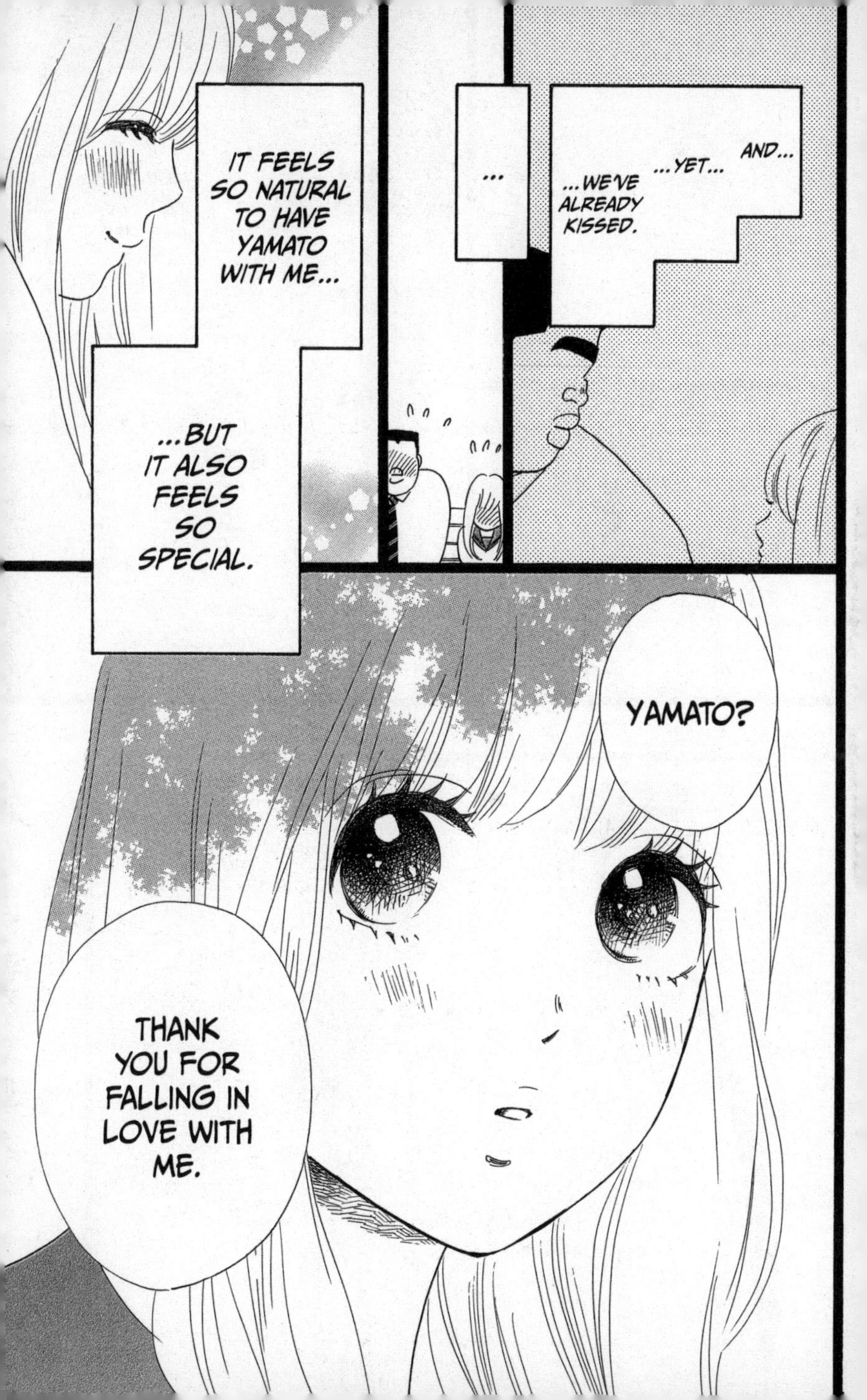
AND...
...YET...
...WE'VE ALREADY KISSED.
...
IT FEELS SO NATURAL TO HAVE YAMATO WITH ME...
...BUT IT ALSO FEELS SO SPECIAL.
YAMATO?
THANK YOU FOR FALLING IN LOVE WITH ME.

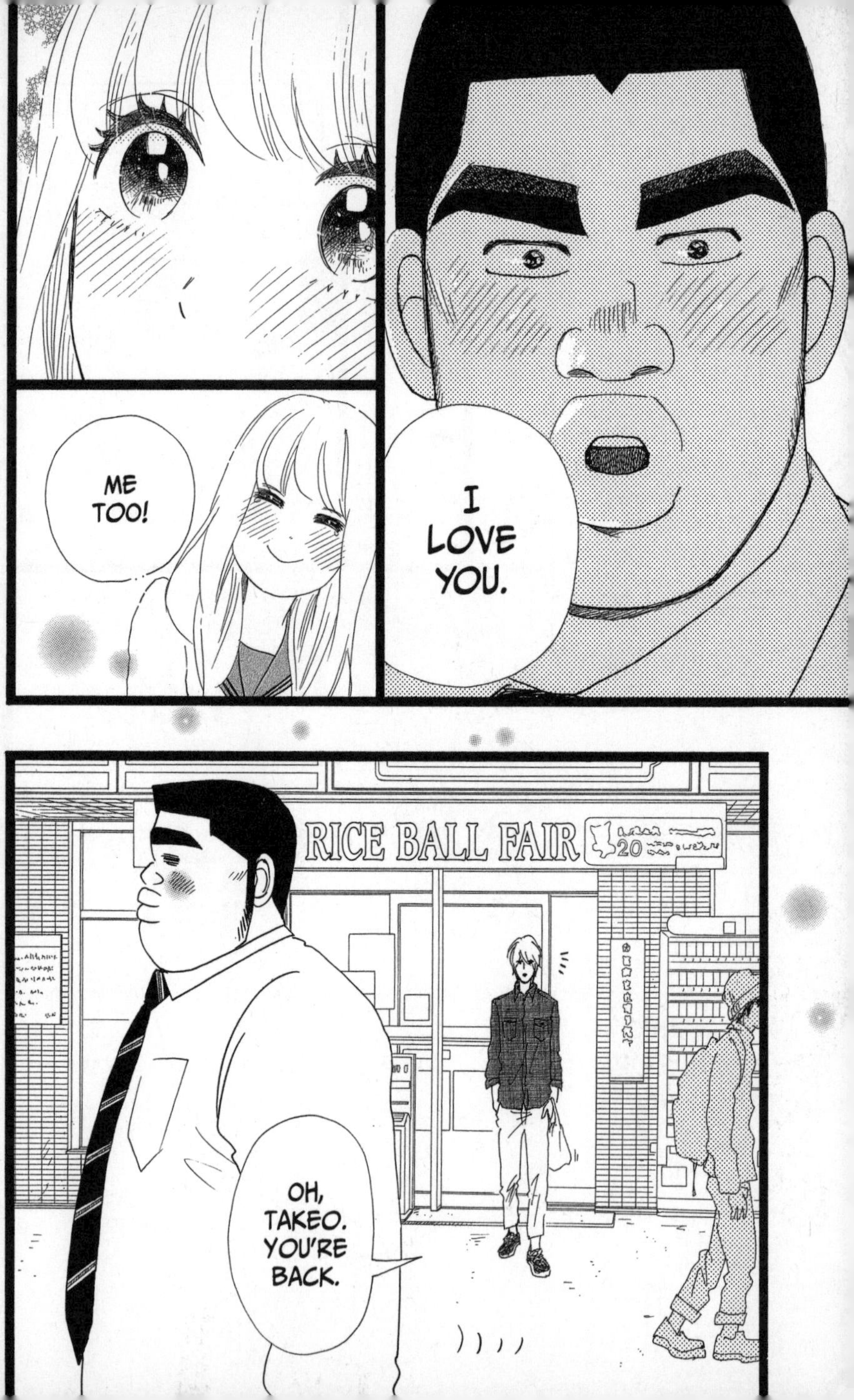
I LOVE YOU.
ME TOO!
RICE BALL FAIR
OH, TAKEO. YOU'RE BACK.

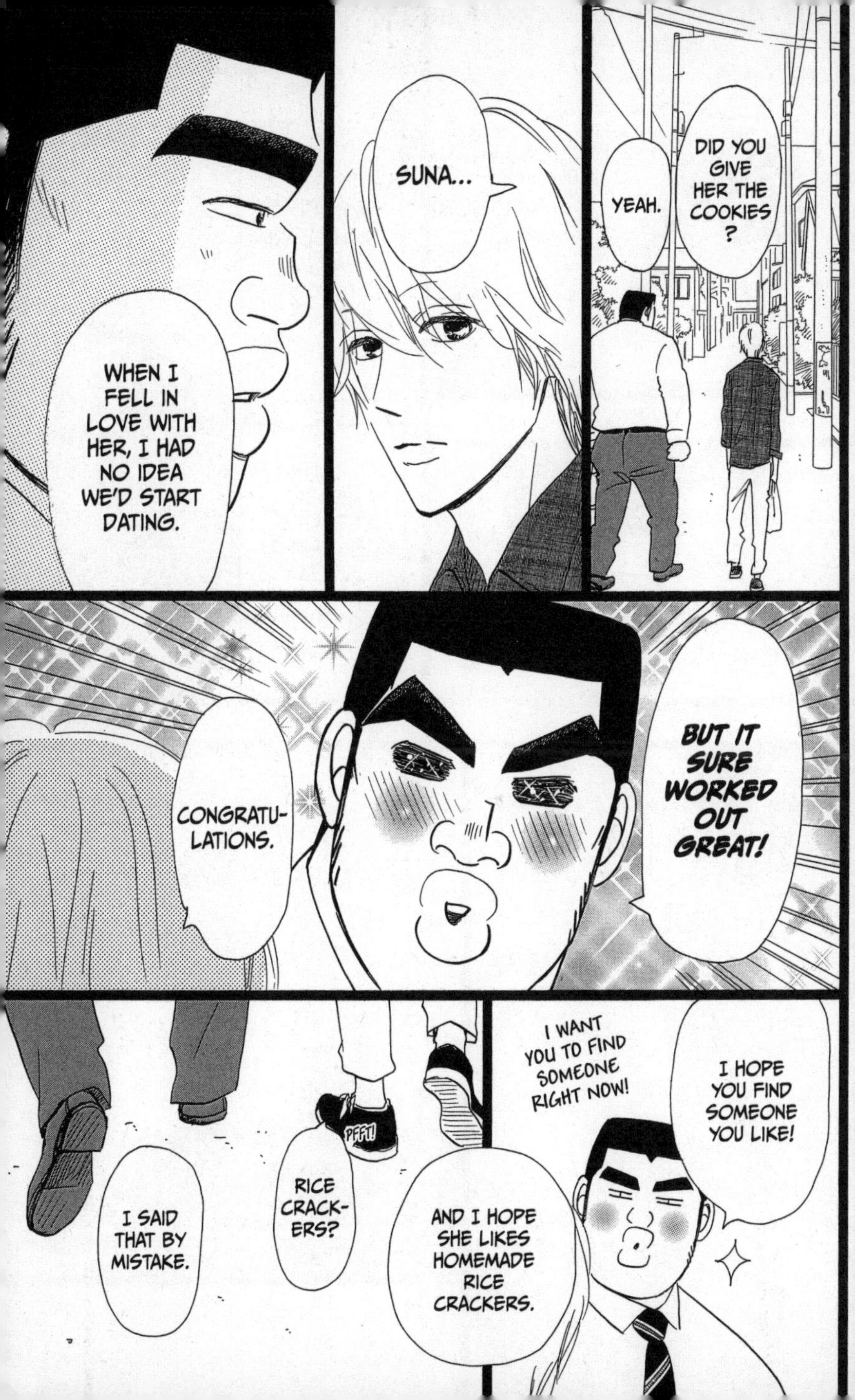

DID YOU GIVE HER THE COOKIES ?
YEAH.
SUNA...
WHEN I FELL IN LOVE WITH HER, I HAD NO IDEA WE'D START DATING.
BUT IT SURE WORKED OUT GREAT!
CONGRATU-LATIONS.
I HOPE YOU FIND SOMEONE YOU LIKE!
I WANT YOU TO FIND SOMEONE RIGHT NOW!
AND I HOPE SHE LIKES HOMEMADE RICE CRACKERS.
PFFT!
RICE CRACK-ERS?
I SAID THAT BY MISTAKE.

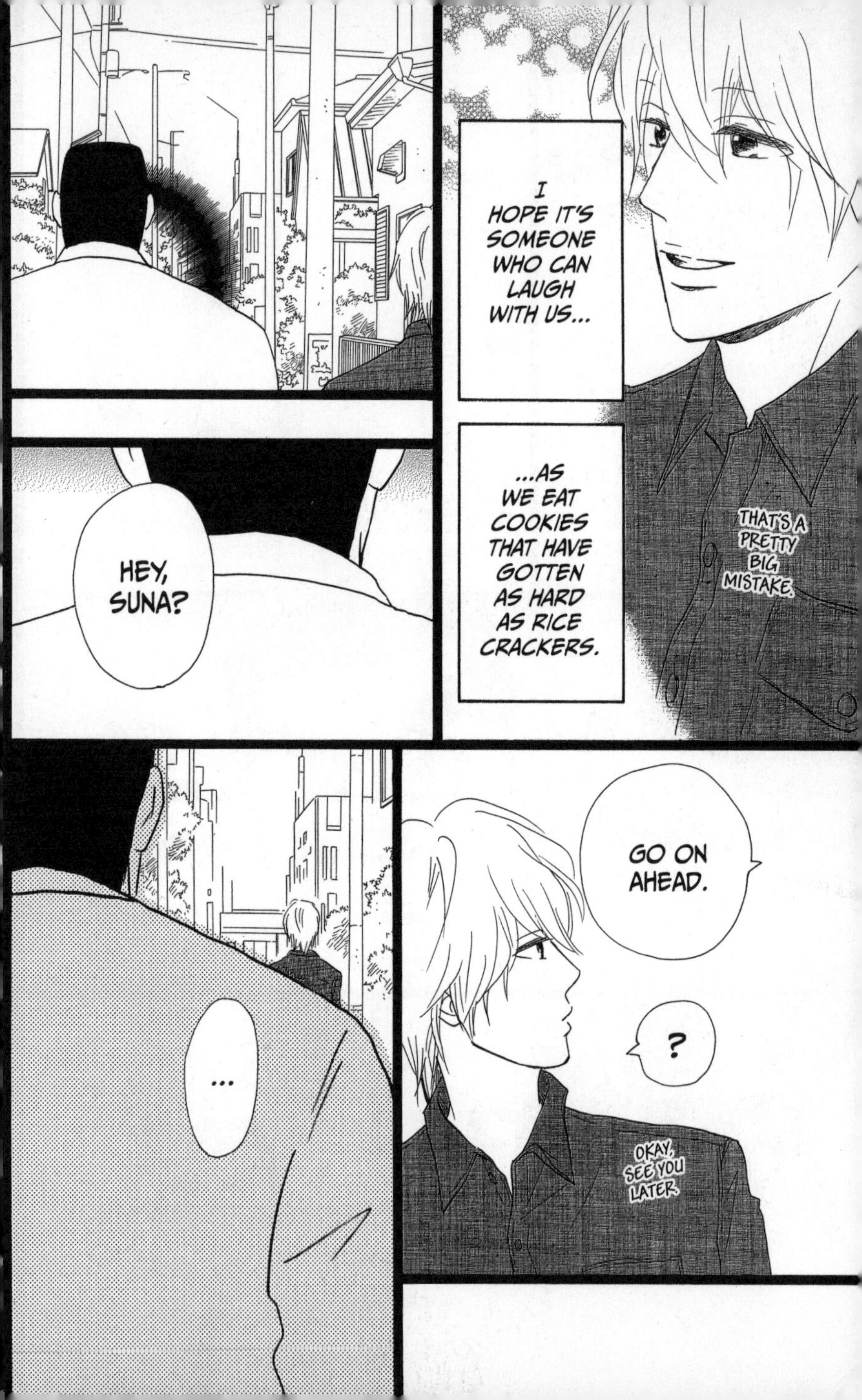
I HOPE IT'S SOMEONE WHO CAN LAUGH WITH US...
...AS WE EAT COOKIES THAT HAVE GOTTEN AS HARD AS RICE CRACKERS.
THAT'S A PRETTY BIG MISTAKE.
HEY, SUNA?
GO ON AHEAD.
?
OKAY, SEE YOU LATER.
...

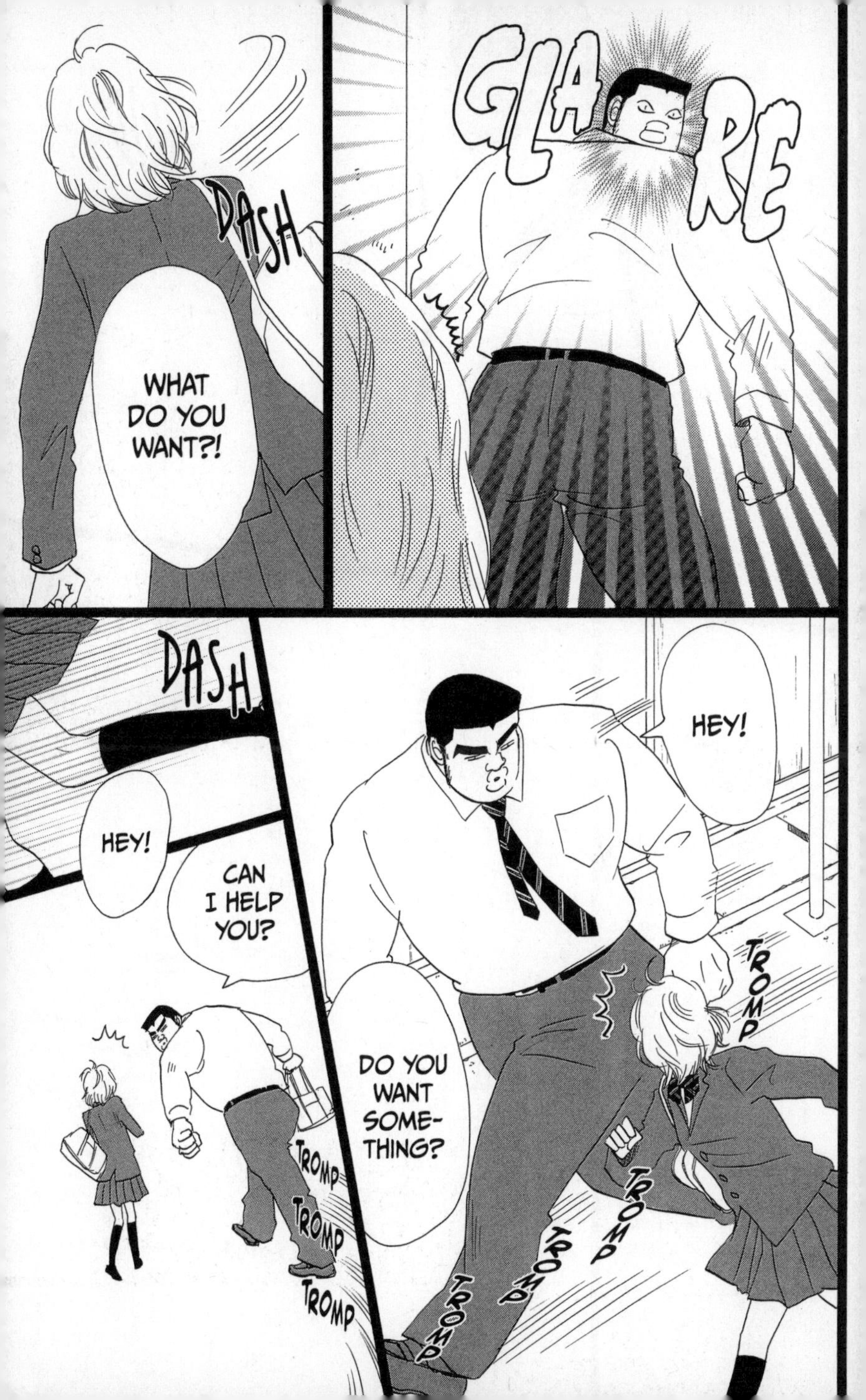
GLARE
DASH
WHAT DO YOU WANT?!
HEY!
DO YOU WANT SOMETHING?
TROMP
TROMP
TROMP
TROMP
DASH
HEY!
CAN I HELP YOU?
TROMP
TROMP
TROMP

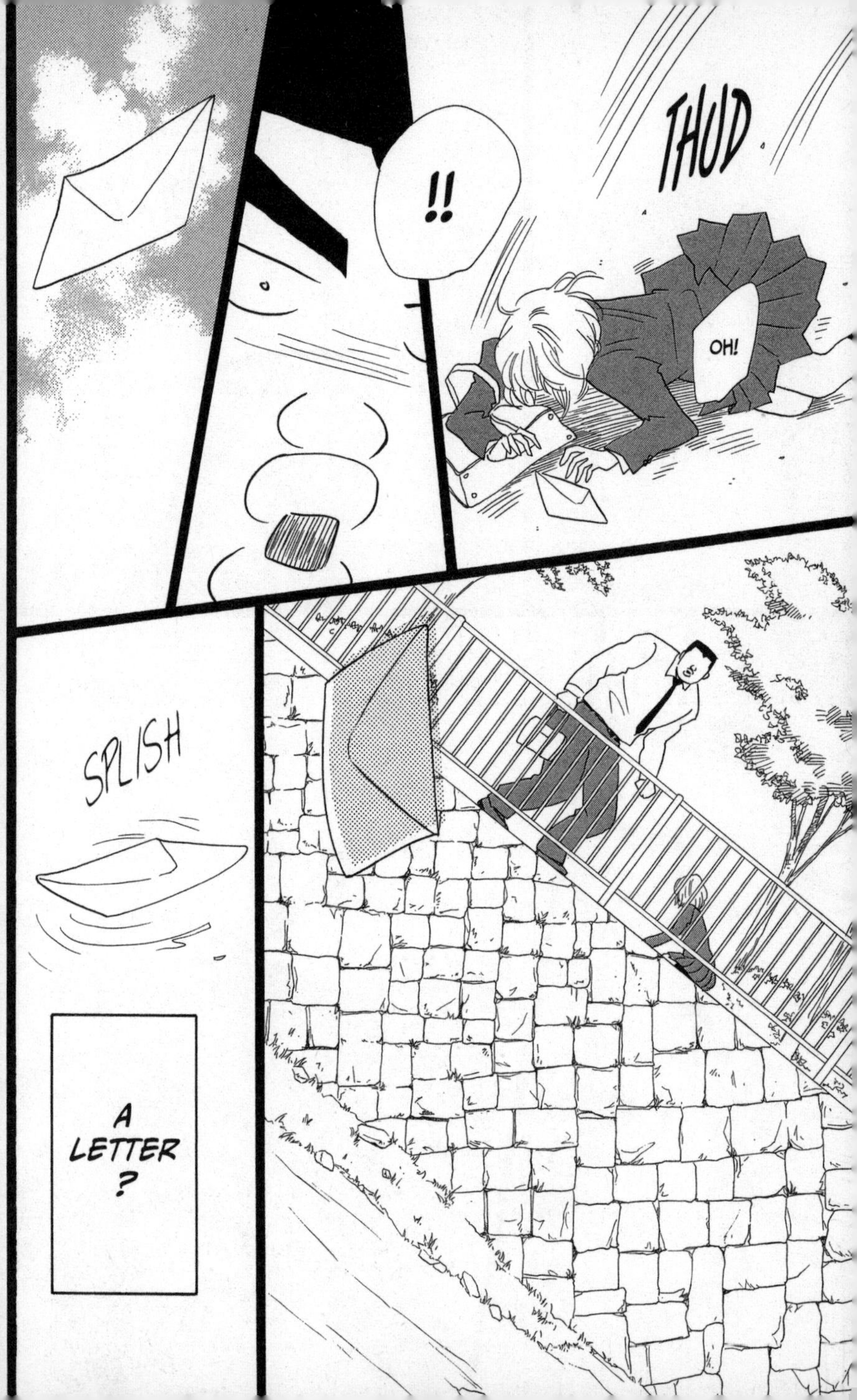
THUD
OH!
!!
SPLISH
A LETTER?

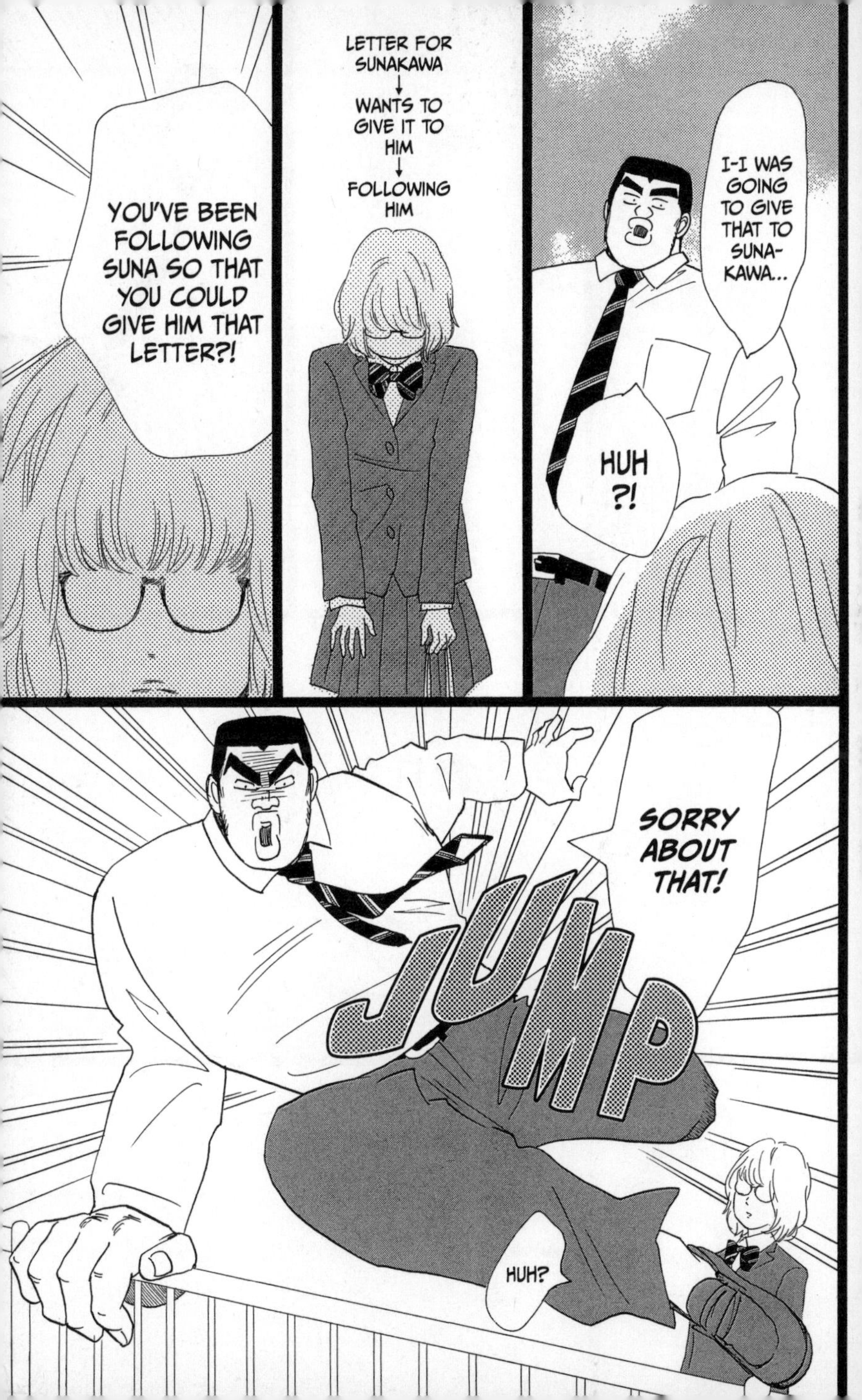
I-I WAS GOING TO GIVE THAT TO SUNA-KAWA...
HUH ?!
LETTER FOR SUNAKAWA ↓ WANTS TO GIVE IT TO HIM ↓ FOLLOWING HIM
YOU'VE BEEN FOLLOWING SUNA SO THAT YOU COULD GIVE HIM THAT LETTER?!
SORRY ABOUT THAT!
JUMP
HUH?

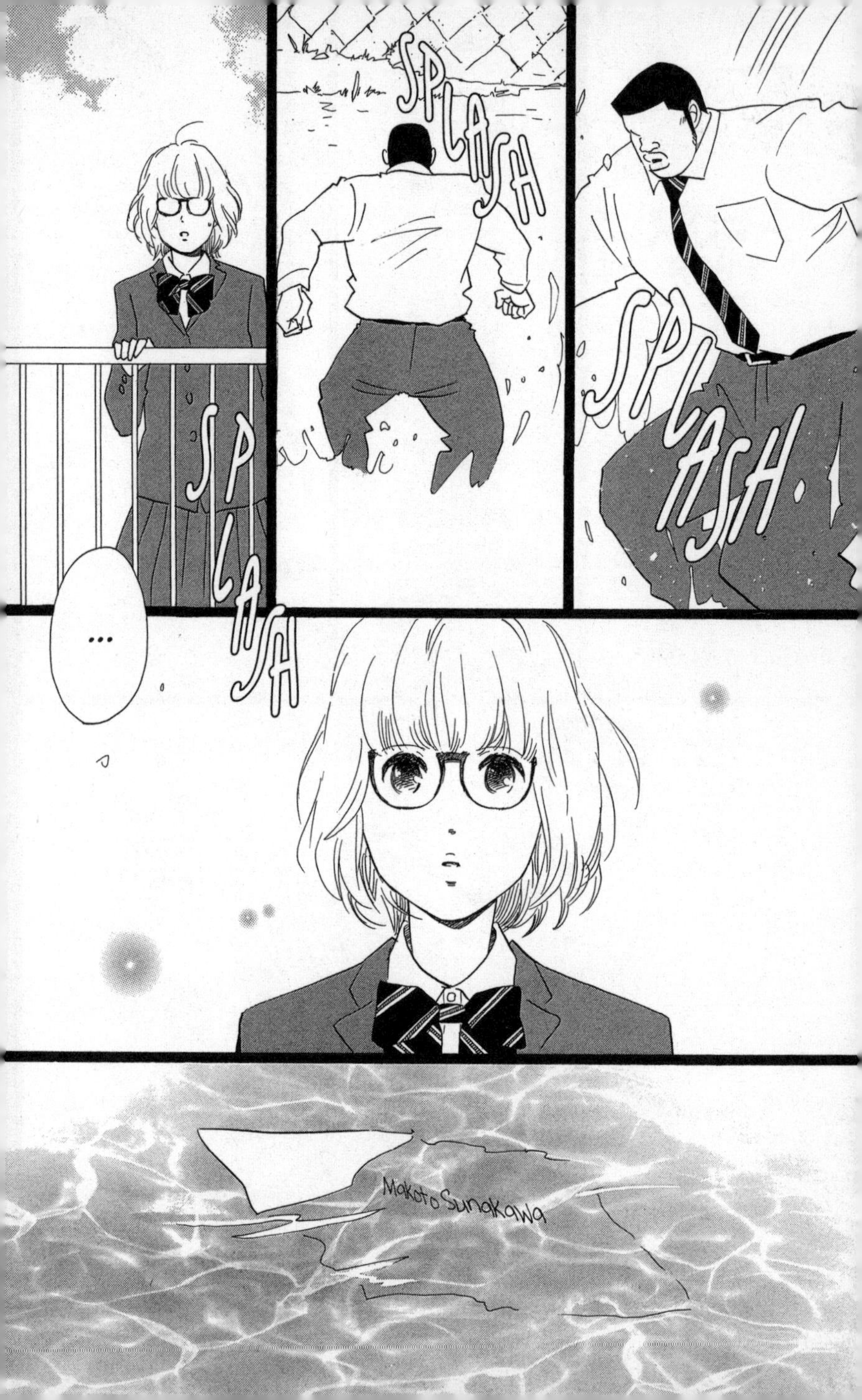
SPLASH
SPLASH
SPLASH
...
Makoto Sunakawa

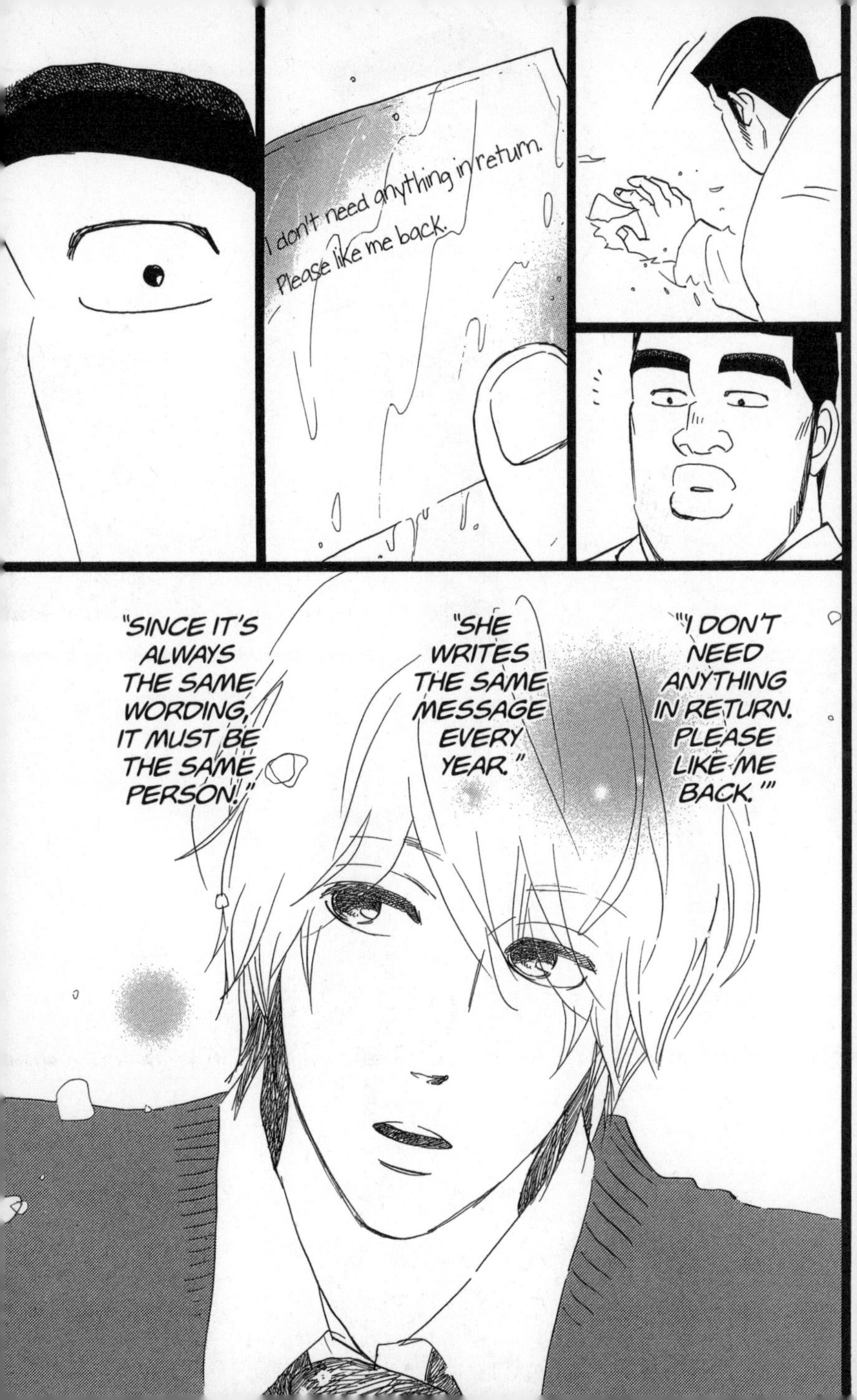
I don't need anything in return.
Please like me back.
"'I DON'T NEED ANYTHING IN RETURN. PLEASE LIKE ME BACK.'"
"SHE WRITES THE SAME MESSAGE EVERY YEAR."
"SINCE IT'S ALWAYS THE SAME WORDING, IT MUST BE THE SAME PERSON!"

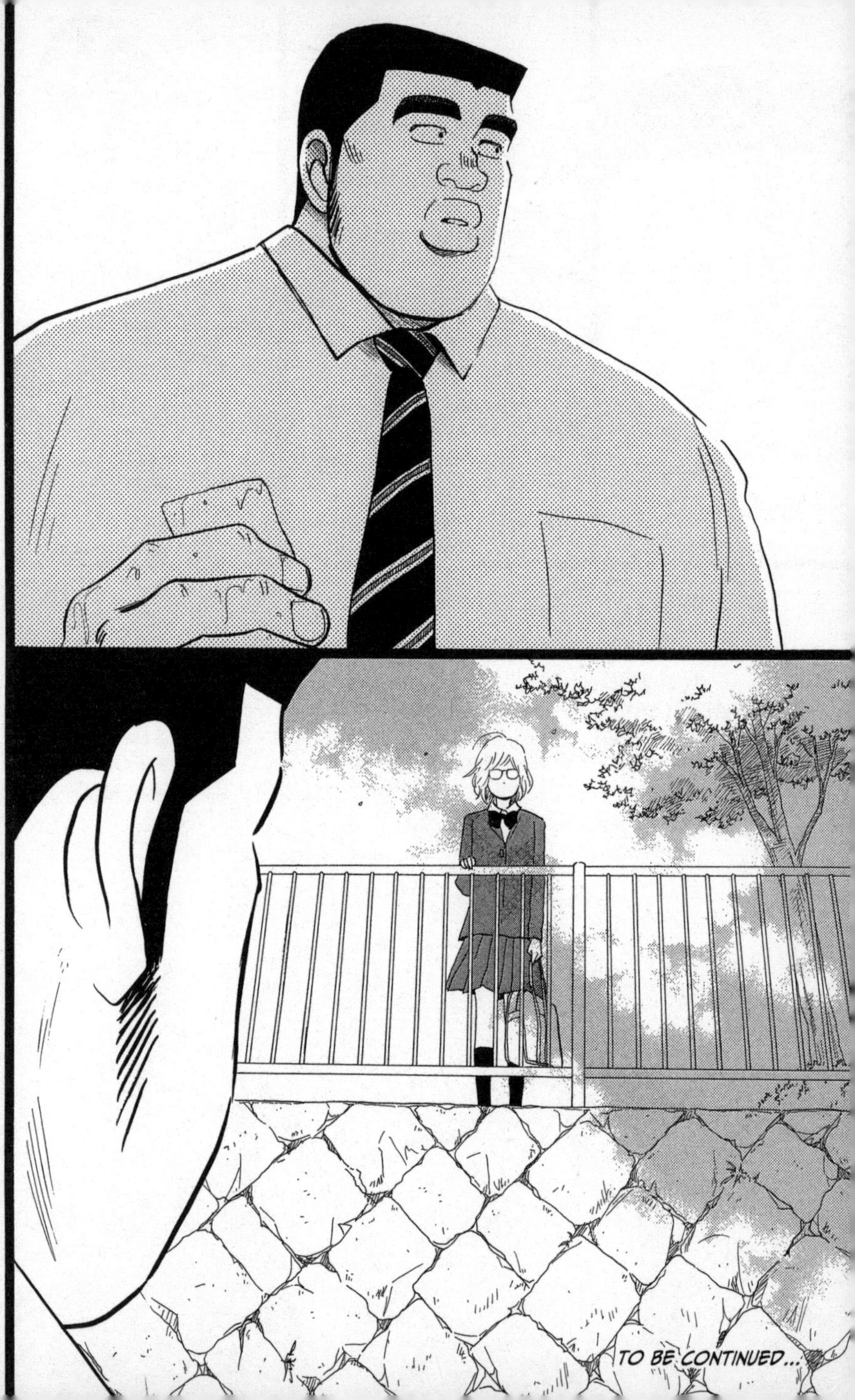
TO BE CONTINUED...

I have the tendency to shorten titles. Even though *My Love Story!!* isn't very long, I'll shorten it to "My!!" when I email my editor. It makes me realize how long I've been working on it. It makes me happy. Whether it be "My" or "Takeo," I'm fine with whatever you call it. I don't mind if you call him "Ta-ke-o," "Tuh-kay-oh" or "Ta-keh-ou." Thank you for your support. And of course, it makes me very happy when you use the full title—My Love Story!!

– *Kazune Kawahara*

ARUKO is from Ishikawa Prefecture in Japan and was born on July 26 (a Leo!). She made her manga debut with *Ame Nochi Hare* (Clear After the Rain). Her other works include *Yasuko to Kenji*, and her hobbies include laughing and getting lost.

KAZUNE KAWAHARA is from Hokkaido Prefecture in Japan and was born on March 11 (a Pisces!). She made her manga debut at age 18 with *Kare no Ichiban Sukina Hito* (His Most Favorite Person). Her best-selling shojo manga series *High School Debut* is available in North America from VIZ Media. Her hobby is interior redecorating.

Thank you for volume 6. It's volume 6!! I've never drawn a manga series that used the same characters for this long before. I'm really happy to be able to spend so much time with such fun people (Takeo and friends). Thank you, everyone and Kawahara Sensei! I look forward to your continued support.

– *Aruko*

MY LOVE STORY!!

Volume 6
Shojo Beat Edition

Story by **KAZUNE KAWAHARA**
Art by **ARUKO**

———————————//———————————

English Adaptation ♡ **Ysabet Reinhardt MacFarlane**
Translation ♡ **JN Productions**
Touch-up Art & Lettering ♡ **Mark McMurray**
Design ♡ **Fawn Lau**
Editor ♡ **Amy Yu**

———————————//———————————

ORE MONOGATARI!!
© 2011 by Kazune Kawahara, Aruko
All rights reserved.
First published in Japan in 2011 by SHUEISHA Inc., Tokyo
English translation rights arranged by SHUEISHA Inc.

The stories, characters and incidents mentioned in
this publication are entirely fictional.

Printed in the U.S.A.

Published by VIZ Media, LLC
P.O. Box 77010
San Francisco, CA 94107

10 9 8 7 6 5 4 3 2 1
First printing, October 2015

www.viz.com

www.shojobeat.com